Rhetoric and the Deco
Recolonization of Eas

MW00679903

By the end of the 1960s the process of decolonization had practically run its course in Southeast Asia. One exception, however, was tiny Portuguese Timor, where notions of self-determination and independence had yet to be generated. In 1974, the Carnation Revolution in Portugal brought about the end of 50 years of dictatorship, and halfway around the world, presented a new opportunity to a small, ambitious proportion of the Timorese population, eager to shape the future of their country.

This book presents a compelling and original perspective on the critical period of 1974–1975 in the history of East Timor. It describes how the language of politics helped to shape the events that brought about the decolonization of Portuguese Timor, its brief independence as The Democratic Republic of East Timor, and its recolonization by an Asian neighbor. Further, it challenges the idea that this period of history was infused with the spirit of nationalism in which the majority of Timorese partook, and which contended with other competing western-isms, including colonialism, communism, neo-colonialism, and fascism. In contrast, the book argues that the Timorese majority had little understanding of any of these alien political abstractions and that the period can be most effectively explained and understood in terms of the contrast between the political culture of Dili, the capital, and the political culture of the rest of the country. In turn, David Hicks highlights how the period of 1974–1975 can offer lessons to government and international policy-makers alike who are trying to bring about a transformation in governance from the traditional to the legal and convert individuals from peasants to citizens.

The result of extensive fieldwork and interviews, this book will be of interest to students and scholars of Southeast Asian studies, international relations, post-conflict studies, and post-colonial studies.

David Hicks is Professor of Anthropology at Stony Brook University, USA, and Life Member of Clare Hall, University of Cambridge, UK.

Routledge contemporary Southeast Asia series

Rhetoric and the Decolonization and Recolonization of East Timor

David Hicks

Routledge
Taylor & Francis Group

LONDON AND NEW YORK

First published 2015 by Routledge

2 Park Square, Milton Park, Abingdon, Oxfordshire OX14 4RN
711 Third Avenue, New York, NY 10017

Routledge is an imprint of the Taylor & Francis Group, an informa business

First issued in paperback 2017

British Library Cataloguing in Publication Data
A catalogue record for this book is available from the British Library

Library of Congress Cataloging in Publication Data
Hicks, David – author.
Rhetoric and the decolonization and recolonization of East Timor/
David Hicks.
    pages cm. – (Routledge contemporary Southeast Asia series; 68)
    Includes bibliographical references and index.
    1. Timor-Leste–Politics and government. 2. Political culture–Timor-
Leste–History–20th century. 3. Rhetoric–Political aspects–Timor-
Leste–History–20th century. 4. Political violence–Timor-Leste–History–
20th century. 5. Decolonization–Timor-Leste. I. Title.
DS649.53.H53 2014
959.87′031–dc23   2014009533

ISBN: 978-1-138-02107-5 (hbk)
ISBN: 978-1-138-47635-6 (pbk)

Typeset in Times New Roman
by Wearset Ltd, Boldon, Tyne and Wear

**To Gwyn Rowley
Instead of "Bullock Cart Days and Irrawaddy Nights";
recollections of Black Forest Tramping and
Mediterranean Nights.**

Also by David Hicks

A Maternal Religion: The Role of Women in Tetum Myth and Ritual
Tetum Ghosts and Kin: Fertility and Gender in East Timor
Cultural Anthropology. With Margaret A. Gwynne
Structural Analysis in Anthropology: Case Studies from Indonesia and Brazil
Kinship and Religion in Eastern Indonesia
Peoples of Timor, People of Timor: Life, Alliance, Death (co-translator)
Ritual and Belief: Readings in the Anthropology of Religion (editor)

Frontispiece The graves near Same (photograph by Maxine Hicks).

[Australian Prime Minister] Whitlam ignored the historical fact that the "educated" have always led liberation struggles everywhere in the world, for this is
their historical and moral responsibility.

(José Ramos-Horta, *Funu*, 1996: 77)

Most arguments about Timor have taken refuge behind popular and fashionable
terms like communism, fascism, nationalism and colonialism. All are too simplistic when applied to Timor and do little to explain a complex topic.

(Bill Nicol, *Timor: The Stillborn Nation*, 1978: vi)

Contents

Preface

This book describes how the language of politics helped to shape events in 1974–1975 that brought about the decolonization of Portuguese Timor, its brief independence as East Timor, and its recolonization by an Asian neighbor. In doing so it draws attention to a fundamental aspect of political and social life at that time that foreshadows politics and society today: the contrast between the values of the capital town, Dili, and those of its hinterland.

By the end of the 1960s the process of decolonization had practically run its course in Southeast Asia. One exception, however, was tiny Portuguese Timor; like the Philippines, a testimonial to a past Iberian glory. There, in contrast with the earlier Indonesian struggle for independence, notions of "self-determination" and "independence" had yet to be generated, and when they did come they would issue from the government of the colonial authority, the Republic of Portugal, and a small segment of the country's population that comprised the educated elite. At the beginning of the twentieth century the Timorese were a colonized population. By the time the century closed, they had advanced to a condition of quasi-independence; "quasi" because they still remained subject to the whims – albeit for the most part, benign – of a foreign authority. In between, they had endured a violent decolonization, won a fleeting independence from their European overlords, and been recolonized, this time by an Asian neighbor. The present book includes a discussion about the manner in which the Timorese responded to the change of government in the mother country and how they created a new political world for themselves during the brief interregnum which separated their two periods of colonial domination, "bookended," as it were, by two dates: April 25, 1974, the day a new regime took power in Portugal, and December 7, 1975, the day the Armed Forces of the Republic of Indonesia, the *Angkatan Bersenjata Republik Indonesia* (*ABRI*), invaded the newly-independent country.

While my professional credentials are those of a social anthropologist who has carried out ethnographic research into the daily lives of Timorese peasant farmers, writing a monograph about a period four decades ago is also to fashion a narrative of a history, or rather, histories; and investigating the events that contributed to the contemporary Timorese polity entails a study of the politics and the political language of that time. This reappraisal, accordingly, would not have been possible without its author transcending the precincts of his own discipline to engage with its sister disciplines of history and the study of politics.

Acknowledgments

This book has endured a long gestation and in writing it I have found myself indebted to many institutions and individuals. I am grateful to the United States Institute of Peace for awarding me a grant (Grant #: USIP-545) to enable me to compose the first draft of this book in 1989 and the Rockefeller Foundation for providing me with a residency at its Villa Serbelloni, Bellagio in 1997 for reworking the manuscript free from academic distractions. I was enabled to continue preparing the book at Clare Hall, University of Cambridge, where I was a Visiting Fellow in 2007. My data were in part based on fieldwork funded by the Wenner-Gren Foundation for Anthropological Research; the American Philosophical Society; and the London Committee of the London-Cornell Project for East and South East Asian Studies which was supported jointly by the Carnegie Corporation of New York and the Nuffield Foundation. My most recent funding was provided by the J. William Fulbright Foreign Scholarship Board, and I thank Mr David Adams for his much appreciated interest in my work. During this period Stony Brook University granted me three sabbatical leaves (1998, 2005, 2011) and a research leave (2007), each allowing me to pursue my research into the history of East Timor. My thanks go to the *Comissão de Alcolhimento Verdade e Reconciliação de Timor-Leste* (Commission for Reception, Truth and Reconciliation in Timor-Leste) or (CAVR), which placed the resources of its invaluable library in Dili, capital of East Timor, at my disposal, thereby making available sources otherwise untapped by previous authors on the period discussed here. Most of all, I am indebted to the Timorese themselves, whether they were individuals I interviewed or not, whose country I have had the considerable pleasure of visiting seven times; and especially to the following for the help they gave me at different times and in various venues: the late Father Jorge Barros Duarte, Luís Filipe F.R. Thomaz, Father Apolinário, Manuel Tilman, Jerry Desousa, José Ramos-Horta, Domingos de Sousa, José Texeira, Sidonio Freitas, Douglas Kammen, the late Francisco Xavier do Amaral, Francisco da Costa Tilman ("Chico"), Victoria Marwick-Smith, José Caetano Guterres, Jean A. Berlie, Charlie Scheiner, Jill Sternberg, Geoffrey Etches, Marion Corbett, Benjamim de Araújo e Corte-Real, Lurdes Bessa, Kym Miller, Dan Groshong, Susan Rodgers, Kirk Endicott, Daniel Varisco, Gregory Forth, Max Stahl, Michael Leach, Andrea Molnar, and Ron Nixon. A very special "thank you" goes to

Maria Rosa Biddlecombe, to the memory of the late Bob Biddlecombe, Luís Francisco de Gonzaga Soares, Tereza da Luz Simões Soares, Fernando da Costa Soares, José Henriques Pereira, and Rosa Maria da Costa Soares for sharing a small part of their lives with my wife and I. I am also grateful to all the persons who agreed to be interviewed. I thank the reviewers who commented on my manuscript; they made valuable suggestions, many of which I have incorporated into this text. I thank Mr John Geizer for drawing the majority of the figures that appear in the text and to Mrs Jean Moreau for the help she gave. My greatest debt is to my wife, Maxine, who shared in almost all the activities upon which my research is based.

I wish to tender my gratitude to the Routledge staff in Asian Studies, who were a great help to me in preparing the manuscript for publication: Dorothea Schaefter, Editor; Jillian Morrison, Associate Editor; Rebecca Lawrence, Editorial Assistant; Amy Ekins, Project Manager at Wearset; and my copy-editor, Melanie Marshall. They did a thorough job.

1 Introduction

1974–1975

The Government of Indonesia untill [sic] now [sic] still adheres to the·following principles [sic]:
  I. The independence of every country is the right of every nation, with no exception [sic] for the people in Timor.
  (Adam Malik, Foreign Minister of the Republic of Indonesia, in a letter dated June 17, 1974 to José Ramos-Horta [Jolliffe 1978:66, courtesy of Helen Hill])

39. [Suharto] – I would like to speak to you, Mr. President, about the other problem, Timor. When it looked as if the Portuguese rule would end in Timor we sought to encourage the Portuguese to an orderly decolonization process. We had agreement with them on such a process and we recognized the authority of Portugal in the carrying out of decolonization and in giving people the right to express their wishes. Indonesia has no territorial ambitions. We are concerned only about the security, tranquility and peace of Asia and the southern hemisphere. In the latest Rome agreement the Portuguese government wanted to invite all parties to negotiate. Similar efforts were made before but Fretilin did not attend. After the Fretilin forces occupied certain points and other forces were unable to consolidate, Fretilin has declared its independence unilaterally. In consequence other parties declared their intention of integrating with Indonesia. Portugal reported the situation to the United Nations but did not extend recognition to Fretilin. Portugal, however, is unable to control the situation. If this continues it will prolong the suffering of the refugees and increase the instability in the area.
40. Ford – – the four other parties have asked for integration?
41. Suharto – – yes, after the UDT [failed insurrection], Indonesia found itself facing a fait accompli. It is now important to determine what we can do to establish peace and order for the present and future in the interest of the security of the area and Indonesia. These are some of the considerations we are now contemplating. We want your understanding if we deem it necessary to take rapid or drastic action.
42. Ford – – we will understand and will not press you on the issue. We understand the problem you have and the intentions you have.
43. Kissinger – – you appreciate that the use of US-made arms could create problems.

44. Ford – – we could have technical and legal problems. You are familiar, Mr. President, with the problems we had on Cyprus although this situation is different.

45. Kissinger – – it depends on how we construe it: whether it is in self defense or is a foreign operation. It is important that whatever you do succeeds quickly. We would be able to influence the reaction in America if whatever happens after we returned. This way there would be less chance of people talking in an unauthorized way. The President will be back on Monday at 2:00p.m. Jakarta time. We understand your problem and the need to move quickly but I'm only saying that it would be better if it were done after we returned.

46. Ford – – it would be more authoritative if we can do it in person.

47. Kissinger – – whatever you do, however, we will try to handle [it] in the best way possible.

48. Ford – – we recognize that you have a time factor. We have merely expressed our view from our particular point of view.

49. Kissinger – – if you have made plans, we will do our best to keep everyone quiet until the president returns home.

50. [No interlocutor named, but presumably, Ford] Do you anticipate a long guerrilla war there?

51. Suharto – – there will probably be a small guerrilla war. The local kings are important, however, and they are on our side. The UDT represents former government officials and Fretilin represents former soldiers. They are infected the same as is the Portuguese army with communism.

(United States Embassy Jakarta Telegram 1579 to Secretary State, 6 December 1975 [Text of Gerald Ford-Henry Kissinger-Suharto Meeting], Secret/Nodis (24). Gerald R. Ford Library, Kissinger-Scowcroft Temporary Parallel File Box A3, Country File, Far East-Indonesia, State Department Telegrams 4/1/75–9/22/76. See also Burr and Evans 2001)

2009

1974 is still alive.

(Bu Wilson: personal communication 2009)

Prelude

As always for the people of Timor, their lives would be changed by others ignorant of their concerns and geographically distant. Shortly after midnight, on April 25, 1974, as the carnations ("*cravos*") were in full bloom in the Portuguese countryside, tanks from Portugal's army, directed by officers in what they called the *Movimento das Forças Armadas* (*MFA*), the "Armed Forces Movement," rolled into the centre of Lisbon. Their troops gained control over the airport, and radio and television centers, and then stormed into the barracks where Prime Minister Marcelo José das Neves Alves Caetano, had taken refuge. He saw no point in resisting, and promptly surrendered to the former deputy minister of the Portuguese armed forces, General António de Spínola. Thus did the curtain fall on the final act in the five decades of a dictatorship Caetano had inherited from his predecessor, António de Oliveira Salazar. By the end of the afternoon, confident they were now Portugal's new masters, the *Movimento das Forças Armadas*, proclaiming the need for calm and patriotism, promised to bestow civil liberties and hold general elections for the National Assembly as quickly as possible. Prominent among their public statements was a condemnation of the colonial policy the overthrown Salazar/Caetano regime had tenaciously pursued over the preceding 13 years. The announcement publicly confirmed what critics had averred for many of those years, i.e., that the bloodshed in the African colonies would never bring about peace, and it promised radical reforms, which would be carried out by a seven-man junta under the leadership of General Spínola. The general and his men received an ecstatic reception from huge crowds of men, women, and children. The soldiers were given cigarettes, food, and newspapers describing the revolution; and elated girls inserted carnations into the barrels of the soldiers' guns. The *Revolução dos Cravos* – the "Carnation Revolution" – had begun.[1]

Liberation of a sort had arrived for the Portuguese, and while there would be many a bump attending the road to democracy, three centuries as a nation-state had developed a sufficiently powerful sense of national consciousness among the populace that, in time, would overcome any threats that might imperil its integrity. The same could not be said for the inhabitants of a barely-known colony situated halfway around the world. Equally impacted by the events of that day and the possibilities they afforded, were the people of Portuguese Timor (Timor Português; today officially "The Democratic Republic of Timor-Leste") who, together with those of Macau, were that European country's last colonial subjects in Asia. While, to many Timorese, the Carnation Revolution brought confusion and an apprehensive sense of insecurity, others – more ambitious and eager to seek their political fortunes – glimpsed an opportunity to play a role in shaping the future of their country. As John Taylor has remarked,

> With the demise of Portuguese colonialism, a nationalist movement emerged, drawing increasingly widespread support by devising policies that were directed toward, and developed aspects of, the indigenous social structure and value system, attempting to form them into strategies for the creation of a national economy and community.[2]

But at the time of the Carnation Revolution, although there were well-educated Timorese who did glimpse a future nation, they comprised hardly more than several hundred individuals in a country of just over half a million people. In contrast with the citizens of the mother country, the Timorese majority (illiterate farmers) had yet to conceive of themselves as participants in a Benedict Anderson[3] "imagined community," or demonstrate that they even comprehended the notion of "national identity." For that matter, they had never even expressed the slightest desire to be independent. So, even in those heady days, as the dawn of liberation was being celebrated in Portugal, a potential fault line in Timorese society could be discerned. On the day of the Carnation Revolution this was no more than hinted at, but over the course of the next 20 months and 11 days the gap between the would-be leaders and their presumed followers would widen at the same time as it deepened, intensifying a division between Timorese and bringing death in its wake. Oddly enough, it was not in the colony itself that a prime agency for that national awareness emerged, but in the capital of the mother country.

In the 1970s, the Portuguese Government initiated a program of scholarships for ambitious young Timorese wishing to study in Lisbon and by April 1974 the governor at that time, Colonel Fernando Alves Aldeia, had sent a hundred or so young persons of both sexes to Portugal. Accordingly, by the time the revolution arrived, a number of them had come to occupy a large apartment located in a high-density outer suburb of Lisbon. This was at first known as the "*Casa de Timor*," the "Timor House,"[4] but, following the revolution, its inhabitants changed its name to the "*Casa de Timores*," the "House of the Timorese," an appellation they believed more attuned to their socialist enthusiasms.[5] Among the residents were individuals destined to earn an eminent place in modern Timorese history: Abílio de Araújo; his wife, Guilhermina dos Santos de Araújo; Francisco Borja da Costa; António Duarte Carvarino (who went by the sobriquet of "Mau Lear") and his wife, Maria do Céu Pereira; Vicente Manuel dos Reis (more usually called "Vicente Sahe"); Hamis Bassarewan; Venâcio Gomes da Silva; and César Maulaka. Two other notables who would soon make their mark on Timorese politics and who shared the same radical political philosophy, Roque Rodrigûes and Rosa Muki Bonaparte, lived elsewhere in the capital. The scholarly disciplines they pursued varied. Carvarino studied law, Reis studied mechanical engineering, and Bassarewan studied civil engineering[6] but for most of them, when the day of the Carnation Revolution dawned, they closed their books. Their future lay, they reasoned, not in a Portuguese classroom, but back home, in Portuguese Timor, where a new political world was waiting its birth.

Background to events

The Portuguese Government had never permitted political activities in the colony, so it was something of a surprise that within a month of the *revolução* three political parties, the *União Democrática Timorense* (*UDT*), the *Associação Social-Democrática Timorense* (*ASDT*) (later named *Fretilin*), and *Apodeti*, blossomed miraculously, as it were, from barren soil, each with its distinctive political platform and offering their fellow Timorese the choice of three possibilities for their future. These possibilities were (a) maintaining a connection of some unspecified kind with the mother country; (b) independence; and (c) incorporation into Portuguese Timor's giant neighbor, the Republic of Indonesia. The speedy emergence of the three parties and their respective platforms had not been anticipated by the *Movimento das Forças Armadas*, but, Governor Aldeia, at the behest of President Spínola, issued a statement on May 28 informing the people of Portuguese Timor[7] that they were at liberty to establish political parties to decide among three alternatives regarding the future status of the territory in an election to be held on March 13, 1975.[8] If the army officers who ran the *Movimento das Forças Armadas* were caught unawares, the overwhelming majority of the population was jolted into a state of puzzlement. By so quickly obliging its inhabitants to make a decision that required more knowledge of democratic politics than they possessed, the government had made its first major policy error in respect of the colony; an error compounded by gratuitously bringing Indonesia into the picture. General support among the Timorese for the incorporation option was, and continued to be non-existent, and apart from one incident, there had never been any indication in the countryside that people desired to become Indonesian citizens.

However that may be, the die was cast. From May 1974 until December of the following year, the three parties attempted to sell their respective agendas to the people in a campaign that developed into verbal skirmishes that eventually resulted in the loss of lives. In part, this came about because during the period in question the political situation in Portugal became increasingly unstable, with changes of president and prime minister, which meant the government could not give the problem of Timor anything like its full attention. The bad policies that resulted included reducing the number of soldiers in the colony and failing to provide Aldeia's successor with the help he needed. The extravagant language of the parties was instrumental in the Indonesian Government's success in persuading a key *União Democrática Timorense* leader, João Carrascalão, to launch an attack on the police headquarters in Dili on the night of Sunday, August 10–11, 1975.[9] This reckless act of insurrection, in Portuguese known as the "*Golpe*," Carrascalão later represented as the birth of what he called the *Movimento Anti-Comunista de Onze de Agosto*, or "Anti-Communist Movement of August 11" (*MAC*), an ad hoc affiliation of the *União Democrática Timorense* and two minor political parties. Its target was *Fretilin*, which retaliated in a war lasting three weeks and ending when its troops drove the *União Democrática Timorense/Anti-Comunista de Onze de Agosto* force over the border into Indonesian Timor, leaving *Fretilin* free to form a de facto government. Given the wretched conditions that beset some regions as a result of the fighting, *Fretilin* leaders displayed impressive competence in re-establishing a measure of administrative order during the three months available to them before the Indonesian invasion, and felt confident enough in their capacity to govern East Timor to declare it independent on November 28. *Fretilin*'s decision gave Indonesia President Suharto verbal ammunition for persuading President Gerald Ford and Secretary of State Henry Kissinger to sanction an Indonesian invasion of the newly sovereign nation in a savage onslaught that eventually caused the deaths of more than a 150,000 Timorese. In July 1976, East Timor, now renamed "Timor Timur" by the Indonesian Government, was incorporated into the Republic of Indonesia as its 27th province.

Traditional authority and legal authority

In identifying different categories of "pure type" political authority, the sociologist, Max Weber, identified among them one category he called "traditional authority" and another he called "legal authority."[10] Traditional authority he averred, rests "on an established belief in the sanctity of immemorial traditions and the legitimacy of those exercising authority under them"[11] A "legal authority" model, on the other hand, depends on a belief in the legality of enacted rules and the right of those elevated to authority under such rules to issue commands.[12] From one perspective we may interpret what happened in 1974–1975 as an attempt by the political elite in the country's capital to convert a "traditional authority" model of governance into a "legal authority" mode. This attempt resulted in bringing into focus the contrast between the political center and the periphery that continues to characterize the political and social structures of the contemporary Democratic Republic of Timor-Leste. The durability of this bifurcation in East Timor lends support for the views of scholars, who like Benedict Anderson[13] question the concept of the nation-state. It also adds weight to the arguments of those who raise doubts about the legitimate application outside the European context of the concept, including Eric Hobsbawm[14] and Ernest Gellner.[15] Jean and John Comaroff[16] too have detected problematic issues in the functioning of the nation-state in non-Western societies by drawing attention to the pressures – "growing fast," they write – that induce "sovereign fragmentation," even in established nation-states. In less secure post-colonial nations, like Burma, the pressures are already well in evidence, as attested to by tensions between the capital and the periphery. These tensions have now emerged as such powerful impediments to the national integrity that one scholar regards them as poised to threaten the nation-state with disintegration.[17] In the period described here we see how an elite group of ambitious politicians, mostly young men, eagerly sought to reconcile the disjunction between the capital and its hinterland; and by examining their strategies, with the benefit conferred by hindsight, come to a clearer understanding of why they failed and how today's government might mitigate its intensity. In this context, the conclusion reached by the author of a recent book, *Justice and Governance in East Timor* sounds a plangent alert. If the institutions of those who reside in the hinterland, it remarks, are "delegitimized and shattered by attempts to socialize [them] into state justice and administrative systems, and if this process ... fails ... there is a risk that a society might be left with no functional systems of justice or public administration at all."[18] The persuasive force of this shrewd assessment is confirmed in the enlightening overview of East Timor recently published by Andrea Molnar, *Timor Leste: Politics, History, and Culture* (2009).[19]

Rhetoric: Timorese, Australian, and Indonesian

Whether defined by *The Oxford English Dictionary, Volume XIII* (2000: 859) as "the art of using language so as to persuade or influence others," or, as Kenneth

Burke would have it, the study of "the art of persuasion,"[20] or by Carrithers[21] and Passes[22] as a use of language that adds to our capacity to understand how people persuade others in pursuing political ends, the study of rhetoric crosses the spectrum of scholarship[23] Yet, in light of the undeniable fact that words came to play a decisive part in helping to encourage resentment against the colonial administration and incite physical violence, accounts of that time have been surprisingly reticent about the function rhetoric played during these 20 months.

The rhetorical forms used by Timorese politicians, officers of the colonial government, Indonesian politicians and generals, and members of the farming population can be seen, in the main, to correspond to three modes of rhetoric Aristotle isolated in his *Rhetorica* as "political rhetoric," "forensic rhetoric," and "hagiography." As various scholars have interpreted Aristotle's understanding of how the persuasive arts are deployed, political rhetoric may be described as anticipating "the future:" it persuades especially on matters involving public affairs. Forensic rhetoric is retrospective; it looks back at the past.[24] Hagiography marshals the resources of language to praise those worthy of acclaim. In 1974–1975 in East Timor, these rhetorical forms were manifested through four media: political programs and party manifestos; narratives (pre-eminently myths); slogans and catchwords; and invective. Complementing and reifying these verbal tropes was an assortment of material artifacts, the most prized of which was the Portuguese flag, the symbolism of which had been assimilated into local institutions.

The educated political elite of Dili, considerably more open to Western influence, typically used words in a rather different way from the illiterate population of farmers (the *ema foho* or *ema lisan*) living in the hinterland. Their political attitudes assimilated philosophical abstractions derived from Western traditions and they spoke in language that used the past as much as it anticipated the future. Most *ema foho* found their present in the past. They followed what they took to be the traditions bequeathed them by their ancestors, which were contained in the language of myth and legend, as well as in more formal language codified in ritual speech. Yet, even so committed to the past as they were, as the new ideas issued forth from the urban centers, ambitious men in the interior and some of its youth, too, were persuaded by the words of party activists, more especially those of *Fretilin* that the time for change had arrived.

Language and -isms

There is a tendency to see in the history of this time an upwelling of something resembling a popular feeling of nationalism fostered by *Fretilin*, and since *Fretilin* eventually became the new government, it is assumed its eventual victory signaled the triumph of this feeling and the acceptance of the party's political philosophy by the majority. This interpretation, I shall argue, misrepresents what happened and is not supported by the facts of ethnography, the historical record, nor political reality. Isolated from the capital, with its 1970 population of 128,000 including *bairo*s,[25] the *foho* was where over 95 percent of the population lived in small local communities called *suku*.[26] Although the peasants' lack of awareness of the outside world and education should make us cautious before accepting the validity of an explanation that assumes their grasp of alien philosophies, some commentators have sought to understand what occurred through the prism of such Western political concepts as "nationalism," "national movement," "communism," "socialism," "colonialism," and "neo-colonialism." Nationalism, originating and most vehemently espoused among the *Fretilin* elite and associated primarily with Dili, eventually touched most parts of the country and was to prove a vital ingredient in inspiring many Timorese to identity themselves as "*the Maubere*"[27] and resist the Indonesian occupation. But this was not so in 1974–1975 for little sense of national consciousness existed in the hinterland. Nevertheless, principally in order to sanction their own policies towards Portuguese Timor, heads of state were persuaded – or they persuaded themselves – that competition between rival -*isms*, directed the course of Timorese politics. The prime minister of Australia, Gough Whitlam[28], to give one example, drummed up support for an Indonesian takeover by alluding to "the left-wing influence in *Fretilin*," and, joining in with President Suharto, other Australian politicians denounced *Fretilin* as the "communist" party.[29] The consequence was that, because international spokesmen and the international media relentlessly construed the power struggle in terms of Western ideologies, parties were simplistically slotted into intransigent pigeonholes by those who read newspapers, watched the news on television, or listened on the radio. The *União Democrática Timorense* came to be identified as the "colonialist" party; *Fretilin* as the "communist" or – more mildly – as the "socialist" party, and *Apodeti* as the "neo-colonialist" party. Surprisingly, far from seeking as strenuously as they could to resist such labels, and oblivious of the damage they were doing to their public images, the leaders of each party inclined to intemperate language that served to reinforce these misappropriated appellations. They even went so far as to append epithets of their own devising, with, for example, *Fretilin* and *Apodeti* stigmatizing the *União Democrática Timorense* as "fascist." Tags like these also furthered the impression that ideology was the motivating impulse behind the political campaign. Nearly 30 years later, Mário Carrascalão, a member of the *União Democrática Timorense's comité central* ("central committee"), asserted that "Ideology ... divided Timorese...";[30] and even a political antagonist of his, a leading *Fretilin* intellectual, Abílio de Araújo, agreed.

Contemporary Timor-Leste

In the chapters that follow we shall see how *Fretilin* emerged as one of several political agencies that have attempted to reshape Timorese institutions over the course of the last 350 years, beginning with the Portuguese Administration – which *Fretilin* replaced – and followed by the Republic of Indonesia, the United Nations, and today's national government. Yet, despite this succession, contemporary Timor-Leste resembles the Portuguese Timor of pre-occupation days in a number of striking ways, two of which are so much a part of the present that the modern nation-state might almost seem trapped in the amber of the past. This parallel I call attention to by having a pair of quotations, one appropriate to 1974–1975 and another to contemporary Timor-Leste, serve as epigraphs for each chapter. The generation that shaped the history of the mid-1970s continues to dominate the political scene, and, regardless of the election, in April 2012, of José Maria Vasconcelos (better known as Taur Matan Ruak) as the new president, José Ramos-Horta, Mari Alkatiri, Mário Carrascalão, Roque Rodrigûes, and, though to lesser extent, Abílio de Araújo, continue to be prominent figures in public life. In the capital, they continue as before, contesting rivalries, often in more acrimonious fashion than is proper in a democracy, much as they were wont to do during the 1970s. At the same time, young men on the streets of Dili are known, on occasion, to resort to more energetic techniques of persuasion, as an earlier generation had done. But what is of greater moment is that – although not as pronounced as in the 1970s – the people of the *foho* continue to remain alienated from the capital. "Traditional" values continue to defy the latest notions issuing from the politicians in Dili, and this parochialism is reinforced by low standards of education. This dualism disturbingly echoes the past, and the tendons linking *foho* and the capital remain too tenuous for a strong nation-state to entertain.

Definitions

Since the terms, "nation," "state," "nation-state," and their congeners are central to my arguments, I need to be clear about the senses I attribute to them. These concepts are subject to varying definitions, of course, and others might be considered just as valid; but for my purposes I find those of Damien Kingsbury the most useful aids in framing the dilemmas faced by the Timorese in the mid-1970s and in contemporary Timor-Leste. "Nation," Kingsbury remarks, "is understood to refer to a group of people who regard themselves as possessing an aggregate political identity, most often based on a shared language (means of conceptualization) and other fundamental cultural signifiers."[31] He defines a state, as "the organizational territory under a political authority and which can (or can attempt to) claim or compel the compliance of its citizens to its laws,"[32] while the combinatory category of "nation-state" implies "a nation of people who claim the state as their collective territorial and institutional expression (or, less plausibly, as an administrative territory that claims a unity of the people within its boundaries)."[33] Accordingly, within the semantic scope afforded by these definitions, I define a "national movement" – such as has, in my opinion, mistakenly, been attributed to the Timorese of those years – as "a popular and organized effort by a group of people to realize an aggregate political identity," with "popular" here being a necessary qualifier. Before we press on, there is one more definition pertinent to my inquiry. Since I shall be using the term "ethno-linguistic group" throughout this monograph, to avoid any possible ambiguity, I should like to note that I employ the term in the sense of "a group whose members share basic cultural traditions and values and a common language, and who identity themselves and are identified by others as distinct from other such groups." Within the compass of this definition, East Timor can be said to have about 15 ethnolinguistic groups, and their principal sociocultural features are summarized in the next chapter.

A few words about the notion of "tradition" are also called for, because the meaning of the term is not quite as self-evident as might be supposed, especially in the context of Timor. While the institutions of the hinterland can be likened to a body of "tradition," some (though not all) of these "traditions" are hybrids resulting from years of interaction with the Portuguese, whereas others are of more recent pedigree.[34] Timorese "traditional" institutions cannot *ipso facto*, then, be assumed to provide an authentic mirror reflecting the past, for although those who dwell in the *suku* may attribute an autochthonous origin to certain of their institutions, the latter's source in the past may actually be of more recent vintage, and derived from colonial experience. Given the presence of the Portuguese for over three centuries, it could hardly be otherwise. To give one example: although an iconic political figure known as the *liurai*, or "king," is typically considered an exemplary instance of a traditional political category, that political category is, in fact, a blend of indigenous "tradition" and European innovation, an instance of a synthetic phenomenon common in Timor-Leste, as elsewhere. Finally, there is the term "institution," which I understand in the sense propounded by Marcel Mauss: "public rules of action and *thought*" [my translation and emphasis].[35]

Credentials

As a social anthropologist, my special interest lies in the domain of ethnicity, and my prime research procedures involve fieldwork as well as archival work. In East Timor my total research in the field has amounted to roughly 30 months, beginning in 1966 with a stay that lasted 19 months. I carried out research in the sub-district of Baucau for a few months, and then in Viqueque for over a year.[36] This initial period of fieldwork was supplemented by three shorter visits, between 1999 and 2001, for a total of roughly two months; a residence of seven months in 2005; an excursion of two weeks in 2007; and three weeks' visit in 2009. These residences provided me with the opportunity to interview men and women who had been involved the events described here, and my interviewees came from diverse points of the socio-political compass. They included members of the political elite, persons from the *ema foho*, Portuguese officials, and foreigners.

Notes

1 BBC. 1974 "On this Day April 25, 1974." http://news.bbc.co.uk/onthisday/hi/dates/ stories/april/25/newsid_4754000/4754581.stm. Accessed May 17, 2014.
2 Taylor (1995: 342).
3 Anderson (1991).
4 Thomaz (1977:40) regards the group of students residing in the apartment as having been so influential in instilling a left-wing ideology to *Fretilin* that he goes so far as to

label the *Casa Timor* "*Fretilin*'s birthplace." Jolliffe (1978: 73) puts the total number of students studying in Portugal at 39.

5 Carrascalão (2006: 50).

6 Araújo (2012: 95).

7 At the time of the Carnation Revolution and for months afterwards, the colony was referred to as "Portuguese Timor" ("*Timor Português*" in the Portuguese language), but as it became clear that its colonial status was in the process of changing, the name "East Timor" gained international currency. This appellation was assimilated into their declaration of independence by the *Fretilin* central committee in November 1975 when it declared independence and "Portuguese Timor" became "The Democratic Republic of East Timor." In this book I shall make use of both names, primarily employing the former when referring to the earliest months of the period described here.

8 Department of Foreign Affairs (1977: 16).

9 Although the term "coup" is often used to characterize the attack on the police headquarters, and even while it did, in effect, terminate Portugal's authority over the colony, the men who organized it claimed not to be seeking the overthrow of the Portuguese Administration. More apt terms might be "insurrection," "revolt," or "armed movement." There has been some discussion concerning when the coup began, i.e., whether on the night of Sunday, August 10, or the early morning of Monday, August 11. Even though military action began just before midnight, since the perpetrators applied the designation "*onze*" ("eleven") to their "Movement," i.e., *Movimento Anti-Comunista de Onze de Agosto*, and most of my informants regarded the coup as effectively commencing in the early hours of the August 11, I follow this convention.

10 Weber (1978: 212–241). I am indebted to Rod Nixon for bringing this to my attention.

11 Weber (1978: 215).

12 Weber (1978: 215). Weber's scheme is subject to various modifications, some imposed by their author at the time he offered them; others, subsequently, by scholars who have argued for or against them; but as polar abstractions they have useful application in the context of numerous local instances, including Timor-Leste.

13 Anderson (1991).

14 Hobsbawm (1990).

15 Gellner (2008).

16 Comaroff and Comaroff (2007: 48).

17 Smith (2006).

18 Nixon (2012: 9).

19 In preparing this book, it became apparent that research, especially at the level of the local communities, needs to be done before anything like a complete picture of the political happenings of those years can emerge. Examples would be the structure of the ties that bound the Dili politicians to the hinterland communities where members of their families lived and the nature of the political ties that bound them to local prominent families and the heads of sub-districts. Very little detail about what went on in these local communities has been published, and it is my hope that this book will encourage investigations along these lines.

20 Burke (1950: 46).

21 Carrithers (2005a, 2005b).

22 Passes (2004).

23 Cf. the *International Rhetoric Culture Project* [www.rhetoricculture.org] (Strecker 2005). Rhetoric's function as a political force is attested to by such appeals made to citizens by leaders like as President Bush who put it to decisive effect in his responses to 9/11 and in justifying his decision to invade Iraq (Carrithers 2005b).

24 Aristotle (1924: 1358a).

25 Dunn (2003: 4).

26 This term has general applicability throughout the Indonesian archipelago and in its particulars has a range of local meanings. For its use in East Timor see page 19.
27 See page 159 and Chapter Nine.
28 Whitlam (1980: 76).
29 That certain of the most vocal of the *Fretilin* elite, more especially Rodrigûes and Reis, were well to the left is however, hardly in dispute. The point I argue, though, is that for the mass of the population ideology was inconsequential.
30 CAVR (2004: 19). Testimony of Mário Viegas Carrascalão.
31 Kingsbury (2005: 88).
32 Kingsbury (1998: vi).
33 Kingsbury (1998: vi).
34 Cf. Hobsbawm and Ranger (1983).
35 Mauss (1968: 25).
36 Hence my frequent references to this sub-district.

References

Anderson, Benedict R. O'G. 1991. *Imagined Communities: reflections on the origin and spread of nationalism*. Revised and extended, ed. London: Verso.
Araújo, Abílio. 2012. *Autobiografia de Abílio Araújo: Dato Siri Loe II*. With José de Assunção Gonçalves. Lisbon: Alétheia Editores.
Aristotle. *Rhetorica*. 1924. W. Rhys (editor and translator). Translated into English under the editorship of W.D. Ross. Robert. *The Works of Aristotle, vol. 112*. Oxford: Clarendon Press.
BBC. 1974. "On this Day April 25, 1974". Available at: http://news.bbc.co.uk/onthisday/hi/dates/stories/april/25/newsid_4754000/4754581.stm. Accessed May 17, 2014.
Burke, Kenneth. 1950. *A Rhetoric of Motives*. New York: George Braziller, Inc.
Carrascalão, Mário Viegas. 2006. *"Timor: Antes Do Futuro."* Dili, Timor-Leste: Livaria Mau Huran.
Burr, William, and Michael L. Evans (eds.). 2001 (December 6). "East Timor Revisited: Ford, Kissinger and Indonesian Invasion, 1975–76," in *National Security Archive Electronic Briefing Book No. 62*. Available at: www.Gwu.Edu/~Nsarchiv/NSAEBB/NSAEBB62/. Accessed May 17, 2014.
Carrithers, Michael. 2005a. "Why Anthropologists Should Study Rhetoric." *The Journal of the Royal Anthropological Institute (N.S.)* 11, no. 2: 577–583.
Carrithers, Michael. 2005b. "Anthropology as a Moral Science of Possibilities." *Current Anthropology* 46: 433–446.
CAVR. *Timor-Leste Massacres: Audiência Pública Nacional*, 19–21 Novembro 2003, 2005 Comissão de Acolhimento, *Verdade e Reconciliação de Timor-Leste (CAVR)*.
Comaroff, Jean and John Comaroff. 2007. Law and Disorder in the Postcolony. *Social Anthropology*, 15 (2): 133–152.
Department of Foreign Affairs. 1977. *Decolonization in East Timor*. Jakarta: Republic of Indonesia.
Dunn, James. 2003. *East Timor: A Rough Passage to Independence*. New South Wales, Australia: Longueville Books.
Gellner, Ernest. 2008. *Nations and Nationalism*. 2nd. Ithaca, N.Y.: Cornell University Press.
Hobsbawm, E.J. 1990. *Nations and Nationalism Since 1780: Programme, Myth, Reality*. Cambridge: The Press Syndicate of the University of Cambridge.
Hobsbawm, Eric and R. Terence (eds.). 1983 *The Invention of Tradition* (Cambridge and New York, Cambridge University Press).

International Rhetoric Culture Project www.rhetoricculture.org.

Jolliffe, Jill. 1978. *East Timor: Nationalism and Colonialism.* Brisbane: University of Queensland Press.

Kingsbury, Damien. 1998. *The Politics of Indonesia.* 1st edition. South Melbourne, Australia: Oxford University Press.

Kingsbury, Damien. 2005. *The Politics of Indonesia.* 3rd edition. Oxford: Oxford University Press.

Mauss, Marcel. 1968. *Oeuvres: 1. les fonctions sociales du sacré.* V. Karady (ed.) Paris: Les éditions de Minuit.

Nixon, Rod. 2012. *Justice and Governance in East Timor: indigenous approaches and the "new subsistence state."* Abingdon and New York: Routledge Contemporary Southeast Asia Series.

Passes, Alan. 2004. "The Place of Politics: Powerful Speech and Women Speakers in Everyday Pa'ikwené (Palikur) Life." *The Journal of the Royal Anthropological Society (N.S.)* 10, no. 1: 1–18.

Pires, Mário Lemos. 1991. *Descolonização de Timor: Missão Impossível?* 3rd edition. Lisbon: Publicações Dom Quixote, Lda.

Smith, M. 2006. "The Paradox of Burma: conflict and illegality as a way of life." *International Institute for Asian Studies (IIAS) Newsletter* 42: 20–21.

Strecker, Ivo. 2005. (August-October) "On Anthropology as a Moral Science of Possibilities." *Cultural Anthropology* 46, no. 4: 650.

Taylor, John G. Taylor. 1995. "The Emergence of a Nationalist Movement in East Timor," in R.H. Barnes, Andrew Gray, and Benedict Kingsbury (eds.). *Indigenous Peoples of Asia.* pp. 323–343; 436–438. Ann Arbor: The Association for Asian Studies.

Thomaz, Luís Filipe F.R. 1977. *Timor: Autopsia de Uma Tragedia.* Lisbon, Portugal: Author, distributed by Dig/livro.

United Nations. 1976 (August). *Decolonization.* A publication of the United Nations Department of Political Affairs, Trusteeship and Decolonization. No. 7.

United States Embassy Jakarta Telegram 1579 to Secretary State, December 6, 1975 [Text of Gerald Ford-Henry Kissinger-Suharto Meeting], Secret/Nodis (24). Gerald R. Ford Library, Kissinger-Scowcroft Temporary Parallel File Box A3, Country File, Far East-Indonesia, State Department Telegrams 4/1/75–9/22/76. See William Burr and Michael L. Evans (eds.). 2001 (December 6) "East Timor Revisited: Ford, Kissinger and Indonesian Invasion, 1975–76," in *National Security Archive Electronic Briefing Book No. 62.* Available at: www.Gwu.Edu/~Nsarchiv/NSAEBB/NSAEBB62/. Accessed April 28, 2014.

Weber, Max. 1978. *Economy and Society.* Guenther Roth and Claus Wittich (eds.). Berkeley: University of California Press. Vol. One.

Whitlam, E.G. 1980. "Indonesia and Australia: Political Aspects," in Ross Garnaut, James J. Fox, Peter McCawley (eds.). *Indonesia: Australian Perspectives.* Canberra: Research School of Pacific Studies, The Australian National University.

Wilson, Bu. 2009. Personal Communication.

2   *Ema Foho, Ema Lisan*

1974–1975

Not all the FRETILIN visits to the countryside were a total success. In their early stages some of the FRETILIN leaders from Dili encountered a number of difficulties in their work in the rural areas.... Some of these difficulties were the sort of problems one would expect to be encountered by any group of western educated young people trying to convince traditionally minded rural people to change their ways.

Hostility was aroused in some areas when FRETILIN leaders made attacks on the "sacred" Portuguese flag. The Tetum word "Malai" means foreigner, it is traditionally used by people in the mountains to refer not only to non-Timorese but also to the people of Dili. FRETILIN leaders had to overcome this traditional hostility towards people from the town before they could get anywhere with their program.

In most cases it required the FRETILIN members themselves coming to a greater understanding of the specifics of Timorese culture, to realize, for example that it was better to tell the Timorese animists that they needed a new lulik, the FRETILIN flag, in addition to the symbols they revered, and to use this as a starting point for explaining what FRETILIN was, rather than to ridicule luliks as superstitious, as some FRETILIN members were inclined to do initially.

(Hill 2002:108–109)

2010

Sacred house inaugurated in Hatobuilico

Uma luliks [sacred houses associated with descent groups or families, though not villages] *in Oecussi, Bobonaro and Lautem are part of the same cultural preservation project.... The total cost is $32,000. Uma luliks are the spiritual center of communities throughout Timor-Leste. Each village* [sic] *uses its* uma lulik *as a gathering place for traditional rituals and as a spiritual resting place for the village ancestors. The United States provides* *financial support for* uma lulik *preservation out of respect for the roots of Timorese national and cultural entity.*

(A notice in *Embassy News*, issued from the Embassy of the United States in Timor-Leste, dated April 23, 2010, accompanied by a photograph of Ambassador Hans Klemm helping with the preparation of a presumably related ritual [United States Embassy 2010])[1]

The politicians of the capital were *"assimilados,"* a Portuguese word that denoted Timorese or Timorese-Europeans (*mestiços*),[2] who had been assimilated into the colonial system and who were literate, possessed a working knowledge of the Portuguese language, professed Catholicism, and bore a European-style name. The contrast with the *ema lisan* could hardly have been greater. The latter lived in a world that appeared more medieval than modern to the journalists who flocked to the colony, and they were to be found in 472 *suku* scattered about the interior.[3] They were subsistence farmers, oblivious to much of what was happening outside their island and even Dili itself, a town very few had visited or declared much interest in. This is an attitude that persists among older persons today. Although over the decades the *ema lisan* had come to assimilate some of the values of the colonial rulers into their "traditions," many institutions unfamiliar to Westerners were included in their *lisan*, which acculturation had not diminished. Unlikely vectors of a nationalistic impulse, local communities professed distinctive *lisan*, each allegedly vouchsafed to its possessors by their ancestors (*mate bein*) whose forensic rhetoric, expressed in myths, legends, and ritual speech, was tangibly supplemented in material artifacts of a sacred character (*lulik*), including the sacred houses (*uma lulik*) and ancient swords (*surik lulik*).

1 Location, geography, and population

The landscape of East Timor has encouraged ethnic diversity as much as it has been a hindrance to communication, a geographical reality, which among other consequences, made it very hard for the political leaders in Dili to control their followers in the hinterland from indulging in excessively violent behavior before, during, and after the war.

Lying between latitude 8° 17′ S and 10° 22′ S and longitudes 123° 25′ E and 127° 19′ E, Timor is part of a chain of islands straddling the equator from Sumatra to New Guinea, bounded by the Wetar Strait to the north (*tassi feto*) and the Timor Sea to the south (*tassi mane*), and located some 250 miles north of the Kimberley region of Western Australia (Figure 2.1). The eastern half of the island, together with the enclave of Oe-Cussi in Western Timor, constitutes the major part of the nation-state of Democratic Republic of Timor-Leste, with the small island of Ataúro, 12 miles north of Dili, and the islet, Jaco, at the extreme eastern tip of Timor, as its outliers. The western half is included in the Republic of Indonesia. By the nineteenth century the Portuguese and the Dutch, who had been contesting the island since the Dutch arrived in February 1613,[4] finally decided to settle upon a formal boundary between their respective spheres of influence in Timor, and they agreed in several boundary treaties. The Treaty of April 20, 1859 delimited the land frontier but left two enclaves, which the Convention of June 10, 1893 was intended to eliminate and mark an exact frontier. Most parts of the boundary were settled in 1898/1899, and those parts that remained disputed were referred to in a conference held at The Hague in 1902 whose results were incorporated in the Convention of October 1, 1904. However, the question of a Portuguese enclave in the Dutch territory remained. A theoretical boundary line was, nevertheless, drawn, and this issue dealt with by a boundary commission. It failed to reach an agreement, and at The Hague, on April 3, 1913, an arbitral agreement was signed by representatives of Portugal and the Netherlands to submit the question to the Permanent Court of Arbitration. This decided the matter, once and for all, on the basis of the concluded treaties and general principles of international law. The sentence (the Arbitral Award or *Sentenca Arbitral*) was rendered on June 25, 1914,[5] and it established the definitive boundary between what was then called "Portuguese Timor" and "Dutch Timor."

The country's imposing interior resembles a prehistoric-like landscape, with stark mountain peaks declining into a multitude of valleys, counterpointed by jagged rocky pinnacles and weird formations that culminate in the summit of Ramelau, at 9,331 feet the island's tallest mountain. Dissected into steep-sided

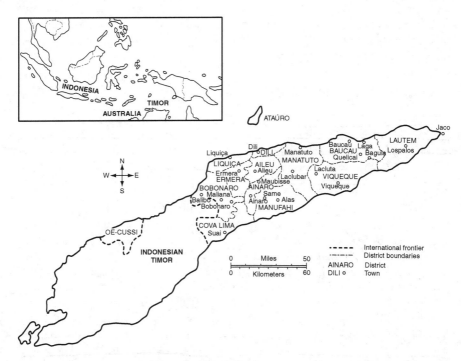

Figure 2.1 Timor and the districts and principal towns in Portuguese Timor in 1974.

ravines, intermeshed with wider valleys, the rugged highlands descend to the southern coast in foothills that spread out as broad alluvial plains as they approach the sea. In contrast, the landscape of the north coast alternates between maritime plains and terraces that drop, on occasion, precipitously, into the Wetar Strait, and the single road that passes along the north coast has to negotiate steep inclines, some of which nudge the passing traffic to the very edge of perpendicular cliffs hovering over the surf. During the dry season, the impression one gets traveling over the few mountain roads is of a brown, sun-baked, desiccated countryside; but with the arrival of the wet season, streams cascade from the central massif through a verdant landscape and drive purposefully over lower elevations to coalesce into rivers that empty into both seas. None, though, is navigable for any significant length. During the wet season, the monsoon makes the southern plain impassable in many places because the overflow from the rivers turns the unpaved roads into quagmires of mud.

The first European to register his impressions of Timor was António Pigafetta, who accompanied Magalhães[6] on his historic voyage around the world in 1515. Pigafetta describes the Timorese as hunters and foragers, who, save for golden ornaments that dangled on silk threads from their ears, went about naked.[7] They had swords and machetes; and bows and arrows. After contact with the Portuguese, the islanders' agricultural resources expanded significantly as the centuries went by[8], until, by the 1970s, the people of Timor practiced the swidden cultivation of crops such as corn, dry rice, green vegetables, sweet potatoes, yams, and other root crops; and cultivated wet rice on flat lowlands or hillside terraces. They also raised buffaloes, pigs, chickens, and dogs. In the closing years of the Portuguese era, some sub-districts had become famous for growing particular crops, Viqueque sub-district, for instance, being celebrated for its coconut palms and Ermera sub-district for coffee. In 1974, dispersed hamlets dominated the landscape, each *suku* following its own *lisan* and having its own particular social identity. However, the Indonesian invasion brought about massive changes, which included villagers being forcibly resettled into concentrated communities where they could be more easily controlled. Today, some families have returned to their traditional homelands.

The agrarian cycle influenced the rounds of daily life and was largely determined by the monsoons. Although the climate appears to be changing now, in the mid-1970s the mean annual rainfall varied from less than 23.4 inches on the northern coast to over 117 inches in the uplands, but seasonal incidence and the unreliability of the rains were more critical than absolute amounts.[9] From about November to May (depending upon location), the Northwest Monsoon brought heavy falls of rain, and from approximately June to October the Southeast Monsoon, blowing off the dry western desert of Australia, dropped an average of only about four inches a month. Seasonal temperatures varied little, unlike altitude. Higher altitudes were appreciably colder than the plains, and, regardless of the season, spending a night in the mountains required warm clothing. In 1966–1967, in the sub-district of Viqueque, rain began falling in November and, with its coming, corn was planted in gardens. Until February, when the crop was harvested, families tended their gardens, weeding the growing crop and protecting it from predatory animals. After the harvest came the planting of dry rice and corn again, followed by continued labor in the gardens, until another bout of harvesting was called for during the dry period in June-July. After that, apart from setting fire to the detritus that had accumulated from the year's work, little needed to be done in the gardens until October when households prepared the soil for the next cycle of planting.[10] During the wet season, families settled down for most days in their garden houses looking after the growing crops, but in July returned to their hamlets which now became the center of their social lives. Except for burning weeds and other such debris that had accumulated over the growing season in their gardens, they remained there until returning to the gardens to prepare the soil for next round of planting.

As often as not, however, the monsoons were irregular, and, whether the rains were delayed or lighter than expected, the consequence was a poor harvest, which meant families might have to depend upon stocks of food put by from previous years or forage in the forests, much like their sixteenth century forbears had done.

2 The administrative structure in 1974–1975

With physical geography presenting a daunting challenge to communication, a centralized political structure in East Timor was difficult to establish, but the colonial authorities tried. By April 1974, the *Província de Timor*, the "Province of Timor," consisted of 13 "*concelhos*" or "districts" (Figure 2.1),[11] which from east to west were Lautem, Baucau, Viqueque, Manatuto, Dili, Aileu, Ainaro, Same ("Manufahi"), Ermera, Liquiça, Cova Lima, Bobonaro, and Oe-Cussi. Each was under the authority of an officer of the colonial government, the *administrador* ("administrator"), who was assisted in his duties by a *secretário do posto* ("secretary of the post"), usually a Timorese or *mestiço*. The administrator, invariably Portuguese, reported to the *governador* ("governor") in the capital, who was the ultimate source of authority, law, and social order, in the colony, and who reported to the government in Lisbon. A district consisted of several *postos* or "sub-districts," each administered by a *chefe do posto* ("sub-district chief"), who, although sometimes a European, was more usually a Timorese. In 1974, there were 58 sub-districts, from one of which, the *posto sede*, the "sub-district seat," the administrator presided over the entire district and serving as his own sub-district chief within it.

A sub-district comprised a cluster of *suku*, each headed by a *chefe de suku* or *liurai*, who reported to the sub-district chief. The *suku* chief was the face of the administration, and although villagers elected the incumbent, their choice required the governor's endorsement. The term *suku* is Malay, and is widely used throughout the archipelago, albeit with different, though overlapping, meanings, which vary according to locality. In Timor in the mid-1970s, *suku* denoted a territorial unit within the administrative structure as well as referring to a social unit that was part of the *lisan*, a group of clans (*ahi matan*) holding certain institutions, rituals, charter myths, totems, and land, in common, and it was here, at the level of the *suku*, that European and Timorese institutions were most intertwined.[12] Although ubiquitous throughout the country, in certain regions the term *suku* had its approximate vernacular counterpart.[13] In the *suku* of Caraubalo, one of seven comprising the Viqueque sub-district, this vernacular term was *fukun*.[14] As a traditional social and political unit, a *suku* consisted of a number of villages (*povoações*[15]), each under a *chefe de povoação* ("headman"), and made up of *knua* ("hamlets").

3 *Lisan*

Whereas each *suku* was regulated by the protocols of its particular *lisan*, certain institutions were pan-Timorese. The most prominent of these were rank, kinship, marriage, gender, age, ritual, and belief, and two anthropologists carrying out field research in different regions at the time of the revolution provide insights into how the *lisan* operated in respect of certain of these institutions. Elizabeth Traube's *Cosmology and Social Life: ritual exchange among the Mambai of East Timor*,[16] which describes the institutions of the Mambai ethnolinguistic group residing in the sub-district of Maubisse, discusses myth, age, and gender in a wealth of detail in a sub-district that became of focal significance in the war; while the unpublished doctoral dissertation of Toby Lazarowitz[17] describes in ethnographic depth the system of kinship and affinity by which the Makassai, of Ossu sub-district, in Viqueque, organized their lives.

Rank

Social inequality operated through a tiered system of social hierarchy that was made up of three hereditary ranks, *liurai, dato* ("aristocrats" or "nobles"), and *ema, ema rai*, or *ema reino* ("commoners"), and, until the earlier years of the twentieth century, a fourth, the rank of *ata* ("slaves"). Victor T. King's definition of social inequality – "the process of unequal distribution of and/or unequal command over key resources such as materials, goods, ritual objects, knowledge and skills"[18] – well describes this feature of the *lisan*. Individuals were ascribed a social status based on the rank of their parents, either father or mother, depending upon whether a patrilineal or a matrilineal regime prevailed, but individuals could elevate their standing by wealth, education, occupation, fluency in Portuguese, professed Catholicism, or sartorial self-presentation. A prestigious marriage, the amount of bridewealth given for one's bride, the antiquity of family ritual paraphernalia, body ornaments, tombs, and honorary military titles bestowed in ancient times by Portuguese governors, were other indices that distinguished families and individuals.

The liurai

Irrespective of affiliation, most party leaders were of *liurai* descent. The word *liurai* literally means "more than the earth," and until 1912, when, after an unsuccessful rebellion, colonial authorities abolished their kingdoms (*rai* in Tetum; *reino* in Portuguese), the Portuguese described the *liurai* as "kings" (*rei* or *régulo*). After their kingdoms were broken up, *liurai* loyal to the Europeans were granted a *suku* from their old kingdom to administer as *chefe de suku*. Since there were more *suku* than kingdoms there were not enough *liurai* to fill every *chefe de suku* position, a lack exacerbated by some *liurai* being ineligible on account of their questionable loyalty. So men in the rank of *dato* were co-opted for the job, and since the title "*liurai*" was applied to the office, although now only as an honorific instead of an inherited title, some *dato* men became eligible to be termed "*liurai*."[19] This has occasioned confusion for some who have written about East Timor, since the term "*liurai*" now applied to two fundamentally different social categories of male functionary: one the "traditional" *liurai*; the other an "honorary" *liurai*, a distinction holding true today, with important political consequences. Despite the abolition of the kingdoms, *liurai* continued to enjoy privileges: they were exempted from *corvée* labor; automatically commissioned as officers in the *Segunda Linha*, the indigenous reserve army that supplemented the regular Timorese Army (the *Forças Armadas Portuguêses em Timor*); and enjoyed most of the few civil service jobs that existed. *Liurai* generally owned more land and livestock than other men, and so had the resources to afford a superior education for their offspring.

Two of the more celebrated *liurai* in Timorese history were an anti-Portuguese, *Dom* Boaventura of Manufahi kingdom who led a serious rebellion in 1911–1912 against the colonial power, and *Dom* Aleixo Corte-Real (1886–1943), of the kingdom of Ainaro, who resisted the Japanese in World War II during the time they occupied Timor (1942–1945) and was executed by them. His name has entered Luso-Timorese history as one of the greatest of heroic pro-Portuguese *liurai*.[20] Their lineages ranked at the very pinnacle of the Timorese social hierarchy, but within many *suku* there was a local hierarchy of such families. In Viqueque sub-district, the da Costa Soares family garnered considerable respect, and during the time of my first fieldwork its patriarch, Miguel da Costa Soares, wielded more influence with the administrator, José Teles, than did his other chiefly colleagues.

The power *liurai* and *chefe de suku* are often said to have exercised has aroused a certain negative attention in some discussions about what was occurring during the closing years of the Portuguese empire, especially as it involved their alleged exploitation of the peasants and the support they are supposed to have given to the colonial administration. While some took advantage of the influence they could exert with the authorities, to the detriment of farmers, their power has been exaggerated. Max Weber defined power as "the chance of a man or of a number of men to realize their own will in a communal action even against the resistance of others who are participating in the action," a definition which, as Victor King[21] has noted, stresses the coercive face of power. In Portuguese Timor, the power of kings was not, however, of this nature. What George Kahin has written about authority in the Javanese context – "A Javanese peasantry ... in most areas ... had been able to force the indigenous nobility to respect its rights…" – resonates in the context of Portuguese Timor as well,[22] and, among the factors that restrained a *liurai's* use of power, was the authority of the elders (*katuas*) in his *suku*. Any consequential decision he might wish to take required their approval, and those of *dato* rank or men who were members of the local *suku* council, a body of male elders that met regularly to discuss local matters. For their part, at sessions of the council, elders issued due notice of *their* wishes to the local *liurai*, and as a body had the authority to recommend to the local administrator that an unpopular *liurai* be censured, or even replaced. Elsewhere, too:[23]

> Timorese political and social reality is based on a system with democratic characteristics, in which the elected chief's power is limited by the general consensus of the elders – Katuas – and generally the possibility of hereditary succession is excluded. Until European influence was felt, Timorese society was organized according to a primitive feudal system headed by a *Liurai* – the monarch.
>
> The heads of villages and groups of villages, the *Liurais*, were freely chosen from among the nobles, forming a powerful wealthy ruling class in which authority and justice were said to repose. The *Liurais* were chosen by their peers, the *Dato*s, who were the descendants of royal families on the side of their father or mother.
>
> The chiefs resolve issues or disputes between people under their jurisdiction and only recur [sic] to the *Liurai* when they cannot find a solution. Family questions are resolved by the oldest – Katuas – of the *Knua*. Besides, the Katuas are the guardians of tradition and customs in a *Knua* or group of villages. They attempt to ensure well-being and harmony among all the inhabitants.
>
> For this reason, in the first phase of the young nation, it will be necessary to accept the most influential *datos* and *liurais* as part of the consulting council of the *Knua*s ["hamlets"]. Administrative divisions should respect the traditional borders of the old kingdoms and their ethno-linguistic divisions, but the number of counties [districts?] can be reduced and villages can become an enlarged *Knua* (not limited only to the family group).
>
> (Costa 1992: 146–147)

Father Apolinário Guterres, an educated Timorese, and Dr. João dos Santos, an anthropologist, reinforce this description:

> In Bunak society we can see in Taz [a Bunak village, evidently the one in which one or perhaps both of them carried out research] an organized miniature state, where family, educational, political, judicial, religious, military, and economic structures are based on a system of lineages. Power is parceled out in consensual fashion. The distribution of functions in Taz has existed since it was founded. The effective and correct exercise of institutional functions in Taz, and the interaction of the diverse social agents

according to traditional customs foster harmony, safety and overall welfare. As a decision-making institution, there exists in Taz the assembly of the council of the chiefs of lineage – the *datomil*/matamil.

(Guterres and Santos 1992:145)

influence ≠ power

This much having been said, I would, therefore, be more inclined to describe Timorese *liurai* as possessing *influence*, "the ability to change events or the minds and decisions of others without necessarily having the formal authority to do so" rather than "power."[24]

Dato *and* ema reino

Day-to-day administration of village life was exercised by the male elders of privileged *dato* families, of which a minority had received an education in the local Catholic primary school. However, facility in the Portuguese tongue was not required for these or for the highest office to which most *datos* could normally aspire, that of village headman. Unlike chiefs, they had few dealings with the colonial bureaucracy. In some sub-districts, the political structure of *suku* took the form of a diarchy. A case in point is Caraubalo, where a pair of leaders, the *makair fukun* and *dato ua'in*, governed *suku* affairs in parallel fashion to that of the *chefe de suku*. In the language of the local *lisan*, the *makair fukun* was metaphorically said to be the "father" of the *suku* whereas the *dato ua'in* was its "mother," the pair presiding over the *suku's* seven villages as "a father and mother look after their children." Their authority lay concealed under the administrative radar, but *lisan* conferred on both *dato* elders considerable influence with the *chefe de suku*, João da Sá Viana, who sought their counsel in major decisions, and without whose backing he could enforce neither his will nor the mandates handed down to him by the administrator.

Most *suku* residents were *ema reino*, commoners who, like *dato*, were obliged to undergo *corvée* labor. In most respects in daily life, there was nothing to distinguish members of this rank from *dato*, and they lived in the same style of house, mixing freely with the latter. Wealth was not a decisive factor in marking the distinction between ranks, and it was not unheard of for some *ema reino*, to be wealthier than men of the other two ranks.

Kinship and marriage

Entrenched in Dili though they might be, the leaders of all parties had to reckon with those *lisan* provisions regulating kinship and marriage, which unlike language, varied little among ethnolinguistic groups, except for certain Tetum- and Bunak-speaking regions, which had matrilineal descent and matrilocal residence rather than the more widespread patrilineal descent and patrilocal residence. Irrespective of the particular form it assumed in a *suku*, descent was the principal factor determining how individuals inherited property, privileges, eligibility for political office, and where a couple resided after marriage. Patrilineal descent resulted in the children becoming members of their father's lineage, and the bridewealth his family gave to that of the bride's also acquired for the bridegroom the right to reside with his father, an arrangement resulting in hamlets composed of male patrikin generation after generation. Land ownership, accordingly, was a function of descent and residence, and was justified in the language of proprietary charter myths narrated, when the occasion called, by *lia na'in* ("lords of the word") of the land owning lineages in question. The majority of ethnolinguistic groups practiced matrilateral cross-cousin marriage, an institution that brought into political, economic, and ritual alliances descent groups of varying degrees of segmentation, be they clans, lineages, or sub-lineage, and – prior to 1912 – *suku* and even kingdoms. This institution, which social anthropologists refer to as "asymmetric alliance," went by the generic term, *barlaque* (or *berlaki*), but most ethnolinguistic groups had their own vernacular term. In use among the various ethnolinguistic groups were the following: *maneheu-umamane* (Kemak), *malu-ai* (Bunak), *fetosa-umane* (Mambai), *feto-mone* (Atoni), *asukai-tupumata* (Makassai), *arahopata-tupurmokoru* (Fataluku), *anaperani-anahata* (Ataúro), *fetosa-umane* or *fetosawa-umamane* (Tetum), *vassau-umane* (Galoli), *uasa-umane* (Kairui), and *oa-sae – uma ana* (Naueti). According to the protocols of these alliances, the bride was considered only as one of the symbolically "feminine" items that made up the set of prestations wife-givers gave to wife-takers, and which were given in exchange for the symbolically "masculine" prestations that wife-takers gave to their wife-givers. The "feminine" prestations included cloth, basketwork, pigs, and, pre-eminently, of course, the woman herself. The masculine prestations included buffaloes, horses, money, golden pectoral discs, and silver pectoral discs. Gifts of the same symbolic character were exchanged at rituals of births, funerals, and other communal occasions.[25] Whatever the segmentary character of the descent groups engaged in these alliances, the latter involved specified mutual obligations encompassing ritual duties, economic assistance, and cooperation in various kind of manual labor. Even as late as the nineteenth century, kingdoms allied in this manner included among its provisions military collaboration, such as Schulte Nordholt[26] has described for the Atoni, of Indonesian Timor: "...in the case of war the bride-receiving ruler could marshal the support of his bride-giver."

This convention of closely-knit kinship and marriage relationships meant that, regardless of whichever party they affiliated with, leaders and followers were more often than not related as kin or affines to one another. Francisco Xavier do Amaral, president of *Fretilin* was married to Lucia, younger sister of a founder of *Apodeti*. Fernandes José Osório Soares was brother-in-law to Pinto Soares; both *Fretilin* leaders.[27] Mário Carrascalão was brother-in-law to the *Fretilin* leader, José Ramos-Horta. *Fretilin*'s Nicolau Lobato was married to the sister-in-law of a Gonçalves, one of Guilherme Gonçalves, the *Apodeti liurai*. The president of a fourth, albeit minor party, the *Klibur Oan Timur Asuwa'in*, José Martins, was a close relative of *liurai* José Hermenegildo Martins, Vice-President of *Apodeti*, and nephew of Guilherme Gonçalves. One result of these interlocking kinship connections – and the same could extend to friendships as well – was that during the war they could prevent prisoners from receiving cruel treatment at the hands of their captors or even save lives. One of my interviewees described how a *Fretilin* man saved a young female friend suspected of supporting the *União Democrática Timorense* from being raped by his colleague by vouching for her *Fretilin* credentials. She also recalled how a *União Democrática Timorense* family was given the opportunity to flee in a truck from *Fretilin* men after being warned by a *Fretilin* friend that his mates were coming for them.[28] Dulce Cruz (sister of the *Fretilin* leader, Vicente dos Reis), a *Fretilin* women, was taken prisoner by the *União Democrática Timorense* in Bucoli, Baucau district, and confined in the Baucau *pousada*.[29] Upon hearing she had not eaten for two days, a *União Democrática Timorense* man, Domingos de Sousa, a long-time friend, consoled her with gifts of food and cigarettes. Friendships also survived the war and the invasion. When *Liurai* Guilherme Gonçalves contracted prostate cancer, José Ramos-Horta bore the cost of his airfare to Portugal for him to receive medical treatment, and later paid for the *liurai's* body to be repatriated for burial in Dili's Santa Cruz Cemetery.[30]

Blood-brotherhood (*ahi-shaun*) also brought individuals and *suku* into relationships that entailed mutual reciprocity and in the seventeen and eighteenth centuries was used by kings and Portuguese military officers to establish political ties. This institution, as we shall later see, was put to rhetorical effect by the leaders of the "out of the mainstream" party, the *Klibur Oan Timur Asuwa'in*.[31]

Gender

Fretilin's agenda for change included adjusting gender conventions of the *foho* to suit the party's political ideology, and although no woman ever entered its superior echelons, four women were afforded the opportunity to contribute to the party's operations. Several, of course, were nurtured in the intellectual world of Lisbon university life and were married to prominent leaders. Maria do Céu Pereira was the wife of António Duarte Carvarino; Isobel dos Reis Lobato was Nicolau dos Reis Lobato's wife; and Guilhermina dos Santos de Araújo was the spouse of Abílio de Araújo. The most publically prominent, Rosa Muki Bonaparte, had returned from Lisbon in January 1975 to become a member of the *Fretilin*'s *comité central*. She was, by all accounts, an enthusiastic active party member, who later represented her party's interests in talks held with the Decolonization Commission[32] on May 7, 1975, and helped establish the *Organização Popular de Mulher Timor* (*OPMT*), the "Popular Organization of Timorese Women." Nevertheless, it was men who determined party policies and ensured they were implemented, and, as it happened, the most conspicuous contribution *Fretilin* women played in East Timor's history was that of political martyrs to the cause. On December 8, both Muki Bonaparte and Isobel dos Reis Lobato were executed on the Dili waterfront by paratroopers of *Angkatan Bersenjata Republik Indonesia*, and their corpses were discarded in the sea. One weakness in the arguments of those who claim that the *ema foho* readily accepted the *Fretilin* line is the failure of *Fretilin*'s challenge to traditional notions about women winning support in the hinterland. There, *lisan* limited women's influence to household matters, and the gender hierarchy remained as firmly installed in its protocols at the end of 1975 as it had been on the day of the Carnation Revolution. But it was not only the tenacity of the *lisan* that worked against change; the dismissive attitudes *Fretilin* operatives had towards *lisan* played its part in producing a "push back" in the hinterland, as is illustrated by a demeaning and sordid incident that allegedly occurred in the sub-district of Remexio, in the hills just south of Dili. There, according to Luís Thomaz, a group of young *Fretilin* men took it into their heads to divest village girls of their clothes, and, after they had been stripped, forced them to parade naked in front of the village.[33] Party leaders are unlikely to have condoned such behavior, but the tenuous communications between the capital and interior worked against keeping its impulsive cadres in line once they were ensconced in the fastness of the hinterland, In contrast with *Fretilin*'s demonstrated willingness to bring women into the public domain, neither the *União Democrática Timorense* nor that of *Apodeti* countenanced the possibility of adjusting the gender hierarchy, and for them gender never emerged as an issue.

Age

But it was not only within the institutional framework of gender that *Fretilin*'s ideology diverged from the values of the *ema foho*. In his account of the Japanese occupation and how nationalism strengthened the resistance movement, *Java in a Time of Revolution*, Benedict Anderson (1972: 1) notes that, "The central role of the *Angkatan Muda* (Younger Generation) in the outbreak of the Indonesian national revolution of 1945 was the most striking political fact of that period." He further remarks: "[Scholars] of the development of nationalism in Indonesia have also stressed the relative newness of this phenomenon in a society where the values of respect for and submission to the aged were traditionally paramount..." Much the same might have been said for Timor during the 1970s. *Fretilin* was youth-orientated at a time and place that was age-orientated. The tensions in this contrast unsettled the more conservative elements of the population, that is to say, the majority of the Timorese, and stirred resentment against *Fretilin* that was compounded by such behavior as that instanced above. Under *lisan* prescriptions, older persons were respected in weighty measure, and while the *Fretilin* leaders were, on average younger than those of the *União Democrática Timorense*, when *Fretilin*, then the *Associação Social-Democrática Timorense*, came to chose its president, the authority of the ancestors persuaded the party to select an older man, the 37-year-old Francisco Xavier do Amaral. Seniority's hold on Timorese life was apparent in every Timorese household one visited. In the absence of the father, his eldest son, were he of adequate years, served as his surrogate, commanding respect and enforcing his authority, when necessary, over both siblings and mother. Still, although respect for age buttressed domestic order, it could also generate its own brand of havoc since paternal or fraternal authority could result in abuse that led to quarrels that caused hamlets to break up. One remark attributed to an elder (*katuas*) during the heat of the campaign that "one has never seen such a thing: imagine what has happened, inside the same family, the father is of one party, one son is of another, and the others are of another,"[34] was most likely to have been generated by indignation that the sons did not follow their lord and master's lead.

Given the importance of kinship in Timorese society, it is hardly surprising that the idiom of kinship was incorporated into the forensic rhetoric of the *ema foho*. Elizabeth Traube describes how Mambai self-imagery portrayed themselves as the "elder brothers" and the Portuguese as their "younger brothers,"[35] an analogy that, incidentally, suggests that, far from regarding their relationship with the colonial authority as one of exploited subordination,[36] Timorese imagined themselves superior siblings.[37] The language of kinship suggesting, perhaps, that the *Fretilin* elite of Dili appeared to the *ema foho* almost as *malai* (the Tetum term for "foreigner") as the Portuguese.

Ritual and belief

Like kinship, affinity, age, gender, and blood-brotherhood, ritual practices imposed mutual obligations on people, and these practices were authorized through the narration of myths and legends. Unlike the residents of Dili, Baucau, and a handful of the more accessible towns, whom the missionaries had been proselytizing for decades, the farming population reposed its trust in ancestral ghosts, souls of the dead, nature spirits, corn souls, buffalo souls, a masculine sky god, and a "mother earth" goddess. These spiritual agencies were legitimized in the *lisan* and credited with the power to confer, or withhold, life's necessities. Of these, the most important were fertility, freedom from sickness, and plentitude in general, to obtain which villages would offer sacrifices in rituals whose successful outcome was certified by the birth of children, good harvests, health, and an increase in livestock. The origins of, and justifications for, these rituals and the beliefs associated with them, came in narratives which described how the first ancestors came by the *lisan* that would govern the lives of their successors, and, among other things, subjected them to a multitude of taboos (*lulik* artifacts and acts) and the veneration of various totems that governed their spiritual lives. The origins of local *suku* and their clans were similarly legitimized in the language of myth and legend.

Central to *lisan* was the concept Émile Durkheim[38] identified as the "sacred," and whose Timorese correspondent was *luli* or *lulik*. Besides meaning "taboo," the term was applied to a wide range of things, including isolated spots in the wilderness dedicated to spiritual agencies; artifacts safeguarded in the sacred houses; the *uma lulik* itself, of course; and a variety of contexts where sacred might encounter its opposite, the secular (*saun*). Included among these *lulik* artifacts were bracelets (*keke*) and necklaces (*morteen*); old porcelain imported from China; old Mexican coins (*pataca*), and war swords. Especially prized among families of highest rank were ancient, yellowed, papers from the Portuguese

Crown bestowing the title of "*coronel*" ("colonel") on *liurai* whom the Europeans wished to honor, sometimes on the occasion of blood-brotherhood rituals that bonded "younger brother" Portuguese individuals with "elder brother" Timorese notables. Of these fetishes none was more revered or held in greater esteem than the Portuguese flag – or fragments of the flag –, the veneration of which several writers have characterized as "mystical." Luís Thomaz suggests the flag might have been regarded as the totem of the Portuguese king and as such regarded as a transcending symbol of the conjunction of mother country and colony.[39] In that case, by asserting the conjunction of the capital (the locus of Lusitanian values) and the *foho*, this *lulik* artifact might be regarded as a counterforce to the disjunctive socio-political rift between the capital and periphery: perhaps even the master trope of Portuguese Timor itself. We get some sense of the sacrosanct quality Timorese had come to invest in this artifact over the course of centuries of interaction with the Portuguese, from the anthropologist, Margaret King, who described one she inspected in a house in Luro sub-district (Lautem district) in 1960–1961 as follows:[40] "From the dim recesses of his house the chief brought us to a small and carefully wrapped bundle which he reverently unwrapped before us. Enclosed within the wrapping was a stained and battered cloth, which as it was unfolded to the light, proved to be a flag. The linen, discoloured with age, bore at its centre a large red cross of coarsely woven cloth, such as sailors might use, and it was sewn to the finer white linen with large, masculine stitches. Printed beneath the cross, in ink now faded to reddish brown were the words: *"Dada por Valenty Correa figa TENENTE DEHES BEILOS A Phoupicão de Luz, Juridcão de Same dada em Luro em 20 a Julio de 1693 annos.*

"Given by Valenty Correa, gentleman, Lieutenant Belos to Phoupicão de Luz, ruler of Same – given at Luro on 20 July 1693."

The flag enveloped a small book, hand-bound in calf, the edges of its pages yellowed and split with age, whose print, still legible, identified it as an abbreviated Missal published in Prague in the year 1660. As the political campaign took its course, the flag-as-symbol was snagged from the cobwebs of a remote political past and fashioned into a useful addendum to the verbal repertoire of the *União Democrática Timorense* and *Klibur Oan Timur Asua'in*. Nor were the *ema foho* alone in attributing a sacred dimension to this red, white, and green fabric. For all their anti-colonial criticisms, when the leaders of *Fretilin* became the de facto government of the new East Timor, yet wished to let the world know they still continued to look upon the Europeans as the *de jure* authority, they were scrupulous about maintaining the ritualistic protocols of the Portuguese flag, which they continued to fly from the government building. And, even as the balance of power was shifting in Dili towards *Fretilin*, and Portuguese soldiers were in the process of leaving the island with all possible speed, a major in a paratrooper brigade sent to Timor by the Portuguese Government, seeing a Timorese man tearing up the national flag to fashion it into a *simulacrum* of a Red Cross flag denounced, in heated words of protest, the perpetrator of the desecration.[41]

Something of *lisan's* political dimensions is seen in the part the *uma lulik* came to play in the political action. The following account, told to CAVR by a *Fretilin* man, Mateus Soares, illustrates how this edifice could be put to political use during the war, and underscores the nightmarish savagery Timorese, in some regions, inflicted upon those against whom they held (oftentimes unacknowledged) grudges.[42] Mateus Soares, so he relates, was in Turiscai when the war broke out, and since news of the revolt in Dili had not yet reached him, he had no idea why *União Democrática Timorense* in that sub-district, and in the nearby sub-districts of Laclubar and Soibada, suddenly began to assault *Fretilin* supporters. They eventually stopped, however, and returned home to Poholau where they had come from, a *suku* that lay on the border between Laclubar and the *suku* of Fatumakerek, where the *União Democrática Timorense* had its headquarters. At no great distance away, Francisco Xavier do Amaral gathered together a delegation of 11 *Fretilin* soldiers, under the command of a *Fretilin* commander, Geraldo Barbosa, to negotiate with the *União Democrática Timorense* force; but when they arrived in Poholau, Soares among them, they were instantly set upon and captured. After being tortured, the captives were taken to the *suku* of Fatumakerek, in Laclubar, where, he relates, the torture continued, and they were not permitted any food or drink. Fatumakerek *suku* had an *uma lulik*, next to which was a grindstone the *União Democrática Timorense* troops used to sharpen their weapons, and they took delight in flourishing their machetes at their prisoners. One day, a man inside the house began to perform a *lulik* ritual, which involved him running out of the house, jumping and shouting while the prisoners remained in a state of dread. When he had completed the ritual, the captives were pulled over to the edge of a ravine, and Soares feared they were as good as dead. He had been roped to another man, and their captors began jabbing away at them with spears, until one soldier threw a machete in Soares' and his companion's direction. It missed the two of them, but cut the cord binding them. Despite having his hands bound together behind his back, and as the soldiers slung stones and spears in their direction, Soares threw himself towards the ravine. One struck Barbosa, but he was still alive when the soldiers tossed him over the precipice. Only three of Soares' friends survived, and he himself managed to escape only because he succeeded in securing a hiding place near a local river where he was later found by Portuguese soldiers who gave him food. The cord binding him had by now embedded itself in his skin, and after he had eaten, he soaked his hands in water to remove it with the help of his rescuers. When they finally managed to extract the cord, a deep wound remained and he suffered hemorrhaging.

The ethnolinguistic groups

Apart from some engrained hostility between the Naueti and Makassai peoples in Viqueque district, which had arisen in the late 1950s, and a tradition of ill-will between the Kemak and Bunak, ethnic rivalry, as such, did not usually translate into physical violence. Not that ethnolinguistic groups did not appreciate their own individuality, for, just as topography limited communication and made political centralization difficult, so too did physical geography foster ethnic and – above all – linguistic diversity as divisive cultural markers. Outside of Dili, each ethnolinguistic group spoke its own vernacular, of which, depending upon the criteria for classification, there were about 15 in East Timor;[43] and some, like Tetum and Makassai, had dialectal variants.[44]

It is understandable that foreign concepts like "communism," "democracy," "fascism," "freedom," and suchlike held little meaning for the rural folk since their equivalents did not exist in the languages of Timor. It was only after the Carnation Revolution, however, that the term *ukun rasik-an* – "independence," "autonomy" – came into circulation in the Tetum language, to accommodate the political changes that it had ushered in and the neologism became a rallying point for the two major parties. The international press identified Tetum[45] as the "language of Timor," but this was very much an exaggeration. True, a Tetum-Portuguese dialect, spoken in Dili, was in some general use around the colony, but this hybrid was far from being the *lingua franca* popularly assumed. As befitting its location, the dialect was known variously as *Tetum Dili* or *Tetum Praça*,[46] and it contained numerous words borrowed from Portuguese. This pidgin form of the Tetum language derived from *Tetum Los*, or so-called "true Tetum," or *Tetum Terik*, a more grammatically and semantically complex dialect altogether, which was spoken along the southern coast of both Timors.

Timorese languages belong to two principal families, the Austronesian, which includes 11 languages, and the non-Austronesian (or "Papuan"), which includes four. Geoffrey Hull, a linguist, derives the Austronesian languages on Timor from an ancestor language (or group of related dialects) spoken in the Muna-Buna-Tukang Besi zone of southeastern Sulawesi ("Moributonia"), and

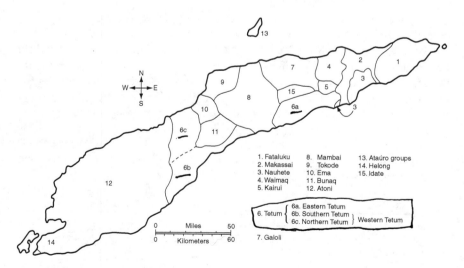

Figure 2.2 Principal ethnolinguistic groups.

suggests that, about the eleventh century A.D., speakers of languages derived from this ancestor language sailed to Timor where they encountered speakers of non-Austronesian languages who had arrived sometime prior to the birth of Christ. With the passage of time, their languages assimilated linguistic traits from the autochthonous languages.[47] The precursors of the Kemak, Tokode, Idate, and Mambai he regards as possibly having originated in Muna and Buton islands, while those of the Tetum and Galoli languages and the Kawamina complex of dialects, taking a less direct route, coming from the four islands of Tukang Besi via Wetar.[48] As for what he calls the "Bomberaians" – speakers of the non-Austronesian languages found on Timor: Fataluku, Makalera, Makassai, and Bunak[49] – in Hull's evolutionary schema, their forbearers originated in New Guinea, perhaps from the Bomberai Peninsular.[50] "While retaining many non-Austronesian features, the four transplanted 'Papuan' languages have been more-or-less assimilated to the Timor Sprachbund made up of Austronesian languages of Celebean [Sulawesian] origin."[51]

When the Portuguese arrived on Timor at the beginning of the sixteenth century they found a patchwork of kingdoms grouped into two confederacies. One, which was called the Servião, roughly corresponded to today's Indonesian Timor and consisted of 16 kingdoms. The other was the Belu Confederation, consisting of 46 kingdoms, with the kingdom of Wehali as its most prestigious. This east/west moiety has, as we have seen, proved resilient through the centuries, manifesting itself as Dutch Timor/Portuguese Timor, Indonesian Timor/Portuguese Timor, Indonesian Timor/Timor Timur, Indonesian Timor/East Timor, and, today, Indonesian Timor/Timor-Leste.[52]

The people of the lisan, the ema foho

Geographically and culturally isolated as they were, and still governed to a large extent by the institutions summarized above, these ethnolinguistic groups were untouched by the ideological currents that had swept the Dutch, British, and French out of Southeast Asia. While the concept of independence had swum into the consciousness of the populace by the end of the twentieth century – as the election of 1999 demonstrated – it took intense persecution by the *Angkatan Bersenjata Republik Indonesia* to really stimulate a sense of national awareness, and, of course, the Church also played its part in bringing this about. This growing sense of nationalism found verbal expression in a term – *mauberism* – that had its origins in the period but grew rapidly as a verbal icon for the growing feeling of national identity. I discuss this term more fully later. A statement such as:

> By the end of 1975, however, and particularly during the period when Fretilin administered East Timor after the departure of the Portuguese, support for the movement had increased dramatically, extending to all ethnolinguistic groups, even the Fataluku people at the eastern extremity of the island

is to lay claim to the future rather than reflect the reality of the period.[53]

After the fighting they had suffered and the social dislocation it had brought into their lives, the Timorese were thankful for the relative stability of the de facto government of *Fretilin* after its forces had defeated the *União Democrática Timorense*. They accepted the new regime as they had done that of the Portuguese Administration, and as they would that of the United Nations. For the most part, villagers were apolitical, and it was only after September 1974, when the first batch of *Fretilin* cadres began to arrive from Dili to start their proselytizing, did they have the opportunity of being introduced to new ideas. And these novelties would be scrutinized through the *lisan* lens. While hardly an authority on Timorese sociology, and a politician with his own agenda, Prime Minister Whitlam was not entirely off the mark in charging that the political elite, as "rulers of the rest of the population," (Whitlam 1980:759) were essentially substitutes for the Portuguese. Remarkably, for its part, *Fretilin* leadership seemed to have bought into this view, as demonstrated by Ramos-Horta's assertion that serves as one of the epigrams for the present monograph.

The aftermath of the revolution had made it obvious that 350 years of Lusitanian colonialism had done little to reconcile the "educated" and the "uneducated," or integrate Dili with its hinterland; and this legacy of disjunction the *Fretilin* leadership moved swiftly to address. They were about to engage on an attempt to convert the Timorese local version of the aforementioned Weberian "traditional authority" model into a "legal authority" model. Although they almost surely did not realize they were embarking on an enterprise comprehensible within terms of this dialectic, *Fretilin* leaders were very much aware that the demands of this conversion entailed their extending the institutions of the new political order they wished to create from the capital into the *foho*.

Notes

1   In the aforementioned epigrams the term *lulik* finds a conspicuous space, and, though it will be considered in more detail later on, a preliminary note of its range of referents is appropriate at this point. *Lulik or luli* refers to things that are "sacred" or "set apart" from the mundane affairs of quotidian life, and thus includes things pertaining to the invisible world of the ancestral ghosts that inhabit the spiritual world. Since the term *uma* includes among its referents "house" and "building," the term *uma lulik* may be rendered as "sacred house" or "ritual house," a building prominent in Timorese conceptions of space, and which came to play a political role in 1974–1975.

2   The term also includes the Timorese-Chinese.

3   Duarte (1988a: 53).

4   Durand (2006: 84).

5   Krieger (1997: 1).

6   He is more generally known to the English-speaking world as "Magellan."

7   Matos (1974: 25).

8   Matos (1974: 17, 18).

9   Ormeling (1957: Figure Five).

10   I describe the cycle of agricultural work as it was in the Viqueque sub-district during the period 1966–1967. Variation occurred across the country.

11   Strictly speaking, the Portuguese term *concelho* refers to a "municipality" or "council."

12 For a discussion of how this system worked, see Hicks (1990: 1–13).

13 The term *suku* and the vernacular term were not exact synonyms because the latter lacked the administrative connotations of the former.

14 Glossed as "node" or "point of articulation."

15 In contemporary usage, the term *povoação* has been replaced by *aldeia*.

16 Traube (1986).

17 Lazarowitz (1980).

18 King (1985: 12–21). Cf. Rousseau (1990).

19 Although there is an assortment of different categories of political leaders that might be characterized as "chiefs" in Timor, when one reads in the press about Timorese "chiefs," it is invariably to these *liurai* that the writer is referring. It will be recalled that, in his dialogue with the two American statesmen, President Suharto mentioned "kings." This was the category of leader he had in mind. It is worth noting, by the way, that those who write about Timorese politics habitually fail to discriminate among the "traditional" *liurai* and the "honorary" *liurai* (see Hicks 2013: 29–30).

20 See Felgas (1956: photograph facing page 152).

21 King (1985: 19).

22 Kahin (1966: 2).

23 The passage that follows is less reliable about the allocation of authority in the *suku*, hamlet, and "village," and the assertion that "the possibility of hereditary succession is excluded."

24 Shea (1988: 3).

25 Hicks (2007a: 239–262).

26 Schulte Nordholt (1971: 388). Asymmetric alliance, though a conspicuous feature of most Timorese social organizations, is not featured in all marriages. For various reasons, in a particular marriage it may not be resorted to, and in such cases this more encompassing system of wife-giver/wife-taker is replaced by a marriage imbued with fewer symbolic, economic, and political entailments. For a discussion of these alternative modes of marriage, see Hicks (2004: 94–102).

27 Nicol (1978: 57).

28 Madeira (2009). Maria Madeira was nine years old and living in Ermera at the time of the coup and could not return to Dili, so she fled to Atambua. Certain other members of her family were in Dili and fled to Darwin. She eventually finished up in Portugal.

29 A government-maintained hotel.

30 Ramos-Horta (Interview 2005).

31 See page 58.

32 See page 112.

33 Thomaz (1977: 73). The author gives no source for this statement.

34 Thomaz (1977: 63). "*Nunca se viu uma coisa assim: imagine que sucede, dentro da mesma família, o pai ser de um partido, um filho de outro, e os outros ainda de outro.*"

35 Traube (1986: 52).

36 But see the contrary opinion of Araújo on page 68.

37 An origin myth Traube (1986: 54–61) transcribes makes this point admirably.

38 Durkheim (1960: 65).

39 Thomaz (1977: 21).

40 King (1963: 156–157).

41 See page 151.

42 CAVR (2005: 20–21).

43 For a comprehensive account of the languages in East Timor, see Hull (1998, 2000, 2004).

44 Unlike East Timor, Indonesian Timor has only four principal indigenous languages, Atoni, Tetum, Bunak, and Kemak.

45 "Tetun," "Tetu," or "Teto" in alternative orthographies.
46 The dialect is also called *Tetum Maka.*
47 Hull (2000: 158; 1998: 149–153).
48 Hull (1998: 149–153).
49 Alternative renderings for Bunak are "Bunaq" and "Buna."
50 Hull (1998: 149–153; 2004: 27).
51 Hull (2004: 27).
52 East Timor is also called *Loro Sa'e,* the Tetum term for "east."
53 Taylor (1995: 337).

References

Duarte, Jorge Barros. 1988a. Timor: *Um Grito.* Odivelas, Portugal: Pentaedro Publicidade e Artes Gráficas, Lda. e Jorge Barros Duarte.

Durand, Frédéric. 2006. Timor: 1250 750 ans de cartographie et de voyages. Editions Arkuiris, Espace, Asie, Toulouse, France: IRASEC [Institut de Recherche sur l'Asia du Sud-Est Contemporaine], Bangkok, Thailand.

Durkheim, Émile. 1960. *Les structures élémentaires de la vie religieuse; le système totémique en Australie.* Paris: Bibliothèque de Philosophie Contemporaine Fondée par Felix Alcan, Press Universitaires de France. 4th edition.

Guterres, Apolinário, and João dos Santos. 1992 [Synopsis of a Paper], in António Barbedo de Magalhães (ed.). *East Timor: Land of Hope Second Symposium on Timor Oporto University (28 April–1 May 1990)* p. 145. Oporto, Portugal: President's Office, Oporto University.

Hicks, David. 2004. *Tetum Ghosts and Kin: Fertility and Gender in East Timor.* Waveland Press, Inc.: Prospect Heights, Illinois. 2nd edition, 2004.

Hicks, David. 2007a. "The Naueti Relationship Terminology: A New Instance of Asymmetric Prescription from East Timor." *Bijdragen tot de Taal-,Land- en Volkenkunde* 163 (2/3): 239–262.

Hicks, David. 2013. "Adat and the Nation-State in Timor-Leste: Opposition and Synthesis in Two Political Cultures," in Michael Leach and Damien Kingsbury (eds.). *The Politics of Timor-Leste.* pp. 25–43. Ithaca, N.Y.: Cornell Southeast Asia Program.

Hill, Helen. 2002. *Stirrings of Nationalism in East Timor: Fretilin 1974–78, The Origins, Ideologies and Strategies of a Nationalist Movement.* Kuala Lumpur and Díli: Contemporary Otford, Otford Press, Ortford (Sydney).

Hull, Geoffrey. 1998. "Basic Lexical Affinities of Timor's Austronesian Languages." *Studies in Languages and Cultures of East Timor* 1: 97–202.

Hull, Geoffrey. 2000. "Historical Phonology of Tetum." *Studies in Languages and Cultures of East Timor* 3: 158–212.

Hull, Geoffrey. 2004. "The Papuan Languages of Timor." *Studies in Languages and Cultures of East Timor* 6: 23–99.

Kahin, George McTurnan. 1966 (1952). *Nationalism and Revolution in Indonesia.* Ithaca, New York: Cornell University Press.

King, Margaret. 1963. *Eden to Paradise.* London: Hodder & Stoughton.

Leach, Michael, and Damien Kingsbury (eds.). 2013. *The Politics of Timor-Leste.* Ithaca, N.Y.: Cornell Southeast Asia Program. pp. 25–43.

Lazarowitz, Toby Fred. 1980. *The Makassai: complementary dualism in Timor.* Unpublished Ph.D. dissertation, State University of New York at Stony Brook.

Matos, Artur Teodoro de. 1974. *Timor Português 1515–1769: Contribuçâo Para a Sua*

História. Lisbon: Faculdade de Letras da Universidade de Lisboa Instituto Histórico Infante Dom Henrique.

Nicol, Bill. 1978. *Timor: The Stillborn Nation.* Melbourne: Widescope International Publishers Pty Ltd.

Ormeling, F.J. 1956. *The Timor Problem: A Geographical Interpretation of an Undeveloped Island.* Groningen and Jakarta: T.B. Wolters, 1956.

Schulte Nordholt, H.G. 1971. *The Political System of the Atoni of Timor.* Translated by M.J.L. van Yperen. Verhandelingen Van Het Koninklijk Instituut Voor Taal-, Land- en Volkenkunde 60. The Hague: Martinus Nijhoff.

Thomaz, Luís Filipe F.R. 1977. *Timor: Autopsia de Uma Tragedia.* Lisbon, Portugal: Author, distributed by Dig/livro.

Thomaz, Luís Filipe F.R. 1981. Notas Linguistics. Lisbon: Thomaz.

Shea, Michael. 1989. *Influence.* London: Sphere Books Ltd.

Taylor, John G. 1995. "The Emergence of a Nationalist Movement in East Timor," in R. H. Barnes, Andrew Gray, and Benedict Kingsbury (eds.) *Indigenous Peoples of Asia.* pp. 323–343; 436–438. Ann Arbor: The Association for Asian Studies.

Traube, Elizabeth G. 1986. *Cosmology and Social Life: ritual exchange among the Mambai of East Timor.* Chicago: University of Chicago Press.

United States Embassy. 2010 (April 23). Press Release: Sacred House Inaugurated in Hatobuilico, Embassy News. Available at: http://timor-leste.usembassy.gov/news-events/press-releases-2010/sacred-house-inaugurated-in-hatobuilico-april-23-2010. html (U.S. Embassy, Dili, Timor-Leste). Accessed April 28, 2014.

Victor, T. 1985. *The Maloh of West Kalimantan.* Verhandelingen van het Koninklijk Institut voor Taal-, Land-en Volkenkunde 108. Dordrecht-Holland/Cinnaminson-U.S.A.: Floris Publications.

Interviews

Madeira, Maria. Interview 2009.

Ramos-Horta, José. Interview 2005.

3   Portugal's legacy and the politicians of Dili

1974–1975

I myself hesitate to accept at face value the claims of the political personalities who have emerged in the <u>first year of political activity in Timor</u>. They have sprung from what appears to have <u>been a political vacuum under</u> the Portuguese. <u>Most appear to represent a small elite class – the educated, the government officials and various other Westernized elements</u>. It may be that this group will be able to win the allegiance of the people of the territory, <u>but their claims are as yet untested</u>. There may well be, below the surface, thoroughly indigenous political forces which would carry the inhabitants of Portuguese Timor in directions different from those on which their present leaders are set.

(Prime Minister Whitman in a letter to Senator Arthur Gietzelt dated 22 April 1975, and quoted in Dunn 2003:129)

2002–2005

RESEARCHER: Senhor A., *may I ask you a "stranger" question?*

CHEFE DE SUKU: *You have lived in our village for almost three years and I am used to your questions. You are welcome. I will try to answer.*

RESEARCHER: *Imagine, you are walking along a road, and at a junction this road splits up into three different paths. And now your* governo *[government] says, "Turn left!" And the Church says "go straight!" And your tradition requires you to turn right! Where would you go?*

CHEFE DE SUKU: *You must respect all three.*

RESEARCHER: *Yes. But sometimes in life there are these difficult situations and you must make decisions. Imagine. Prime Minister Alkatiri says, "go left!" Bishop Basílio says "go straight", and the old men of your uma lulik (sacred house) demand, to go right: Which track would you follow?*

CHEFE DE SUKU: <u>*We really must respect the* governo *in Dili, the religion*</u> katoliko <u>*[Catholic religion] and our*</u> tradisaun *[traditions] – but <u>if the situation is really, really hard, I think, I can never do anything against <u>my sacred house. Everybody</u> must respect the</u>* lisan *(traditional law).*

(Loch 2009: 95)

Unimportant in the eyes of successive governments of Portugal and as a consequence, neglected, Portuguese Timor had always been the "invisible" colony about which politicians in faraway Lisbon cared very little and begrudged the cost of keeping even more. After traveling around its *suku* for four months in 1861, Lord Alfred Russel Wallace registered his impressions:

> The Portuguese government of Timor is a most miserable one. Nobody seems to care the least about the improvement of the country, and at this time, after three hundred years of occupation, there has not been a mile of road made beyond the town, and there is not a solitary European resident anywhere in the interior. All the government officials oppress and rob the natives as much as they can, and yet there is no care taken to render the town defensible should the Timorese attempt to attack it. So ignorant are the military officers, that having received a small mortar and some shells, no one could be found who knew how to use them; and during an insurrection of the natives while I was at Delli [*sic*] the officer who expected to be sent against the insurgents was instantly taken ill! and they were allowed to get possession of an important pass within three miles of the town where they could defend themselves against ten times the force. The result was that no provisions were brought down from the hills; a famine was imminent, and the Governor had to send off to beg for supplies from the Dutch Governor of Amboyna [*sic*].[1]

A visitor to the Portuguese colony in the year of the *Revolução dos Cravos* would have recognized a family resemblance to Wallace's portrayal in, above all, the fault line between the capital and its hinterland that impressed him so much. But by 1974 the administration was showing signs of taking its colonial responsibilities rather more seriously, most conspicuously in that greater attention was being paid to the territory's infrastructure. Although still subject to the disruptions brought about by floods, landslides, and the collapse of bridges, communications had improved somewhat, and something resembling a modern system of roads was starting to bring the district capitals into closer contact with Dili. Even so, however, because such advances usually favored the capital, the ensuring disparity made the polarity all the more striking. Whereas the streets in Dili were sealed and its inhabitants enjoyed electricity, the populations in the districts were obliged to rely upon the initiative of their local administrator, with the result that districts differed considerably in the development of their infrastructures and local economies. Viqueque town in 1966 showed what improvements might come about under the direction of an energetic administrator. Dr. José Teles had used the resources at his disposal to construct a furniture factory, install water tanks and running water, and encourage local people to make traditional artistic artifacts for a tourist industry he was attempting to build. The sort of commitment to the colony such as Teles displayed was uncommon, though, and the administration had yet to devise an effective and reasonable plan for systematic improvements throughout the colony, and, while a new bridge would be constructed in one district, travelers might risk their lives trying to make their way across crumbling, ancient, wooden bridges or attempting to ford perilous watercourses in a neighboring district. For Timorese and Europeans alike, the country's shoddy roads and bridges, and its rulers' ineptitude, provided a fertile source of anecdotes. Among the stories that circulated during my first visit were the following. The first concerns the fate of an ambitious scheme that was poorly conceived and badly executed in Manatuto. The principal river in this district debouches into a dauntingly wide estuary, which in the 1960s could only be crossed by a vehicle driven by an experienced driver adept at bouncing it (and his passengers) from one boulder to the next. In the wet season, passage was just possible at times when the rainfall had stopped in the mountains and the elevated level of the river had sufficiently abated to make an attempt at passage feasible. But even then, the driver's deftness could be seriously taxed as he negotiated the boulders and strained against the river's powerful current, which continually threatened to sweep the vehicle and its passengers northwards into the Wetar Strait. The 81-mile journey between Timor's two largest towns, Baucau and Dili, could take more than half a day.[2] In the mid-1960s, therefore, the administration decided to have a bridge constructed, and to that end employed a Portuguese engineer to carry out the job. He succeeded in laying down the foundations of the bridge, and constructing the span itself, but was unable to complete the work before the next wet season. The onslaught from the millions of tons of floodwaters that poured down from the central massif caused what had been built to be washed into the sea. Undeterred by this catastrophe, when the next dry season arrived, the engineer tried again, but with the same result. The second anecdote illustrates the lack of vision by an administration trapped in the mindset of the previous century. It concerns a crude system of signaling relied upon to prevent collisions at a particularly dangerous site on a road only 20 miles from Dili, at a place where the road rises abruptly in a series of tight bends cut into a range of cliffs that drop suddenly into the sea. Since the road was extremely narrow and circuitous, to prevent two vehicles, coming from opposite directions from confronting each other on the same stretch, a sentry had been stationed at each end of its narrowest part to telephone his colleague when a vehicle arrived on his side. His was a 24-hour vigil.

As with roads and bridges, so too with education. Although, by the early 1970s, more pupils than ever before were being taught in the schools, illiteracy remained widespread,[3] and few children ever made it to secondary school. Institutions of advanced education were scarce; though there was one that did provide an exceptional education. Tellingly, however, it was not a government institution, but one run by the Church. Here, at the Jesuit seminary of *Nossa Senhora de Fátima*, a few miles south of Dili, many leading politicians of both the *União Democrática Timorense* and *Fretilin* were schooled; but even for its well-educated graduates, few jobs existed in the more prestigious professions in the civil service or in teaching, a shortage that bred resentment against the colonial government by those who had received a good education, yet had not found a job adequate to that education.

The year before I went into the field, a civil servant in Lisbon had told me that for the Portuguese Government "Timor is a bore." No senior cabinet minister had ever visited the colony, and two decades later José Ramos-Horta would recall, with justification, that "Portuguese attitudes towards East Timor ranged from condescending paternalism to outright disrespect for the rights of the people of East Timor to self-determination."[4] Even some Timorese succumbed to this dismissive attitude, more than one person informing me, when things were not working out as well as I had hoped, that "*Timor hanessan ne'e*," i.e., "This is Timor. How can you expect anything to go right, function properly, or generally act as it should here?" – an attitude some Europeans used to justify their own incompetence or laziness. For them, the saga of the River Manatuto Bridge was cause for amusement rather than embarrassment.

The antinomic character of the relationship between Dili and the *foho*, described by Alfred Russel Wallace, had been in existence many years before he arrived on the island. The hegemonic authority of colonialism was contained within the capital itself, with only two or three small outliers along the coast affirming its claims. Elsewhere, the European presence was scarcely even nominal, with *liurai* asserting themselves when and wherever they desired, while at the same time paying nominal tribute to the colonial government as a token of their putative submission. At the core of the Portuguese military force were the indigenous militias who were controlled by pro-colonial *liurai*, and it was these that were deployed against *liurai* that rebelled. This dependence upon Timorese soldiers, and the fragility of Dili's defenses, was not lost on the kings in the hinterland. Between 1847 and 1863, the majority of kingdoms along the north coast engaged the colonial army in sundry skirmishes, with the kingdoms of Cotobaba and Maubara usually being in the vanguard.[5]

The arrival of a new governor, José Celestino da Silva (1894–1908) shook the status quo.[6] At the time he assumed office, Portuguese Timor was administered from the Portuguese colony of Macau, and almost from the time he arrived he sought to change this relationship of subordination and report directly to Lisbon. He was a forceful man and inside two years had achieved his goal. As for the colony itself, Governor Silva decided that the kings had given his predecessors far too many headaches, and began a series of military campaigns to bring them to heel. The struggle lasted for 12 years, and had its setbacks, but Silva showed himself as forceful in dealing with the rebel kings as he was diplomatic in negotiating with the government in Lisbon. The colonial authorities now reorganized the colony into commands (*comandos militares*), each administered directly from Dili, and by 1908 there were 15: Batugadé, Bobonaro, Maubara, Liquiça, Aipêlu, Hatolia, Manufahi, Central do Sul, Central do Norte (with its "seat" first in Motael and afterwards in Aileu), Remexio, Manatuto, Baucau, Viqueque, Lautem, and Oe-Cussi.[7] For any serious attempt at administering the colony, this was a move in the right direction; but it was not enough to stop *Dom* Boaventura, the *liurai* in Manufahi, from attempting another rebellion. The rebellion came in 1911–1912, three years after Silva had been replaced as governor by Filomeno da Câmara de

Melo Cabral. *Liurai* Boaventura was finally defeated, and with his defeat the administration was well placed to consolidate its authority and lessen the threat of future rebellions.[8] The kingdoms were dismantled and with it the position of *liurai*, though the *suku* within each former kingdom remained as a territorial unit of administration. *Liurai* regarded as loyal to the colonial authorities were installed as *chefes de suku* or appointed to the higher position of *chefes de posto*.

As time went by, and the fear of rebellions became increasingly remote, the colonial administration gradually began to assume a less military character, so that by January 1934, the military commands had been pre-empted by a system of civil administrative regions (*circunscrições*), and when the Japanese invaded, the colony was being administered through the single district (*concelho*) of Dili and six *circunscrições*.[9] From east to west, these *circunscrições* were Lautem, São Domingos, Manatuto, Suro, Fronteira, and Oe-Cussi. The Japanese retained this system during their three years' occupation (1942–1945), and only in 1966 was there further reorganization. With the exception of Oe-Cussi, which remained an administrative region, the *circunscrições*, became districts in their own right.

Like the Portuguese before them, the Japanese exploited the rivalries among the kings and *chefes de suku*, some of whom sided with the occupiers, whereas others stayed loyal to the Portuguese. Others preferred to remain neutral. Loyalty to their former masters cost some kings their lives, as happened to *Dom* Aleixo Corte-Real,[10] and *liurai* in Viqueque, Atsabe, and Bobonaro, who were executed, though, in some instance, the victims were more anti-Japanese than pro-Portuguese. Three years of occupation devastated Timor, and not all deaths were caused by the invaders. As an omen for the future destruction that would be visited upon the populace during the militia rampages of 1999, armed militias of Timorese surrogates for the Japanese army – the "Black Columns" (*colunas negras*) as they came to be called – ravaged the hinterland, destroying houses and killing whomsoever they wished. Among the collaborators was Arnaldo dos Reis Araújo, who was jailed for nine years by the Portuguese when they reclaimed their colony.[11] A little over 30 years later, *Apodeti*'s future president climaxed his political career when he was made first governor of Timor Timur after the Indonesia invasion. Following a pattern that *União Democrática Timorense* and *Fretilin* supporters would replicate in 1974–1975, and the militias would follow in 1999; the Black Columns selected as their preliminary targets villagers living in *suku* traditionally at loggerheads with their own. As was to be the case in the mid-1970s, these marauders were for the most part men who had no jobs or had not received what they deemed sufficient advancement in the administration.

After 1945, the only serious incident that might be considered a rebellion was that in 1959. Many of the details of the event remain obscure, but the drama provided gist for the anti-colonial attitudes of several prominent leaders of *Fretilin* and *Apodeti* to exploit what they chose to cast as an anti-colonial rebellion for their own political ends.[12]

Portuguese Timor in 1974

Like the African colonies, Timor was not officially designated in the Portuguese Constitution as a "colony," but as a "*província ultramarina*" ("overseas province"), a status redefined by the Overseas Organic Law of 1972 in order to deflect anti-colonial denunciations by Third World leaders, which had intensified during the 1960s.[13]

Lisbon's indifference to Portuguese Timor is apparent in the uneven quality and accuracy of official statistical data available on the colony, and so its demographic make-up in the mid-nineteen-seventies is not as exact as one would like. This is the case not only with regard to the ethnic breakdown of the population, but also in terms of headcounts. Official figures give a 1970 total population of 610,541[14] and official estimates for 1974 number 650,000, though Catholic Church figures for the same year put the figure at 680,000, including over 97 percent ethnic Timorese.[15] In Farol, near Dili's lighthouse, lived several hundred Muslims, mostly traders, who usually had little interaction with persons outside their community, and this population included Mari Alkatiri, who, in 2001, became the first prime minister of East Timor. The *Delegação de Timor do Instituto Nacional de Estatística* gives the following 1973 figures: total population 646,155, including about twenty thousand Catholics, 2,400 Protestants, and 910 Muslims. Europeans numbered 1,500, and there were about seven thousand Chinese and two thousand *mestiços*.[16] Of the combined Timorese and *mestiço* populations, 91 percent were non-literate, and of the 9 percent literate, only a small minority had received more than a primary education.[17] The 1970 census records that about 76 percent of Timorese were self-employed farmers cultivating their own gardens and rice fields, 15 percent worked for a family as domestics, and nine percent were salaried, mostly employed as civil servants or in some position associated with the bureaucracy.[18] The majority of Europeans in 1970 were either soldiers or civil servants working in the territory for a limited time.[19] Like other foreigners, they were called *malai*[20] by Timorese, and over half of them resided in Dili, which was credited with a 1974 population of about twenty thousand.[21] Apart from the handful of civil servants who administered the districts, some teachers, priests, nuns, and soldiers, the only Europeans in the interior were the settlers, many residing in Ermera and Liquiça, the two districts most favorable for the cultivation of coffee. The total population of permanent European settlers numbered no more than 50, and the land they occupied totaled less than 301,384 acres, 1.4 percent of the total territory.[22] There was only one large-scale capitalist enterprise, the *Sociedade Agricola Patria e Trabalho* (*SAPT*), half of which was owned by the state, and grew 40 percent of East Timor's coffee, a reality also contradicting *Fretilin*'s claims.[23] The only other major Portuguese capitalistic enterprise was the *Sociedade Orientale do Transportes e Armagéns* (*SOTA*), which handled wholesale and retail activities. Private coffee planters grew 10 percent, and the remaining 50 percent of coffee was grown by Timorese peasants. Except for the coffee region, the economy of Portuguese Timor was of a subsistence nature, with production in the hands of the *ema foho*.

Fretilin's arguments to the contrary,[24] apart from the *Sociedade Agricola Patria e Trabalho*, the European settlers were too few in number to impose their economic interests on the local population, and it was the Chinese who were the dominant commercial force in the colony. Descendants of immigrants who had begun to establish themselves in Timor as early as the seventeenth century, they remained faithful to the language and culture of their homeland, and owned 98 percent of the retail establishments and controlled more than 75 percent of the external commerce. Less tight-knit than the Muslims, they nevertheless formed a fairly closed community and usually avoided involving themselves in European culture or integrating into that of the Timorese. They were uninterested, for the most part, in politics, and were generally viewed unfavorably by the rural population, which regarded them as exploiters.

The incompetence, and occasionally the abuses, that plagued the colony's administration aroused some criticism of the Europeans by the Timorese elite, but most knew that Timor's economy depended on Portugal, which – assisted by subsidies from Angola and Mozambique – provided one-third of the public expenditures of the colony, amounting to 120 *contos* a year. This was six times more than Portugal collected from Timor, which provided only 15,000- to 25,000 *contos* annually.[25] Despite this, *Fretilin* leaders alleged that the Portuguese were gouging their country, and they believed it to be true, so that, while anti-colonial antagonism among the rural people was rare, by the end of the 1960S it was decidedly discernible among the men who were to form the *Associação Social-Democrática Timorense* and *Apodeti.* José Ramos-Horta, for one, envisioned no possibility of advancement in the civil service or of putting his education to use in the prevailing political status quo, and he later characterized his fellow disaffected as "an incipient national organization." He makes no mention of the *ema lisan* experiencing the same alienation from the Portuguese.

The *Forças Armadas Portuguêses em Timor* and the *Segunda Linha*

A prime contributor to *Fretilin*'s triumph over the *União Democrática Timorense* was the support given by the *Forças Armadas Portuguêses em Timor*, a military organization usually described in English as the "Timorese Army," which, until the early 1970s, was mainly composed of European officers and men and recruits from the African colonies.[26] It included infantry, an artillery battery, and a cavalry unit equipped with light armored vehicles. In the early 1970s, Timorese men became eligible to join the ranks of the *Forças Armadas Portuguêses em Timor*, and by 1975 several had been elevated to the rank of non-commissioned officer. But for all that, only Europeans could be officers, and they were few in number, which is hardly surprising since the total number of European troops never amounted to more than about 2,500 men.[27] Until about two weeks after João Carrascalão's insurrection, when the army swung its weight decisively behind *Fretilin*, the political affiliation of the indigenous members in the *Forças Armadas Portuguêses em Timor*, was not clear-cut.

Although *Apodeti* commanded no support among either men or officers, most Timorese soldiers may have inclined more to the *União Democrática Timorense* than to *Fretilin*. So, too, did a minority of European officers, but the anti-Fascist attitude of most tended to make them rather more inclined towards *Fretilin*. The most striking phenomenon affecting the *Forças Armadas Portuguêses em Timor* before the night of August 10, 1975 was the steady attrition of its European contingent as they were steadily repatriated, a process that continued until only about 200 soldiers, including about 70 combat troops remained.[28] So few had they become that the Portuguese Government, at the request of Governor Pires, augmented them at the end of March with a detachment of a platoon of parachutists and some administrative staff sent from Portugal, and then in late July, a second platoon.[29] At the same time, the number of Timorese men in the ranks steadily increased until by 1974 the latter numbered about 3,000. The following year, the first Timorese recruits were commissioned and elevated to the rank of *alferes* ("second lieutenant"). James Dunn,[30] Australian consul in Dili from January 1962 to 1964 and a member of a fact-finding mission sent to East Timor by the Australian Government in 1974, is of the view that, by inducting Timorese into the army, the Portuguese contributed to the growth of political awareness among some of the more educated men. Non-commissioned European officers and second lieutenants carried out the bulk of military instruction, and many of these men, educated in Portuguese universities, tended, for the most part, to be of left-wing persuasion. Some formed personal relationships with the Timorese soldiers entrusted to them, and inculcated anti-Salazar/Caetano notions into their thinking. Attempting to improve primary and secondary education, the colonial administration used some of these university-educated army officers to supplement civilian teachers, and by 1973 90 *escolar militares* ("military schools") had been established. While these military adjuncts were never conspicuous, their influence was significant, and many passed on their liberal ideas in the classroom. On the other hand, although they privately deplored the low level of development on Timor, the poverty of the Timorese, and the Chinese business monopoly, senior European officers tended to be loyal to the Salazar and Caetano regimes.[31] The sentiments of the junior officers and men gradually spread through the army, though it was not until after the attack on the garrison (*quartel-general*)[32] on the night of August 10, 1975, that the Timorese troops threw themselves and their weapons decisively behind *Fretilin*.

Providing a backup for the regular army was the indigenous military reserve, the *Segunda Linha*, which consisted of about 7,000 men.[33] Conscription was compulsory for all Timorese males, with only *liurai* being eligible for the rank of officer.

The *Revolução dos Cravos* and its aftermath

However "bored," disinterested in, and largely ignorant of, their last remaining Asian colony the Portuguese Government may have been before the *Revolução dos Cravos*, its occurrence intruded itself into the previously insignificant Asian colony into the new anti-colonial government's agenda. The Provisional Government was organized by the *Junta de Salvação Nacional,* ("National Salvation Junta"), which was made up of seven army officers, Francisco da Costa Gomes, Jaime Silvério Marques, Diogo Neto, Carlos Galvão de Melo, José Baptista Pinheiro de Azevedo, António Rosa Coutinho, and their leader, António de Spínola, who became president. These men had no formal party affiliations, and they remained in office from April 25 to May 16. Their work included abolishing the more repressive institutional apparatus of the fascist regime, but there were no purges. Spínola was a military man; a political moderate faced with the immediately pressing problem of how to deal with the colonies, particularly Angola, Mozambique, and Guinea-Bissau, which had been fighting for independence for years, and by July the government had committed itself to embarking upon a process of gradual decolonization. Portuguese Timor, however, was a special problem, not only because it was so undeveloped, but, paradoxically, because there was no independence movement already existing with leaders ready to form a government.

As suggested earlier, the gradual disintegration of public order in Portuguese Timor during the 20 months following the Carnation Revolution can, to some extent, be accounted for by the instability prevailing during that time in Portugal itself. This helps explain the lack of decisiveness shown while Spínola was president, and why, after the failure of the insurrection, Governor Pires sent urgent requests to Spínola's successor, Francisco da Costa Gomes, without receiving responses. The mother country and the colony were on parallel tracks, though, unlike what happened in Timor, no crippling political violence broke out. In 1974 Spínola had published a book, *Portugal e o Futuro,*[34] that excited general interest by arguing that Portugal should divest itself of its colonies. This bold argument him brought about his political celebrity and was what opponents of the fascist regime wanted to hear, so that when the left-wing young officers of the *Movimento Forças Armadas* decided upon who should be their leader this public reputation was one factor in their choosing him.[35] However, their own political views – much to the left of the political spectrum – were at odds with his more centrist inclinations. His ideology has been characterized by Kenneth Maxwell[36] as evolutionary and favoring a gradual decolonization of the Portuguese overseas possessions. In contrast, the *Movimento Forças Armadas* officers' ideology was revolutionary and in favor of immediate decolonization. The revolution itself obscured this divergence; but as the months went by the cleavage became increasing a political issue, and though he made attempts to retain his office, Spínola was forced out on September 30, 1974. From that time on the radical position of the *Movimento Forças Armadas* officers dominated the government, and a communist, Vasco dos Santos Gonçalves, eventually became Gomes' prime minister. In July 1975 – when the colony was at its most critical period of all – there was a two-month struggle for power in Lisbon between Gonçalves and his supporters and the more moderate left-wingers in the government. "Last weeks' developments certainly did not signal a right-wind revival. But the country's drift toward Communism had clearly been checked and perhaps reversed, leaving socialists of a non-communist stripe as the big winners."[37]

During the five months he held office Spínola seems to have entertained the idea of converting Timor into some sort of "Associated Territory" or "Federal State," an idea not all that dissimilar from the initial platform the *União Democrática Timorense* decided upon at its creation, though rather different from that of the *Associação Social-Democrática Timorense*, and decidedly at odds with its subsequent platform when it evolved into *Fretilin*. Major Silvério Henrique da Costa Jónatas, a leading officer in the *Movimento das Forças Armadas*, in Portugal, is reported to have said later that if Spínola had not been ousted, *Fretilin* would have been in trouble because the president had a real dislike of that party.[38] But Spínola proved too conservative for the younger officers in the movement, who began to waver in their support of him, and then withdrew it. The president's followers countered in September by seeking to remove what they saw as the more dangerous left-wing officers from key positions in the government, and they failed, and Francisco da Costa Gomes, his predecessor's army chief of staff and another officer with no political affiliations, assumed office. He served as president for most of the time the campaign in Timor lasted, leaving office on July 13, 1976, the month East Timor was incorporated into Indonesia as the republic's 27th province. Decidedly more left-wing than his predecessor, Gomes worked with the *Movimento das Forças Armadas* to bring Portugal's domestic politics and foreign policy more in line with the latter's socialistic bent. They wasted no time granting independence to the African possessions,[39] but realized Timor was a special case. Unfortunately for the *União Democrática Timorense*, Spínola's vague plan held no appeal. Whatever they might say in public, the new rulers of Portugal favored either outright independence or integration into Indonesia, and with the passing of the months, and regardless of Lisbon's indignant reaction to the eventual invasion, the government's actions suggested their preference was for incorporation.

Also out of luck was Fernando Alves Aldeia, who had been appointed governor in January 1972.[40] A few days before the revolution he had publicly described the army officers as a bunch of "undisciplined" soldiers, an untimely imprudence that resulted in his being replaced by Lieutenant-Colonel Níveo Herdade. From all accounts Aldeia was a conscientious administrator who was relatively popular with both Timorese and Europeans.[41] Pires himself is of the opinion that had Aldeia been retained as governor he might have been able to quell the disorder ("anarchy" as he calls it) that developed in the capital after his departure.[42] It was not until July 15 that his acting successor, Níveo Herdade, replaced him, by which time the three parties were already coming to dominate the political stage and the administration's control over the colony was already starting to weaken.[43] Herdade's mission was to try implementing a plan – if a rather uncoordinated cluster of ideas can be characterized as such – that Spínola seems to have been working on for modifying the status of Portuguese Timor from that of a colony into something resembling an associated territory or a federal state. Spínola appears to have invested some confidence in the acting governor's executive capabilities, and Herdade might have sidestepped into the governorship in his own right. However, he antagonized almost everyone with his "dictatorial manner and ultra-conservative views,"[44] and a public demonstration he contrived in Dili to boost his image convinced Spínola to bring him back to Lisbon. In effect, the country was left with no colonial administration, and political leaders were free to indulge themselves. What they did, and what they said, would be closely monitored in Indonesian and Australian political circles.

It was to Governor Aldeia, however, that the duty fell to announce to the Timorese that the government was offering them the three choices, and that they would do so in the form of a referendum, or plebiscite,[45] to be held under the auspices of the Portuguese military on March 13, 1975. The scheme, as one might suppose, underscores how little the Spínola government really understood about the socio-political realities of the colony; but to more conversant observers what might happen in the intervening period was anybody's guess. Under the Portuguese Constitution, the only political party that could legally exist was the government's party, the *Acção Nacional Popular* (*ANP*), the "National Action Party," so few Timorese had never had the opportunity to gain political experience in politics. Lisbon would inform the leaders of the *Acção Nacional Popular* of its will, and they would do what they were told. Two Timorese, though, did have some experience of governmental politics, though not of the democratic sort. Before the revolution, Mário Carrascalão and Francisco Lopes da Cruz had been members of the Timorese branch of the *Acção Nacional Popular*, and afterwards founding members of the *União Democrática Timorense*. Other politically ambitious men also responded with remarkable speed to the revolution, and though political novices and in the absence of any political tradition in their country, they formed three rival parties. These were not called "parties," however, because the law that effectively reserved that designation exclusively for the *Acção Nacional Popular* had yet to be repealed; so the new political formations were called a "union," a "front," and an "association." For their part, the people of the *foho*, who had even less knowledge of what Western-style politics consisted of, remained out of the political loop.

The politicians of Dili

The difference between Whitlam's "political personalities that emerged," i.e., the elite, and the people was evident as early as May, as the members of the former came together in their respective caucuses. Although they were culturally *assimilados*, in that they spoke Portuguese, were literate, and conscious of the political circumstances of the sociological context in which they found themselves, some were *mestiços*, so one might have supposed the distinction between the latter and "full-blood" Timorese to have emerged as a political rallying cry as the competition heated up later. But, as things turned out, the distinction was not exploited in campaign utterances, most likely because the two most prominent parties, *Fretilin* and the *União Democrática Timorense*, had their share of both. Mari Alkatiri was of Yemen parentage, for example, while Francisco

Xavier do Amaral and Francisco Lopes da Cruz were full-blooded Timorese. José Ramos-Horta and the Carrascalão brothers (João, Mário, and Manuel) were *mestiços*. But whether full-bloods or *mestiços* all of the *assimilados* came from socially privileged circumstances, being either of *liurai* families or families of wealth. Some, like Xavier do Amaral, Nicolau dos Reis Lobato, and Guilherme Maria Gonçalves of *Apodeti*, were advantaged by both rank and wealth, with an experience of life as uniform as it was unrepresentative of the populace. The capital, though, afforded fertile ground for change, and it was here that the majority of the politicians had their principal residences. The town served as a locus for political activity after May, a fact that impressed journalist, Bill Nicol. "Dili was the place for me to be." he pronounced, "Politics were to be found in the capital, not the countryside."[46] Even those of its residents who were not politically inclined were literate, and, since many had been educated to at least primary school level, some were reasonably fluent in Portuguese. Although sharing with *ema lisan* an inclination for the status quo, the majority had come into contact with Europeans, and were, to varying degrees, aware of social change and understood themselves to be on the verge of entering the wider world.

Most *liurai* were content to remain local figures, but the aspiring politicians of *Fretilin* and *Apodeti*, though not those of the *União Democrática Timorense*, realized that to secure the votes of the *ema lisan* they needed to reach out from the capital and engage the hinterland in their ambitions. The leaders of the *Associação Social-Democrática Timorense* had demonstrated that they understood this imperative as early as September 1974, shortly after the party changed its name to *Fretilin*, by sending their cadres on promotional missions into the *foho*. *União Democrática Timorense* leaders discovered the political need for this strategy only towards the end of the year, by which time *Fretilin* had entrenched itself too deeply in some of the sub-districts for them to undermine their rival. Other than being the first party to form, the lethargic leaders of the *União Democrática Timorense* were always lagging behind *Fretilin*, never taking the initiative in the campaign,[47] a political failing they extended into the international domain. The contrast was clear-cut. As early as June 17, 1974, José Ramos-Horta had visited Jakarta, where he was invited to an audience with Adam Malik, the Indonesian Minister for Foreign Affairs; whereas it took until the following April for any *União Democrática Timorense* leader to show up in this most crucial of all capitals, when Lopes da Cruz and César Augusto da Costa Mousinho flew there.

Associação Social-Democrática Timorense/Fretilin

The leaders of *Fretilin*, like those of the *União Democrática Timorense*, while sharing many common political views, among them a firm commitment to the cause of nationalism, often differed in their convictions. Some, like António Carvarino, Vicente dos Reis, and Roque Rodrigûes, for example, were fairly extreme left-wing politicians who embraced views in accord with Marxism and

Maoism; Abílio de Araújo, though espousing left-wing opinions, was more mod-
erately to the right of them; Francisco Xavier do Amaral might be characterized
as left of center; while Ramos-Horta favored a slightly right of center perspective. Indeed, Ramos-Horta would not have been out of place in the *comité
central* of *União Democrática Timorense*, though professing a decidedly anti-
Portuguese bias. *Fretilin* leaders were nationalists above all, but they represented
a spectrum of options regarding the place of the State in society. To characterize
the *comité central* of the party as "communist," as the Indonesian generals and
President Suharto did, therefore, was thus a gross misrepresentation of political
reality, as was the Indonesian allegation that they were a group of atheists. Carvarino and Reis probably were, and, most likely, Ramos-Horta, but not Araújo[48]
and certainly not Xavier do Amaral.

Francisco Xavier do Amaral, who continued as president of his party after it
became *Fretilin*, was born in the Mambai-speaking sub-district of Turiscai, and at
37, was about 15 years older than the average age of his co-party founders.[49] In my
interview with him, Xavier do Amaral stated that the Japanese occupation had
stopped him from attending primary school at the usual age and that he always
lagged three years behind his fellow pupils, an apparent handicap he turned to his
advantage by using it as a tool for manipulating the colonial authorities.[50] When his
real age rendered him eligible for military service he claimed he was three years
too young to be conscripted.[51] As did many of the political leaders, from the Catholic primary school at Soibada, in Manatuto district, the finest primary school in the
country, which he entered at 13, he went to the *Nossa Senhora de Fátima* seminary.
He then went to Macau to begin a course of study for the priesthood, which
included philosophy, theology, and Latin in preparation for a vocation as a lay
father; but soon came to regard the Church as an organization more concerned with
aggrandizement than an agent for dispensing charitable works. He especially
detested the Concordat, an agreement between the Portuguese Government and the
Holy See by which the Church agreed not to publicly criticize repressive imperial
policies in exchange for a license to permit its missionaries exclusive rights to pros-
elytize in the colonies. In Xavier do Amaral's opinion one consequence of this
bargain was that ecclesiastical authorities remained silent about abuses, an acquies-
cence causing him to question his vocation. He sought counsel from his bishop as
to the propriety of his continuing with it, and notwithstanding the prelate's advice,
abandoned his studies in 1963, and returned to Dili where he taught school. In the
capital, Amaral's activities extended beyond the classroom. At various times, he
worked as a customs officer at the Dili Harbor Authority; as adviser to the "court,"
i.e., the administrative legal system; and as a counselor to the police force. The
legal job brought him in an income of 3,000–5,000 *escudo*s a month – more than
the salary the governor himself received – and he became a wealthy man by Timorese standards. Unlike many *Fretilin* leaders, he therefore benefited from the colonial regime; but, like them, he felt dissatisfied with the colonial status quo. Rather
than make money, he told me, his new vocational aspiration, which he declared to
be "to work for the people of East Timor" (some of whom called him "the
teacher"), resulted in him deciding to do what he could to spread his political

convictions throughout the land. He therefore resigned his job. Xavier do Amaral said he had read Marx, but properly noted that understanding Marx was not the same thing as following him; and in our interview I had the impression that his antagonism towards the Catholic Church was directed at the hierarchy not at Christian ideals or belief in an absolute divinity. Another complaint was that, abetted by the Church, the Portuguese had imposed a system of taxation on the Timorese. This made it possible for the colonialists to expropriate fertile land and the coffee it yielded because, with little cash to pay taxes, Timorese had no option but to pay the government in kind, which, at first was limited to parcels of land. When, in subsequent years, all the land had been surrendered, he said, and there was nothing with which to pay taxes, farmers were obliged to work for the administration. The *liurai* acquiesced in this system, he contended, and helped the Europeans take advantage of their own people, a collusion that had sorely vexed him.

Xavier do Amaral was no less admonitory about the attitudes of the staff at the Nossa Senhora de Fátima Seminary. He alleged that they discriminated against Timorese teachers when promotions were made; and he was aggrieved by what he saw as the unnecessarily harsh reprisals taken against the Timorese rebels by the colonial Administration after the 1959 "uprising." On this score, Helen Hill adds that the earlier rebellion by Boaventura may have further fueled his resentment.[52] Populist aspects of Catholic social teaching influenced his intellectual attitude, too, for though rejecting the institutional role of the Church, as it operated under the Portuguese Government, in speaking about *Fretilin*'s platform he used to remark, "We work as Jesus did, amongst the people."[53] A capable orator who was alleged to be especially deft at exploiting his purportedly "profound knowledge of the common people's problems, aspirations, and way of thinking" to win over an audience, Xavier do Amaral's talents were a pragmatic complement to those of Nicolau dos Reis Lobato, who became vice-president of their party. The latter was no great public speaker and decidedly less well-known, but he was a tireless and methodical organizer. He had not been a member of a clandestine anti-colonial group that had come into existence in Dili in January 1970, and included among its members Nicolau Lobato, Borja da Costa, Justino Mota, José Ramos-Horta, and Mari Alkatiri.[54] But he was respected by persons of different political stripes, both Timorese who were anti-colonialists and – despite the criticisms of the administration he published in the Dili magazine, *Seara* – those who leaned towards the Portuguese. Still, he tested the tolerance of the administration to breaking point on one occasion with a particularly unabashed anti-colonialist article he published under the pseudonym "Ramos Paz," an indiscretion that brought about the magazine's suspension.[55] The choice of Xavier do Amaral for the position of president of the *Associação Social-Democráta Timorense* was thus logical enough,[56] and his house near the Santa Cruz Cemetery came to serve as *Fretilin* headquarters,[57] with countless political meetings held there.

Fretilin's vice-president, Nicolau dos Reis Lobato, was born on December 7, 1952, in Bazartete, a sub-district of Liquiça district. After a primary education at the Soibada institution, he attended the Nossa *Senhora de Fátima* seminary with the intention of studying law in Portugal. However, his father was only a Catholic catechist, so he did not have the financial means to fulfill this ambition, and after his five years at the seminary ended he went to work at the Agricultural Department in Dili. Following a year there, he went to the Department of Finance where, between his duties, he studied economics and contributed to the *Seara*. He also joined the anti-colonial group. Lobato had intended studying economics overseas, but the Revolution made him decide to remain in Timor and try to influence events here, and so in August he resigned his job and went to work full time for the *Associação Social Democrática Timorense.* After the party's transformation into *Fretilin*, Lobato was entrusted with the task of setting out the party's economic and agricultural policies, a set of ideas that included forming "cooperatives."[58] the first of which was in Bazartete, his home sub-district. During the campaign Nicolau Lobato's public profile increased steadily, and by the time *Fretilin* became the de facto government in the October of the following year, he was generally regarded as the most distinguished of all Timorese political leaders, not excepting President Xavier do Amaral. Unlike Fernandes Lobato was not a communist, but was characterized by Ramos-Horta as a "secular Christian Marxist, like the theology of Latin American priests."[59]

His younger brother, Rogério dos Reis Fátima Lobato, was born a year later, and, after receiving an education at the Soibada School and *Nossa Senhora de Fátima* seminary, became a teacher of English at a primary school in Dili, and was present at the founding meeting of the *Associação Social Democráta Timorense*. When the *Forças Armadas Portuguêses em Timor* began recruiting Timorese, Lobato joined up, and eventually became one of only eight of his countrymen to rise above the rank of sergeant. He was one of the first recruits who trained to become a second lieutenant and during his training displayed qualities of leadership and personal discipline that greatly impressed his European officers, who saw in Lobato a natural leader of men. He knew how to get them to follow him, a knack that stood *Fretilin* in valuable stead when it needed to push back against the *União Democrática Timorense's* makeshift army in the days following the latter's attack on the police headquarters. During the war Lobato demonstrated an aptitude for warfare and provided leadership that was a decisive factor in *Fretilin*'s victory.

Rogério Lobato's contributions to *Fretilin* were not confined to the military, either. He was energetic in sponsoring the National Union of Timorese Students, the *União Nacional de Estudantes de Timor* (*UNETIM*), which furnished *Fretilin* with an unlimited number of committed enthusiasts who established *Fretilin*'s presence in the sub-districts, and fortified its presence in the capital. As early as September 1974, these students (who included boys from the Dili schools as well as the university) went out and worked in the cooperatives, taught in "instant" makeshift schools they created, and went about spreading the party's anti-*União Democrática Timorense's* gospel. The students took somewhat longer to make their mark in the capital, but by the end of December, and increasingly throughout the remainder of the campaign, they were a raucous fact of Dili life. The demonstrations they staged became a constant feature of street life, and with their incantatory chants of *"fascista"* ("fascists"), directed at the Portuguese, they became one of the forces that sapped the political will of the administration and military.

Another co-founder of the *Associação Social Democráta Timorense* was its *secretário geral*, Alarico Jorge Fernandes. Older than most of the leaders, having been born in 1943 to a Timorese mother and a Portuguese *deportado*[60] who had helped Australian commandos during World War II, he, too, was an alumnus of Soibada and *Nossa Senhora de Fátima*. Fernandes had visited the mother country as a member of a youth delegation, and, after his return in the 1970s, he obtained a civil service job in Dili, and then studied radio operations in Darwin for six months. His next employment was at the Baucau international airport. A close friend of the radical Catholic priest, Father Rocha, a disciple of the Colombian Marxist priest, Camillo Torres, Fernandes seems to have been influenced more by radical currents within the Catholic Church than most of his *Fretilin* colleagues. So much so that he came to the attention of the Bishop of Dili, José Joaquim Ribeiro, who sought to have him expelled from Timor by the colonial authorities in October 1974.[61] In the CAVR hearings he was identified by Ramos-Horta as a communist.[62]

The personal background and education of Mari Alkatiri differed from those of his colleagues. One of ten siblings born in the Arab section of the capital on November 26, 1949, to parents from southern Yemen, he received his earliest education at a mosque school in Dili before moving to a primary school run by the Portuguese Government and, upon graduation, to the Dili High School. After helping to establish the anti-colonial group, he traveled to Angola in 1970 to study surveying. There, he met members of the Popular Movement for the Liberation of Angola (*Movimento Popular de Libertação de Angola* or *MPLA*). Had he made a serious effort to get to know them he might have acquired more political acumen than he was naturally blessed with, a talent that could have served him well in his later career as a politician; but both he and the rebels were suspicious that the other party might be a colonial secret police agent. However, when he became part of *Fretilin*'s *comité central*, his experience in Angola qualified him as its expert on African politics. Acknowledged relatively early on in his career as a tough negotiator, Alkatiri would later claim his unwillingness to compromise was the reason the Indonesian Government never invited him to Jakarta. Whether this claim was justified or not, moderating his political ideals was anathema to Alkatiri, and this attitude prevented him from compromising with Nicolau Lobato, Ramos-Horta, and other more moderate members of his party. It gave *Fretilin*'s opponents ample linguistic ammunition for stigmatizing *Fretilin* as intransigently "communist." After *Fretilin* declared independence Alkatiri became East Timor's Minister for Political Affairs, and, 27 years later, after the Indonesian occupation had waxed and waned, the nation-state's first prime minister.

Future Nobel Laureate, minister for foreign affairs, prime minister, and president, José Manuel Ramos-Horta, was to eventually emerge as the most successful of the founding fathers of the Democratic Republic of Timor-Leste. He was the most skillful politician, a resourceful man who combined idealism, ambition, and pragmatism, and who had an instinct for successful public relations no other politician came close to matching. One of 12 children, Ramos-Horta was born in December 1949, to a Timorese woman and a Portuguese *deportado* who had been exiled to Timor for opposing Salazar. Ramos-Horta's political career can partly be understood as a result of inheriting from his mother a steely determination to rise above the status of a colonial subject and from his father political values grounded in the tradition of Western liberalism. These two influences melded to create a politically-conscious young man who, while barely out of his teens, became an outspoken voice for independence. His early education was in the Dili primary and high schools, and even while in his final year he began contributing to the *A Voz de Timor*.[63] As another founding member of the anti-colonial group, Ramos-Horta had been interrogated by the *Polícia Internacional e de Defensa do Estado* (*PIDE*), Portugal's political police, before the end of 1970 for publicly criticizing colonialism.[64] His final critical sally came at a party when he advised Europeans he was talking to about Timorese politics that they would be fighting a war in Timor as well as Africa if they were not careful, an indiscretion that caused Governor Aldeia to exile him. The governor did, however, allow him to select his country of exile. He chose Mozambique, intending to connect up with the Liberation Front of Mozambique (the *Frente de Libertação de Moçambique* or *Frelimo*), but like Alkatiri in Angola discovered a lack of compatibility with the local independence movement. The colonial authorities permitted Ramos-Horta to write journalism, though he was subject to a tight vigilance that included political censorship. With characteristic curiosity he explored his new surroundings avidly. Ramos-Horta also whiffed racism in the colonial air, and made a point of emphasizing that, although the Portuguese claimed that discrimination was non-existent in their colonies, blacks and whites were segregated on beaches and buses, and only black people served as waiters.[65] Exile enriched his political education in addition to making his appetite for the political arts all the keener. In particular, by having to work under the close scrutiny of the authorities while remaining true to his political convictions, Ramos-Horta acquired a sense of diplomacy that always eluded Alkatiri, and by the time he returned to his native country he was developing into a shrewd and pragmatic political operator. Indeed, in 1974–1975, he, Nicolau Lobato, and, possibly Xavier do Amaral, were the only ones *Fretilin* possessed. In Africa, Ramos-Horta learned the need to adjust ideals to suit the exigencies of political reality and how to cultivate the powerful, and was so successful he convinced the colonial authorities he should no longer be regarded as a threat; so they reduced the length of his exile and permitted him to return home earlier than scheduled. Back in Timor, his increased political maturity developed further as he continued his machinations in a more clandestine manner. His growing maturity also helped *Fretilin*'s advancement in the propaganda war against its political rivals, and in later decades, in the United Nations' corridors of power, he worked with some success to persuade international leaders to recognize his country's right to self-determination.

Ramos-Horta returned to writing articles in the *A Voz de Timor* and rejoined the anti-colonialist group. Despite his improved sense of diplomacy, he continued to have lapses, when an occasional lack of tact overcame caution, suggesting that his political education was incomplete. There was the venting of ill-considered frustrations, and, once more, he went too far, and, early in 1974 after an Australian journalist published a careless off-the-cuff comment of his, Aldeia called him into to his office and notified him he was going to be exiled again. He puckishly requested that he be assigned Australia as his destination, but before he received the inevitable rejection, the *Revolução dos Cravos* intervened. In his *Hari-Hari Akhir Timor Portugis*, Indonesian Consul Eliza Meskers Tomodok[66] recounts his awareness of Ramos-Horta's anti-colonial activities in the period before the Carnation Revolution, and suggests it indicates the potential for internal conflict within the colony, even before the three principal parties formed.[67]

If José Ramos-Horta's and Francisco Xavier do Amaral's chosen medium for expressing their anti-colonial opinions was the colonial press, Abílio Araújo favored pamphlets as the forum for articulating his views and also music and verse. He was not a journalist, but an intellectual. Araújo's educational path proceeded through the Dili high school and *Nossa Senhora de Fatima*.[68] He became prominent by his stern anti-colonial commentaries, whose denunciations exceeded those of either Alkatiri or Xavier do Amaral. Araújo had gone to Lisbon in 1971 on a scholarship to study economics, and was there when the *revolução* broke out. Seeing the opportunity to put his philosophical ideas into practice, Araújo flew to Dili and at once joined the *Associação Social Democráta Timorense*, under whose auspices he began designing a campaign in the sub-districts to promote village education. As well as a polemicist, Araújo was also something of a literary artist, and he collaborated with a fellow-party member and Lisbon student, Francisco Borja da Costa, in turning traditional Timorese oral verses into patriotic songs. Still, it was his non-fictional politics tracts that established his reputation as an opponent of the status quo. Among his most famous was the first analysis of East Timor history written by a Timorese. This appeared in 1974 with the title, *As Elites em Timor*, a translation of which, *Timorese Elites*, was published the following year. In 1974 Araújo returned to Lisbon where he resumed his studies and prepared a handbook on how to teach reading and writing to illiterate villagers. In an interview he gave a Dili newspaper in 2005 Araújo, although remaining unrepentant about his contribution to the radical language he resorted to in the earlier period, denied he was a communist.[69] He conceded that he "drank a little of this water," i.e., the revolutionary, anti-Vietnam War activism, and Marxist language of the sixties, but preferred to view himself as a "nationalist" (*uma nacionalista*) rather than as a communist.[70] This self-attribution is probably true.[71]

Abílio Araújo's collaborator, Francisco Borja da Costa, was born in October 1946 at Fatuberliu, in the Eastern Tetum-speaking region. Son of the *liurai* of Same, he was another product of the Soibada primary school and *Nossa Senhora de Fátima* seminary. From an early age Costa loved writing poetry and he included in his verses hopeful anticipations of independence, dreams that led to his collaborating with Araújo. In 1964, he left the seminary to work for the administration, and four years later was inducted into the army where he remained until 1971. Costa described his military training as a "good experience," because it gave him confidence to speak out against what he saw as racial discrimination.[72] Returning to work in the administration, Costa began a research project of his own into anti-Timorese discrimination in employment practices and joined the anti-colonialist group. He said his real politicization came about when he visited Lisbon in September 1973 and, while living in the *Casa de Timor*, witnessed the *Revolução dos Cravos* first hand. This made him determined to create a new Timor, and he wasted no time arranging at the *Casa de Timor* and in other forums, occasions for publicizing the aspirations of the *Associação Social Democráta Timorense*. Returning to Dili in late 1974, Costa became a regular contributor to *A Voz de Timor* and was later appointed secretary for information in *Fretilin*'s *comité central*. He was killed on the first day of the Indonesian invasion.

António Duarte Carvarino was born in 1949 and after attending Dili High School traveled to Lisbon in 1972 with the intention of studying law and philosophy. At first, his friends tended to be Africans, and he even went so far as to claim that, for a time, the African colonies were more familiar to him than his own country. But at the *Casa de Timor* he learned from his fellow students of the existence of the *Associação Social Democráta Timorense*, and in September 1974, together with his wife, Maria do Céu Pereira, returned to Timor about the time the *Associação Social Democráta Timorense* was changing its name to "*Fretilin*." In October 1975, the Indonesian publication *Sinar Harapan* published photographs of he and his wife, under the label "Maoists from Lisbon,"[73] a tag Francisco Xavier do Amaral, who also described Carvarino as an atheist, later endorsed in his interview.[74] Like the other Lisbon students, Carvarino was influenced by the writings of Amilcar Cabral, Samora Machel, and other leaders of the African liberation movements, and he was so impressed by the Brazilian Paulo Freire's ideas on education that he determined to apply them to East Timor. He used his position on *Fretilin*'s education committee to establish the first schools in the party's literacy program, and although he was probably more grounded in Marxism than his *Fretilin* colleagues – an increasing number of books written by European Marxists had begun to be published after the *revolução* – he does not seem to have tried very hard to make *Fretilin* a party entirely committed to Marxist principles. Carvarino met his death at the hands of Indonesian soldiers in early February 1979.

Vicente dos Reis, son of the *liurai* of Bucoli, a *suku* about two and a half miles west of Baucau, was from the Makassai ethnolinguistic group, and attended the Dili High School before leaving for Portugal in 1972 with a scholarship to study engineering. Another *Casa de Timor* student, he abandoned his studies and flew back to Timor in September 1975, and, like António Carvarino and Maria do Céu Pereira, was portrayed in the Indonesian media as a leading light of the "communist" wing of *Fretilin*. Unlike the other returning students, Reis did not immediately settle down in Dili, but went to live in Bucoli with his parents where he publicly reclaimed his indigenous family name of "Sahe." With help from his brother and sister, who were local teachers, Reis established various community groups, some of which discussed politics, and credited himself with having founded "local cultures," including songs and dances. Given that "cultures" (presumably he was referring to *lisan*) had existed for an untold number of generations before ever he was born, this was something of an audacious claim. There was an unintended irony here, too, since *Fretilin*'s political agenda, by seeking to impose exogenous institutions on villagers challenged *lisan*. Towards the end of the year, Vicente Reis moved to Dili where he became a science teacher in the local technical school, and helped Rogério Lobato build a student union, the *União Nacional de Estudantes de Timor*.

In May 1974, a 24-year-old *mestiço* with a Goan father and Timorese mother called Roque Rodrigûes was a lieutenant in the army. Although he never was a resident in the *Casa de Timor* at the time of the *revolução*, Rodrigûes knew its residents well and as an articulate man with practical experience of Mozambique, where he had served as a lieutenant and had become acquainted with the *Frente de Libertação de Moçambique*, he acquired something of the status of a "*guru*" among them.[75] In the judgment of Hamish McDonald he "contributed an African-style socialist ideology" to *Fretilin*'s "demand for immediate independence."[76] To Xavier do Amaral he was a firm communist.[77]

Two other persons were more prominent than most *Fretilin* members. Justino Mota, a *mestiço*, came from Timorese-African-European descent, and was another member of the early anti-colonial group. Rosa Muki Bonaparte was the most active of the *Fretilin* women. She left the *Casa de Timor* for Timor early in 1975 and immediately joined the party. As noted she became secretary of the *Organização Popular da Mulher Timor*, the "Popular Organization of Timorese Women," and died at the hands of the Indonesian Army during the assault on Dili.

Writers typically characterize the *Fretilin* leaders as being of diverse linguistic and local backgrounds, but their biographies reveal most were Mambai, Tetum, Kemak, or Makassai, and their party discussions and public utterances were usually conducted in *Tetum Dili*. Few were Fataluku, Kairui, Naueti, or Waimaha.[78]

That much having been said, the leaders of all the parties shared important qualities. All came from elite families, and although having family ties in the *foho* – Alkatiri was an exception – none could claim convincingly to be an *ema lisan*.[79] None emerged from farmer stock or had known what it felt like to till the soil. How could they, since the majority boasted *liurai* pedigrees and belonged to families of sub-district chiefs or officers of the European administration whose wealth could afford an education for them at Soibada and at *Nossa Senhora de Fátima*? All were urban men whose social *milieu* was the capital.[80] Even Vicente Reis in Bucoli kept in touch with what was going on in Dili before eventually moving there. Youth, as we have noted, was another common trait of the leaders. Francisco Xavier do Amaral, the three Carrascalão brothers, and a few others apart, most of the men were in their twenties. Especially in respect of *Fretilin*, this quality has attracted attention from many observers, some remarking it admiringly;[81] others deprecating it, and attributing to the party's youthful character what they regarded as the party's naivety and excesses. Prime Minister Gough Whitlam, a politician with considerable influence at his disposal, was decidedly of the latter school. Luís Thomaz,[82] for his part, preferred to call attention to the youthfulness of its *followers*. He noted that the necessary "manpower" to enact *Fretilin*'s platform in the sub-districts came from students, whose exuberant exhortations were, at times, reinforced by dint of strong-arm persuasion. It was not in the *foho*, though, that this human weapon was most effectively used. In Dili there was a deep reservoir of youths looking for trouble who vied with one another in striving to subvert adult authority, and who graduated from fiery utterances to physical intimidation in tumultuous street demonstrations.[83]

Such, then, were the leaders of *Fretilin*. They varied in the nuances of their convictions, and like their rivals some modified their ideas in response to the changing requirements of the campaign; but a common conviction was carved in stone. *Fretilin* would not tolerate any form of colonial dependency, and even in the closing months of 1975 – when its *comité central* repeatedly called upon the governor to reassume Portugal's administrative responsibilities – party leaders never reneged on *Fretilin*'s commitment to independence. In contrast, *União Democrática Timorense* leaders adjusted their platform repeatedly throughout the campaign, until, listing too heavily in the choppy waters of Dili politics, they finally brought their agenda into line with *Apodeti*'s, and sought integration (albeit a conscripted one) with the Republic of Indonesia.

União Democrática Timorense

Socially elevated though they were, the politicians of *Fretilin* nevertheless tried to characterize their opponents as privileged surrogates for the Portuguese. The truth, however, is that for all their professed admiration of Lusitanian values, the members of the *União Democrática Timorense comité central* neither considered themselves, nor sought to be, fully-committed agents of Portuguese colonialism.[84] With the passing of the months, as they witnessed the failure of the colonial administration to maintain order and came to realize how little interest President Gomes had in the fate of the Timorese, the attraction of retaining ties with Portugal gradually diminished.

The majority of these men held jobs in the administration that were of higher status and typically better paid than those of most of those *Fretilin* leaders who had managed to find employment,[85] and, unlike the latter a few, most conspicuously, Mário Carrascalão, were also businessmen. Francisco Lopes da Cruz, editor of the *A Voz de Timor*, the only newspaper in the colony, at 33 years of age, he was party president. As member of the *Acção Nacional Popular*, Lopes da Cruz had some experience in politics and its maneuvers, albeit of a non-democratic nature.[86] Lopes da Cruz attended *Nossa Senhora de Fátima*, and although he did not graduate, this was not through a lack of ambition, as was demonstrated by his becoming a non-commissioned officer in the *Forças Armadas Portuguêses em Timor* in April 1975. Nevertheless, it was not until the following year, when his party and *Fretilin* came together in a coalition and he became ever-more attracted to the cause of integration that Lopes da Cruz's influence was felt. Vice-President César Augusto da Costa Mousinho, the Dili mayor, another member of the *Acção Nacional Popular*, had won political advancement because the colonial authorities trusted him and he had the reputation of being solidly conservative, and a man willing to work doggedly for political power.

Two other activists of the *União Democrática Timorense* were a pair of brothers, sons of a communist youth leader deported in the 1930s who had married a Timorese woman. The most politically astute was 37-year-old Mário Carrascalão, at the time of the *revolução* a wealthy coffee planter and employed as a forestry engineer. His political skills were forged during his term as vice-president of the *Acção Nacional Popular* and a spell as Portuguese Member of Parliament, an accumulation of experience that would have made him automatic choice for *União Democrática Timorense* President; but those attending the party's inaugural meeting judged it more prudent to select a man less closely identified with the colonial regime. Carrascalão's qualities as a politician were seen at their best during the Indonesian occupation, when the government in Jakarta appointed him governor of Timor Timur, a position he held from 1982 to 1992. But it was, of course, his younger brother, João Viegas Carrascalão, born in 1945 in Liquiça, who was destined to play the most decisive role of any *União Democrática Timorense* leader, and this was detrimental to both his party and to the people of Timor. Although reputedly candid and straightforward, he was inclined to impetuosity and was not given to taking advice.[87] He was out of the country when the party came into existence and only returned when the campaign was at an advanced stage and became the *comité central* member responsible for foreign relations. A third brother, Manuel Viegas Carrascalão, participated little in the campaign.

Still another *Nossa Senhora de Fatima* alumnus and civil servant was the *secretário geral*, Domingos de Oliveira, who at the time of the *revolução* occupied a minor position in the customs department of the Dili Harbor Authority. He reportedly had business interests in coffee estates.[88]

Apodeti (Associação Popular Democrática Timorense)

Dislike of the Portuguese and anticipation of preferment under a future Indonesian Administration were the principal factors motivating the men who founded *Apodeti*. Although Dili served as their base of operations, two were active in the *foho*, a fact that made them particularly well placed to function as conduits between the two regions. As local *liurai*, *Dom* Guilherme Maria Gonçalves was a man with some – albeit overrated – influence in Atsabe, a Kemak-speaking sub-district in Ermera district, and he used what he possessed to promote *Apodeti*'s cause among local *ema lisan*. Despite having left primary school after his fourth year,[89] Gonçalves was a figure of some celebrity, if only because, alone among the *liurai*, he resembled the old-style pre-1912 kings in having responsibility for more than a single *suku*, a distinction evident in his honorific title of *raja*.[90] There was more to his credentials than his grand political status, for he was reputed to be one of the wealthiest *liurai* in the colony. Yet his and his family's reputation were sullied. Gonçalves' two sons, Lucío and Tomás, had run afoul of the law in the early 1970s, when they were accused of crimes that included murder, arson, and rape, and for which the administration had sent them to prison.[91] Having no reason to look with favor upon the Portuguese, the three men considered the Indonesians to hold out a lot more promise for their advancement, and Tomás, as it happened, had already had some dealings, of a dubious nature, across the border. One person I interviewed suggested, as another factor in their decision to join *Apodeti*, that *liurai* Gonçalves joined *Apodeti* in order to have his sons, whom the Indonesian authorities had caught in Atambua smuggling cattle, treated leniently. But regardless of their motivations, Gonçalves and his sons became dedicated *Apodeti* men, and for some weeks prior to the invasion Tomás Gonçalves energetically participated in the *Angkatan Bersenjata Republik Indonesia's* incursions into East Timor.[92] The president of *Apodeti*, Arnaldo dos Reis Araújo, was quick to see the advantage of having Gonçalves in the party. His governing more than one *suku* seemed to impart to him a singular and prominent bully pulpit from which to promote *Apodeti*'s platform throughout the entire sub-district of Atsabe. As it turned out, though, the *raja* was more unpopular than he was liked, and only a handful of his *suku* supported *Apodeti*. Of the 12 *suku* in Atsabe, two (Tiar Lelo and Atu Dame) had the strongest allegiance to the Gonçalves family, with the institution of asymmetric alliance a powerful factor in securing loyalties.[93] Other *suku*, where the institution of asymmetric alliance also endowed political support, oscillated in their support. Some, like Laclo *suku*, would passively oppose and even avoid public displays of acknowledging the Gonçalves family's authority and legitimacy; attitudes justified through recourse to the foundation myths of Atsabe, which differed between the *liurai* family and its *suku*, and the other Atsabe *suku*.

Liurai Arnaldo dos Reis Araújo, cattle rancher and substantial landowner in the Tetum sub-district of Zumalai (Cova Lima district), near Suai town, had taught for eight years in an elementary school in Oe-Cussi and worked as a teacher of Malay during the Japanese occupation. When the Portuguese returned after the war, they imprisoned Araújo for collaboration with the enemy, despite his claim that he was coerced, and, after his release, he turned to farming, enjoying such success that he was wealthy enough to educate his three children in Portugal. Soon after the invasion, the Indonesians appointed Araújo as head of Timor Timur's provisional government.

In the interior, two other men were contributing *Apodeti* operatives. *Apodeti*'s vice-president, *liurai* José Hermenegildo Martins, a coffee plantation owner in the Mambai and Kemak district of Ermera,[94] and Araújo's son, Casimiro dos Reis Araújo.[95] More influential than any of these, however, was a man whose base lay in Dili, 37-year-old José Fernandes Osório Soares. Soares served as the party's planner and *secretário geral*, and, as chief executive, oversaw the party's day-to-day administration, propaganda, and finance.[96] A school teacher who had also worked for the *Assistência Social*, the government health agency, Soares engaged in protracted efforts to undermine *Fretilin*'s claim to be the anti-colonial party by trying to present *Apodeti* as the authentic face of Timorese anti-colonialism. Like the two Araújos, Soares spoke some Indonesian,[97] and was yet another *Apodeti* leader with something of a checkered past. Rumor had it that Soares had been fired from his job after being accused of rape and that he had been dismissed from another job for fraud.[98] For his part, Soares accused the Europeans of framing him because of his pro-Indonesian views.[99] Yet, whatever his moral flaws may have been, Soares combined three qualities that made him *Apodeti*'s most effective impresario. He had ideas; he was a capable manager; and he worked ceaselessly, a combination that produced *Apodeti*'s draft manifesto and contributed to shaping the party's administrative structure. *Apodeti* had a small executive committee, empowered with authority to act on behalf of the entire organization, and its members were Arnaldo dos Reis Araújo, José Hermenegildo Martins, and Casimiro dos Reis Araújo, each of whom had been selected by Soares who considered they would make impressive figureheads.[100] The party's *comité central*, with six members, was the smallest *comité central* of the three major parties, with Pinto Soares, a 37-year-old customs officer its most important member, an advantage he enjoyed by virtue of being Osório Soares' brother-in-law.[101] Pinto Soares was the man entrusted to run the *Apodeti* campaign. Another functionary, Abel Belo, a Makassai from Baucau, as a reputed veteran of the 1959 "uprising," contributed to the party propaganda that exploited that ambiguous fragment of history.

Klibur Oan Timur Asuwa'in and the other parties

The only politician of significance in the *Klibur Oan Timur Asuwa'in* was its president, the *mestiço* José Martins, one of the less influential founders of *Apodeti*, but who, perhaps because he realized he had less authority than he aspired to, later joined the *Klibur Oan Timur Asuwa'in*. A Mambai-speaking son of the Ermera district *liurai*, Martins had resided for some time in Portugal, where he worked for an evening paper, the *Diário Popular*, and in Timor acquired a reputation for political shiftiness. This notoriety originated when he was seen to enjoy the confidence of the anti-colonial Indonesian Government operative, Louis Taolin, with whose agents he collaborated until he was exposed.[102] His unreliability was confirmed following Carrascalão's attack on the police headquarters, when in his capacity as leader of the *Klibur Oan Timur Asuwa'in* he switched tracks and formed a coalition with the *União Democrática Timorense* and *Apodeti*, a move that forced him into Indonesian Timor with them under duress from the pursuing *Fretilin* army.

The Decolonization Commission did not recognize the *Klibur Oan Timur Asuwa'in* as a legitimate party, any more than it officially registered the existence of two other parties that flittered in shadowy fashion across the political scene before becoming lost in obscurity. Not that it made much difference. Neither the *Partido Trabalhista* nor the *Associação Democrática Integração Timor-Leste-Australia* were with serious purpose, though President Suharto found use for their nominal existence when he appealed to President Ford and Henry Kissinger for the United States' permission to invade.

Certain other men, indigenous and foreign, were to have varying degrees of input into what happened during the period discussed in this monograph, and we shall meet them in due course. Those introduced above, however, were the prime Timorese influents in the politics that decided the fate of Portuguese Timor.

Notes

1 Wallace (1883: 196–197).
2 Today the time taken is under three hours.
3 According to Dunn (2003: 26), though he provides no source for his data, there were over 57,000 (50 percent of school-age children) studying in 456 schools and in 1974 there were about 1,200 children in secondary education preparatory schools. He also records that in the latter year over 1,000 students were enrolled in institutions of a secondary education nature. See also Hastings (1975: 25–26).
4 Ramos-Horta (1996: 57) His charge of "paternalism," however, is ironic given that the self-same attitude was held by *Fretilin*.
5 Durand (2002: 56).
6 A magnificently-researched source for this, and other periods of Timorese history, will be found in Figueiredo (2011).
7 Felgas (1956: 319).
8 For an account of the war, see Pélissier (1996: 262–264).
9 The principal difference between the two categories of administrative unit was that a district possessed an administrative center or municipality (*município*). The Indonesian correspondent of district was *kabupaten*.
10 See Martinho (1947).
11 He claimed his term of imprisonment had been 28 years (Dunn 1996: 31).
12 I consider this rhetorically fertile episode in the history of Portuguese Timor in more detail further on.
13 Krieger (1997: 18).
14 Metzner (1977: 250).
15 Dunn (2003: 3).
16 But see Duarte (1988a: 42). He provides no source for his figures.
17 Duarte (1988a: 42).
18 Thomaz (1977: 23–24).
19 Thomaz (1977: 23).
20 The term can be qualified by adding the suffixes *mutin* ("white") or *xina* ("Chinese") to the radical, e.g., *malai mutin* and *malai xina*.
21 Jolliffe (1978: 16).
22 Thomaz (1977: 23).
23 Thomaz (1977: 22–23).
24 See below.
25 Thomaz (1977: 27).
26 Alternatively referred to as the "Portuguese Army."
27 Dunn (2003: 35).
28 Dunn (2003: 36).
29 Pires (1991: 152, 153).
30 Dunn (2003: 36). Dunn returned to East Timor in October and November 1975 as the leader of the Australian Council for Overseas Aid (ACFOA) which performed relief work following the civil war, and attempted to assess what the longer-term aid requirements of the Timorese might be.
31 Dunn (2003: 36). There were only two prime ministers under the "*Estado Novo*" (or "New State"), which lasted from 1933 to 1974. António de Oliveira Salazar served as prime minister from July 5, 1932 to September 25, 1968; Caetano from September 25, 1968 to April 25, 1974. Both were members of the National Action Party.
32 Or to give it its complete designation, the *Quartel-General Exército Português* ("Portuguese Army Garrison" or "Army Headquarters").
33 Dunn (2003: 35).
34 Short title: *Portugal and the Future.*

35 The *Movimento Forças Armadas*, just formed, made the decision on December 1, 1973, to overthrow the Caetano Government, and its radical program was approved by a secret assembly in Cascais, a town to the west of Lisbon, on March 5, 1974 (Maxwell 1975: 29).

36 Maxwell (1975: 31).

37 Willenson with Acoca (1975: 45).

38 Ramos-Horta (1996: 46).

39 For an account of the political developments that followed in the first 12 months after the revolution see Maxwell (1975).

40 United Nations *Decolonization* (1976: 14).

41 Jolliffe (1989: 30).

42 Pires (1991: 31–32).

43 According to Luís Filipe F.R. Thomaz (1977: 65), Aldeia, though publicly lauded for his excellent work in government, was brought down because he had incurred Arnão Metelo's enmity. However, given his earlier criticism of the army officers it is likely he would have been marked for dismissal in any case.

44 Ramos-Horta (1996: 47).

45 Department of Foreign Affairs, Republic of Indonesia (1977: 16).

46 Nicol (1978: 1).

47 Other than the assault of August 10–11, of course; and this initiative ended in disaster.

48 In his intriguing autobiography Araújo recounts his devotion to the Church in no uncertain terms (Araújo 2012: *passim*).

49 For this section and for most of the following information on the *Fretilin* politicians, see Hill (1978: 73–83).

50 Amaral (Interview 2005).

51 Amaral (Interview 2005).

52 Hill (2002: 61).

53 Hill (2002: 74).

54 Cf. Hill (2003: 52–53).

55 *Seara* was a Catholic magazine, published in Dili, featuring articles that covered a wide diversity of topics. Ethnographic themes were well represented before the end of the 1970s when articles of a more political nature began appearing on its pages. These expressed the views of such contributors as Ramos-Horta, Francisco Borja da Costa, Inácio de Moura, Manuel Carrascalão, Amaral, Domingos de Oliveira, Alkatiri, Nicolau Lobato (Jolliffe 1978: 55–56). Since the journal was published by the Catholic Church, it was not subject to the stringent censorship to which its editors would otherwise have been exposed, but Xavier de Amaral went over the line.

56 Ramos-Horta ranked him with Nicolau dos Reis Lobato as among the most serious intellectuals in East Timor and the only two gifted with leadership qualities (Ramos-Horta 1996: 34).

57 Carrascalão (2006: 79).

58 Discussed further on.

59 CAVR (2006 Part 3: 28). Lobato was killed by Indonesian military on the last day of December 1979.

60 A *deportado* was an opponent of the Salazar/Caetano regime who had been exiled to one or other of the Portuguese colonies.

61 Hill (2002: 74–75).

62 CAVR (2006 Part 3: 28).

63 A newspaper printed in Dili that circulated from August 1959 to 1975. At the time of the unsuccessful coup, its editor was Fernando de Almeida do Carmo, a moderate political figure whose political affiliations were reputed to incline to *Fretilin*, and during the campaign *A Voz de Timor* generally supported that party. Carmo proved himself one of the more capable military commanders after the failed insurrection.

64 Ramos-Horta (1996: 6). In 1968 the *Polícia Internacional e de Defensa do Estado* changed its name to the *Direcção Geral de Segurança*.
65 O'Dwyer (1974: 4).
66 An Alorese, who was Indonesian Consul, in Dili, from 1972 to 1976.
67 Tomodok (1994: 61–65).
68 See Araújo's autobiography (Araújo 2012).
69 Araújo (2005: 7).
70 In 1977, Araújo followed up with a companion volume, *Timor-Leste: os loricos voltaram a cantar*, in which he again presented his distinctive interpretation of Timorese history under the colonialists.
71 *Integrasi* (1976: 93) characterized both Araújo and Borja da Costa as "Maoists."
72 Jolliffe (1976: 8).
73 Hill (2002: 66).
74 Amaral (Interview 2005). Ironically, the Indonesian governmental report, *Integrasi*, (1976: 93) evidently sought to smear Amaral himself in this regard, by drawing attention to a photograph of him sitting next to "a Maoist student from Lisbon."
75 Nicol (1978: 102–103).
76 McDonald (1981: 192).
77 Amaral (Interview 2005).
78 Interestingly, in light of the current controversy about a reputed division between "westerners" versus "easterners" (see Hicks 2009), these ethnolinguistic groups are located in the eastern part of the country (Figure 2). José Alexandre Gusmão (today Kay Rala Xanana Gusmão) was born in Manatuto, a Galoli-speaking region, but he played virtually no part in the campaign until after August 1975, and then in a military rather than in a political capacity.
79 Carvarino and Reis adopted *ema lisan* names, but did so not because they had decided to actually become people of the *foho*, nor that they envisioned themselves as such, but rather to enhance their radical credentials by trying to assimilate them into the category of "the people."
80 "They were the first generation of Timorese to benefit from the expansion in educational opportunities which took place from the mid-sixties," and the "first generation immigrants into Dili" (Hill 2002: 68).
81 Jolliffe (1978).
82 Thomaz (1977: 40).
83 These, it might be remarked, foreshadowed the *manifestaun* of April and May 2005 when young men from all the Timorese districts marched on the capital in a demonstration that threatened to bring down the government of Mari Alkatiri (Hicks 2010). In contrast with 1974–1975, however, the latter demonstrations were not marred by violence. The following year, adolescent anger did find an outlet in more than mere demonstration, when street fighting by youthful roustabouts dominated the streets of Dili, and the atmosphere of violence culminated, in 2008, in an assassination attempted on President Ramos-Horta.
84 Quite the contrary, as the eventual shift to embrace *Apodeti* and the Indonesian cause, after the *Golpe*, was to show – however insincere it may have been.
85 Francisco Xavier do Amaral was the most prominent exception.
86 He provides an account of his activities in the autobiography *Aku dan Timor Timur* (1998).
87 Assis (Interview 2007).
88 United Nations (1976: 8).
89 Duarte (1988a: 54).
90 The Malay equivalent of *régulo*.
91 Ramos-Horta (2005 Interview).
92 Upon the death of his father, Tomás became the new *liurai* (Fernando da Costa Soares Interview 2005).

93   I am grateful to a reviewer of an early draft of this book for this and the following information on Atsabe.
94   A kinsman of José Martins of the *Klibur Oan Timur Asuwa'in*.
95   Nicol (1978: 57).
96   Nicol (1978: 57).
97   Nicol (1978: 57).
98   Ramos-Horta (1996: 32).
99   On this score, Ramos-Horta (1996: 32) was inclined to believe him.
100 Nicol (1978: 57).
101 "and 'yes man'" in Nicol's (1978: 58) estimation.
102 Jolliffe (1978: 284).

References

Araújo, Abilio de. 1975. *Timorese Elites*. J.M. Alberto (translator). Jill Jolliffe and Bob Reece (eds.). Canberra: Jill Jolliffe and Bob Reece.

Araújo, Abílio. 1977. *Timor Leste: os loricos voltaram a cantar*. Publisher: author.

Araújo, Abílio. 2005. "É um imperativo rever a nossa Constituição." *Jornal Nacional Semanário*. 28 May. pp. 1, 6–7. Dili, Timor-Leste.

Araújo, Abílio. 2012. *Autobiografia de Abílio Araújo: Dato Siri Loe II*. With José de Assunção Gonçalves. Lisbon: Alétheia Editores.

Carrascalão, Mário Viegas. 2006. *"Timor: Antes Do Futuro."* Dili, Timor-Leste: Livaria Mau Huran.

Delegação de Timor do Instituto Nacional de Estatística. 1973. Instituto Nacional de *Estatístic*: Lisbon.

Duarte, Jorge Barros. 1988a. Timor: *Um Grito*. Odivelas, Portugal: Pentaedro Publicidade e Artes Gráficas, Lda. e Jorge Barros Duarte.

Dunn, James. 1996. *Timor: A People Betrayed*. 2nd edition. Sydney, Australia: ABC Books for the Australian Broadcasting Corporation.

Dunn, James. 2003. *East Timor: A Rough Passage to Independence*. New South Wales, Australia: Longueville Books.

Department of Foreign Affairs. 1977. *Decolonization in East Timor*. Jakarta: Department of Foreign Affairs, Republic of Indonesia.

Durand, Frédéric. 2002. *Timor Lorosa'e Pays Au Carrefour de l'Asie et Du Pacifique Un Atlas Géo-Historique*. Marne la Vallée Cedex 2; Bangkok, Thailand: Press Universitaires de Marne-la-Vallée; IRASEC [Institut de Recherche sur l'Asia du Sud-Est Contemporaine], Bangkok, Thailand.

Felgas, Helio A. Esteves. 1956. *Timor Português*. Lisbon: Agencie Geral do Ultramar.

Hastings, Peter. 1975 (April). "The Timor Problem." *Australian Outlook*. 29(1): 18–33.

Hicks, David. 2009. "'*Ema Lorosa'e*', '*Ema Loromonu*': identity and politics in Timor-Leste," in Christine Cabasset and Frederic Durand (eds.). *East Timor: How to Build a New Nation in Southeast Asia in the 21st Century?*" pp. 81–94. Research Institute on Contemporary Southeast Asia (IRASEC & CASE): Bangkok, Thailand.

Hill, Helen. 2002. *Stirrings of Nationalism in East Timor: Fretilin 1974–78, The Origins, Ideologies and Strategies of a Nationalist Movement*. Kuala Lumpur and Díli: Contemporary Otford, Otford Press, Ortford (Sydney).

Jolliffe, Jill. 1976. "Introduction," in Francisco Borja da Costa. *Revolutionary Poems in the Struggle Against Colonialism*. pp. 7–18.

Jolliffe, Jill. 1978. *East Timor: Nationalism and Colonialism*. Brisbane: University of Queensland Press.

Jolliffe, Jill. 1989. *Timor, Terra Sangrenta*. Colecção Memória Memórias. Lisbon, Portugal: O Jornal.

Krieger, Heike (ed.). 1997. *East Timor and the International Community: Basic Documents*. Cambridge: Cambridge University Press.

Loch, Alexander. 2009. "Nation Building at the Village Level: First the House, then the Church and finally a modern state," in Christine Cabasset and Frederic Durand (eds.). *East Timor: How to Build a New Nation in Southeast Asia in the 21st Century?* pp. 95–104. Research Institute on Contemporary Southeast Asia (IRASEC & CASE): Bangkok, Thailand.

McDonald, Hamish. 1981. *Suharto's Indonesia*. Blackburn, Victoria, Australia: The Dominion Press and Fontana/Collins.

Martinho, José Simões. 1947. *Vida e morte do régulo timorense D. Alexio*. Lisbon.

Maxwell, Kenneth. 1975 (April 17). "The Hidden Revolution in Portugal." pp. 29–35. *New York Review of Books*. New York.

Metzner, Joachim. 1977. *Man and Environment in Eastern Timor*. Development Studies Centre, Monograph 8. Canberra: The Australian National University.

Nicol, Bill. 1978. *Timor: The Stillborn Nation*. Melbourne: Widescope International Publishers Pty Ltd.

Pélissier, René. 1996. *Timor en guerre. Le crocodile and les Portugais (1847–1913)*. Orgeval: Pélissier.

Pires, Mário Lemos. 1991. *Descolonização de Timor: Missão Impossível?* 3rd edition. Lisbon: Publicações Dom Quixote, Lda.

Ramos-Horta, José. 1996. *Funu – The Unfinished Saga of East Timor*. Lawrenceville, N.J.: The Red Sea Press, Inc.

Spínola, António de. 1974. *Portugal e o Futuro. Análise da conjuntura nacional*. Lisbon: Arcadia.

Thomaz, Luís Filipe F.R. 1977. *Timor: Autopsia de Uma Tragedia*. Lisbon, Portugal: Author, distributed by Dig/livro.

Tomodok, E.M. 1994. *Hari-Hari Akhir Timor Portugis*. Jakarta: Pustaka Jaya.

United Nations. 1976 (August). *Decolonization*. A publication of the United Nations Department of Political Affairs, Trusteeship and Decolonization. No. 7.

Wallace, Alfred Russel. 1883. *The Malay Archipelago: The Land of the Orang-Utan and the Bird of Paradise, a Narrative of Travel, with Studies of Man and Nature*. London: Macmillan and Co.

Whitlam, E.G. 1975. Unpublished Letter dated April 22, 1975 to Senator Arthur Gietzelt quoted in Dunn (2003:129).

Interviews

Amaral, Francisco Xavier do. Interview 2005.

Assis, Rudy de. Interview 2007.

Soares, Fernando da Costa. Interview 2005.

4 Rhetoric and its agenda

1974–1975

These parties [União Democrática Timorense, Fretilin, Associação Popular Democrática Timorense] were nothing but words.
(Francisco Ximenes, Vice-President of *Klibur Oan Timur Asuwa'in*. [Nicol 1978:54])

2006

Words make war.[1]
(Maria Dias, quoted and translated by Silva 2010:102)

These politicians and their political parties, as products of the culture of Dili, found the capital their most obvious initial forum as a sounding board from which to broadcast their opening agendas. These came forth in a series of documents, constructed from political convictions that appeared to have been genuine enough, and were intended as something resembling articles of faith as much as political platforms in the strict sense, although *Fretilin*'s, even in that initial exchange of philosophies, had already begun to assert its platform in language somewhat more robust than its two main rivals. In due course, however, the latter's own verbal cadences would follow suit, and the epithet "communist" would become as much of the sloganeering as that of "colonialist" and "neo-colonialist."

The political language of the programs

Although coming months would see the politicians emphasizing one or other passages they more especially favored in their respective party's agendas, amend segments, and even disown policies previously advocated, the founding documents reveal clearly enough the initial differences between the policies of *Fretilin*, the *União Democrática Timorense*, and *Apodeti*.[2]

Given the acrimonious phraseology, the tone of which increased from September 1974, and in light of the misleading hyperbole in the international press at the time – the respective manifestos reveal a number of similarities, especially between *Fretilin* and the *União Democrática Timorense*, that many observers at the time and later failed to remark. Although the latter's manifesto favored an orientation "towards a federation with Portugal, with an intermediary stage for the attainment of independence," at the same time, it also advocated "self-determination for the Timorese people." Not that this inhibited *Fretilin*'s words of censure, and even after the two parties had formed what proved an uneasy coalition the party harped on the "colonial" character of its rival, and, after their coalition disintegrated, returning to this refrain with increased acerbity.

The *Apodeti* program, which in some respects was hardly divergent from the socialist-inspired goals of *Fretilin* and at certain points consonant with that of the *União Democrática Timorense*, was brief. After a prologue in which the "failure of the Portuguese colonisation of Timor" was stated and the "view of ending the 400-year old Portuguese occupation" proclaimed, the manifesto went on to announce the foundation of the party to maintain 13 "rights," including the teaching of Indonesian as a compulsory subject at all secondary schools; the "just distribution of wealth by the government"; "just employment with fixed minimum salary"; the "exercise of labour's right to strike"; and "direct voting in general elections in accordance with the principle of [electoral] regulations." Unexpectedly, perhaps, the list included the right "to enjoy the Portuguese language and civilization as well" and the "freedom of religion with particular respect to Catholic churches..." Like *Fretilin*, *Apodeti*, too, claimed a wide constituency, but whereas *Fretilin* claimed to represent *all* Timorese, *Apodeti* more modestly (yet still incorrectly) claimed to be the "representative of [*only*] the majority of the 600,000 Timorese people..."[3]

The *União Democrática Timorense* program consisted of a mere two "articles" and conveys the impression of not having been thoroughly thought out. Included among its provisions were the "accelerated promotion – proceeding in the shadow of the Portuguese flat [*sic*] – of the social, economic, cultural and political development of the Timorese people"; "self-determination for the Timorese people orientated towards a federation with Portugal, with an intermediary stage for the attainment of independence"; the "integration [*sic*] of the Timorese people through the use of the Portuguese language"; "defence and enrichment of the Timorese culture"; "just distribution of income"; "democratisation of Timorese life," and "rejection of the integration of Timor into any potential foreign country." In its preamble, the document states that "the final objective of the party" is "through our propaganda" to "enlighten those [inhabitants] of the interior, and for UDT delegates to give knowledge to the Timorese people."[4]

Although the leaders of the *União Democrática Timorense*, and others, have suggested that *Fretilin* would be content with nothing less than immediate, out-and-out independence, *Fretilin*'s manifesto shows that, although that party demanded "I. IMMEDIATE RECOGNITION OF INDEPENDENCE *DE JURE* BY THE PORTUGUESE GOVERNMENT," this insistence was tempered by a sense of pragmatic restraint.

FRETILIN interprets independence *de jure* as the formal recognition that the only way for the future of East Timor is *total independence*. Until this is achieved, FRETILIN will have the co-operation of the Portuguese Government to implement the program of reconstruction and economic growth of the country. FRETILIN will discuss with the Portuguese Government the best form of this co-operation.

The document added that, there is to be "immediate decolonisation ... in order to achieve de facto independence," and concluded with a reference to the timeline for independence: "IV. PROCLAMATION OF INDEPENDENCE." ... FRETILIN reserves the right to decide the date of the proclamation of independence of East Timor."[5]

Fretilin's platform, then, did not push for an unqualified, immediate, liberation, but contained the provision that there would remain a relationship with Portugal until such time as the Timorese might be competent to govern themselves. Nor was this the only ground common to the two parties. Their policies regarding the conduct of international relationships overlapped, as did even some domestic matters. Although the *União Democrática Timorense*'s provisional statutes were less specific than *Fretilin*'s about those changes they would bring to the emerging nation, like *Fretilin*, it was concerned with the "social, economic, cultural and political development of the Timorese people."[6] Even the tone of the proviso that this "Accelerated promotion" would be "proceeding in the shadow of the Portuguese flat [presumably "flag"]" was not much more deferential than *Fretilin*'s concession, and, for the *União Democrática Timorense*, Timorese life would be subject to "democratisation." No specifics were given, though it would appear that the party was decidedly less inclined, at first, to trespass upon matters involving *lisan* than *Fretilin*.

While *Apodeti*'s platform, whatever common points it had with its rivals, differed significantly in that it alone advocated integration, even its proclaimed goal of integration was not quite as unconditional as has been generally perceived. It called for "An autonomous integration into the Republic of Indonesia in accordance with international law," rather than an incorporation based upon the Indonesian Constitution, which, in fact, made no provision for autonomy. This was a reality that became apparent in July 1976, when integration *did* come about, and the *Apodeti* leaders found that the former Portuguese colony's status was far removed from that which they had had in mind two years earlier. Again, the party was not as fervently anti-Lusitanian as conventional wisdom holds, as the strong assertion of rights in respect of the Portuguese language and civilization demonstrates. As things turned out, of course, integration resulted in *Bahasa Indonesia* becoming the official language of Timor Timur and Portuguese being deleted from school syllabi.

That much said, the three programs had significant differences in their political range, detail, and verbal extravagance, and these variations were all of a piece with their physical dimensions. The *União Democrática Timorense*'s program filled a single page; *Apodeti*'s rather more than two pages; *Fretilin*'s all of nine. This difference in scale resulted, to some extent, from the fact that the *comité central* of *Fretilin* contained members who had been discussing political philosophy for several years and who wished to draw as detailed plan as they could, given the need to quickly counter the *União Democrática Timorense's* program, of what future they envisaged for an independent East Timor. But it was also lengthened by its creators' resort to extravagant verbal flourishes. *Apodeti*'s statement, for its part, included only one disingenuous phrase: "the existing culture of traditional mysticism of our Timorese ancestors which has been forgotten." While it is not apparent what "traditional mysticism" might have been, if the expression was intended to refer to the *lisan*, or more exactly, in this particular formulation, to *lulik*, then the statement – whether by purpose or ignorance – sounded a false note. *Lisan* flourished, as we have seen, and would continue to flourish even after the last Indonesian soldier had departed the country in 1999.

Tellingly prominent in the *Fretilin* manifesto was the claim to be a "front" and its distinctive view of Timorese history. Since its manifesto was the most well thought out and complex of the three, and because it was *Fretilin* that would eventually form a Timorese government, it merits an extended analysis.

> FRETILIN struggles against colonialism and any form of domination of our people. We struggle for a humanitarian existence, for our development and for our lives. But this struggle cannot be conducted if the people are factionalized. We remember very well that the disunity of our forefathers caused their defeat. We will not repeat the same ever. We will go forward in unity. [...] For this, it is urgent and necessary that all people participate in the Revolutionary Front of Independent East Timor (FRETILIN).[7]

In their choice of name for their party, "*Fretilin*," its founders were making a point of using language to align its political stance with that of *Frelimo*, the left-wing independence party in Mozambique, and as *Frelimo*, refer to their party as a "front." They saw their party as the institutional expression of a movement embracing the entire population, and thus it was apt to call it a "front" instead of a "union," or "association."[8] It followed, therefore, that since *Fretilin* spoke for the Timorese, a popular plebiscite or referendum would be redundant. This audacious assertion lacked legitimacy in September 1974, and is unlikely to have been true even a year later when *Fretilin* had apparently gained more support in the hinterland. The claim was repeated later in a communiqué issued by the *Fretilin–União Democrática Timorense* coalition on March 18 of the following year, by which time, the fortunes of the *União Democrática Timorense* had declined to the extent that its leaders were willing to accede to *Fretilin*'s demands and, in doing so, reinforced *Fretilin*'s assertion.

Although East Timor had never been a nation in the sense in which Kingsbury defines the term, and its population was devoid of any notion of possessing a national consciousness, *Fretilin* asserted that "...it is urgent to awake the CONSCIOUSNESS OF THE NATION," a call that spoke of the Europeans' "wars of oppression and subjugation, accompanied by the exploitation and of the rape of the riches of the people." The demand refers to the "various uprisings and rebellions, over the long 500 years [*sic*] of colonial domination registered and proved irrefutably the strong spirit and desire for independence which tied together our forefathers." However, these "uprisings and rebellions" had, according to the historical record, resulted at least as much from *liurai* conflicting ambitions among themselves as the desire to get rid of a handful of Europeans. Even the call to battle made by some kings in the closing years of the nineteenth century and early years of the twentieth century involved, in many cases, local rivalries as much as it did animosity against the *malai*. Abílio de Araújo's influence is apparent here, for his *Timorese Elites* makes precisely the same assertions.[9] Araújo cites in that pamphlet "tribal feuds," by means of which the Portuguese were able to divide the Timorese and so dominate them. Contemporary descriptions of the time, though, depict the kingdoms being in a state of chronic warfare even before the Europeans arrived. He continues with other powerful indictments. "Through the exercise of colonial power we gradually lost our land, our women were maltreated, we were reduced to lives of slavery and obscurity, our culture stagnated, our lives were full of misery and hunger, leading to premature death [*sic*]." This was inventing a past that had never existed, and brought into the present a threatening prefiguration of the future that awaited the *ema lisan* if they were permitted to vote in a "divisive" referendum. *Fretilin*'s version of democracy was one in which the democratic choice would be enjoyed exclusively by a few; in the "Recognition of *Fretilin* as the only legitimate representative of the people of East Timor."[10] Officially, the *Fretilin*'s *comité central* was responsible for the manifesto, but apart from Araújo we cannot tell who else contributed ideas, though its radical language accords with the political ideology of Carvarino, Reis, Rodrigûes, and Alkatiri. The pamphlet misrendered the present, too, in asserting that "The Revolutionary front of East Timor (FRETILIN) is a fore-front movement which interprets *the profoundest aspirations of the people of East Timor to be free from political, cultural and economic colonisation and other forms of domination and exploitation* [italics supplied]."

Heedless of *lisan's* continuing vitality, the manifesto fostered the illusion that the colonialists had subverted Timorese traditions,[11] an image that enabled *Fretilin* to position itself as the protector of people whose culture was not "modern" enough, and whose histories had shown them to be gullibly weak. In this respect, the *Fretilin* program contained another contradiction. While insisting on its commitment to maintain a Timorese "culture," it also advanced a policy designed to radicalize the lives of the *suku* inhabitants. Among other ways, this would be accomplished by the *Fretilin* cooperatives, which, by controlling production, distribution and consumption, would "be the base of the economic and social life of East Timor." Nor did the plan to modify traditional Timorese agricultural practices cease there, for a sweeping "agrarian reform" was in the works. "All large farms [presumably the commercial plantations, especially those growing coffee] will be expropriated and returned to the people" [*sic*]. Not that "the people" would actually get to acquire the land, because the land "[would] be used within the co-operative system." As with large farms, so, too, with "fertile lands" in general. "[T]hose not under cultivation will be distributed to the people [*sic*] and will be utilized in co-operatives by state enterprises." *SAPT* was the obvious target there. Portuguese owners would be replaced by *Fretilin* operatives, which meant that the *ema foho* would continue missing out. "Traditional institutions of justice will be preserved and protected," i.e., *lisan* would be permitted to continue; *but* would be "improved by international law." In other words, *lisan*, too, would be subjected to fundamental alterations to bring it into conformity with precepts emanating from the *malai*.[12]

Nor were the ethnic Timorese the only people for whom the framers of the new order had plans. Sharing, at least, with the *ema lisan*, resentment of the success of the Chinese, *Fretilin* intended to stop their "commercial exploitation," by controlling prices and introducing a new fiscal system. Neither was the international domain neglected. Although not directly identified, the statement, "The rejection and energetic repudiation of neo-colonialism and all forms of alienation of the country to any potential foreign power," was an obvious reference to Indonesia. *Apodeti* and its supporters in East Timor were also served notice they were included in this stern proscription: "organisations and groups which support the annexation of the country to a foreign power will be forbidden to exercise political activities."

In foreign affairs, *Fretilin* intended to give greater importance to its neighbors in Southeast Asia than had the colonial power, and – hardly surprisingly – the party looked forward to establishing "fraternal" ties with the *Movimento Popular de Libertação de Angola, Frente de Libertação de Moçambique*, and *Partido Africano da Independência da Guiné e Cabo Verde*."

Paradoxically, at the same time as they wished to alter the *lisan* of the Timorese, two *Fretilin* leaders, at least, held certain aspects of it in respect and revealed a devotion for those who followed it. Abílio de Araújo and Francisco Borja da Costa, sought inspiration in poems, songs, and motifs from the hinterland; most famously manifested in the song, "*Foho Ramelau*" ("Mount Ramelau"), the Tetum words of which came from Borja da Costa and the music from Araújo.[13] In 1974–1975 its words and music served to carry *Fretilin*'s message of national awareness into the sub-districts, and in later years would inspire young nationalists in their struggle against the Indonesian occupation.

Having taken a preliminary examination of the kind of political language used in the platforms of the three main parties, let us now see how the parties that created these manifestos came into existence, starting with the first party to appear.

The *União Democrática Timorense*

Within ten days of the news of the *Revolução dos Cravos* reaching Dili, several dozen men decided that the overthrow of the fascist regime meant their country's future might include space for their political ambitions. On the evening of

May 11, 1974, 23 or so among them assembled in the house of Domingos de Oliveira and formed the *União Democrática Timorense* and its *comité central*.[14] The *União Democrática Timorense* program that they fashioned reflected the minds of men who had more-or-less succeeded in winning a place for themselves in the colonial world, and included men with differing ideas about what their new party's political platform should be. Domingos de Oliveira and Mário Carrascalão favored an *autonomia progressiva* (a "progressive autonomy") to independence within a community of Portuguese-speaking nations. Others preferred to maintain the status quo, but with some small changes. Others wished to leave the status quo intact. The ubiquitous José Ramos-Horta was there, "more by coincidence than design," so he says, a presence fortuitous for us since he is able to give us a shrewd insider's version of that historic meeting. It was here that Mário Carrascalão was passed over in favor of Lopes da Cruz, a choice that would in time facilitate Indonesian ambitions. Nevertheless, Carrascalão level-headedness was acknowledged by his being placed in charge of the organizing committee (*"commissão organizadora"*), which was tasked to prepare the ground for consolidating the party after it had been formally established. Domingos de Oliveira was selected the party's *secretário geral*.

Mário Carrascalão had initially proposed calling the party the *União Luso-Timorense* (the "Luso-Timorese Union") but Ramos-Horta, ever attuned to the importance of political language and imagery in public relations, pointed out that such a name implied that Portugal would remain a presence in the country, and counseled those present to come up with a name that had a less conservative sound. Rather quickly, the name *"União Democrática Timorense"* was settled upon. That the party's founders were not wholeheartedly committed to the colonial past is confirmed by Ramos-Horta, who records that even though Mário Carrascalão had originally proposed that Lusitanian name, he wanted little more than to retain some sort of link with the mother country for as long as possible, and did not dismiss the option of independence. Unlike typical meetings of the future *Fretilin*, there was little by way of feisty debate about political philosophy, and this initial meeting was not in the least contentious. "Just to be polite," César Mousinho asked Carrascalão to exactly say what democracy was. When Carrascalão hesitated, Oliveira began an exegesis of the etymology of the word *demos*.[15]

Some who assembled in Oliveira's house that evening had been accustomed to gather together in the *Associação Desportiva e Recreativa "União,"* the "Sporting and Recreational 'Union' Association," a club founded in the 1950s by Father Ezequiel Enes Pascoal, the only institution of its kind in Dili that was not some mere branch of a parent outgrowth in Lisbon.[16] Luís Thomaz, an official at the club for some two years and among whose functions it was to ensure its membership did not run foul of the governor, recalls that, while some members may have met privately to discuss political issues, politics was rarely openly mentioned.[17] It appears from what he says that, to the extent politics *was* discussed, attitudes inclined to be more reformist than revolutionary, with the general sentiment inclining more towards autonomy within some sort of association with Portugal rather than outright independence. The draft of the *União Democrática Timorense* platform quite impressed Ramos-Horta, as had the assurance Mário Carrascalão had given that the option of independence remained. "I had strong reservations about the politics of most of the group's founders; their love for Portugal was distasteful to me. However, I thought I could work within the group to steer it to the right course."[18] Despite his inclination at the time, Ramos-Horta decided not to join. Afterwards, he immediately left for Xavier do Amaral's house where, according to Carrascalão, men who had not been at Oliveira's house were waiting, and they devised a plan of action against the newly-formed party.[19]

The *União Democrática Timorense* formally announced its platform on the first day of August,[20] but although the party's program tended to have a ductile character, never, at any time before September 1975 did its leaders look upon the integration option with any favor. Their public language was even more anti-Indonesia than *Fretilin*'s, and in later stages of the campaign further inflamed the campaign by broadcasting the rumor that certain *Fretilin* notables, including Ramos-Horta, were actually pro-Indonesian. Interestingly, apropos of this attitude towards Indonesia, Ramos-Horta himself credits Mário Carrascalão with an emotional statement made in Dili in May 1974, during a meeting between East Timorese political leaders and two senior Portuguese army officers.[21] In response to a comment made by one advocate for integration, Carrascalão is said to have replied, "In my view, integration with Indonesia would be treason! Portugal is the only country with which we have cultural affinities!" Ramos-Horta joined him in denouncing José Osório Soares. As a measure of its flexibility, the *União Democrática Timorense* later adopted the slogan *ukun duni-an*, a Tetum expression that translates as "we will govern ourselves." Nonetheless, 18 months later, as noted earlier, the *União Democrática Timorense* leaders, pressured by their Indonesian controllers, reversed themselves and, in what became known as the "Balibo Declaration," formally requested integration from the Indonesian Government.

In Portugal, in contrast with his immediate predecessor, the centrist, António de Spínola, President Francisco da Costa Gomes was unsympathetic to the *União Democrática Timorense*'s policy of maintaining ties with the mother country. For him, the party's all too gradualist approach to independence was incompatible with the *Movimento das Forças Armadas*' policy of "dynamic decolonization," so from the time Gomes came into office, on September 30, 1974, he saw to it that the Portuguese Government inclined to policies that benefited their chief rival, the party that wanted independence.

As an example of the language through which dedicated supporters of the *União Democrática Timorense* framed their opinions about the party and its place in East Timor's future at that time is the personal testimony of one Timorese I interviewed, Mrs. Maria Rosa Biddlecombe.[22] Her account reveals how some well-educated persons in that party regarded the political benefit of cooperation between *Fretilin* and the *União Democrática Timorense*, and offers a counter-argument to the assertions made by many journalists and academics that the Portuguese Government was the principal party at fault for the calamitous turn the process of decolonization took. The guilt, she avers, lay with *Fretilin*. From the very beginning of the time its elite starting bruited the pros and cons of the three options, Mrs. Biddlecombe was convinced Portuguese Timor lacked the political resources for speedy independence. Delivered in a style of anti-*Fretilin* rhetoric typical of a *União Democrática Timorense* loyalist, and one that brings Fidel Castro into the picture, she contended that "No one in their right minds, and [*sic*] being realistic [would] give independence to these people [*Fretilin*] because giving them independence then, the next day [after independence Timor] would be full of Cubans...." And she was in no doubt that the majority of the *Fretilin* leaders *were* communist "Horta might not be, but the others were."[23] Mrs. Biddlecombe was of the opinion that a premature early independence would have resulted in a communist takeover, aided and abetted by communist countries. She maintained, correctly, in my view, that had Timorese leaders been able to come together, Indonesia would not have had the "excuse" to invade.

> I think if the Portuguese flag was still there [rather than having been replaced by the flag of independence in November 1975 Indonesian probably wouldn't [have] come in because as soon as *Fretilin* took the flag down and the Portuguese garrison left Timor to [go to] Ataúro. That [was] it ... they just walked in ... and there was a good excuse for them ... we made out own bed ... we can't keep on blaming [Portugal] ... Portugal was broke and made a big mess in [its]own country as well ... [it] became ... [a] democratic country but I think in one year they [changed] the government about four or five times.... They wanted to go back home, but if the Timorese leaders [had been] united then, Indonesia wouldn't [have had] an excuse to get in ... when you think rationally how could we be independent then in '74, [and] stand up on our own two feet?

Associação Social-Democrática Timorense/Fretilin

If the men who founded the *União Democrática Timorense* eschewed speculation about the nature of government and social abstractions, the founders of the *Associação Social Democráta Timorense* reveled in debate about political theory and enjoyed the play of ideas for, like Araújo, some were decidedly of an intellectual turn of mind. It is not surprising, then, that the party they created was more grounded in conceptual thinking than their rival's nor that their manifesto was more detailed. They were, however, realistic enough to think through the practical implications resulting from the economic backwardness of their country and the immensity of the challenge they faced in attempting to bring Portuguese Timor into the modern world, and so, *pace* Mrs. Biddlecombe, they thought the country could dispense with a lengthy stage of *autonomia progressiva* and still transform itself into a viable nation-state.

Taking advantage of the revolution in Portugal, early in May, José Ramos-Horta and a few professional men and civil servants helped to organize a laborers' strike for higher wages, and the experience of working on the strike committee gave Ramos-Horta's colleagues a taste of political activism in an executive capacity.[24] This experience may have played a part in their decision to follow the example of the men who had founded the *União Democrática Timorense*, which they saw as a challenge to their own political philosophies. And so, on May 20, 1974, about a dozen of them gathered in Dili to found what became the *Associação Social-Democrática Timorense*, among them Francisco Xavier do Amaral, Nicolau Lobato, Rogério Lobato, Justino Mota, Mari Alkatiri,[25] and José Ramos-Horta. Some were former schoolmates who had gone their own ways in the years before 1974, yet who continued to exchange ideas when they hung out at the *Associação Desportiva e Recreativa "União."* Some, as we have seen, had, like Xavier do Amaral, done rather well under the colonial system, but others had not prospered and were, in consequence, disgruntled young men; Mari Alkatiri and Justino Mota prominent among them. Differing experiences and ideological heterogeneity might have made one expect the group would find it hard to find unity, but in the end it came, in a unanimous call for independence. For the moment, their differences were glossed over, and only later would re-emerge when the party was reborn as *Fretilin*. Ramos-Horta has gone on record as remarking that in those early days "Marxism was far from our minds," and at that time an impartial judge would have concurred with him. He writes that, except for Nicolau Lobato and possibly Alkatiri, no one had read Marx or Lenin,[26] and for his own part disclaims any taste for the "abstract extravaganzas" his more radical colleagues relished: "...social democracy to us and to me particularly, seemed closest to the ideal. It stood for social justice, equitable distribution of the wealth of the country, a mixed economy and a democratic political system."[27] Robust discussion eventually resulted in the aforementioned draft manifesto,[28] and it was accepted by everyone. As he was, in his estimation, instrumental in helping the founders of the *União Democrática Timorense* to fix upon a more diplomatically acceptable name for their party, so Ramos-Horta claims to have played a determining role in shaping the second party's draft manifesto. Its partial convergence with that of the *União Democrática Timorense's*, was not far from the position advocated by Mrs. Biddlecombe, but was, of course, as things turned out, to be superseded by the more radical *Fretilin* document. It may be read as a somewhat vaguely – even conservatively – worded call for independence, with no time-frame specified; the founders envisioning a period of perhaps ten years before they thought Timor would be ripe for independence.[29] A decade or so, they reasoned, would give them adequate time for administrative, judicial, and economic reforms; enable them to include among their leadership people from outside their elite circle who would also be capable of running the country; and establish international contacts in the areas of commerce, economic aid, and cooperation.

José Ramos-Horta floated the possibility of the *Associação Social Democrática Timorense* merging with the *União Democrática Timorense*, a precocious attempt at a coalition which might have produced a better outcome for the future of East Timor, but his colleagues feared that, with their greater political experience, the *União Democrática Timorense* leaders would end up controlling them.[30] His proposal was rejected out of hand.

The name "*Associação Social Democrática Timorense*" reflected accurately enough the values of a number of the men assembled there that evening, and immediately attracted the support of young people as well as that of the lowest wage earners, to whom Ramos-Horta and his colleagues had rendered assistance in their strike. But whereas the support of these outsiders was unconditional, the same cannot be said for António Carvarino, Vicente dos Reis, and Abílio de Araújo, any more than it was acceptable to Roque Rodrigûes. Indeed, when Carvarino, Reis, and Araújo arrived from Lisbon on September 11[31] they already had an alternative program that they had devised while in Portugal. In their view a social democratic association was not the most adequate for organizing a movement for independence, and Araujo proposed an alternative manifesto and political program of his own called the "*Frente Unida para a Libertação e Independência Nacional*" (*FULIN*), the "Front for National Liberation and Independence." When they met with Ramos-Horta, Alkatiri, Xavier do Amaral, and Nicolau Lobato that day, Araújo urged the party to accept the plan. It was not accepted, and *Fretilin* was born. According to Ramos-Horta, the *Associação Social Democrática Timorense*'s "social democracy" was altogether too much of a "bourgeois doctrine that did not represent the real interests and aspirations of the common people."[32] As it was quickly to turn out, the choice of the words "front" and "revolutionary" in the new name served to agitate the concern of the Indonesian generals and projected an image of extreme radicalism that did not reflect the more moderate character of the *comité central*. For all his uninhibited polemic against the Portuguese, Abílio de Araújo also made the statesmanlike recommendation that an alliance with the *União Democrática Timorense* and *Apodeti* be formed, arguing that they must all be united to achieve independence.[33]

When the founders contemplated whom to consider for the position of president of *Fretilin*'s organizing committee, an office that was, in effect, that of party president, one popular candidate was Nicolau Lobato, a young man who was beginning to be talked about as a future leader. Three factors weighed against him: his attendance at the *Associação Desportiva e Recreativa "União"* get-togethers had been too sporadic for the more dedicated members; his public profile was still relatively low; and his youth.[34] Francisco Xavier do Amaral, of course, did satisfy that age criterion, and, given his popularity with many Timorese, was the natural choice. However, he was reluctant to accept the nomination, and although he eventually agreed to serve, in a matter of days, suffering from a case of "buyer's regret," he called the local government printing house where the list of members of the organizing committee was being printed, to withdraw his name. The director of the printing house phoned Ramos-Horta who, fearing the party's viability would be in jeopardy without the respected name of a senior man to lend it credibility, phoned Xavier do Amaral and urged him to keep his name on the list. Xavier do Amaral acceded to his request. The claims of Nicolau Lobato were not forgotten, however. He was elected vice-president. "There was no disagreement on anyone's part about the choices of Xavier and Nicolau as our leaders."[35] Thus it was that the *Associação Social Democráta Timorense* had emerged as the second party to contest the future of Portuguese Timor.

Apodeti

Midwife of the third party's birth was the *Movimento Forças Armadas'* chief representative in the colony, Major António Carlos Arnão Metelo, *Estado-Maior do Comando Militar de Timor* ("Chief of Staff") and *Chefe do Estado Maior das Forças Armadas* ("Chief of the General Staff of Armed Forces").[36] On May 27, three dozen men came together in his house in Dili, and chose Arnaldo dos Reis Araújo as president of a party they at first called the *Associação Para a Integração de Timor na Indonesia (AITI)*, the "Association for the Integration of Timor into Indonesia." This was considered a shade too blatant for public taste, and the party was quickly renamed the *"Associação Popular Democrática Timorense" (Apodeti)*, the "Timorese Popular Democratic Association." It proved decidedly unpopular with the Timorese and could hardly be considered democratic since it quickly became a dependent of an autocratic government.

Major Metelo had been commissioned by President Spínola to serve as the *Movimento das Forças Armadas'* delegate in Portuguese Timor, and had been entrusted with the task of beginning the process by which the colony would be decolonized. By July, Governor Aldeia's criticism of the army officers in the weeks prior to the revolt in Lisbon had resulted in his ceding influence in the colonial Administration to Metelo, who emerged as its most powerful figure. Metelo was a man to be reckoned with, and there is little doubt that *Apodeti* benefited considerably from his patronage. So intimate was Metelo's association with the party that some Timorese referred to him as *"Apodeti nia aman"* (*"Apodeti's* father"),[37] and the question has been posed as to why, as a representative of the *Movimento das Forças Armadas*, he would encourage the aspirations of the Indonesian generals. Jorge Duarte speculates that his "strange initiative" might have resulted from the *Movimento das Forças Armadas'* decision to feed the Timorese to the wolves.[38] For his part, James Dunn was told by Metelo that although *Apodeti* enjoyed little support among the populace, he had "an obligation to be protective of *Apodeti"* because the Indonesian option had to be clearly presented to the Timorese so as not to antagonize the Indonesian Government which might then be provoked into undermining the process of decolonization.[39] Mário Pires's answer is consistent with what Metelo told Dunn. He points out that, on May 13, Governor Aldeia created a *"Commissão para a Autodeterminação de Timor"* (the "Commission for the Self-Determination of Timor") the intention of which was to bring about the legalization of the several political associations that appeared to be coming into existence in order to avoid clandestine activity and possibly violence. The result was that *Apodeti* came to be recognized as a legitimate political party, and since Arnão Metelo had been appointed the commission's president, he became identified as its mentor and supporter.[40] In July, with the support of and under the control of the Indonesian authorities,

Apodeti began publishing a journal, *O Arauto de Sunda*, and began radio transmissions from Atambua and Kupang.[41] Metelo was eventually recalled to Portugal where he subsequently served as vice prime minister under the Marxist prime minister, Vasco dos Santo Gonçalves.

Before he left, however – and this only served to increase the suspicion that he favored *Apodeti* – Arnão Metelo was said, during the course of a reception at the Indonesian consulate in Dili, to have suggested that at least some members of the *Movimento das Forças Armadas* were willing to hand the colony over to Indonesia. Since the *Movimento das Forças Armadas* regarded Indonesia as having a repressive, right-wing government, this solution may have seemed ideologically inconsistent for its members; but it was expedient. The Portuguese Government would be rid of an expensive and profitless albatross, and the *Movimento das Forças Armadas* would be relieved of a vexing problem, since a Timorese plebiscite might suggest a precedent for the African colonies. As things stood in May 1974, the government of Portugal faced the awkward possibility that the Timorese would vote for the *União Democrática Timorense*, which would mean that Lisbon would probably be obliged to keep a colony it wished to rid itself of. This possibility came about because *Apodeti* did not seem to be receiving support in the sub-districts (and there was no reason to suppose its standing would improve) and the government of Indonesia was not pushing its policy of integration as aggressively had been anticipated.[42]

Like the *Associação Social Democrática Timorense*, *Apodeti* also had some claim on the past; in the form of the 1959 "uprising," but of more practical significance in the years immediately prior to the *revolução* were the machinations of its consul in Dili, Elias Tomodok, who continually sought to ferment anti-Portuguese sentiment. The extent to which he directly interfered with the administration has yet to be determined, but anti-colonial Timorese never failed to find a sympathetic ear at the consulate to air their resentments. Timorese inclined to integration were, above all, welcome, as one might expect, but José Ramos-Horta also met clandestinely with the consul on "numerous occasions," usually nocturnally to escape the surveillance of the *Polícia Internacional e de Defensa do Estado*. Ramos-Horta's relationship eventually soured when Tomodok threw his support behind *Apodeti*, and the future president of Timor-Leste came to see him as, "an extremely corrupt individual" inhibited by "no moral restraints to hinder him in gathering a fortune and gaining more political clout back in Jakarta."[43] Later, his contempt for the man intensified upon discovering that Tomodok had been "responsible for the climate of intrigue, uncertainty and fear that began to prevail in East Timor in early 1975," allegations later reinforced when the Secretary of the Indonesian Consulate, a character called Saate was identified as a recruiter of supporters for pro-integrationists.[44]

But even as Tomodok sought to win recruits for *Apodeti*, so was José Ramos-Horta doing the same on behalf of *Fretilin*, maneuverings that even included an attempt to seduce José Soares. The bait he dangled before the *Apodeti* leader was the promise that a *Fretilin* government would make *Bahasa Indonesia* compulsory in schools, and after allowing village people time to understand what integration meant, in practice, for their lives, would permit them to consider that option. Soares was intrigued enough by the proposal to agree to attend a meeting of the *Associação Social Democrática Timorense* and even served as co-chair at the meeting with Ramos-Horta and Xavier do Amaral. Tomodok, however, managed to keep Soares on the side of pro-integration, and continued his intrigues until Soares assumed responsibility for *Apodeti* strategy.[45] About José Soares' character, opinions are divided. In contrast with Ramos-Horta, who had a low opinion of the man, Jill Jolliffe describes Soares' reputation among those who knew him as that of an honest man who stood up for the educated people in the *suku*, and, though pressing for integration was said to have opposed it being forced down the throats of the Timorese.[46]

Apodeti, too, included men of somewhat differing political views, though they were not as diverse as those of the other two parties. As noted earlier, some men favored out-and-out integration whereas others imagined an East Timor that was at one and the same time both independent and yet a province of Indonesia. Demonstrating their seriousness about the integration option, members of the *Apodeti comité central* went to Jakarta and spoke with Ali Murtopo, who, in July, sent his deputy, Aloysius Sugiyanto, pretending to be a marketing officer, to Dili to gather information about the political parties.[47] For several months Sugiyanto kept visiting Portuguese Timor, on each visit talking with the leaders of all three parties, not only with those of *Apodeti*.

Statistics showing the strength the party commanded are untrustworthy, as, for example, Soares' wildly optimistic June 1975 estimate of between 30,000 and 40,000 supporters.[48] Given the general unpopularity of *Apodeti*, its leaders were understandably not at all confident of winning the plebiscite, and their insecurity helps explain the virulence of its utterances on *Rádio Dili*, and why, in early 1975, with Jakarta's connivance, the party began recruiting Timorese in villages near the border for military training at Atambua.[49] Months later, their training completed, the recruits returned to East Timor and began a campaign of house-burnings, random killings, and coercions to intimidate villagers into seeking refuge across the border. The campaign was supported by radio transmissions from West Timor that made use of rumors that Indonesian warships had begun to land troops on the island to begin the process of forced integration, and that all who resisted would be exterminated.[50] In a year's time this is exactly what did occur.

The *Klibur Oan Timur Asuwa'in* (*Kota*)

The *União Democrática Timorense*, *Fretilin*, and *Apodeti* did not have the campaign exclusively all to themselves. October 1974 saw several men, some of whom were *liurai*, discussing the feasibility of fourth party, an ambition that hinted there might exist other values available for exploiting by politically shrewd operatives. The party so strongly identified itself with the privileges traditionally accorded the *liurai*, it was initially known as the *Associação Popular Monárquica de Timor*, "The Popular Monarchic Association of Timor";

but, as was becoming customary by now, its name changed. The change occurred on November 20, and the *Associação Popular Monárquica de Timor* became the *Klibur Oan Timur Asuwa'in (Kota)*, the "Association [or Congregation] of the heroic sons of Timor."[51] The leaders spent the next month organizing the party before they formally announced its existence in a flamboyant rally celebrated on January 26.[52] Its leadership consisted of a president, the aforementioned 49-year-old, José Martins, formerly of *Apodeti*, and a vice-president, Francisco Ximenes,[53] a Galoli-speaker from Laleia, in Manatuto district.

The foreign press all but ignored the *Klibur Oan Timur Asuwa'in*, with Bill Nicol the single exception, and from him we have most of our information about this curious political phenomenon. The party's platform, in his estimation, might have appealed to the *ema foho* because it responded to *lisan*. Among its throwbacks to tradition was a plan for establishing a "popular" monarchic form of national government in which *liurai* would be elected to a parliament – an institution unknown to *lisan*, it might be noted – which would elect its own leader who would preside in the capacity of a *quasi* monarch. Through an indirect electoral process, each "tribe"[54] would select a "chief from a hereditary line of males," every one of whom would elect the parliamentary representatives from among their own constituents, and these would elect the king. By this procedure "The Monarchists believed this would dispose of the need for political factions."[55] The *Klibur Oan Timur Asuwa'in* planned to modernize and democratize the more autocratic components of *lisan* while "preserving tradition." "...historical lines of authority, with the chiefs at the top, [would] be maintained, even strengthened. But the chiefs would be elected, giving the people some say in their affairs."[56]

Unrealistically, Nicol considered the *Klibur Oan Timur Asuwa'in* to have had serious potential for attracting the support of the Timorese populace, but its leaders failed to capitalize on their party's possibilities and took too long to get going.

> ...slow and naive, it took them a long time to decide even that they should form a political movement ... October 1974 was the first they thought about it, and it was not until 10 months after the Portuguese revolution that the group actually surfaced.[57]

But by then whatever chances they had for challenging the major parties had evaporated.

The name *Klibur Oan Timur Asuwa'in* was a piece of forensic rhetoric. The association of the acronym "*Kota*" with the meaning "fort" conjured up the idea of *lisan* institutions being defended from some outside force, an image that might appeal to *ema lisan*; and the vague allusion to monarchism was intended to strike a cord with *liurai*. *Klibur Oan Timur Asuwa'in* would have had a major expansion if it had been established earlier, so Bill Nicol speculates, especially if the party had been able to recruit civil servants in the administration to its leadership. Even so, despite its assorted handicaps, the *Klibur Oan Timur Asuwa'in*

January demonstration attracted thousands who acknowledged their commitment to *lisan* institutions and reveled in the long-standing influence the Portuguese had had on the these institutions.[58] They did so in their own style of imagery, embellishing their speech by displaying *lisan* artifacts from their various *uma lulik*. Prominent among the latter were those patent letters issued by the Portuguese to the *liurai* centuries earlier, which affirmed the demonstrators' connections to the colonial past. In light of the role the image of the *uma lulik* would come to play as a potential symbol of the nation during the first decade of Timor-Leste's independence,[59] it is interesting that the *uma lulik* proved an irresistible artifact for men so wedded to "tradition"; the leaders of *Klibur Oan Timur Asuwa'in*, for example, choosing to conduct their business in one.[60] Like the two *Klibur Oan Timur Asuwa'in* leaders, the *liurai*, so they claimed, descended from the *topasses*[61] and as such held exclusive rights to perform *lisan* rituals.[62] The compelling power of *lisan* is apparent in the images displayed in the demonstration:[63]

> It was January 26, 1975.... About 10,000 people had gathered in front of the administration palacio [*sic*] in Dili in support of one of Timor's least-publicized political movements. The demonstration was unexpected. As a spectacle, it surpassed the best-organized rally that any of the major political parties, including Fretilin, could turn on in the capital. We could hear the chanting and beating of drums three or four blocks away.... An Australian woman, Frances Swan, joined us as we watched.... "They want to have a monarchy in Timor.... Each tribe in the mountains is led by a king and the Monarchists want one of these to rule the country, you know, as king of the Timorese." ... Colour parties [*sic*] carried tattered Portuguese flags which I was told were over two centuries old. One group carried some moth-eaten documents and cloth protected within a large glass-covered picture frame. I was to find out later that the overall gathering was an attempt by the Monarchists to show the administration the sort of support the group could muster. It was more than a mere demonstration. It was a show of force. In theory, the Monarchists could have attracted the largest number of supporters of any political movement in East Timor. Yet they were a dismal failure.

Like the Mambai concept of elder brother/younger brother, the party had an "extremely favorable" attitude towards the mother country, which it idealized as Portuguese Timor's "true benefactor."[64] In an interview he had with Ximenes, Nicol came away with the impression that, though not without some excess, the vice-president's words carried a more authentic ring than either *Fretilin*'s or *Apodeti*'s, including, as it did, a genuine evocation of the *lisan* institution of blood-brotherhood (*ai moruk*) and the reverential esteem in which the Portuguese flag was held:

> They [the Portuguese] came with the cross and the people accepted the cross of Christ. The people mixed their blood with the Portuguese blood. When

the Portuguese were satisfied that the people needed their friendship they handed over the chiefs, to each group of tribes [*sic*], the military armor, the bastion and the flag. The people had lived separately. But the Portuguese, doing this, joined the people together. So the Monarchists say: 'We welcome the Portuguese.'[65]

A hyperbolic invention of the past, as creative as that of *Fretilin*'s and *Apodeti*'s, but one whose images drew upon the hierarchical character of the *lisan*, Francisco Ximenes' reconstruction incorporated more than its fair share of illusions, but what the founders of the *Klibur Oan Timur Asuwa'in* had in mind bore somewhat greater fidelity to *ema lisan* values than those of the other parties. And, although open to the charge of lacking sophistication, the party's platform converged more with the parochial conservatism of rural Timor than any of the three main parties.

Nicol describes the setting of his interview:[66]

A rusty old Portuguese sword hung on the unpainted cement wall above Ximenes' head.... The interpreter refused to translate any of my questions which were obviously critical of the Portuguese Administration. He just glared at me briefly and asked if there was anything else I wanted to know.

In words that went further than that of the earlier language of the *União Democrática Timorense*, the leaders of the *Klibur Oan Timur Asuwa'in* appealed to the Portuguese Government not to abandon them. "...Only release [us] when our people feel apt to enter alone, with security, with confidence and with head erect.... We want Portugal to remain until the country is economically and politically prepared for independence" ... "We want a special independence with close ties to Portugal."[67] Ximenes believed that were the Portuguese to suddenly abandon their island ("suddenly" here being roughly 50 years) the traditional lifestyle of the people would be "drastically undermined." They envisaged the Europeans as a necessary component of an integrated complex of history, land, people, and culture. To avoid vitiating its integrity, Timor had to become an autonomous "state" in a "neo-colonial" (Nicol's terminology) Portuguese commonwealth.[68]

This vision gave *Klibur Oan Timur Asua'in* "tremendous potential" to make their mark, in Nicol's judgment, but "few people ever heard of them," in part because the administration denied the party access to *Rádio Dili*.

The party leaders could not see that they would never be allowed to use *Rádio Dili* for publicity. Blind to reality, Ximenes told me that "Once the governor lets us use the radio to speak to the people, *União Democrática Timorense* and *Fretilin* will lose support. The people will come behind us. We will win..." And well they might have.... But they were out in the cold, and that's where they would stay.[69]

More realistically, a less laudatory opinion was that of Jorge Duarte, who regarded the party leaders as men obsessed with self-promotion and espousing a vague and utopian monarchism.[70]

Perhaps the *ema foho* also saw through them, as well, for the party failed to win the support of enough people to pose any sort of threat to the other parties.

The *Partido Trabalhista*

If the *Klibur Oan Timur Asua'in's* impact on the political scene was barely perceptible, that of two other parties, as remarked previously, was virtually nonexistent. The fifth day of September 1974 saw the formation of the *Partido Trabalhista Timorense*, the "Labour Party," by a few men[71] who hoped to attract the *ema lisan*, but who were completely ignorant of the social reality of a hinterland populated exclusively by conservative farmers not by a discontented proletariat. Nor did it help that these would-be political leaders had no notion of what constituted a political party. With an undefined platform, no coherent ideology, and an undetermined leadership, they were unable to muster the support of more than around ten persons,[72] and after the administration denied the party recognition, they threw in their lot with the *União Democrática Timorense*. But a year later, as with the *Klibur Oan Timur Asua'in* and the three main parties, the Indonesian Government professed to recognize it as one of the parties representing the will of the majority of Timorese and made its representatives add their signatures to the Balibo Declaration.[73]

The *Associação Democrática Integração Timor-Leste-Australia (Aditla)*

As if a workers' party was not insufficiently improbable, an entity whose creators named the *Associação Democrática Integração Timor-Leste-Australia* [*Aditla*], the "Democratic Association for the Integration of East Timor with Australia," somehow managed to force its way into existence in November 1974. The group was the brainchild of a businessman by the name of Henrique Pereira, who, exploiting Timorese-Chinese fears about *Fretilin* and Indonesia, proposed that Australia should incorporate East Timor into the commonwealth. The Australian Government would have nothing to do with the proposition.

Summary remarks

At their inceptions, then, the *Klibur Oan Timur Asuwa'in* and the *União Democrática Timorense* were the parties most closely identified with Portugal. According to Jorge Duarte, around May 1974, 230 *suku* out of the 472 *suku* supported the *União Democrática Timorense*, amounting to perhaps 50 percent of the indigenous population,[74] and he argues that "The *União Democrática Timorense* rapidly reunited the principal 'values' of Timor, thereby conquering with ease almost the entire totality of the Timorese population of the interior." Duarte traces this support to the influence of "tradition," remarking that "this strong implantation of the *União Democrática Timorense* in the mass of traditional Timorese" was a function of (a) the social organization and traditional values of Timor; (b) the positive Portuguese orientation of the party; and (c) the influence of the Catholic missions.[75] Even José Ramos-Horta concedes the hold *lisan* exercised on the politics of the time among the *ema foho*, remarking that the *União Democrática Timorense* had the "automatic" support of "traditional" chiefs when it was founded.[76] He adds, though, that "As in colonial Africa, where tribal rulers who were puppets of the colonial regime lost their power when independence came, the so-called Timorese 'traditional' chiefs saw their fortunes fading within months of the Lisbon coup."[77]

In Jill Jolliffe's view the *União Democrática Timorense's* links with the *ema lisan* were less authentic than *Fretilin*'s: "Even accepting the nominal commitment of *União Democrática Timorense*, as their programme evolved, to some measure of social change, there was little which could link the leadership to a popular movement [*sic*] of the people of the interior."[78] There was, of course, no popular movement at that time, and it was only after *Fretilin* began its campaigning in the interior after September 1974 that villagers began to be exposed to the new ideas that were coming from Dili. Jolliffe correctly notes that the effects of centuries of what she characterizes as "Portuguese indoctrination" should not be underestimated, illustrating this characterization by remarking the custom of older Timorese bowing when passing a European, and noting that in the early months after the revolution, the *União Democrática Timorense* had support in the interior despite the "chasm [*sic*] which separated the leadership from the mountain people."[79] This support Jolliffe detects as indicating "the strength under the old order of the social authority of *chefes de posto*, hoteliers, and plantation owners in each local area," even though few actually lived in the more isolated areas.[80] She is also on the mark in observing that, "if the repercussion of Lisbon events was slow to reach Dili, it took even longer to affect the hinterland." The "social authority" was most entrenched, she adds, (a) in the coffee-growing district of Ermera, where the Carrascalão brothers and Lopes da Cruz were based, and which was an employment centre for wage laborers; (b) the prosperous rice producing region of Maliana; and (c) in Maubisse, which was a military, administrative, and commercial centre. Even in the final stages of the campaign, when support for *Fretilin* seemed to be escalating elsewhere, these were the places that remained loyal to the *União Democrática Timorense* longer than elsewhere.

It has often been assumed that, as the Portuguese withdrawal became increasingly pronounced in 1975, sub-district chiefs tended to become advocates for the villagers they administered. This occurred in some sub-districts,[81] but this did not occur everywhere, in part because the colonial administration usually picked chiefs from sub-districts other than those for which they had been given responsibility, and in many instances had no ties of kinship or affinity with its residents. Often they did not even know the local tongue or much about local *lisan*.

Like non-traditional *suku* chiefs, sub-district chiefs were administrative appointees whose offices had been stamped into the "traditional" indigenous system by the administration and hence projected into the *lisan*. As a result, their impact on local matters tended to pale in comparison with the influence *liurai* like Miguel da Costa Soares, Gaspar Nunes, of Maubara, or even Guilherme Gonçalves (in a few *suku*) might bring to bear. Such leaders were also in daily contact with villagers, and so *suku* chiefs who often provided the most effective channels of communication between villagers and the administration came from traditional *liurai* stock.[82] In the mid-1970s, because they functioned at a higher bureaucratic level, the sub-district chiefs tended to be too removed from their constituents to have daily interaction with them, and "non-traditional" *chefes de suku*, who resided among the *ema foho*, lacked the required family lineage pedigree that would have conferred upon them some measure of moral authority. A similar situation continues today,[83] with some non-elected "traditional" *liurai* exercising more influence than government appointees or even democratically, but non-"traditional," *chefes de suku*.[84]

Nothing in the *lisan*, of course, had prepared villagers for formulating views about "independence," "colonialism, "neo-colonialism," "integration," and "nationalism," and, despite having devised the scheme for a political referendum, the administration made little attempt at informing the Timorese about these novel concepts. Nor did all Portuguese administrators remain neutral. In Luís Thomaz's – hardly unbiased – view, the *União Democrática Timorense* brought together most of what he refers to as "the positive values of Timor." He argues that the party "easily won over" the *ema lisan* and the majority of *liurai* because, "independent of the pressures brought to bear by the kings," the *União Democrática Timorense*, of all the three parties, was the only one that seemed least likely to meddle with traditions, including the cult of the flag.[85] This satisfaction with the status quo was consistent with Spínola's presumed inclination to confer "Associated Territory" or a "Federal State" on Portuguese Timor, and all of a piece with the *União Democrática Timorense's* platform. On the other hand, this conservatism clashed with, and was to be subverted by, the radical ideology of the *Movimento das Forças Armadas*. Committed to divesting itself of the colonies, the *União Democrática Timorense* was an inconvenient obstacle to swift decolonization; *Fretilin*'s platform was a lot more congenial, and even *Apodeti*'s was something Lisbon could live with.[86] So, bent upon breaking the colonial mold, the government dispatched to the colony three officers, the replacement for Governor Aldeia, Mário Pires, and his two colleagues, Major Francisco Mota, and Major Silvérico da Costa Jónatas. They arrived on November 18, 1974, charged with a brief to bring about decolonization as quickly as possible.

With their respective platforms in place, the three parties' next step was to find a constituency outside Dili. Campaigning was now in order, and the elite needed to reach out from the political center into the hinterland, where values were different. In this task one party would easily prove itself the most adept.

Notes

1 "*São as palavras que fazem a guerra.*"
2 They are reproduced in Jill Jolliffe's *East Timor* (Jolliffe 1978: 325–338). They would appear to be translations; but the translator is not identified, and one can only assume the original language in which they were written was Portuguese. The *Fretilin* manifesto formally promulgated the *Associação Social Democrática Timorense's* change of name, and was officially enacted on September 12, 1974. The "Provisional Statues" of the *União Democrática Timorense* gives the place and date, "Dili, August 1st, 1974." The date of *Apodeti*'s program is not given.
3 Jolliffe (1978: 325–327).
4 Jolliffe (1978: 337–338).
5 Jolliffe (1978: 327–336).
6 In fact, the platforms of both parties shows evidence of having been fashioned in haste; hence the changes they underwent. That of *Apodeti* remained more stable.
7 Jolliffe (1978: 331).
8 They could not, of course use the designation, "party".
9 Discussed in more detail in Chapter 9.
10 The non-Dili, indigenous, elites, however, also come in for criticism since they acceded to the demands of the colonialists.
11 Cf. Jolliffe (1978: 334).
12 An account of the formation of the three parties and their manifestos is given in Pires (2013: 31–55).
13 Araújo (2012: 107–108). This very popular song was published in Borja da Costa's *Revolutionary Poems in the Struggle Against Colonialism* (1976), which, in vivid imagery used the majesty of Timor's highest peak ("What is greater than your majesty?") to foster the spirit of nationalism in the "*ema maubere*." Employing both the resources of forensic rhetoric and political rhetoric, it combined somber reflections on the past-as-present ("Why, Timor, are your children enslaved?") with uplifting prospects of a future destiny ("Awake! Take command of our land") (Hill 2002: 75). Cf. Duarte (1988b).
14 Carrascalão (2006: 26–27); Duarte (1988a: 53); Pires (1991: 38–39); Ramos-Horta (1996: 29).
15 Ramos-Horta (1996: 30).
16 Not all members of the *Associação Desportiva e Recreativa "União"* were present at the birth of the *União Democrática Timorense*. One notable absentee was Francisco Xavier do Amaral.
17 Thomaz (1977: 34).
18 Ramos-Horta (1996: 34).
19 Carrascalão (2006: 26).
20 As Jill Jolliffe (1978: 76–77), following Dunn, has remarked,

> UDT has generally been regarded as the proponent of continued Portuguese rule. However, the party had never overruled the possibility of independence. Its original program called for "progressive autonomy" within a Portuguese federation, allowing for the possibility of eventual independence in "15 to 20 years."

21 Ramos-Horta (1996: 31).
22 A member of a celebrated *liurai* family who lived in Viqueque town when my wife and I first carried out our fieldwork, and who, in the days of fighting that took place in Dili after the armed movement, escaped to Darwin, and eventually married a very successful businessman.
23 Biddlecombe (Interview 2005).
24 Hill (2002: 59–60).
25 Jolliffe (1989: 31, 34).

26 He seems not to have known about Xavier do Amaral's reading, however.
27 Ramos-Horta (1996: 34–35).
28 See Appendix A in Jolliffe (1978).
29 Ramos-Horta (1996: 35).
30 Ramos-Horta (1996: 37).
31 Araújo (2012: 112). Venâncio da Silva, another student from Portugal, accompanied them.
32 Ramos-Horta (1996: 35).
33 Araújo (2012: 113).
34 "We desperately needed an older person with some intellectual standing to give our group an air of respectability and maturity. Our patriarchal society had no respect for a bunch of young people." (Ramos-Horta 1996: 35).
35 Ramos-Horta (1996: 36).
36 Carrascalão (2006: 31) refers to him as *Chefe do Estado Maior do Exército Português*, in Timor, and *Presidente da delegação local do Movimento Forças Armadas*.
37 Carrascalão (2006: 16); Cascais (1977: 16).
38 Duarte (1988a: 55).
39 Dunn (2003: 47). Whatever the truth, from the time he arrived, Metelo was not a popular man. The Timorese and the military alike "detested" him (Carrascalão 2006: 15, 31).
40 Pires (1991: 37).
41 Pires (1991: 42).
42 Thomaz (1977: 65).
43 Ramos-Horta (1996: 32).
44 Thomaz (1977: 41).
45 Ramos-Horta (1996: 32).
46 Jolliffe (1989: 31).
47 Conboy (2003: 196–197).
48 Nicol (1978: 60–61).
49 Elsewhere, in the sub-districts, except for Uato Lari and Uato Carabau, *Apodeti* campaigned very little, in part because their advocates feared being physically assaulted. Jolliffe (1989: 32).
50 Ramos-Horta (1996: 33).
51 Duarte (1988a: 57).
52 Nicol (1978: 53).
53 Duarte (1988a: 57) refers to him as "Tomás Ximenes."
54 By "tribe," Nicol presumably means "*suku*."
55 Nicol (1978: 52).
56 Nicol (1978: 52). But see pages 20–23: villagers of a *suku* already had a powerful influence in *suku* matters.
57 Nicol (1978: 54).
58 Cf. Nicol (1978: 51).
59 See Hicks (2008) for a discussion of the iconography of the *uma lulik* in contemporary East Timor.
60 Jolliffe (1978: 118.)
61 *Topasses* were *mestiços* of Timorese-European descent who, for several centuries starting around the seventeenth, wielded a great deal of power in Timorese politics and trade. Some families were especially prominent, the most influential being the Hornay family and the da Costa family.
62 Thomaz (1977: 42).
63 Nicol (1978: 51–52).
64 Nicol (1978: 52).
65 Nicol (1978: 52–53).
66 Nicol (1978: 53).

67 Nicol (1978: 53–54).
68 Nicol (1978: 54).
69 Nicol (1978: 54).
70 Duarte (1988a: 57).
71 Duarte (1988a: 57); Jolliffe (1978: 68); Thomaz (1977: 42).
72 Duarte (1988a: 57); Jolliffe (1978: 68).
73 See Chapter 8.
74 Duarte (1988a: 53). He gives no source for these figures.
75 Duarte (1988a: 53).
76 Here, he appears to be referring to *liurai*.
77 Ramos-Horta (1996: 30–31).
78 Jolliffe (1978: 77).
79 Jolliffe (1978: 78). She seems not to wonder why, if such a "chasm" existed, *ema foho* would find sufficient enough commonality with the party to support it in such numbers.
80 Jolliffe (1978: 78).
81 James Dunn (2003: 35) has remarked that the *chefes de posto* sometimes combined with the *chefes de suku* to resist the "oppressive demands of the *liurai.*"
82 Hicks (1990: 1–13). One example was Miguel da Costa Soares, who was both a *liurai* and also the *chefe* of Uma Ua'in de Baixo *suku* in Viqueque sub-district.
83 Hicks (2013: 35).
84 That is, officials elected by the villagers themselves.
85 Thomaz (1977: 36).
86 Duarte (1988a: 54).

References

Araújo, Abilio de. 1975. *Timorese Elites*. J.M. Alberto (translator). Jill Jolliffe and Bob Reece (eds.). Canberra: Jill Jolliffe and Bob Reece.

Abílio, Araújo. 2012. *Autobiografia de Abílio Araújo: Dato Siri Loe II*. With José de Assunção Gonçalves. Lisbon: Alétheia Editores.

Carrascalão, Mário Viegas. 2006. *"Timor: Antes Do Futuro."* Dili, Timor-Leste: Livaria Mau Huran.

Cascais, António M. Cravo. 1977. *Timor: Quem é o Culpado?* Portugal: Braga Editora, LDA.

Costa, Francisco Borja da. 1976. *Revolutionary Poems in the Struggle Against Colonialism*. Translated by Jill Jolliffe (editor) and James J. Fox. Sydney: Wild and Woolley.

Duarte, Jorge Barros. 1988a. Timor: *Um Grito*. Odivelas, Portugal: Pentaedro Publicidade e Artes Gráficas, Lda. e Jorge Barros Duarte.

Duarte, Jorge Barros. 1988b. *Timor Jeremiada*. Lisbon: Pentaedro Publicidade e Artes Gráficas, Lda. e Jorge Barros Duarte.

Dunn, James. 2003. *East Timor: A Rough Passage to Independence*. New South Wales, Australia: Longueville Books.

Evans, Grant. 1990. *Kinship and Religion in Eastern Indonesia*. Gothenburg Studies in Social Anthropology 12. Gothenburg: Acta Universitatis Gothoburgensis.

Hicks, David. 1975. "Eastern (Portuguese) Timor: Independence or Oppression?" Australian Union of Students, Melbourne.

Hicks, David. 2008. "Afterword: Glimpses of Alternatives: The *Uma Lulik* of East Timor," in "Against Belief?" *Social Analysis* 52 (1): 166–180. Special Issue, Simon Coleman and Galina Lindquist (eds.) London.

Hicks, David. 2013. "Adat and the Nation-State in Timor-Leste: Opposition and Synthesis in Two Political Cultures," in Michael Leach and Damien Kingsbury (eds.). *The Politics of Timor-Leste*. pp. 25–43. Ithaca, N.Y.: Cornell Southeast Asia Program.

Hill, Helen. 2002. *Stirrings of Nationalism in East Timor: Fretilin 1974–78, The Origins, Ideologies and Strategies of a Nationalist Movement*. Kuala Lumpur and Díli: Contemporary Otford, Otford Press, Ortford (Sydney).

Jolliffe, Jill. 1978. *East Timor: Nationalism and Colonialism*. Brisbane: University of Queensland Press.

Jolliffe, Jill. 1989. *Timor, Terra Sangrenta*. Colecção Memória Memórias. Lisbon, Portugal: O Jornal.

Nicol, Bill. 1978. *Timor: The Stillborn Nation*. Melbourne: Widescope International Publishers Pty Ltd.

Relatório do Governo de Timor. 1981. Presidência do Conselho de Ministros, Lisbon, Portugal.

Pires, Paulo. 2013. *Timor: Labirinto da Descolonização*. Lisbon: Edições Colibri.

Queer Space: Centers and Peripheries Conference. 2006.

Ramos-Horta, José. 1996. *Funu – The Unfinished Saga of East Timor*. Lawrenceville, N.J.: The Red Sea Press, Inc.

Silva, Kelly Cristiane da. 2010. "Processes of Regionalisation in East Timor Social Conflicts," in Paulo Castro Seixas (ed.). *Transition, Society and Politics in Timor-Leste*. pp. 123–136. Porto: Universidade Fernando Pessoa.

Thomaz, Luís Filipe F.R. 1977. *Timor: Autopsia de Uma Tragedia*. Lisbon, Portugal: Author, distributed by Dig/livro.

Interviews

Biddlecombe, Maria Rosa. Interview 2005.

5 April–December 1974

1974–1975

The Fretilin *of 74–75 was a movement or national front. Today it has transformed itself into a party. Thus, in 1974–1975, the slogan proclaiming* "Fretilin *is the People and the People is* Fretilin" *had a social and political base and the state of the historical development of that time. In a colonial society all those who resisted and desired national liberation were the People and* Fretilin *was the only force that advocated national independence.*

(Araújo 2005: 7)[1]

2006

Spirits and Ancestors, rise up to look after these people [the ema lisan]! Bones that are scattered everywhere stand up. Blood that was spilt everywhere, unite again to see those who want to destroy the people, who want to see the people suffer forever, who always want to see the people dead. Show yourselves, show your power! Your child is here, who implores you to look after the People, to liberate this People from the yoke of the bloodthirsty.

From a speech delivered on June 22, 2006, by President Gusmão, on national television, criticizing what he regarded as the manipulation of voting procedures by *Fretilin* and Prime Minister Mari Alkatiri's handling of the violence.

(Translated and reproduced in Silva [2010: 104–105])

During the period from April to December 1974 the principal parties sought to come to grips with the unexpected situation brought about by the Carnation Revolution and tried to decide what their goals would be and the strategies they would devise to reach them. But the responses to the change in government in Lisbon that the Republic of Indonesia might contemplate would be the foremost reality with which the Timorese leaders would be forced to contend over the forthcoming months.

Indonesian perspectives

Indonesian attitudes towards Portuguese Timor had been inconsistent over the years; and remained so. The Constitutional Committee of 1945, basing its argument largely on the myth that the island had once been part of the Majapahit Empire adopted the policy that Portuguese Timor was part of a pan-Indonesian nation, which also included West New Guinea, North Borneo, and Malaya.[2] During Indonesia's struggle for independence this notion was all but forgotten, and the colony was mostly ignored thereafter. The Carnation Revolution changed all that. Immediately the revolution occurred, acting in response to new reports about what had happened, the vice-chairman of the Indonesian Parliament, John Naro, the Development Unity Party an amalgamated Muslim party (*Partai Persatuan Pembangunan*, the *PPP*), who was closely associated with Ali Murtopo, recommended that "the Indonesian Government takes preliminary steps and finds a special policy on Portuguese Timor so that finally that area will once again return to Indonesian control".[3] By June 1974 the attitude of Jakarta was of pressing concern for the Timorese politicians and for the Australian Government. The Australian Department of Foreign Affairs started quietly advising journalists that the Indonesian Government had "considerable strategic anxieties about Portuguese Timor" for it was concerned that if it attained independence the country might be unable to resist external influences threatening to Indonesia because it would be economically and militarily weak.[4] Should that occur, Jakarta feared the national unity of Indonesia would be weakened as the result of the diversity of the many ethnic groups in Indonesia, and the former colony might became a base for foreign incursion into Indonesia. This was the period when the Indonesian Government regarded with much suspicion China and its communist regime. By June 1974, it looked to Jakarta as if the process of decolonization encouraged independence and that it would need time to create a campaign for integration, even as the *União Democrática Timorense* and *Fretilin* were beginning to arouse something like a sense of national identity among literate Timorese.

The young Timorese anti-colonialists in the years immediately preceding the *Revolução dos Cravos* had hoped Indonesia might assume the role of sympathetic provider of assistance for any move they might make to bring about Portuguese Timor's independence,[5] as attested to by Ramos-Horta's clandestine liaisons with Tomodok.[6] But by that month their illusions were beginning to dissipate as they listened with apprehension to what Jakarta and Canberra were saying.

President Suharto had to take into account many influential voices in his country, typically competing, in his decision about what approach to take with the colony, and the most powerful of these voices were those of "the generals." So that in order to understand the nature of the political forces at play in Indonesia the Timorese leaders, the Portuguese Government, and Prime Minister Whitlam were dealing with, we need to have some idea of the role of the generals.

A detailed assessment of the personalities who exercised influence on President Suharto is given by David Jenkins.[7] He notes that the Indonesia leader depended on the services of about a dozen key military officers, each of whom controlled tightly organized and often mutually antagonistic pyramids of authority There was a "core group" of influents in the mid-1970s, composed of the following men: Lieutenant (later general) Amir Machmud; Lieutenant General (later general) Yoga Sugama, head of *Bakin*, the State Intelligence Coordinating Board; Lieutenant General Ali Murtopo, deputy head of *Bakin*; Admiral Sudomo, chief of staff (later commander) of *Kopkamtib* (*Komando Operasi Pemulihan Keamanan dan Ketertiban*, the Operational Command for the Restoration of Security and Order); Major General (later General) Benny Murdani, assistant for intelligence to the minister of defense; Lieutenant General Sudharmono, State Secretary; Lieutenant General (later General Darjatmo, chief of staff for non-military affairs at the Ministry of Defense; Lieutenant General Ibnu Sutowo, the president director of *Pertamina*, the state-owned oil company; and, perhaps, one or two others. Within Suharto's core group was an inner group, whose membership changed from time to time, and of which Murtopo, Murdani, Sudomo, and Yoga Sugama were the most influential. Maraden Panggabean could work closely with Suharto, but was not numbered among the president's closest confidants. One key feature of the core group was the predominance of officers with an intelligence or security background, and Murtopo, Murdani, and Sugama held extraordinary security powers. The result was that in 1974–1975 the foreign policy of Indonesia was "shaped to a quite extraordinary degree by intelligence and security officers."[8] This offended senior officers at the Ministry of Defence and Security, and sharpened traditional rivalries between officers from the intelligence branch of the army and officers from its operations branch, a competition that seemingly attained its maximum in November-December 1975.[9] Murdani, without the knowledge of important members of the operational staff, drew up the plans for invading Portuguese Timor. The deputy commander of the armed forces, General Surono Reksodimedjo, knew nothing of the plans, and the *Kostrad*[10] commander, Lieutenant General Leo Lopulisa, was in Paris when the invasion took place, and was never asked if his troops were ready.[11] Bypassing *Kostrad* and the intelligence community, Suharto relied upon troops in *Kopassandha* (*Komando Pasukan Sandi Yudha*), the Special Warfare Force Command, a force that consisted of four groups (*grups*): two *Parakom* (para-commando) groups, each made up of 1,800 men; and two *Sandhi Yudha* (secret warfare) groups, each about 550–600 men. The two *Parakom* groups were stationed in West Java; the two *Sandhi Yudha* groups were stationed in Unjung Padang.[12] In selecting his *Kopassandha* troops for covert military work in Portuguese Timor, the president was relying on soldiers that, while capable of penetrating enemy territory, were not as capable as regular infantry troops at retaining the territory they had won,[13] a weakness that became apparent during the tussle for ground during the incursions into the East Timor borderlands that the Indonesian made in October 1975.

The reaction of the generals and Adam Malik was of particular concern to the *Fretilin comité central*, all the more so since John Naro had called upon the government to start working towards "the return of East Timor to the fold of the Republic," a verbal image of a mythological past that resounded with Benny Murdani and his fellow generals.[14] It was, in part, to counter Naro's provocative challenge, that Ramos-Horta flew to Jakarta on June 17 to meet whichever representatives of the Indonesian Government would receive him.[15] The first excursion into Indonesian politics a Timorese had yet made, this initiative reflects the self-assurance of the younger, national aspirant, and, although ostensibly a private affair, the visit signaled that Ramos-Horta was starting to emerge as party spokesman for foreign affairs. Breaking his journey in Kupang, he talked with the governor of the province of Nusa Tenggara Timur, El Tari, in what, by all accounts, was a cordial meeting. Ramos-Horta gained the impression El Tari was "decidedly sympathetic to an independent East Timor," and recounts that the governor declared himself "satisfied with the colonial boundaries."[16]

El Tari offered Ramos-Horta the services of an aide to accompany him, his nephew, Louis Taolin, a character who would play a duplicitous role in the months to come. Son of the king of Insana, a district in Indonesian Timor, and an ethnic Atoni, Louis Taolin was a well-known Dili figure, closely linked with Elias Tomodok in his capacity as an official of *Bakin*, on whose behalf he intrigued tirelessly.[17] In the Indonesian capital, Taolin escorted Ramos-Horta around for the entire two weeks the *Fretilin* leader remained there, and the Indonesian media publicized the visit. The popular news magazine *Tempo* and the daily newspaper *Sinar Harapan* put Ramos-Horta on their covers, and by so doing generated sufficient publicity to induce Adam Malik to invite Ramos-Horta to meet with him. Before their meeting, Ramos-Horta lunched with John Naro and six other Indonesian officials, and Naro, while conceding that the Timorese should be able to determine their own future, forebodingly, made the prediction that "just like in Irian Jaya," the Timorese would decide to "rejoin their brothers in Indonesia."[18] In his meeting with Ramos-Horta, Adam Malik tacked in a different direction, informing him that he had read *the Associação Social-Democrática Timorense's* platform and was sympathetic to its professed goals. For his part, Ramos-Horta sought to dispel any concerns Malik might have entertained about an independent East Timor. He told Malik that as a government the party would seek a close relationship with Indonesia, cooperate in all areas and at all levels, including foreign affairs and security, and always take Indonesia's interests into account. Adam Malik brought up the possibility of East Timor joining the Association of Southeast Asian Nations (ASEAN), and Ramos-Horta unhesitatingly assented to the proposition, though this issue would later become a bone of contention within *Fretilin* because António Carvarino, Roque Rodrigûes, Vicente dos Reis, and Mari Alkatiri regarded the association as a bastion of imperialism.[19]

Next day, the two politicians reconvened, and this time, exchanged gifts from their respective countries. Ramos-Horta offered a silver-plated sword to Malik and received a bundle of 50,000 *rupiahs*, handed over with the comment that the money was a donation to *Fretilin*. Ramos-Horta then broached the most important matter of all: a written assurance that the government of Indonesia would support East Timor's right of self-determination. Ramos-Horta notes that he did not dare suggest the content of the message; he left his unstated implication open for Malik to interpret. With no further ado, Malik agreed to draft a letter, inviting Ramos-Horta to pick it up the following day.[20] When he came to collect it, the *Fretilin* leader saw Malik sign the letter. It read:

> The Government of Indonesia until now still adheres to the following principles:
>
> I   The independence of every country is the right of every nation, with no exception for the people of Timor.
> II The Government as well as the people of Indonesia has no intention to increase or to expand their territory other than what is stipulated in their Constitution.
> III (...) whoever will govern in Timor in the future after independence, can be assured that the Government of Indonesia will always strive to maintain good relations, friendship, and cooperation for the benefit of both countries.

Translated into Portuguese and Tetum, and later read over Rádio Dili, the letter "calmed the fears of the Timorese community, for it was a clear affirmation of his Government's position on the question of East Timor. It went even further than I expected inasmuch as it seemed to favor independence over any other alternative."[21] The statement "...whoever will govern in Timor after independence..." seemed to preclude the other two options. Ramos-Horta referred Malik to what Naro had said, and the minister retorted that it was he who represented Indonesia's foreign policy, not Naro, and promised to talk to the latter.[22] Whether Adam Malik was deceiving the Timorese or whether he was sincere at the time, his subsequent actions repudiated the affirmation he gave to Ramos-Horta that day in Jakarta.

Regardless of the assurances Malik had given José Ramos-Horta, other influential men had the ear of President Suharto and would lobby him for different responses to events as they unfolded. Whether Malik had been honest or not over the course of the months that followed, Suharto would hear their arguments. Not that any favoured Malik's putative response: virtually all advocated the incorporation of the colony into the Republic of Indonesia. But alternative strategies and tactics for achieving that outcome would be pressed upon him. For his part, the canny Suharto was in no hurry to decide what was the more advantageous option. Three seemed to stand out: seeking a political solution by employing the rhetoric of diplomacy; waiting upon events and trusting that the colony would fall into Indonesia's hands; attempting a military solution. Each could be conjoined with attempts to undermine the stability of East Timor.[23]

The *União Democrática Timorense* and *Fretilin* and the Australian Government

Although Prime Minister Gough Whitlam's government had no legal authority over the Portuguese colony, geopolitics did give him and his cabinet an impelling interest in its future, impelling because of the potential political threat, some ministers thought, presented by the Republic of Indonesia.[24] The Australian Government's interest in the unexpected problem of East Timor caused by the *revolução* was marked by a sense of apprehension. East Timor was Australia's nearest foreign neighbor, and its next closest neighbor, Indonesia, was the strongest power in Southeast Asia. From the very first, the Australian Government regarded the independence of Portuguese Timor as an unviable possibility, and, as Portugal showed disinterested incompetence as the months rolled by, Whitlam found his cabinet, perhaps with reluctance, increasingly preoccupied with what was happening – or might happen – across the Timor Sea. Shortly after the *Revolução dos Cravos*, the Spínola Government had attempted to include Australia in its decolonization plans, but Whitlam, not wanting to risk alienating Suharto, whom he thought might suspect Australia had designs on the colony, rejected the initiative. Whitlam's view was that since there had been no movement for independence prior to the *revolução*, the three political parties that had had blossomed overnight could not be taken seriously. Accordingly, from the time it became clear that the Portuguese Government wished to liberate its colonies, he favored integration.[25] The *União Democrática Timorense* leaders sensed the danger in this kind of skepticism, and in July responded by proposing to the *ASDT* that they form a common front. José Ramos-Horta, Nicolau Lobato, Domingos de Oliveira, and a few other politicians met in Ramos-Horta's mother's house in Dili, and the *União Democrática Timorense* men expressed a willingness to establish an alliance.[26] The meeting was amicably adjourned, and a second one scheduled for a week later. Ramos-Horta recalls how, in the interim, reservations that had frustrated an earlier proposal he had made about the two parties uniting resurfaced. Francisco Xavier do Amaral was receptive; Nicolau Lobato less so, and Mari Alkatiri outright hostile. Although a coalition eventually did come about, these men were to retain these fundamental attitudes about such an alliance throughout the campaign, and these attitudes were consistent with their views on a range of issues. Ramos-Horta and Alkatiri voted on opposite sides on many occasions, with Justino Mota usually siding with Mari Alkatiri. This Ramos-Horta/Alkatiri stand-off persisted after independence.

Unsurprisingly, therefore, a second meeting never came about, though the effective cause was trivial. When the *ASDT* leaders attempted to set up a meeting with Domingos Oliveira they were informed he had gone off to inspect his rice plantations in Gleno Valley,[27] and felt snubbed enough to immediately abandon any thought of a union. "*Fretilin*'s abrupt decision to move ahead [change its name and shift its agenda to a more radical incline] without *União Democrática Timorense* because of such a minor incident," Ramos-Horta later wrote, "reflected our collective immaturity."[28] Ramos-Horta was "disappointed" by the failure of this initiative, yet admits he did not fight hard to alter the minds of his colleagues. As he put it, he "simply lacked the courage." It would have made no difference, though. Ideological differences between the *União Democrática Timorense* and *Fretilin* politicians had, by September, been reinforced by too much personal ill-will for any accommodation to be likely. For the present at any rate.

In July 1974, José Ramos-Horta, who had no prior contacts with Australian politicians, academics, or political activists, decided to try to change the policy of the Australian Government, and he thought the most effective way to do so was to visit government officials in Canberra. En route, he was given a warm reception in Darwin by James Dunn, a constant advocate for the Timorese, who introduced him to his political colleagues. However, when Ramos-Horta arrived at the capital the frigid reception he received from government officials dispelled any illusions he might have harbored about his party's receiving the support of the Australian Government. Prime Minister Whitlam told him, in no uncertain terms, that an independent East Timor was unviable, a judgment Whitlam later confirmed in a letter dated April 22, 1975:[29]

> Political parties emerged in Portuguese Timor for the first time a few weeks after the coup in Lisbon.... The leaders were mostly *mestiços* who had spent some time in seminaries and the army and who often seemed to be desperate to succeed the Portuguese as rulers over the rest of the population.
>
> (Whitlam 1980: 759)

As far as they go, Whitlam's characterizations are accurate enough; but they were beside the point. Unrepresentative of the majority of the Timorese population *Fretilin* leaders were, but for better or worse, East Timor now had it own politicians who, though lacking political maturity, were seriously intent on contributing to their country's future.

By contrast, when he met with President Suharto in Wonosobo, a town in Java, from September 5 to 7, Prime Minister Gough Whitlam was accommodating. At their first of two meetings to coordinate their policy regarding East Timor, Whitlam affirmed his conviction that the best solution was that Indonesia incorporate East Timor. This opinion he reiterated when he discussed the issue with António de Almeida Santos, the Minister for Interterritorial Coordination (*Ministro da Coordenação Territorial*), in Canberra, the following month. President Suharto's consent would be necessary, he insisted, for any plan the Portuguese might have for the colony, since Indonesia had "party principal" status in the process of decolonization. If the independence of East Timor were unacceptable to Indonesia, it would *ipso facto* be unacceptable to Australia. As a token of his concern that Australia might discommode Suharto, and heedless of requests made by Lisbon, Whitlam refused to reopen the Australian consular office in Dili that had been closed in 1971. José Ramos-Horta, as official *Fretilin* representative, "repeatedly raised" the issue with the Foreign Affairs Department in Canberra as well as with a number of Australian members of parliament, but his requests were dismissed. Whitlam feared that even such an apparently insignificant act like opening the office might cause Suharto offence. President Suharto, however, had not at this stage committed himself to an Indonesian takeover.

For their part, until early in 1975, *Fretilin* leaders "always thought that somehow Australia would support our independence and that after independence we could count on millions of dollars in Australian aid."[30] The *ema lisan* attitude was one of indifference. Many families had nostalgic recollections of the soldiers whom they helped fight the Japanese, but these were counterbalanced by recollections of how their ancestors had given their lives to save foreigners who had arrived uninvited from the land to the south. Nor had they sufficient knowledge about Australia to realize that country's potential as a source of economic assistance.

Fretilin's *comité central* argued that an independent East Timor was in Australia's best interests, a claim that did, in fact, hold some weight, since before World War II the Australian Government had understood the island's potential for serving as a bulwark, even if more symbolic than empirical, against a Japan invasion of the island continent, and it was not entirely outside the bounds of the imagination to suppose it might have to serve that purpose against Indonesia at some future time. But Whitlam showed little inclination to take this argument seriously. What counted was the immediate geopolitical reality that the prime minister was determined to make no move that might antagonize Suharto.[31] By the time the second meeting of the two heads of state took place, which occurred between April 3 and 5 of the next year, in Townsville, party leaders had come to accept the fact that Australia was likely to support whatever action the Indonesia Government chose to take, not that President Suharto had decided upon a violent incorporation of East Timor, and, indeed, he apparently told the prime minister that Indonesia would not resort to force.

In the weeks before the invasion, some cabinet members urged the prime minister to remind Suharto of this promise; but Whitlam said nothing, and the advice of those like Richard Woolcott, Australian Ambassador to Indonesia, proved more persuasive.[32] Woolcott reminded his boss that there was "a settled Indonesian policy to incorporate Timor," and warned him that Suharto would not be happy with any *communiqué* that "he might regard as a lecture or even a friendly caution:"[33]

> [Australia's] policy's should be based on disengaging ourselves as far as possible from the Timor question; getting Australians presently there out of Timor; leave events to take their course and if and when Indonesia does intervene act in a way which would be designed to minimize the public impact in Australia and show privately understanding to Indonesia of their problems ... I know I am recommending a pragmatic rather than a principled stand, but that is what national interest and foreign policy is all about.

The position of the United States

Of the nations that became most involved with the problem of Portuguese Timor, the United States was the least directly concerned. But it regarded an independent East Timor under *Fretilin* as threatening its interests in three ways: (a) the country might emerge as a "Cuba of the South Seas"; (b) its achieving independence might destabilize Indonesia by encouraging separatists; and (c) that the U.S. Navy's freedom to send its submarines through the deep Ombai–Wetar Straits north of Timor might be threatened.[34]

The *Associação Social-Democrática Timorense* becomes *Fretilin*

Even as early as a few weeks after May's inaugural meeting, the more radically inclined members of the *Associação Social-Democráta Timorense* had begun questioning the propriety of their party's name since it did not, they felt, reflect their political philosophies. They wanted a name that projected an image of a political entity that represented all Timorese, and so they decided upon the "*Frente Revolutionária de Timor-Leste Independente*," "the Revolutionary Front for an Independent East Timor."

When it came to drafting the more radical elements in their revised program, its authors took as models the African liberation movements for some of their most important ideas and their party's new name. Accordingly, such phrases as "the pillaging of our mineral riches,"[35] "the occupation of our best lands by the colonialists,"[36] and "the tribalism that the colonialist feeds," became part of their political language.[37] The charges apparently referred to foreigners removing small amounts of gold in some parts of the island, minor oil extractions, and the coffee plantations owned by the *Sociedade Agricola Patria e Trabalho* and some individual planters, accusations which were more appropriate in the African context. There were other weaknesses in their arguments. In that they concerned control of the means of production by the state, i.e., the nationalization of private enterprise, Marxism and Maoism had much less relevance. East Timor had no industry, there was nothing to nationalize, and there were few landlords from whom to liberate the land. Nor did the writers acknowledge that most Europeans, namely, the soldiers on conscription, could not get back to Portugal fast enough; and that comparatively few Portuguese had ever settled in the colony permanently. The document won acceptance from the assembly and the reshaped, distinctly more radical platform was unanimously adopted. Ramos-Horta managed to sneak in a "hopeful" reference to the party's "continuing adherence to social democracy," but when the wording of the text reached Lisbon, the phrase drew a rebuke from more extremist members in Portugal for whom the reference to "social democracy" was "in sharp contradiction" to the rest of the manifesto,[38] as indeed it was.

Arguably, the most dynamic radical in this early stage of *Fretilin*'s campaign was Roque Rodrigûes. He was not especially popular among his colleagues, as it happened, for they regarded him as brash and something of a "know-all," while his continual upbraiding of the Church offended some of the Catholics in the party.[39] But Rodrigûes had the capacity to argue – and argue cogently – for his ideas with a passionate conviction that some of his colleagues found persuasive. What he had learned from the *Frente de Libertação de Moçambique* in Africa had convinced him that the Maoist policy of land reform, based on agricultural cooperatives and consumer cooperatives, was what Timor needed; and with the renaming and reorientation of the *Associação Social-Democrática Timorense* he figured the time had arrived to put his ideas into practice. Incorporated into *Fretilin*'s manifesto was a plan he himself had largely conceived, which involved creating agricultural cooperatives in the *foho*. Nicolau Lobato was very much taken with this idea, and although Rodrigûes had claims to have originally thought up the plan, the wary ambiguity in which the mercurial reformer was held by his colleagues made them entrust executive responsibility for this initiative to Lobato. The Bazartete cooperative opened in October,[40] with students and dissatisfied, unemployed, poorly-educated, young men, supplying the necessary workforce. Their inadequate education had prevented them some of them from obtaining jobs requiring literacy and the ability to speak Portuguese, and many hung about the streets of Dili where they formed vagrant groups in search of excitement.[41] Although supposed to teach modern agricultural methods to the farmers, as urbanized youth they were as ignorant of modern agricultural methods as they were of Timorese agricultural practices; yet ignorance in no way undermined their self-confident presumptions. So peasants who had tilled the soil since childhood were expected to defer to ill-equipped youngsters. According to the provisions of the "reformed" land system implemented by Nicolau Lobato "…areas under co-operative cultivation were [to be] collectively worked at *suco* level with the use of shared implements," and "It was proposed that land tenure remain with the constituent families."[42] However, according to local *lisan*, households already owned land, which they had acquired by patrilineal or matrilineal descent; and kinship groups already cultivated them collectively when cooperation was required. The elite's tendency to ignore *lisan*[43] and their misunderstandings of *foho* culture were also illustrated in *Fretilin*'s proposal that half the produce of a family's gardens and fields be expropriated by the state, in the form of an innovation called the "*suco* consumer co-operative." Hardly surprisingly, local people resented these intrusions into their social life, and Lobato was subsequently to remark that villages were suspicious about cooperatives.[44] The conservative character of the people made them reluctant to welcome new ideas introduced by young persons from outside their world. The moderate Nicolau Lobato, perhaps influenced by Araújo's writing, attributed this reluctance of farmers to accede to *Fretilin*'s designs to their earlier, unhappy, experiences with Portuguese and Japanese collectives, but he provided no evidence in support of his thesis. He apparently was unaware that, like all farming communities in the Indonesian archipelago, Timorese agriculturalists had embedded the values of reciprocity deeply in *suku* life, a concept verbalized throughout the islands as *gotong royong*. Rural Timorese had nothing to learn from *Fretilin* operatives about the moral value of cooperation.[45]

The agricultural cooperatives scheme was complemented by another campaign, one aimed at a real scourge, illiteracy. The goal of the literacy program was to teach the illiterate to read and write Tetum in three months. As *secretário geral* of the Education and Cultural Affairs Committee, António Carvarino was empowered with the task of putting the program into effect, and he succeeded in establishing several schools. But since almost the entire population was illiterate, a sweeping national program undertaken by a central government and employing an army of trained teachers would have been required to do an effective job. *Fretilin* had at its disposal only a few dozen young men without any experience in teaching, and had the resources to operate in only a few sub-districts, so it is unsurprising that their efforts resulted in no enduring returns. Although this plan, too, was an integral part of the party's campaign strategy for winning over the *ema lisan*, unlike the cooperatives, the program was more appreciated by the *ema lisan*.[46] Indeed, it may have shifted the balance in *Fretilin*'s favor in some *suku* initially disposal to the *União Democrática Timorense* or otherwise party-neutral, but, even so, the presumptions of the young and the heavy-handedness in which the campaign was conducted antagonized local senior men and made them more reluctant to cooperate with the cadres than they might otherwise have been.

Infusing some socio-political theoretical insight into these programs were ideas originally propounded by the Brazilian educational specialist, Paulo Freire. These formed a body of ideas collectively known as the *"conscientização política,"* the "process of developing political consciousness,"[47] and, as implemented in East Timor, meant that *Fretilin*'s cadres included in their instruction sessions about agricultural and educational reforms discussions about the radical policies of the *Movimento das Forças Armadas* and the three options. Army officers from Dili, called "dynamic groups" (*grupos dinamizadores*), augmented the students' teaching, and instructed *ema lisan* about local elections that had been devised as a first step towards the plebiscite to elect a constituent assembly that would determine the future political status of East Timor.

The students labored with enthusiasm to build schools and help organize the cooperative schemes, and constructed health centers where they taught nutrition and hygiene, and from which they "mobilized" paramedics for campaigns to vaccinate local people. The *ema lisan*, by and large, approved of these initiatives, for they promised to bring about an improvement in their lives, and Ramos-Horta is correct in asserting that they "...differentiated *Fretilin* from the *União Democrática Timorense*," but whether he is as accurate in his blanket claim that they "...established our popularity in the remote mountain interior," is open to question.[48]

Although the cooperative and education programs did not achieve their creators' goals, as components of a political strategy they did succeed in raising *Fretilin*'s profile in the *foho*. To such an extent that by January *União Democrática Timorense*'s initial, albeit passive, popularity among the *ema lisan* had been threatened enough for the *União Democrática Timorense comité central* to start thinking about how they might survive as serious competitors. Thus, they began to reconsider the desirability of collaboration with the opposition.

Going hand-in-hand with *Fretilin*'s busy activity in the *suku* was the work its operatives and supporters carried out in Dili, in both words and deeds. *Fretilin* promised the party would help every Timorese person "actively contribute to the political life of the country," and, energized by its earlier triumph in establishing the country's first trade union, the *Fretilin comité central* founded another two unions, the *União Nacional de Estudantes Timorense* (the National Union of Students) and a teachers' union.

Nevertheless, Nicolau Lobato, Francisco Xavier do Amaral, and José Ramos-Horta remained dissatisfied with the progress the party was making. *Fretilin* needed an authentic national following that transcended mere name-recognition in those sub-districts where their cadres were already active. The profile of the party needed to be elevated in *all* sub-districts. A campaign of propaganda to blanket the districts was the strategy they devised, and here the *Rádio Dili* would serve as an essential tool.[49] But, as it happened, the first propaganda from this forum came from the militants, and it brought forth such outrage from the *União Democrática Timorense* and *Apodeti*, which considered their language both slanderous and racist, that in November the administration suspended *Fretilin*'s broadcasting rights.[50] This reversal in *Fretilin*'s fortunes lent hope to some optimists in the *União Democrática Timorense* that they might yet regain the initiative they appeared to be surrendering in the *suku*. Indeed, had the *União Democrática Timorense* leaders seized this opportunity and begun promoting their party more vigorously there, they might have won back at least some of their initial support. But even when some of its leaders made excursions into the *suku* their desultory appearances displayed nothing resembling the verve of the cadres.

In the hinterland, therefore, while the excesses of the cadres acted as something of a restraint on *Fretilin*'s popularity, they did not prevent the party from making significant strides in its ambition to win the support of Timorese in both *suku* and the capital. This was, in part, because, from September onwards, the cadres' dynamism in the hinterland was complemented by the fiery language of the party militants in the capital, and the more moderate persuasions of the respected Xavier do Amaral, Nicolau Lobato, and Ramos-Horta. *Fretilin* leaders also joined the cadres in excursions into the *foho*, and in those places their evangelistic fervor reinforced the verbal enthusiasms of the young men. It also happened that a few, genuinely politically motivated villagers, were excited enough to help propagate the new ideas from the capital and so added their weight to *Fretilin*'s cause. A majority of men, however, disinterested in abstract and foreign ideologies, listened to the political language being deployed in the capital, witnessed the antics of the cadres, and reflected upon the opportunities that this talk and action had opened up for them to exploit. They saw this challenge to their personal status quo, not as did the village elders, something to resist, but as a means by which they could gain at the expense of their neighbors. As in the sub-districts of Uato Lari and Uato Carabau,[51] and the *suku* of Gari-Wai,[52] with the passing of the months, old grudges came to be revived and heated words exchanged.

Meanwhile, back in Dili, despite the wealth of publicity they were generating, and regardless of their initial success in shifting the party leftward, António Carvarino, Abílio de Araújo, Mari Alkatiri, Vicente dos Reis, and Roque Rodrigûes had found themselves marginalized in the party's decision-making body, the *comité central*.[53] For instance, although, as *secretário geral* of the education and cultural affairs committee, Carvarino had the executive authority to implement the education program, his position was not one from which he could determine party policy.[54] On the other hand, their more influential place in the *comité central*, endowed Xavier do Amaral, Nicolau Lobato, and Ramos-Horta with the power to weaken their more extreme proposals. Still, as the radio transmissions showed, they could not stifle the militants.[55]

As we have seen, kinship and affinal links could moderate the ferocity of political rivalries, and the *Associação Social Democráta Timorense* leaders were, at least initially, friendly enough with their rivals, and even, though in a more cautious way, the *Apodeti* leaders. But this comity was sorely tested after September, when *Fretilin* rhetoric began to assume a more threatening tone. When, eventually, coarse threats like "death to traitors" and "burn the traitors" began to be daubed on the walls of Dili buildings, goodwill between the parties was more evident by its absence than by its presence, new and violently inflected utterances duly registered in Lisbon and Canberra – and in Jakarta.

Although not incorporated into the final version of the party platform, adopted in late November,[56] the terms *"mauberism"* and *"the Maubere"* were the most evocative verbal expressions of *Fretilin*'s commitment to the rural people, and, like them, distinguished it from its rivals. I shall analyze the nature of the terms later, but they refer to the way in which *Fretilin* ideology portrayed the *ema foho*, the *"maubere,"* i.e., downtrodden people who had been exploited by the Portuguese colonialists. The concept had been in circulation before the change in party name, and gained considerable traction after the invasion and proved to have an important function in uniting the Timorese against the Indonesian Government and instilling a sense of nationalism among the populace. But in 1974–1975 it had yet to become a major verbal force.[57]

Rhetoric from Portugal

The language employed by the Portuguese side added its own contribution to the political scene. When Francisco da Costa Gomes became president it might have appeared that the prospects for *Fretilin*'s advancement had now become somewhat rosier. His more centrist predecessor had shown himself mildly disposed towards the *União Democrática Timorense*, after all, whereas the new president was decidedly a man of the left. Moreover, it was clear that he was a president determined to hasten the process of decolonization. However, the political calculus was not quite as clear-cut as *Fretilin* leaders may have thought, since two alternative perspectives offered themselves to the ministers in Lisbon.[58] Senior civil servants who had spent some time in the colony and realized the Timorese were ill-equipped for immediate independence took the view that a continuing, though, temporary, Portuguese presence was necessary if an orderly transition into a new polity was to come about. Opposed to this view was a heterogeneous group of socialists and communists, including Gomes, who argued for a more rapid decolonization. Some among them were convinced that, whatever eventually happened, Portuguese Timor would, in any case, be assimilated into Indonesia anyway. The questions were whether it would be brought about through negotiations between Lisbon and Jakarta; whether it would be a peaceful or violent assimilation; and when it would occur. As far as they were concerned, any outcome was acceptable just as long as it could be accomplished with at least some appearance of legality and no loss of face for the mother country. Independence, on the other hand, was "atrociously unrealistic." Unfortunately for *Fretilin*, this feeling – albeit not so unequivocally – was shared by the socialist President Gomes and his prime minister, Vasco dos Santos Gonçalves. It was also entertained by many in the *Movimento das Forças Armadas*, a senior member of whom is reported as having remarked to Portuguese journalists that, "Timor doesn't justify more than a few lines."

When, therefore, in mid-October the *Movimento das Forças Armadas* dispatched the civilian lawyer, Dr. António de Almeida Santos, Minister for Interterritorial Coordination to Timor to assess the situation, his report of how the Timorese felt about the options disturbed the calculations of cabinet members as much as the words he used when addressing the Timorese outraged them. Santos had arrived in Australia, on October 13, where he consulted with government officials, before leaving for Jakarta on October 16. He stayed in the Indonesian capital for three days, talked with Ali Murtopo, and then flew to Dili, where he arrived on October 20. Upon touching down he found himself engulfed in the largest popular demonstration in all of Timor's history, an event that amazed him. Rapturously greeting him were Dili residents and thousands of *ema lisan*, some of whom had traveled on foot for days from all parts of the *foho*, thrilled at the opportunity to welcome only the second cabinet minister ever to have set foot in the colony. Something of the esteem in which they held the mother country's representative can be gauged from the following, poignant episode.[59] While António Verdial, headman of Manumera, a Mambai village, was in Dili to greet the minister, *Fretilin* supporters from the nearby town of Same attacked his village and burned down his house, a beautifully carved building he had devoted the better part of a decade to constructing. Informed of his loss while still in the capital, Verdial retorted that he had left home to pay his respects to a Portuguese minister and could not return to inspect the damage until he had done so.

Among those witnessing Santos' arrival at the Dili airport that day was Mrs. Biddlecombe. In my interview with her, she told me she interpreted the crowd's reaction to Santos' speech as a moving upwelling of patriotic devotion to the mother country.[60] Some who had traveled from far away to await his arrival had been in the capital for more than a week before his plane touched down, and had exhausted their food supplies food. "But nobody left ... they wanted to hear what this minister had to say," she reported. Those who wanted to keep ties with the mother country made their feelings known by displaying their *lulik* Portuguese flags brought out from their *uma luliks*. One careless fellow was unfortunate enough to walk on the shadow cast by a fellow demonstrator's flag, and was beaten up for insulting the sacred artifact.

The ministers' ignorance of the colony and the lack of interest they felt for the people living there is apparent in the opinions Santos reputedly expressed before he left for Portuguese Timor in which he likened the colony to a huge ship, afloat in the ocean, and draining money from Portugal. The enthusiasm that that he encountered that day changed his mind – for a time, at least – and caused him to declare that he had left Portugal, come to the other side of the world, and had found Portugal again. He went on to recount the glories of the mother country's past and how a country whose population in the fifteenth century was about that of his country's second largest city, Oporto, had nevertheless been able to place its citizens throughout the entire world, remain a presence in Africa and India, sought to break into the mysterious universe of China, and had, finally, arrived on their island. Santos concluded by adding that Timor would be what the Timorese wanted their country to be. If Timorese wanted to remain with Portugal they could stay with Portugal. If they wished to be independent, they could be independent. If they desired union with Indonesia, they could join Indonesia. Any choice they made would be respected by the Portuguese Government. Santos noted, gratuitously perhaps, and decidedly undiplomatically, that should they wish to be part of Indonesia it would be just like changing one's tailor. They would be going from one colonial power to another: from a European master to an Asian one. If they wanted to be independent they needed to be realistic. Independence might be a bit too early to talk about, and he could not see out-and-out independence as a viable option. "For Timor there is only one way, federation with Portugal." Everyone clapped and clapped, "no end," said Mrs. Biddlecombe, who went home convinced that the *União Democrática Timorense* party "had won" the campaign for the hearts of the Timorese, a feeling she attributed to the sense of the occasion conveyed by the crowd that day. Some Timorese girls, she noted, danced all the way in front of Santos' car to the Government Palace.[61]

Even as Santos was delivering his message, however, President Gomes, Prime Minister Gonçalves, Foreign Minister Mário Soares, and *Movimento das Forças Armadas* officers were finishing up meetings with Ali Murtopo, during one session of which Gomes reportedly confided to Murtopo that the independence option was "nonsense."[62] The news of Santos' speech was, as one might expect, a serious embarrassment, and the cabinet complained that, "The minister had talked too much."[63] Even before his plane left Timor for the return trip to Lisbon, Santos received a telegram from Gomes advising him that it would be "convenient" were he to refrain from making public statements that, by emphasis or even reference, placed independence on the same level as the other options. The president was devising his own plans for the future of the colony, and, although neither certain nor set in stone, they were not what the Timorese or *Fretilin* leaders had in mind. And so it came about that, as a first step towards putting them into effect, two months later, he sent a new governor and his two assistants to Dili. Whatever form decolonization might take, they were charged with the task of bringing it about; and whether the integration option would be encouraged by the trio, or whether they would find, after their arrival, that independence might not, after all, be so unrealistic a resolution to the problem of Portuguese Timor, were questions that, even now, remain unresolved.

The four months, August to November 1974, was a decisive period, with parties and governments laying down the foundations for the policies they would adopt and the procedures by which they would try to fulfil them. In Portuguese Timor, there was, of course, the adoption of the name *Freilin* by the *Associação Social-Democráta Timorense* made (on September 10), and its signal that it was transforming itself from a left-of-center party of a social democratic cast, to one that was committed to a more radical socialism The September 30 replacement of the centrist, Spínola, by the socialist Gomes and the communist, Vasco dos Santo Gonçalves becoming prime minister was duly registered with the *comité central* of the *União Democrática Timorense*. They could see now that the left-wing was in control of the mother country's overseas' policy, and that the *Movimento das Forças Armadas* was thoroughly set upon liberating Portugal from its colonies as quickly as possible. Whatever the strength of their previous commitment to retaining links with Portugal, the *União Democrática Timorense*'s leaders now realized they needed to abandon any such notions. Independence was now their goal. Then, finally, there was the arrival of the three new administrative officers from Lisbon.

The leftward trend taken by *Fretilin* and by Lisbon did not escape unnoticed in Jakarta, and one consequence was Murtopo's bringing together some of his associates in October for a Security Council meeting in Jakarta to create *Operasi Komodo*.[64] This was a clandestine intelligence operation designed to destabilize the colony as a way to incorporate it into the Republic. Murtopo then was deputy head of *Badan Koordinasi Intelijen Negara* (*BAKIN*), or National Intelligence Coordinating Agency,[65] and head of the Special Operations Command (*Opsus*), the agency responsible for establishing *Operasi Komodo*.

The trio from Lisbon

The exact nature of the political philosophies and agendas the trio from Lisbon brought with them have never been clearly established. It may be that they were not particularly enthusiastic about the integration option, and since, in Thomaz's opinion,[66] the *Movimento das Forças Armadas* had in actuality commissioned them with the task of "exporting the revolution," they may, in fact, be seen as favoring – or coming to favor – *Fretilin*. Within a matter of days, the governor lifted the ban on *Fretilin*'s radio transmissions and António Carvarino and Roque Rodrigûes took advantage of this apparent support to intensify their vilifications of the *União Democrática Timorense* and *Apodeti*.[67] Whether substantial or putative, this perceived support for *Fretilin* was resented by the other two parties, and eventually was seen as so thoroughly detrimental to the interests of the *União Democrática Timorense* that it became a major factor driving João Carrascalão to take the violent steps he did in August 1975 and the demand he made to Pires that the governor expel his two colleagues from the colony. As *Fretilin* leaders verbally assaulted their rivals on the radio, the party cadres promulgated the party's message in the countryside, and local political opportunists, who had began to uncover or manufacture grievances by which to intimidate their neighbors, added their voices. For whatever reason, the administration was unwilling to restrain these forceful activists, and without support from the governor and the army district administrators and sub-district chiefs had, in a number of regions, by year's end, grown too intimidated to maintain order. In these insubordinate sub-districts, *Fretilin* operatives arrogated the authority the administration was, in effect, beginning to relinquish, and *Fretilin* cadres saw the opportunity of asserting themselves, by, for example, monitoring the movements of *suku* residents by setting up roadblocks.[68]

Forty-three-year-old Mário Lemos Pires had been promoted from the position of lieutenant to colonel prior to his appointment as governor because the government thought the promotion would enhance his status in his new capacity.[69] He was not identified with the *revolução*, nor was he a member of the *Movimento das Forças Armadas*, and he chose not to make any political convictions he may have held public. Since he had been regarded as friendly to Spínola, some observers interpreted his politics to be somewhat to the right, and it may be that, even though President Gomes had appointed him to the post, Pires may have detected a lack of complete trust on his part. Certainly, Lisbon never relied on his counsel nor tendered him much support in the way of military resources to carry out his mission. This slightly uneasy relationship might explain why, from the moment of his arrival, Pires seemed politically more distanced from his two colleagues and subordinates than one might have expected, a position that approached that of marginalization at times, and rendered him less effective than he might have been in pursuing any policy he may have devised. Thomaz considered that he lacked the qualities required of a leader,[70] while Bill Nicol, who interviewed him in March 1975, regarded him as little more than figurehead whose public assurances that the Portuguese would leave only when the Timorese wished was a sham.[71] These came soon after his arrival as Pires was traveling around the districts and learning for himself how anti-integration people really were and how sincerely they wanted the colonial presence to remain.[72] Nevertheless, his enlightenment did not prevent him from working with Jónatas and Mota, behind the scenes, to expedite what they took to be President Gomes' "exit strategy," though one more inclined in favor of *Fretilin* than *Apodeti*.[73] This inclination is suggested by his swift action in lifting the ban on *Fretilin* transmissions, as well as in the appreciative words of Ramos-Horta, who considered him, "a liberal, decent and bright officer," a judgment that may also be colored by a suggestion Pires had made that the two principal parties merge into a coalition.[74]

Pires's first task was to form a cabinet that would assist him and his two colleagues in the task of decolonization. With himself as its leader, he appointed, among others,[75] Major Adelino Rodrigûes Coelho, Head of the Military Cabinet of the Commander-in-Chief and Head of the Governor's Cabinet;[76] Major Queiroz Martins Barreto, General Chief of Staff of the Independent Territorial Command of Timor,[77] another officer who had worked in a previous Timorese administration (1968–1970); Lieutenant Colonel José Angelo Texeira de Magalhães, Military Commander-in-Chief of Timor;[78] and Dr. Libânio Pires, ex-*secretário geral* of Guiné-Bissau and member of the Committee for the Decolonization of Guinea-Bissau under the presidency of General Spínola.[79] In the cabinet – as well as outside it – Mota and Jónatas, however, were his principal associates, and their actions exerted a decisive influence on the history of Portuguese Timor.

Major Francisco Fernandes da Mota, was 38 years old, and had come to Timor with a wealth of colonial experience. He had served as a lieutenant (*tenente*) in Goa where he had been captured during the Indian invasion, and in 1968 had been assigned to a stint in Timor.[80] After spending a few months in Ossu, he was transferred to the capital as head of military intelligence at the army headquarters. Two years later, Mota was in Angola where he served a term before returning to Lisbon, where he became a prominent participant in the *Movimento das Forças Armadas'* plot to overthrow Caetano. His work for the *revolução* earned him a respected status in Lisbon political circles, and General Spínola invited him to join his staff, a patronage that did not stop Spínola's successor, Prime Minister Vasco Gonçalves, from sending him to Timor.[81] In Pires' cabinet, Mota became Chief of Cabinet for Political Affairs and Special Assistant to the Military Cabinet of the Commander-in-Chief, in effect, holding the portfolio for political affairs.[82]

Also 38 years old, and no stranger to the colony, Major Silvério Henrique da Costa Jónatas had served as a captain in Oe-Cussi from 1969 to 1971 before being sent to Mozambique and Angola, from whence he returned to Lisbon where he, too, became a member of the *Movimento das Forças Armadas*. Unlike Mota, however, he only joined just before the *revolução* broke out, and so carried somewhat less political clout than did his colleague. Nevertheless, as one of the 200 officers involved in the movement, Jónatas was rewarded with the rank of major, and he became a member of the elite military body, the Continental Operational Command (*Comando Operacional do Continente* or *COPCON*), the organization entrusted to safeguard Portugal's internal security. Jónatas was one of several junior officers whose advancement had been endangered by the reduction in the Portuguese armed forces from something like 200,000 to around 30,000 when the African wars came to an end, so unlike Mota, whose career was well underway, Jónatas' mission gave him an opportunity to further his career prospects. Pires entrusted him with the running of the gubernatorial cabinet's Social Communication portfolio, a critically important commission since it made him not only responsible for managing the mass media,[83] but effectively placed the two media propaganda outlets for the parties, *Rádio Dili* and the *A Voz de Timor*, under his control.[84] His new office conferred upon him a status that, in a formal sense, was equivalent to Francisco Mota's.

Although the portfolios of Mota and Jónatas already endowed them with more influence than those of the other members of the cabinet, from the outset they and Pires were determined to ensure that they, rather than their colleagues, kept the wheels of power securely in their hands, so that no sooner had the cabinet had been created and the portfolios assigned, than they decided to reorganize it. With Pires as its president, they established a huge military council, containing no fewer than 44 members, some of whom were to be elected, others appointed by Pires, and justified this unwieldy creation on the grounds that the council would democratize the Timorese armed forces much in the same spirit as the *Movimento das Forças Armadas* had democratized the military in Portugal. Hence its nickname, "the *MFA* in Timor."

The cumbersome council, perhaps as planned, showed itself to be dysfunctional. Its members rarely found time to meet and as a group it lacked any kind of executive authority. In practice, Governor Pires ignored those decisions it did sporadically manage to make if they did not have his cabinet's approval. Mota and Jónatas took advantage of its impotence to operate independently, with Mota, in particular, using his authority to put into effect the policies of the *Movimento das Forças Armadas*. Because Pires knew that Mota had well-established Lisbon connections, he gave Mota virtually all the slack the major desired. At its first meeting, held in January, the military council created a five-man executive commission, called the "Coordinative Commission of the *Movimento das Forças Armadas*," to advise the council and Pires himself, and from then on, "Both invariably accepted what it said," especially since the only operational full-time members were Mota and Jónatas.[85]

To facilitate decolonization the administration created the *Commissão de Descolonização de Timor (CDT)*, the "Commission for the Decolonization of Timor," an instrument through which Governor Pires hoped to facilitate consultation with the political parties.[86] It included representatives of the *União Democrática Timorense*, *Fretilin*, and *Apodeti*, and was divided into various sub-committees, each having as its portfolio a special area. The most important of these were the areas of the economy, administration, and education. Authority lay with the chief of the cabinet, the army commander, and the members of the commission.[87] But for all the high expectations, and although the commission sought to project an image of neutrality, it was accused of reflecting the ideology of the *Movimento das Forças Armadas*,[88] and promoting the interests of *Fretilin*.

Major Mota was the principal mover and shaker in these bodies, although Jónatas, too, helped decide their procedures and how policies should be implemented.[89] The influence the government had was channeled through Mota and Jónatas; so much so that Major Luís Cadete, who was, for a time, Pires' head of military intelligence, declared that Mota and Jónatas' actions met with the *Movimento das Forças Armadas's* approval. "The MFA programme gives no timing for independence of the colonies [and so Mota and Jónatas] interpreted this as a minimum period. The aim would be to have a minimum cost and minimum liability over time."[90] As though to confirm this judgment, Major Mota is reported to have remarked to his aides early in 1975, "We will be out next year."[91] As it turned out he overestimated.

Of the problems the Portuguese faced, the most urgent was how to get the three political parties talking together to discuss the implementation of the process of decolonization. Their desire to do so without delay was prompted by the increasingly savage exchanges among them, which had by now become so pervasive and dangerous there were fears that serious violence was becoming inevitable: "Political circumstances [were degenerating] in the territory itself from around April–May 1975"[92] [...] "the boiling point was quickly approaching."[93] However, there was one hopeful development. The *União Democrática Timorense* and *Fretilin* had formed a coalition in the New Year; and it was this apparent reconciliation that encourage the committee to anticipate an initial schedule of talks for May 7. *Apodeti*, however, refused to participate. The objective of the first meeting was to consider the feasibility of creating a transitional government in the context of independence and planning a local consultative assembly to advise on such matters. But before the meeting could take place, the coalition between the *União Democrática Timorense–Fretilin* dissolved, and the Portuguese Government took advantage of the break-up to invite representatives of the Indonesian Government to attend, thereby moving the discussion into the realm of international diplomacy. The planned decolonization talks were to take place, not in Dili, but in Macau, between June 26 and 28. *Apodeti* agreed to attend, and this time, it was *Fretilin*'s turn to stage a boycott.

Although *Fretilin*'s platform – a short period during which the Portuguese administration would continue to administer the emerging colony and train prospective leaders of the new nation-state, followed by independence – was consistent with the administration's goal of decolonization, for Major Mota, even this relatively brief period of transition was excessive. So he can hardly have been quite the hard-line pro-*Fretilin* devotee João Carrascalão considered him to be. Still, he did deliberate more with the *Fretilin comité central* leaders than with those of the other parties, and one can readily see how he gave the impression of being more inclined to the left than he actually may have been. As one Portuguese diplomat summed him up: "Mota is progressive, definitely not a reactionary. This makes it understandable why he might support *Fretilin*. Lemos Pires cannot be seen to favour any of the parties. He must be detached. Mota, on the other hand, is involved." He added that Lemos Pires "has very similar, socially advanced ideas like Mota. Mota is more outspoken."[94]

Certainly, Francisco Mota made few public appearances and never granted foreign journalists interviews. "He was a smooth back-room operator who went about his business quietly, efficiently, and with as much diplomacy as possible. His impact on Timor was enormous."[95] Mota's and Jónatas' contributions to the process of decolonization were influenced by their relative sympathy with the *Fretilin* cause (though not its timeline) and through the "reforms," as they termed them, they brought to the administrative structure changes inspired more by their *Forças Armadas Portuguêses em Timor* ideology than from any realistic appraisal of the country's capacities or needs.

With Pires' backing, Mota's and Jónatas' changes in the structure of the administration gave *Fretilin* an advantage over their rivals, and the party benefited from them. Ramos-Horta confirms, with evident appreciation, the heavy impact they had: "Timorese with years of experience in the bureaucracy, but until then restricted to minor responsibilities, were justly [*sic*] promoted to senior posts" while "directorship posts," until then an exclusive preserve of Europeans, were rendered accessible to Timorese.[96] Changes came from other quarters, as well. The young politician was "impressed with the dynamism and dedication of the *Forças Armadas Portuguêses em Timor* officers and other experts who were engaged in the task of preparing the country for the future"; adding, with evident satisfaction, that inside 12 months "much was accomplished." Ramos-Horta admiringly concludes that Pires, Jónatas, and Mota accomplished all this without receiving much assistance from Lisbon, but omits to mention that, that although short with material help, the Portuguese Government, had commissioned the trio to decolonize East Timor, and, subject to that mandate, gave them a free hand to do pretty much what they wished.[97]

The Portuguese Government further assisted the cabinet in its work of weakening the established colonial system by repatriating the European component of the *Forças Armadas Portuguêses em Timor*. Two months before the insurrection the army had been reduced to 74 combat troops and commando battalions, which meant that had these been the only resources available to him, Governor Pires did not have the military capacity to squelch the escalating street demonstrations in Dili that preceded the revolt. But he did have 40 paratroopers at hand, and, though few in number, they were veterans of the African wars. But the two platoons of parachutists were never deployed to any effective purpose, other than to protect the European population after the armed movement. The attitude of the European military that prevailed after that date was aptly captured in the words of one of them, Captain António Ramos, who, when asked by a reporter if the *Forças Armadas Portuguêses em Timor* would resist an Indonesian invasion, replied, "We would tell them … come in!"[98] – a sentiment that may have resonated with Major Mota despite his left-wing leanings.

Although José Ramos-Horta claims that the trio tried to remain impartial, and dismisses the argument that the Indonesian Government and the *União Democrática Timorense* favored *Fretilin*, Jorge Duarte not only considers that they boosted the fortunes of that party, but accuses the trio, together with Arnão Metelo (whom he considered their ideological soul mate), as being the authors of the entire crisis. He attributes to Pires the remark, "We are working to abandon Timor,"[99] and he adds that, upon being informed that *Fretilin* had declared that Aileu, a district where *Fretilin* operated with the greatest license, was a "*zone libertada*" (a "liberated zone"),[100] Pires' reported response was to characterize it as "an interesting experience."[101] In Duarte's view, December 1974 was the month when social order and political stability openly revealed their first signs of fracturing, and although Ramos-Horta[102] dismisses the "instability" allegation as exaggeration, the army's depletion, the widespread sense of impending disaster, and the use of such rhetoric as "liberated zones"; would appear to substantiate Duarte's opinion.[103] The account given by the administrator of Ermera, Adriano de Almeida Gominho about the situation in his district and in the neighboring "liberated zone" of Aileu district makes clear that by December *Fretilin* street demonstrations were getting out of hand even as the authorities in that district at that time were making some effort at keeping the two main parties apart.[104] Even so, by the end of that month local Chinese merchants had closed their shops out of fear of *Fretilin* attacks and departed for Dili. The Timorese soldiers, he notes, unconditionally supported that party, so they could not be expected to keep *Fretilin* at bay.

A potent force for news in any country lacking newspapers or a non-partisan radio or television station has always been rumor, and by December rumor had so come into its own in East Timor that it wielded a rhetorical power that could not be disregarded. As one example, shortly before the year ended, word circulated that Francisco Xavier do Amaral was assigning 3,000 troops to Turiscai, the sub-district in which he was born, to slaughter local *União Democrática Timorense* farmers. There were denials, rejoinders, and iterated denials, at the time, and, years later, when I questioned him, Xavier do Amaral claimed that the rumor was an invention of Mário Carrascalão's.[105] There would be plenty more rumors in the forthcoming months.

By late January, the *União Democrática Timorense's* political language had adopted the strident tone of *Fretilin*'s, and now that its *comité central* knew the Portuguese Government was not on its side, the "colonial" party was beginning to incorporate some of the anti-colonial diatribes of *Fretilin*'s into its own denunciations. In attempting to take back the competitive edge they had squandered by their lassitude *União Democrática Timorense* leaders were now representing their party as "a liberation movement" that would sever their country's ties with the mother country. They had seen how *Fretilin*'s use of the word "independence" was gaining currency in the hinterland, and with the scales now fallen from its leaders' eyes they knew Governor Pires intended to abandon the colony as soon as possible.[106] They saw their vision for East Timor's future overlapping with *Fretilin*'s. For their part, moderates in the *Fretilin comité central* began to recalibrate their strategy. They imagined they might, after all, accrue some benefit from being allied with the *União Democrática Timorense*. Publicly, nothing happened that might have led a casual observer to anticipate any fundamental change in the dynamics of the political scene. Nevertheless, as the final year of European colonization drew to a close, the campaign was about to take a major turn.

Notes

1 *"A FRETILIN de 74–75 era um MOVIMENTO ou FRENTE NACIONALISTA. Hoje transformou-se em Partido. Por isso, em 1974–75, o slogan proclamado de que a FRETILIN é o POVO e o Povo é a FRETILIN tinha base social e politica e estádio [sic] do desenvolvimento histórico de então. Numa Sociedade colonial, todos quantos resistiam e queriam a libertção nacional eram Povo, e a FRETILIN era a única força que advogava a Independência Nacional."*

2 McDonald (1981: 191).
3 McDonald (1981: 193).
4 McDonald (1981: 193).
5 "inspired by Indonesia's earlier independence struggle against the Dutch, and because of its geographic proximity" (Ramos-Horta 1996: 26–27).
6 See Tomodok (1994) for his own version of what happened in Portuguese Timor.
7 Jenkins (1984: 20–32).
8 Jenkins (1984: 24).
9 Jenkins (1984: 24).
10 *Komando Cadangan Strategis Angkatan Darat* (Army Strategic Reserve Command).
11 Jenkins (1984: 24).
12 Jenkins (1984: 28). *Kopassandha* was known until February 17, 1971 as *RPKAD, Resimen Para Komando Angkatan Darat*, the Army Para-commando Regiment). In 1985 it underwent another change of name, becoming *Kopassus* (Jenkins 1984).
13 Jenkins (1984: 24–25).
14 Ramos-Horta (1996: 64).
15 Ramos-Horta (1996: 41).
16 Ramos-Horta (1996: 41).
17 Jolliffe (1978: 286).
18 Ramos-Horta (1996: 64).
19 Ramos-Horta (1996: 42).
20 Ramos-Horta (1996: 42).
21 Ramos-Horta (1996: 43).
22 Ramos-Horta (1996: 64).
23 See pages 167–168.
24 The policy and attitudes of the Australian Government towards East Timor have been described and discussed in numerous publications, among the most useful being Australian Government Department of Foreign Affairs and Trade (n.d.); Kimura (2012); Tarcznski (2009); Roff (1992); and Way (2000).
25 Jolliffe (1978: 258–259).
26 Ramos-Horta (1996: 36–37). I use "*ASDT*" and "*Fretilin*" interchangeably.
27 18 miles to the west of Dili.
28 Ramos-Horta (1996: 37).
29 See the epigraph heading Chapter Three.
30 Ramos-Horta (1996:43). In due course, this is what actually occurred; but only after Indonesia left East Timor a quarter of a century later.
31 Cf. the Chinese proverb that the historian, Charles Boxer (1960: 355), quoted 14 years earlier: "when the lips are gone the teeth will feel the cold."

32   Secret cables from 1974, released in 2000, show that Gough Whitlam, then Australia's prime minister, was supportive of an Indonesian takeover yet keen for the East Timorese to decide their own fate, albeit for the sake of appearance.... "I am in favour of incorporation, but obeisance has to be made to self-determination. I want incorporation, but I do not want this done in a way which will create argument in Australia which would make people more critical of Indonesia," Whitlam told Indonesian president Suharto.

(Tarczynski 2009: 1–2)

33 Ramos-Horta (1996: 78).
34 Tanter (2001: 206).
35 "pilhagem da nossa riqueza mineira."
36 "ocupação das nossas melhores terras pelos colonos."
37 "o tribalism que o colonizador alimentou."
38 Ramos-Horta (1996: 37).

39 Of Rodrigûes, Bill Nicol wrote: "To him, anyone in any way opposed to the independence of Timor was an enemy of the state, a traitor" Nicol (1978: 107).

40 For details about *Fretilin*'s agricultural cooperatives and its literacy campaign see Hill (2002: 63, 67, 83–87, 106, 113, 124, 156) and Jolliffe (1978: 100–106).

41 The same desire for a job, but not work, prevailed after Timor-Leste became a nation-state on May 20, 2002; but by then the numbers of male youth was considerably higher.

42 Jolliffe (1978: 103).

43 Despite Araújo and Borja da Costa's undoubted devotion to many aspects of it.

44 Jolliffe (1978: 103).

45 Cf. Hill's (2002: 84) reference to Grant Evans, who visited Timor in October 1974 and described how Nicolau Lobato was working in Bazartete, about 30 miles from Dili, with a cooperative consisting of about 50 persons. They shared tools and collectively worked their private plots, with no tractors. Apart from the organizing zeal of a politician from Dili, in its general idea, this description could have fitted any location in Timor at any time in its recorded history.

46 *Fretilin* wrote its programs for agriculture, literacy, and health around November. The literacy program had, however, had begun to be prepared as early as May 1974 (CAVR 2006 Part 5: 15). It was put into practice in January 1975 (CAVR 2006 Part 5: 15; Hill 2002: 109–110) in the community of Namuleco, Aileu District.

47 Jolliffe (1978: 321).

48 Ramos-Horta (1996: 39).

49 A radio station founded by the government that had begun broadcasting on a limited frequency from Dili in 1959.

50 Nicol (1978: 84).

51 See pages 176–178.

52 See page 176.

53 As did the lesser known, Jorge Tomás Carapinha, a European radical.

54 Nicol (1978: 106).

55 Cf. Thomaz (1977: 39–40).

56 Hill (2002: 75). She points out that certain of the Lisbon students had opposed the adoption of *mauberism* as the ideology of the *Associação Social-Democrática Timorense* because they favored a more class-based analysis of Timorese society and feared *mauberism* might develop into an ideology that could be incorporated by, and serve neo-colonial interests. For a discussion of the significance of this term, see Chapter 9.

57 CAVR notes that "When first used in 1974–1975, the term 'Maubere' was considered by East Timorese linked to UDT as racially divisive, marking 'pure-blooded' East Timorese against mixed-race 'mestizos.' The Commission heard testimony from senior former members of the UDT party, who described the term *Maubere* as a source of serious division in society" (CAVR 2006 Part 3: 27).

58 Ramos-Horta (1996: 47).

59 Thomaz (1977: 67).

60 Biddlecombe (Interview 2005).

61 Bill Nicol's account is similar. He describes how thousands of villagers gathered to listen to Almeida, many bringing their treasured ancient Portuguese flags with them, and, apart from those educated Timorese already committed to the cause of independence, like Francisco Xavier do Amaral, exuberantly expressing their desire to remain Portuguese (Nicol 1978: 175). In response, Santos told them

> It is part of our policy that the wishes of the population will be respected, and if the wish is that of Timor being connected to Portugal, it will be connected ... if there is another wish, it will also be respected. But I take from here the conviction that there is not really another wish.

(Nicol 1978: 175)

62 Ramos-Horta (1996: 69).
63 Biddlecombe (Interview 2005).
64 Named after the world's largest lizard, most of which live on the eastern Indonesian island of Komodo (*Varanus komodoensis*).
65 *ABRI's* intelligence collecting agency.
66 Thomaz (1977: 67).
67 Thomaz (1977: 38–40); Duarte (1988a: 56). The latter assigns responsibility for the anarchy that ensued, not only to *Fretilin*, but also to Pires, Mota, Jónatas, and the leaders of the *Movimento das Forças Armadas*.
68 A policy that critics of the colonial system had admonished the Portuguese for doing.
69 Nicol (1978: 179–180).
70 Thomaz (1977: 67).
71 Nicol (1978: 177).
72 Ramos-Horta (1996: 47–48).
73 Desousa (Interview 2005); Nicol (1978: 177).
74 Nicol (1978: 84).
75 Chrystello (1999: 71).
76 *Chefe do Gabinete Militar do Comando-Chefe e Chefe do Gabinete do Governador.*
77 *Chefe de Estado Maior do CTIT (Comando Territorial Independente de Timor).*
78 *Comandante Militar do CITimor.*
79 *Ex-Secretário General da Guiné-Bissau e membro do Comité de Decolonização da Guiné-Bissau.*
80 Nicol (1978: 180–184) is my principal source for the following characterization of Mota and Jónatas.
81 A senior Portuguese diplomat in London remarked that "Mota is very friendly with Gonçalves, who appointed both he and Lemos Pires to Timor. Mota did not want to go to Timor. He was chosen to go before Spínola left the cabinet" (Nicol 1978: 181).
82 *Chefe do Gabinete de Assunto Político e Adjunto do gabinete militar do Comando-Chefe.*
83 *"Pasta da Communicação Social."*
84 Nicol (1978: 180–182).
85 Nicol (1978: 182–183).
86 CAVR (2006 Part 3: 30).
87 The press officer of the Administration, Chris Santos, described its function in the following words: "The Military Council formed the *Comissão de Descolonização de Timor* ... The idea is that the governor is too busy and gives his work to the committee for advice," but in reality, "the decolonization commission was formed by but was independent of the military council. As well as merely 'advising' the governor, it acted on his behalf where it wished" Nicol (1978: 183).
88 See Nicol (1978: 183).
89 As Nicol (1978: 183) summed it up:

> The result of this reorganization of the administration was a circular power base for Mota and Jónatas, who dominated each segment: the governor and cabinet; the decolonization commission; the military council, and the co-coordinative commission of the MFA. It was a base from which Mota in particular was able to exert great influence over both the governor and the local political parties. As Chris Santos told me one day, "He [Mota] has the contacts with the parties. He corresponds with the parties. If the governor wants to see the parties, the organisation is done through Mota."

90 Quoted in Nicol (1978: 183–184).
91 Nicol (1978: 183).
92 Jolliffe (1978: 113).

93 CAVR (2006 Part 3: 37).
94 Nicol (1978: 184).
95 Nicol (1978: 184).
96 Ramos-Horta (1996: 48).
97 While, of course, doing nothing to check Malik's interference in the process of decolonization.
98 See the explanation for this reduction given by Ramos-Horta (1996: 48–49), who regarded the reduction of troops as being the single most damaging mistake Lisbon committed in 1974, a strategy he interprets as part of a conscious policy to facilitate a takeover by Indonesia.
99 *"Estamos a trabalhar para abandonar Timor"* (Duarte 1988a: 59).
100 That is to say, an area purged of *União Democrática Timorense* supporters, both indigenous and colonial.
101 *"era uma experience interessante"* (Duarte 1988a: 59).
102 Ramos-Horta (1996: 49).
103 Arnão Metelo later remarked to Ramos-Horta (1996), "At that critical time, we wanted to assure Angola's independence under *MPLA*. That was our big concern before we were toppled from office. So, I lost contact with the Timor process."
104 Gominho (2006).
105 Amaral (2005 Interview).
106 Ramos-Horta (1996: 30).

References

Araújo, Abilio [sic]. 2005. "É um imperativo rever a nossa Constituição." *Jornal Nacional Semanário.* 28 May. pp. 1, 6–7. Dili, Timor-Leste.
Australian Government Department of Foreign Affairs and Trade. n.d. *Historical Documents Volume 23: Australia and the Indonesian Incorporation of Portuguese Timor, 1974–1976.* Available at: www.dfat.gov.au/publications/historical/volume-23/. Accessed February 14, 2014.
Boxer, Charles. 1960. "Portuguese Timor: A Rough Island History." *History* 10: 349–55.
Burke, Kenneth. 1950. *A Rhetoric of Motives.* New York: George Braziller, Inc.
CAVR (Commision for Reception, Truth and Reconciliation). 2004. "CAVR Update/ December 2003–January 2004" (including Appendix 2: Report on Hearing on Internal Political Conflict, 15–18 December 2003. Available at: www.cavr-timorleste.org/updateFiles/english/cavrUpdate-Dec03Jan04-en.pdf. Accessed February 7, 2014.
CAVR (Commision for Reception, Truth and Reconciliation). 2006. Chega! *Final Report of the Commission for Reception, Truth and Reconciliation in Timor-Leste (CAVR).* Available at: www.etan.org/news/2006/cavr.htm. Accessed February 8, 2014.
Chrystello, J. Chrys. 1999. *Timor Leste: 1973–1975, O Dossier Secreto.* Matosinhos, Portugal: Contemporânea Editora.
Godminho, Adriano de Almeida. 2006. *Timor Paraiso do Oriente (Memórias de um malaio – estranho).* Ebook by author.
Hill, Helen. 2002. *Stirrings of Nationalism in East Timor: Fretilin 1974–78, The Origins, Ideologies and Strategies of a Nationalist Movement.* Kuala Lumpur and Díli.
Jenkins, David. 1984. *Suharto and His Generals: Indonesian Military Politics 1975–1983.* Monograph Series (Publication no. 64) Cornell Modern Indonesian Project. Southeast Asia Program, Cornell University, Ithaca, New York.
Jolliffe, Jill. 1978. *East Timor: Nationalism and Colonialism.* Brisbane: University of Queensland Press.

Kimura, Tomohiko. 2012. *Australian Foreign Policymaking Towards the East Timor Question From April 1974 to January 1978: a re-examination.* Unpublished Doctor of Philosophy thesis. Canberra: University of New South Wales.

McDonald, Hamish. 1981. *Suharto's Indonesia.* Blackburn, Victoria, Australia: The Dominion Press and Fontana/Collins.

Ramos-Horta, José. 1996. *Funu – The Unfinished Saga of East Timor.* Lawrenceville, N.J.: The Red Sea Press, Inc.

Roff, Sue Rabbitt. 1992. *Timor's Anschluss: Indonesian and Australian Policy in East Timor 1974–1976.* Lewiston, New York; Queenton, Ontario; Lampeter, Wales: The Edwin Mellen Press Ltd.

Silva, Kelly Cristiane da. 2010. "Processes of Regionalisation in East Timor Social Conflicts," in Paulo Castro Seixas (ed.). *Transition, Society and Politics in Timor-Leste.* pp. 123–136. Porto: Universidade Fernando Pessoa.

Tanter, Richard. 2001. "East Timor and the Crisis of the Indonesian Intelligence State," in Richard Tanter, Mark Selden, and Stephen R. Shalom (eds.). *Bitter Flowers, Sweet Flowers: East Timor, Indonesia, and the World Community.* pp. 189–207. New York: Rowman & Littlefield, Publishers, Inc.

Tarczynski, Stephen de. 2009. Australia: Complicit in East Timor – Records. January 27. www.globalissues.org/news/2009/01/27/448. Accessed February 15, 2014.

Thomaz, Luís Filipe F.R. 1977. *Timor: Autopsia de Uma Tragedia.* Lisbon, Portugal: Author, distributed by Dig/livro.

Tomodok, E.M. 1994. *Hari-Hari Akhir Timor Portugis.* Jakarta: Pustaka Jaya.

Interviews

Biddlecombe, Maria Rosa. Interview 2005.
Desousa, Jerry. Interview 2005.

6   *A Coligação* and its aftermath: January–July 1975

1974–1975

Politics in this country is … there's no such thing. Umm. They don't know what politics is. They've been [...] they've been … dragged children in on this, they've … how they've … a person becomes a member of a political party is [that] a delegate goes up in the country there and says, "You, you, you, you, you, you, you have to have a card." "But we don't want a card." "But you have to have one." "Oh! All right!" And so when they do have the card … they are given a card that looks like a card they get here when they become a certain age … the government supplies them with an identity card and on this card … this is their passport, so to speak, and they have to treasure that card because they pay about … uuh … 190 escudos every year tax, and it's marked on this card and if they lose that card and they don't pay … tax they pay a double amount … if they lose the card, so they protect this card and wrap it in plastic and they carry it around as if it were something very special like we treat a passport. Well, now, they … receive a card which is similar and they do exactly the same with this card. You know, it's a legal document which they have been handed and they treasure this thing a lot, and that's all … the … that's involved, politically they don't know what the party wants to do or anything because they don't understand politics. It's like trying to … to teach politics to a three year old child. He'd just look at you and that's about it!

(Favaro, 2003)

2007

On Election Day, I saw many Timorese exiting the polling station and proudly exhibiting their finger with the ink mark that signified he or she had voted; in the following days, many others still showed their proof of voting with a smile on their faces. Marred with difficulties and problems as they were, the elections of 2007 were a major success: they were organized by the Timorese authorities themselves, supported by international aid, as a form of expression of sovereignty; they took place in the regular period prescribed by the Constitution, in spite of a serious crisis that paralyzed much of the country in 2006; they drove large numbers to vote without fear of disturbances; they showed the vote to be stable and consequential (and presumably not easily subject to forms of manipulation); and they returned a new majority and therefore a new government who succeeded the previous one in a peaceful manner.

(Feijó 2009: 137)

By January 1975, the growing popularity of *Fretilin* in the *foho* was matched by *União Democrática Timorense's* increasing anger at *Fretilin*'s rhetorical style and the aggressive way its cohorts in the capital and the *suku* were carrying out its agenda. Convergent with the apparent fracturing of the colony and fears Governor Pires and his cabinet were executing their government's plan to abandon it, was the external threat. *Operasi Komodo* was in operation by January 1975, with propaganda of a menacing nature being transmitted from a radio station in Kupang into the colony, stigmatizing *Fretilin* as communist and accusing the Portuguese Administration of victimizing what was characterized as the pro-Indonesian majority.[1] As villagers began to migrate into Indonesian Timor, the Indonesian press exploited their presence by referring to their status as "refugees" and the Indonesian Consulate became openly supportive of the *Apodeti* cause. The result was that by late February the Indonesian Government's official press agency *Antara*'s verbal onslaughts attained a fevered pitch, with excited reports from its "special correspondent".[2] The Australian media, meanwhile, quoted Canberra intelligence sources that suggested Jakarta might be preparing to invade.

To keep abreast with current thinking inside the Indonesian Government, Francisco Mota flew to Jakarta. What he heard in Indonesia's capital was not good news for *Fretilin* for, soon after his return, he said during one *Fretilin dinamizacão cultural* session in Dili, that his discussions in Jakarta had convinced him that although Indonesia would allow *Apodeti* or the *União Democrática Timorense* to govern East Timor, a *Fretilin* administration would be out of the question.[3] This did not surprise Ramos-Horta. He had suspected for some time that the generals would use any apparent collapse of civil order as an excuse for an invasion, and the announcement induced him to try and persuade the more centrist *Fretilin* leaders to make overtures to the *União Democrática Timorense* about a possible *coligação* or "coalition." Over the objections of his radical colleagues, two unpublicized meetings in the first fortnight of January bore fruit when Xavier do Amaral wrote out by hand on a torn scrap of paper a list of six conditions *Fretilin* required for a partnership:[4]

1   Independence.
2   Rejection of integration into Indonesia or with any other power.
3   Portugal as the only foreign party in the process of decolonization of Timor.
4   Supervision by the United Nations.
5   Cooperation with Portugal in the cultural, technical and economic development of Timor.
6   Non-interference and co-operation with nations of the geographic area.

The fifth item was the only concession actually set down in writing by the *Fretilin* negotiators, who considered it too trivial to impede an alliance. The president delivered the note to Francisco Lopes da Cruz, and, for Xavier do Amaral, this marked "the beginning of the coalition."[5] He verbally informed Lopes da Cruz when he gave him the note that *Fretilin* was willing to drop its demand for immediate independence *de jure* and would agree to a transitional period of from five to eight years. Two months later, he confirmed his promise in writing. For their part, *União Democrática Timorense* leaders looked upon the concession as a "major victory."

Only the precise terms of the agreement needed to be drawn up, and in several short, informal, meetings negotiators for the two sides agreed to challenge the *Apodeti* platform directly. However, from the beginning, unity was undermined by *Fretilin*'s determination not to share power equally in any future government. *Fretilin* demanded two-thirds of the anticipated governmental portfolios, including those of the economy, treasury, foreign relations, security, and defense. The *União Democrática Timorense* would get the minor portfolios. Bargaining was thus difficult and protracted. *Fretilin* hard-liners would not budge from their positions, and the *União Democrática Timorese* leaders were resolutely set against tamely acceding to their demands. Then, when the negotiations had reached a critical stage, Governor Pires engaged in the discussions with the pragmatic suggestion that the two parties leave aside for later determination, the more thorny issues that separated them.[6] Ever resourceful, Ramos-Horta submitted a new version of the proposal to the respective leaders, one that included provisions that there would be neither verbal onslaughts on each other's parties nor physical threats against their supporters.

So, with no major changes in their basic understanding, the coalition formally came into existence on January 20, and a new political card had been dealt the Indonesian Government. The more intractable issues were, indeed, discussed over the course of the next two months, though in a desultory manner.

Mário Carrascalão, who did not participate in the discussions, was greatly surprised to hear about it, but he welcomed it.[7] He saw it as reflecting "exactly" the soul of the Timorese people. In theory, he writes, the *coligação* might come to function as a "red carpet" on which *Fretilin* and the *União Democrática Timorense* would lead them to independence.

While conceding that Xavier do Amaral and Nicolau Lobato had fully participated in the majority of the discussions with the *União Democrática Timorense* leaders, Ramos-Horta credits himself with most of the more laborious diplomatic work. This included, he says, "softening those *Fretilin* leaders suspicious of any such alliance," and persuading the *União Democrática Timorense* leaders a coalition was in their best interests. He portrays himself as the honest broker contriving to bring together more obdurate men, some of who were convinced the coalition was not compatible with their ideologies. But Governor Pires' cabinet seemed as pleased as "the general public" that *Fretilin* and the *União Democrática Timorense* were showing signs of political maturity.[8] "Always," writes Ramos-Horta, "with an eye on Canberra, I hoped that the coalition would strengthen the position of our Australian friends who favoured an independent East Timor."[9] The coalition, he claimed, included virtually every educated Timorese and, considerably more dubiously, represented "the vast majority of the population." Unfortunately for the future of the *ema foho*, this show of "political maturity" had, as one of its results, encouraging the *Angkatan Bersenjata Republik Indonesia* generals, having now suffered a setback to their hopes that the two pro-independence parties would mutually destroy themselves and open the door for *Apodeti*, to apply pressure to what they, correctly, saw as the two weak links in the alliance, Lopes da Cruz and César Mousinho.[10]

The *Fretilin* leaders took advantage of the coalition to further their own party's advancement, and even Ramos-Horta admits *Fretilin* benefited most from the alliance. The coalition, he remarks, opened up "previously blocked" *União Democrática Timorense* strongholds, because "UDT supporters were always less solid, more easily swayed than *FRETILIN* supporters, who were more politically conscious."[11] Shortly after the formal birth of the coalition *Fretilin* leaders demonstrated their advantage over the *União Democrática Timorense* when they set down in writing, for the first time, what they considered a reasonable period for transition to independence and presenting it to their partners. Their *União Democrática Timorense* counterparts readily assented. This agreement, bearing the title "*Joint Communique Issued By The Coalition Revolutionary Front Of Independent East Timor And Timorese Democratic Union*," was signed by Francisco Xavier do Amaral and Francisco Lopes da Cruz in Dili, and dated March 18, 1975.[12] While the denunciations the document contained were directed as much at Indonesia as towards Portugal (hyperbolic language derived from the *Fretilin* manifesto), the statement reveals a major negotiating triumph over the *União Democrática Timorense*. The government's pledge to the people that they would have a plebiscite to choose among the three options was to be rescinded, the two parties jointly declaring themselves to be "the legitimate [*sic*] representatives of the people of East Timor"; "…independence is the only possible way for real liberation of the people from exploitation and oppression of any form." The coalition averred to be "interpreting the will of the overwhelming majority of the People of East Timor for National Independence…," and that "*Fretilin* and *União Democrática Timorense* also rejected any questioning of the right of the people to independence implied in a referendum, a so-called 'act of free choice:' 'nobody should ask a slave if he wants to be free!'" The *União Democrática Timorese* had moved beyond assimilating *Fretilin*'s language; it now accepted its claim to be de facto custodian of the *ema lisan*. Whatever the people of the hinterland might wish was of much less concern to both parties than their own platform. Politicians from the capital knew what was best; and that being the case, the *ema lisan* had but small claim on their own futures.

The *communiqué* contained the announcement that, in the path to full independence (Jolliffe 1978: 339):

1   A transitional government was to be formed by a High Commissioner, representing the President of the Portuguese Republic and would consist of an

equal representation of the Portuguese Government, FRETILIN and UDT. During this period a reform of all internal administrative and political structures would take place.

2   The minimum period of the transitional government would be three years, but the period was subject to extension if circumstances warranted.

3   General elections for a Constitutional Assembly would take place after the process of decolonisation had been completed.

Already, however, even as the two signatures were drying, the coalition had begun unraveling.

José Ramos-Horta, falling back on his experience as a journalist, was Xavier do Amaral's writer for most of the latter's speeches as well as the majority of *Fretilin*'s propaganda, letters, press releases, and various *communiqués*. During the campaign, he was typically industrious, and recounts how a "handful of us did all the work," which made this part of the campaign an especially "trying and exasperating period," all the more so since he expended much energy and time accompanying the other two leaders into the *suku*.[13] But his labors bore fruit. In contrast, even though they could see that *Fretilin* was making converts in the sub-districts, Mário Carrascalão, Lopes da Cruz, and João Carrascalão continued to visit the hinterland only rarely. Even when they undertook excursions, the *União Democrática Timorese* had nothing like the literacy program to provide its leaders with the focal purpose that might appeal to villagers or provide them with an established local base from which to spread their message. Their lethargy fused with their increasing resentment at the popularity the other party was enjoying until it reached the point when they started to revert to same kind of anti-*Fretilin* invective they had employed before the coalition. Some of it came with *ad hominem* attacks, while others were as uncalled for as they were spiteful. Consider the case of Lucia, the wife of Françisco Xavier do Amaral. Bored, it may appear, with the interminably tedious political sessions *Fretilin* leaders kept having in her house, when the *Fretilin* president left Dili to campaign in the *suku*, she took advantage of her husband's absences to indulge in a tryst with a kinsman of his. Returning home unexpectedly one day, her husband caught the pair in *flagrante delicto*. *União Democrática Timorense* leaders heard of her indiscretion and broadcast – quite literally – the news to all of East Timor, courtesy of the *Rádio Difusão Portuguesa de Dili*, appending the message that if a so-called leader cannot rule at home – as *lisan* requires a husband to – how can he govern his country?[14] Nevertheless, Xavier do Amaral survived and, more significantly, *Fretilin* continued its upward trajectory.

Meetings between Portugal and Indonesia

Since the *Revolução dos Cravos*, Ali Murtopo had tried to win the Portuguese Government's support for the generals' strong opposition to the independence option. With the advent of *Fretilin* and the change of government in Lisbon,

President Suharto sent Ali Murtopo as head of a delegation to Lisbon in October to find out what the new government had in mind for the colony. They held the aforementioned secret talks with President Gomes, Prime Minister Gonçalves, Foreign Minister Mário Soares, and Jorge Campos, a senior official in the foreign department[15] on October 14–15, and it was on this occasion that Costa Gomes declared the independence option as "nonsense." The conciliatory tone of the meeting suggests the reason why Gomes had counseled Almeida to stop encouraging that option. The delegation, according to Indonesian sources, came away from the meeting convinced that the Portuguese Government at the very least was not in favor of maintaining its relationship with the colony and even that the incorporation option was viewed in a positive light, though they recognized the Portuguese insistence that the wishes of the Timorese people must be considered as paramount.[16]

A second meeting took place on March 9, in another secret but more informal meeting called by the Portuguese Government because it had become disturbed by the provocative, covert actions by *Operasi Komodo*. Besides Santos, the Portuguese delegation included Major Victor Alves (Minister without Portfolio); Secretary of State for Foreign Affairs Jorge Campinos, and Major Mota. Heading the Indonesian delegation was Ali Murtopo, who forced the issue. Murtopo argued that (a) the only guarantee of stability in the region would be East Timor's integration with Indonesia; (b) a joint Portuguese and Indonesian administration should be created to advise the governor and persuade the local population to accept integration with Indonesia; and (c) Portugal should not internationalize the problem of Portuguese Timor. Ali Murtopo reinforced his argument with the reminder that the Portuguese delegates had appeared skeptical about East Timor's capacity to be independent, and reminded his opposite number that colonialism was contrary to the *Movimento das Forças Armadas'* philosophy. Maintaining colonial ties was unacceptable.[17] For their part, the Portuguese seem to have told Murtopo that Timorese support for integration was weak, and that it was neither possible nor acceptable for the Portuguese Government to deliver the populace to Indonesia in disregard of the populace's own preferences. They also rejected a joint Portuguese/Indonesian administration that Murtopo had proposed. Ali Murtopo's rejoinder warned that the people of West Timor were putting pressure on Jakarta to takeover East Timor, and that some were prepared to invade on their own account. He provided no evidence in support of his contention.

According to Ramos-Horta, the Portuguese negotiators sought to deflect a possible invasion by assuring the Indonesians they would not object if Indonesia waged a political campaign inside East Timor.[18] Internationalizing the issue would have been an obvious way to have frustrated the Indonesian Government's plan to annex the colony; but the government of Portugal did not take advantage of this strategy. Had it done so, the United Nations might well have intruded itself into the ongoing struggle for East Timor, and the history of the former colony might have been different.

The diminution of the colonial authority

The restructuring of the established system of administration, noted earlier, was an important tool in the Governor's cabinet's implementation of the decolonization mission. But, whatever its faults, the old order, though paternalistic, had, to some extent, come to a workable relationship with the *lisan* institutions of rank, kinship, marriage, gender, age, ritual, and belief and, under the *Pax Lusitania*, had prevented traditional blood feuds between the *suku*, transcended their ancient grudges in a common system of order, and established a stable colonial organization. With the changes introduced, the colonial government sapped its own authority, and with the removal of the European officers from the Timorese Army, the more reckless followers of *Fretilin* and the *União Democrática Timorense* were increasingly able to unfetter their instincts. The innovatory links anticipated between the *Forças Armadas Portuguêses em Timor* and villagers were never forged and sub-district and *suku* chiefs were at liberty to exercise their ambitions.[19] *Fretilin* leaders and their cadres, in Dili and in the hinterland, had already understood that this degrading of the existing system placed the cabinet in danger of relinquishing authority to whomsoever might wish to seize it and the downsizing of the army suggested to them that the Administration lacked the will to enforce the law and maintain order. This perceptive reading of what was going on emboldened them further, while in the sub-districts the aforementioned opportunists saw openings for striking out on their own. As the authority of *suku* chiefs diminished, and that of *suku* councils' waned, so did disaffected individuals, families, and groupings of disparate kinds – descent groups, ad hoc gangs, and the like – feel free to refuel old grievances[20] and indulge recently invented ones.[21] The cabinet encouraged these responses even more by improvising local "commissions" intended to complement the *conscientização política* campaigns. To this end, they arbitrarily dismissed *suku* chiefs judged too supportive of the colonial government and replaced them with *Fretilin*-inclined local rivals or high-profile *faux*-politicians who had made their mark in rowdy gatherings as often as not fomented by *Fretilin* cadres. As administrative officers became ever more impotent, *Fretilin* consolidated its standing in sub-districts and enhanced its growing reputation as the party that counted the most. Nevertheless, in sub-districts where the cadres distracted farmers from planting or tending their crops or challenged *lisan* protocols too brazenly, the party's behavior, as previously remarked, provoked resentful backlash. This could also occur in Dili, as in *Fretilin*'s overreaching on the education commission. Although this body did include members of all three parties, *Fretilin* saw the chance to advance its own agenda by seeking to align the commission's activities with the party's literacy program, which was by now well underway. Other than the party representatives themselves, the commission's members were supposed to be politically neutral, but the political background of the members suggested otherwise. Within a week of its creation *Fretilin* had managed to include a second lieutenant from the *Movimento das Forças Armadas* (who had spent only a few weeks in Timor), his wife, and the chief of the *Serviços de Educação*, a young Timorese seminarian drop-out whom Luís Thomaz describes tartly as having exchanged St. Thomas for Lenin.[22] When they discovered their colleagues included these people, the *União Democrática Timorense* and *Apodeti* representatives resigned. The *União Democrática Timorense* and the Church tried, but failed, to prevent this kind of exploitation from happening, any more than they were able to match the aggressive verbiage of the cadres. By March, *Fretilin*'s influence had gained momentum. *União Democrática Timorense* and ecclesiastical initiatives did meet with the occasional success, however. In May, after robustly publicizing *Fretilin*'s manipulation of the education issue to inculcate left-wing ideas in the *suku*, they were able to incite students, members of the *Liga de estudantes para a valorização de Timor* (*Lesvalt*), the "League of Students for the Appreciation of Timor," into demonstrating in the streets of the capital, which they contested with students from the *Fretilin*-supporting *União Nacional de Estudantes de Timor*. Although overtly uncommitted politically, the pro-Church students supported, and had the backing of, the *União Democrática Timorense*, which also seemed to have enjoyed the allegiance of most school children. These particular street demonstrations were the most threatening up to that time, and after an exceptionally destructive clash, Governor Pires shut down every establishment of learning in Dili. At the same time, he abolished the education commission.[23] Even before the governor's action, the doors of the Dili high school and the *Escola Técnica* had been closed, and most of the European teachers, many of whom were *licenciados* (officially certified teachers) or *bachareis* (graduates with a Bachelor of Arts degree), had been replaced by youths whose sole credentials were a secondary school education, not being a European, and a commitment to *Fretilin*.

Mrs. Biddlecombe described how Dili grimly dissolved into disorder. After *Fretilin*, she recollected, had told "students to close the schools and go up to the mountains to partake in the agricultural revolutionary system in which everyone lives off the land," chaos had befallen the town. In

> the schools no more, you know, law and order. Finished! Pupils no longer went to school on a regular basis; instead they demonstrated daily, abandoning the books that had been used in the Portuguese schools. Every morning part of the curriculum [had] involved singing the Portuguese national anthem before going into class, but *Fretilin* put a stop to that.[24]

The unfavorable impressions *Fretilin* was generating abroad were reinforced by the standard anti-colonial discourse ("colonial exploitation" and so forth) that resounded from the students through the streets of the capital in May and June. It was the same in those sub-districts controlled by Fretilin. *União Democrática Timorense* supporters were provocative, too, and Governor Pires, lacking support and guidance from Lisbon, took no decisive action to impose order.

The alleged collusion between the Decolonization Commission and *Fretilin* was a festering bone of contention for members of the *União Democrática Timorense* like Mrs. Biddlecombe. In an interview, she expressed no doubts that the administration collaborated with *Fretilin*, citing the willingness of the former to accede to the demands made by the party's militants that all Portuguese individuals be considered agents of colonialism, and as such be dismissed from whatever official positions they might occupy.[25] She offered as one example José Teles, the progressive administrator of Viqueque district during my first period of field research. Teles had departed for Portugal with his wife sometime after ceasing to be administrator, but returned to Dili alone after a year to work in a non-administrative, but consequential, public job involving economics. Sometime before the Carnation Revolution he had been invited to lecture at the technical college in Dili; after the overthrow of the Caetano regime, the college administration rescinded the invitation. Teles left Timor.

The coalition breaks up

The month of May saw support for the *União Democrática Timorense* continuing to wane in the *foho*, a development not lost on Ali Murtopo and General Surono Reksodiredjo, deputy commander-in-chief of *ABRI*, and Colonel Aloysius Sugiyanto, who were troubled by the threat the *coligação* posed. So, in a scheme to divide the two allies, the Indonesians invited members of both parties to Jakarta: José Ramos-Horta, Alarico Fernandes, Francisco Lopes da Cruz, and César Mousinho. This was the first time that the *União Democrática Timorense* had engaged with the Indonesian Government. Ramos-Horta suggested they all travel as one and coordinate their work, but Lopes da Cruz demurred, a decision suggesting a wavering commitment to their union. More politically astute than Lopes da Cruz, their Indonesian hosts had arranged for the two parties to travel on different planes, and had organized meetings on different days.[26] Ramos-Horta and Fernandes landed in Jakarta first; Lopes da Cruz and Mousinho arriving only as their colleagues were about to leave. The two parties were accommodated in separate hotels, but the wily Ramos-Horta managed to ferret out their partners' hotel and found them in the hotel lobby, waiting for the Indonesians to take them to a meeting. "Their Indonesian escorts could not disguise their surprise and annoyance..."[27]

Ali Murtopo and General Surono talked with Ramos-Horta and Fernandes. To discern Ali Murtopo's intentions, and to reassure him once more that *Fretilin* posed no threat to Indonesia, the Timorese leaders promised that an independent East Timor would not lend support to any separatist group. General Murtopo, however, had taken the measure of his guests and seemed to understand how deep was the fault line between *Fretilin* and the *União Democrática Timorense*, and nothing they could say would deflect him from encouraging Suharto to annex the territory. This ambition was signaled by the public relations campaign the Indonesian Government waged while the four Timorese politicians were in Jakarta, and which was designed not only to dramatize Indonesia's "good will" towards the Timorese people, but also to exacerbate the differences between the four Timorese spokesmen. Press photographs showed the *Fretilin* delegates meeting with Murtopo, visiting assembly lines, and museums, while the *União*

Democrática Timorense delegates were accorded no public acknowledgement.[28] At the Center for Strategic and International Studies (*CSIS*), a think-tank of Mur-topo's, Ramos-Horta tried hard to convince Liem Biau-Kie, a Chinese Catholic, that Indonesia did have a fighting chance to win over the hearts and minds of the people were it only to cease its clandestine operations and concentrate on pro-jecting a positive image of Indonesia, their meeting merely confirmed Ramos-Horta's fears. From that moment on, Ramos-Horta's strategy was to buy time:[29]

> My hope was that if military intervention could be delayed, we would have time to make East Timor a focus of international attention. Only this could prevent an Indonesian invasion. However, all of our assurances of friend-ship, cooperation, membership in ASEAN, a foreign policy that was tanta-mount to a "Finlandization" of East Timor – all fell upon deaf ears. In retrospect, I cannot see what assurances and concessions we could have offered to buy our own survival. The Indonesians realized that time was running out for them. APODETI had proved to be irrelevant and ineffective in promoting Indonesia's interests.

For their part, upon returning home following a diplomatic stopover in Australia, Francisco Lopes da Cruz and Caesar Mousinho brooded resentfully over their party's growing weakness and its campaign failure; and foresaw having little influence in any future government they might form with *Fretilin*. They also mulled over the Indonesians' confident claims that Suharto had now decided to annex East Timor, and that only Jakarta could prevent *Fretilin* from dominating East Timor. They began to take seriously the argument that integration was the only realistic option, and while keeping their reflections secret, during the first three weeks of May they did urge Mário and João Carrascalão that the *União Democrática Timorense* must withdraw from the coalition.

For their part, the more radical elements in *Fretilin* were also having second thoughts. On May 24, Ramos-Horta wrote to Jill Jolliffe that,

> We are having now a lot of troubles [*sic*]. The reactionaries [Lopes da Cruz and Mousinho] are trying to divide us, launching rumours among the members, pamphlets accusing some of being communists, opportunists, etc.... We are getting full control of East Timor, but indeed ... UDT and APODETI are trying hard to undermine FRETILIN.... I am trying hard to keep it [the coalition] because if it breaks, we shall have a lot of troubles here, even bloodshed. The only one that can win from such a situation will be APODETI. I have been working hard to keep unity in the Party and to keep the coalition, but time will come when the tensions explode...[30]

Several weeks before the break-up finally occurred, the two parties had been involved in a series of "joint commissions" to resolve the issues that threatened their union, which included the vexed problems of verbal assaults and physical violence. Now, Lopes da Cruz included in his argument to the Carrascalão brothers that *Fretilin* leaders were continuing to permit virulent propaganda and ignore the provisions that barred physical assaults on *União Democrática Timorense* supporters. The Carrascalão brothers could not refute these assertions.[31] Pettiness and vanity could be detected in Lopes da Cruz, too. Several months earlier, Australian journalists had apparently treated Lopes da Cruz with less respect than he felt they had treated the leaders of *Fretilin*, and this personal slight he politicized and projected onto the wider political stage.[32] On May 26 the *União Democrática Timorense* announced it was withdrawing from the coalition. Carvarino, Rodrigûes, Araújo, and Reis were ecstatic, and Vicente Reis was said to have jumped for joy.[33] Gratification was not confined to the radicals in *Fretilin*. The generals could now play off one party against the other and lambast *Fretilin* on the radio while quietly undermining its credibility in Canberra and Washington diplomatic circles with enhanced accusations of irresponsibility and communism. Ramos-Horta understood it for the disaster it was.[34]

> The afternoon after we received UDT's letter informing us of its decision to terminate the coalition, I went to see Governor Lemos Pires in his office. I expressed my deep concern about the sudden development and asked his help. My idea was that with his intervention, both FRETILIN and UDT could remove our respective "radical elements" and restore the coalition. Lemos Pires, always astute and prudent, but sympathetic to an independent East Timor, answered: "I'll put them in the plane and send them to Portugal" – but only after we took the necessary action; he would not intervene unilaterally. I then approached my "moderate" allies within Fretilin who supported the idea. However, we should not move if the UDT moderates would not move against their own extremists of the right. I approached João Carrascalão on this subject and his hesitation was most disappointing. While considering this "internal coup," I also realized then that the so-called "radicals" were our best cadres; much was owed to their enthusiasm and ideas. However, I was prepared to move against them for the sake of tranquility in East Timor during that crucial period. Relations between myself and the "radicals" were deteriorating rapidly and the idea of cleaning up the mess was therefore even more urgent. But things did not turn out as I had hoped. Following a Central Committee meeting, I was assigned to go to Australia. I advised Alarico Fernandes, the leading conservative element in Fretilin, to handle the situation and pursue the idea with João Carrascalão. On our part, I knew we could have neutralized the radical left without any difficulty and, more important, without violence. We could have achieved it in a Central Committee meeting since I had secured the support of Xavier do Amaral and Nicolau Lobato. However, this "palace coup" never took place simply because the UDT wasn't prepared to do likewise with its own "radicals" of the right.

Later, Andrew Peacock, Australia's Shadow Minister for Foreign Affairs, told Ramos-Horta that everyone thought the end of the coalition was due to the influence of the radicals; but Ramos-Horta says this was only half true.[35] He contends that although the radicals had increased their influence in *Fretilin* at the same time as his influence was somewhat diminishing, there "was not a remote possibility" *Fretilin* would have evolved into a "communist front" as the Indonesian authorities were alleging. Francisco Xavier do Amaral and Nicolau Lobato had lost none of their authority in the party and their moderate leadership had the backing of the "vast majority" of *Fretilin* supporters in denying "the radical group" a power base. When *Fretilin* finally emerged as the de facto government this became clear.

It was, at the time, that deciding to become more actively purposed in the process of decolonization, the Portuguese Government announced the Macau meeting of delegates of the three parties to consider the country's future. The meeting was expected – correctly as it turned out – to have important implications, but *Fretilin* decided to boycott it. For *Fretilin*, *Apodeti*'s inclusion made any discussion of decolonization meaningless since *Apodeti* was merely a surrogate for Indonesia and, in their view, for neo-colonialism. This was the worst decision made by *Fretilin* leaders during the 20 months' campaign, for their absence cost them the chance to argue for their agenda and parry counter-arguments in a full formal setting with international participants. They lost the opportunity to publicly expose flaws in the platforms of both their rivals. They might even have given Prime Minister Whitlam second thoughts about their *gravitas* and convinced President Gomes they had sufficient maturity to govern. The pro-*Fretilin* newspaper, *A Voz de Timor*, not only faulted their decision, but, after the meeting had ended, even declared the talks to have amounted to a victory for the *União Democrática Timorense*.[36] Notwithstanding *Fretilin*'s declaration that, since it would send no participants, the party could not be held to any commitments made by the attendees, by dealing themselves out of the negotiations they played right into the hands of the Indonesians. This was because the Macau talks, which were held from June 26 to 28, included not only the *União Democrática Timorense*, *Apodeti*, and the Portuguese delegation (of which the principal members were Almeida Santos, Major Vitor Alves, and Dr. Jorge Campinos), but also an Indonesian delegation, there by invitation of President Gomes. Now, the Indonesian Government had an official say in the future of the colony.

However, absent or not, the *Fretilin* cause was not completely lost. Although the meeting had resulted in a draft document, called the *Constitutional Law for East Timor*, which Almeida Santos had prepared after consulting with the other participants, it was still provisional. It included the word "independence," and proposed the installation of a transitional government, a provision that transgressed the covert understanding Portugal and Indonesia had arrived at earlier, so the possibility for a future adjustment that met with *Fretilin*'s favor was there. In addition, although *Fretilin*'s delegates were not in attendance, the Portuguese representatives had previously touted the relevance of *Fretilin* input into negotiations concerning "any formula and timetable" that required working out. As it happened, the document contained much that met with the approval of the *Fretilin* leaders. Under its provisions, a Portuguese high commissioner and five assistants, three of whom would be Timorese, would be appointed, and an advisory council representing the Timorese people would be elected. The *Fretilin comité central* also approved of the decision to hold general elections the following year to elect members of a constituent assembly that would draft a constitution to determine the colony's future status. And why not?: "We were confident that the outcome of any free election would be heavily in our favour," Ramos-Horta averred, "[and] for this reason, we agreed immediately with the basic provisions of the Macau agreement and set out to intensify our grassroots work in the countryside."[37]

Unknown to *Fretilin*, however, and something that would likely not have occurred had the party been represented in Macau, were secret discussions between the delegates, which resulted in a decision to redraft the original decolonization statute in such a way as to give Indonesia just over a year, with *Apodeti* as its agency, to persuade Timorese to vote for the integration option. Should persuasion fail and the *Angkatan Bersenjata Republik Indonesia* invade, the understanding was that the Portuguese would abandon the colony.[38] When informed of the agreement Governor Pires, Major Mota, and Major Jónatas did not dissent.

These plans were announced publicly on July 17,[39] and included among them was a decision to call elections for the district councils on July 29.[40] The news of this infuriated Sugiyanto, who was working with *Operasi Komodo*, "*Fretilin* had gotten advance funding from Portuguese leftists to order hundreds of campaign buttons from Macau," he complained, "We rushed to make shirts that Apodeti could give away as gifts."[41]

Other *Fretilin* backers, besides *A Voz de Timor*, criticized the boycott. One soldier in the *Forças Armadas Portuguêses em Timor* was so incensed, he accused Xavier do Amaral, Nicolau Lobato, and Ramos-Horta at a public meeting of being informants for the Portuguese secret police. To counter such divisive trends within the party, *Fretilin* leaders joined the students in criticizing the *União Democrática Timorese*, and, recalling that he had once been conscripted as a soldier to fight against the *Frente de Libertação de Moçambique*, they denounced Lopes da Cruz as being nothing more than a "lackey of colonialism."

Overwrought language from both the elite and the mobs had by now combined to inhibit reasonable public discourse, and their supporters in the *foho* showed the same penchant for provocative language. By June, with the restructuring of the administrative system all but accomplished in the sub-districts and with it the evisceration of their authority, some *liurai* and *suku* chiefs could not prevent threats or even, at times, violent actions occurring. In Railako the sub-district chief was murdered.[42] Governor Pires was troubled enough about the potential for violence in certain sub-districts where local conditions encouraged volatility, that he traveled into the *foho* to persuade the populace that Portuguese authority still existed. Tellingly, however, Pires went with an escort of soldiers, a display that astonished villagers, for no one had ever seen a governor of Portuguese Timor who needed protection when he visited them.[43] Back in the capital, disruption to public life continued to be the order of the day, and Pires' lapsed authority was graphically demonstrated in a bizarre confrontation that took place at the Church of San António de Motael, which lies close by the Dili's waterfront. Some *Fretilin* cadres perceived the church as an insultingly prominent icon of colonialism, and so one day some decided the time had come for the "people" to make a statement. They managed to persuade a few disgruntled soldiers from the *Forças Armadas Portuguêses em Timor* to help them occupy it, and together the ragtag joint task force set forth in trucks for the cathedral. Before they reached the citadel, however, just 100 yards short, their leader fell off the vehicle he was hanging from, fracturing his clavicle; an incident the "people" interpreted as divine intervention. God, it seemed, was a *União Democrática Timorese* man.[44]

Less miraculous, perhaps, but indicative of the volatility of the months of May and June, was a confrontation that occurred on June 10 between soldiers in the *Forças Armadas Portuguêses em Timor* who supported *Fretilin* and their colleagues who backed the politics of Mayor Mousinho, the most visible *União Democrática Timorese* colonial officer in the government. While their superiors played cards, the *Fretilin* troops abandoned the army garrison in Taibesse, and headed towards the town centre apparently intending to stage some kind of *coup d'état* against the mayor. When they arrived, they were met by the police commandant (*Commandante da Polícia*), *tenente-coronel* Rui Alberto Maggiolo Gouveia, a lieutenant-colonel in the Timorese Army and Police Commandant, who told them not to behave stupidly; and with that bland admonishment they meekly returned to Taibesse. They were not disciplined.[45]

As the agitation roiled the streets of the capital and *foho*, three key *Fretilin* figures were out of the country. Nicolau Lobato had left for Mozambique in April, and continued on to Lisbon; and Francisco Xavier do Amaral and Mari Alkatiri had gone to Lourenço Marquês, to attend Mozambique's Independence Day celebrations on June 25, courtesy of the *Frente de Libertação de Moçambique*.

Apodeti's campaign

Not only did *Apodeti* lack substantial support anywhere other than in the few *suku* already identified, Arnaldo dos Reis Araújo and José Soares showed no interest in campaigning in the *foho*.[46] Even from the time the party came into existence, *Apodeti* rarely campaigned in head-to-head fashion against its two rivals in the sub-districts, or even very much in Dili. Of necessity, the basic strategy of the *Apodeti* leaders was to ingratiate themselves with the Indonesian Government, and to this end, Arnaldo dos Reis Araújo had visited Jakarta in June 1974, where he stayed, for five months, at Indonesia's expense. José Soares arrived somewhat later. Although confident that whether they convinced the Timorese or not to support integration the territory was going to be taken over anyway, the two men were too ambitious to let the future make its own case. When Araújo returned from Jakarta, accordingly, he encouraged his spokesmen to commence a war of words against their rivals. They were doing so when Mário Pires, Francisco Mota, and Silvério Jónatas arrived and began to keep a wary eye on them. This scrutiny the *Apodeti* leaders attempted to turn to their advantage by alleging that *Apodeti* supporters were being intimidated by the *Movimento das Armas Forças* to advantage *Fretilin*.[47] Almost from the beginning of its serious collusion with the *Apodeti* leaders, starting on February 18, 1975, the Indonesian Government issued propaganda via *Antara*, and three days later *Apodeti* inveighed on *Rádio Dili* against "collaborators" inside the administration, accusing both "colonialist," and what they called "neo-colonialist," of "leftist intimidations" that denigrated *Apodeti* leaders for their political beliefs.[48] During the transmission time allocated to his party, José Soares alleged that the colonial authorities were giving *Fretilin* and the *União Democrática Timorense* "secret protection and treating them with special respect.... Because of fear and force it will be difficult and painful for *Apodeti* to win..."[49] Soares read the contents of a telegram he said would be sent to the United Nations:

> A majority of the people of Portuguese Timor, who support the objectives of *Apodeti*, fear intimidation and oppression by the collaborators of the Portuguese Government in the mountains and interior of the colony so that the genuine will of the people can [*sic*] be changed by the use of force. There is disorder and violence in some regions and assassinations in the region of Atsabe...

Enlivening his words with the sound effects of rifle and machine-gun fire, Soares pleaded for foreign assistance (i.e., from Indonesia): "We are convinced of the need for attention and intervention to avoid the possibility of a second massacre [*sic*] like that in Viqueque in the year of 1959."[50] This was going too far, and next day the administration suspended the party's radio privileges for 45 days, a punishment President Suharto and *Apodeti*, naturally cited as further proof of intimidation. In the words of Soares, "*Apodeti* is oppressed. We cannot express ourselves freely," ignoring the fact that *Apodeti*'s propaganda was given as much license as party leaders could have wished for on Radio Kupang. Night after night, in language designed to intimidate *ema lisan* and elite alike, transmissions in Portuguese, Tetum, and other Timorese languages from Radio Kupang extolled the wonders of Indonesia and the might its military commanded.[51] Violence was threatened against the "communists," and Jakarta's determination to ensure the people of Timor would enjoy a new future within the Republic was repeatedly emphasized.[52]

Soares' telegram from Dili to the United Nations was sent off on February 26, and was followed up with two more at weekly intervals. Each accused the Portuguese authorities of attempting to stifle the genuine desire of the Timorese for integration by seeking to maintain colonialism "under another label." The second and third telegrams included the comment that "our political programme on the official radio has been prohibited for 45 days."[53] The second telegram also alleged:

Telegrams from apodeti

Confirmed facts are as follows. A. Homicides in the region of Atsabe. B. Examination not only of some residences of supporters as in Ermera in the residence of vice-president of *Apodeti* on the night of 26.1.75 and 27.1.75 but also in villages where the supporters are intimidated as in Manatuto, Oe-Cussi, Liquiça. In the region of Oe-Cussi the armed forces arrested and tied and imprisoned some supporters with the purpose of frightening the people. C. Hundred of natives and Chinese with Portuguese nationality ran away to Indonesia and other countries caused by oppression and intimidation.

Articles in *Antara* reinforced the claims, adding that the refugees from Atsabe had been forced to flee across the border to safety and had now become political refugees. What was not stated was that, although villagers had undeniably crossed over the border, they had done so at the behest of *Liurai* Guilherme Gonçalves, who had bribed them with offers of free drink and women.[54] The allegation that "refugees" had sought refuge in Indonesian Timor, nevertheless, gave the authorities in Jakarta further grist for coordinating their propaganda with *Apodeti*'s. And this they needed to do, because by February 1975 even Ali Murtopo had come to realize that *Apodeti*'s boast that the party represented the population was off the mark, and that the party's constituency was never going to be sufficiently large to bring about a widely-supported integration. In any event, by that time, the Indonesian Government had decided to change its strategy of relying entirely on rhetoric. It had other weapons to bring about integration. The Indonesian Government now had Timorese "refugees" to train as guerrillas who would soon come to be part of a complementary campaign of subversion, this time in crude physical terms, to *Operasi Komodo*. It was called *Operasi Flamboyan*.

Dili and the *foho*

For its part, *Fretilin*, too, was now incorporating into its exhortations aggression of a more systematic nature than it had previously resorted to. From Nicolau's cooperative in Bucoli, the party's cadre of young people had extended their hegemony throughout most of the sub-district of Aileu, where they had set up roadblocks to check travelers' party affiliations. Although the town of Aileu itself remained a *União Democrática Timorense* stronghold until August 17,[55] *Fretilin* spokesmen, in the statement that Governor Pires had found so "interesting," were able to proclaim that the entire sub-district was a "liberated zone," and note that their cadres were now pushing into the neighboring sub-district of Dili to claim Remexio, an upland sub-district some 17 miles southeast of the capital, as another liberated zone. Inside these spaces, the young men labored not only to undermine local *lisan* but also undertook "revolutionary" measures to encourage villagers to abandon what the young men dismissed as their "bourgeoisie" inhibitions. António Carvarino, Roque Rodrigues, Vicente dos Reis, Abílio de Araújo, and Mari Alkatiri, and the *comité central* may not have sanctioned this sort of harassment, but by now *Fretilin* youth in search of excitement and reinforced by adults looking to avenge their personal grievances were unstoppable. The difficulties bad roads and paucity of telephone lines offered to party leaders trying to keep track of what was going on in the *foho*, would only multiply as the weeks went by, and further distanced the hinterland from the capital.[56]

These excesses caused the *União Democrática Timorense* and *Apodeti* to complain to Governor Pires, and he promised to open inquiries, though he took no action to quell them. The governor found his justification for refusing to take any action that might have been decisive in the Portuguese Government's policy of "*timorizacão das forças armadas*" (the Timorization of the armed forces) as the result of which the military contingent of European soldiers in the Ossu and Maubisse barracks had already returned to Portugal, and the military police had degenerated into an undisciplined rabble, slouching about in groups so volatile that in an unprecedented – and never duplicated show of unanimity – the three parties joined forces to urge the governor to expel them from the country. Governor Pires had the paratroopers under his command, but he refrained from using them, as he was to do after the insurrection and during the war, when violence was a good deal more deadly than students demonstrating. He also had use of two Alouette helicopters, which had arrived not long before; and then there was the *Segunda Linha*, still under the command of European officers. Here, though, there was a caveat. A substantial number of the non-commissioned officers were *Fretilin*, and the propaganda impact of the *dinamizacão cultural* made it by no means certain they could be counted on to remain neutral. The governor was not entirely blind to the danger that the student rioting in the streets might spread to the rest of the colony, however, and he requested Lisbon for two companies of special troops and a war-boat to support any move he might venture. But they were never sent, and would furnish him with an excuse, reiterated many times in public, why he did not intervene. Given his refusal to deploy the forces he did have, the governor's most likely justification for requesting these additional resources was not to restore order or for punitive measures, but as a show of deterrence. A "show of deterrence" was about all it would have been, because by now *Fretilin*'s leaders were disregarding Pires and his cabinet from their considerations, a contumacy that fueled the anxieties felt by the *União Democrática Timorense* leaders. None were more concerned than João Carrascalão.

Mário Pires' policy of not firmly intervening did nothing to reduce tensions and indeed added to the confusion. At one point during a journey into the *foho* in June he publicly discounted the assurances given by his own government that the Macau agreements were final. The agreement, he told his audiences, "did not matter to the Portuguese."[57]

By March *Operasi Komodo* was set on breaking up the coalition by winning over the *União Democrática Timorense comité central*. Sugiyanto had been working on Lopes da Cruz, and by June it appears he was already persuaded to go along with integration. On July 25, João Carrascalão and Domingos de Oliveira flew to Jakarta for talks with Ali Murtopo to "seek clarification of the Indonesian position and to obtain an assurance from the Indonesians that independence would be accepted by them if the Timorese chose it.[58] This meeting was to have a decisive bearing on Carrascalão's thinking. Lopes da Cruz met them in the capital when they arrived, and they conferred with the Indonesians on August 2. These included Murtopo, Sugiyanto, and another *Angkatan Bersenjata Republik Indonesia* officer. The Timorese were obliged to endure a harangue against *Fretilin*, which the Indonesians called "a communist movement," and were told that *Fretilin* leaders planned a rebellion on August 15.[59] When that occurred, Indonesia would act, they were told.[60] João Carrascalão later claimed that he and Oliveira had sought to dissuade Murtopo and Sugiyanto of these notions, arguing that the left-wing rhetoric they were hearing from *Fretilin* was coming from less than a handful of men, and that the politics of the majority of the *comité central* was moderate. Their arguments fell on deaf ears.[61] Ali Murtopo reiterated what amounted to a threat, but craftily added that, "Indonesia would close its eyes to any move by the anti-communist parties to correct the situation." On August 6, the three of them arrived back in Dili, by which time Lopes da Cruz had decided to throw in his lot with the Indonesian Government, a change João Carrascalão and Domingos Oliveira had already suspected. Which was why they kept him in the dark about the enterprise they had decided upon, and which they were shortly to put into operation.

Other than the *Revolução dos Cravos* and the Indonesian invasion, the *União Democrática Timorense's* armed insurrection was the most violently decisive event in the colony since World War II. Until that night in early August, common sense might have prevailed over unrealistic schemes sufficiently for the leaders of both parties to have cobbled together some sort of compromise that may have convinced the Indonesians the two parties had settled their differences and that Jakarta was facing a more-or-less united front. The Indonesian Government would have been dismayed, as it had been earlier by the formation of the coalition, but had the parties showed a token attempt at unity, their apparent comity would have denied President Suharto and the *Angkatan Bersenjata Republik Indonesia* diplomatic cover for an invasion, and President Ford, Kissinger, and Whitlam might have entertained a few qualms about condoning it. But, instead of some kind of reconciliation, hostility between the parties put the capital in an ugly mood that month, and, in the absence of reliable news, rumor was at a premium. Through people telling and retelling rumors among themselves fears fed upon fears, and the most implausible narratives were repeated as authentic from mouth to mouth. One rumor was as trustworthy as another, and anything seemed possible. The most viral rumors anticipated a coup, or a revolt, or a massacre, and, it was taken for granted that whatever denouement the forthcoming days would bring, blood would be shed. In the *foho*, too, things were hotting up. On July 26, following a major rally in Dili, *União Democrática Timorense* supporters, down from the *foho* for the event, were set upon by *Fretilin* youths when they returned.[62] In Dili *União Democrática Timorense* supporters spread word *Fretilin* planned to occupy Dili and kill all the anti-*Fretilin* Europeans, Chinese, and *mestiços* they found. A variant of this rumor was one that Governor Pires himself had helped circulate. In one public talk[63] the governor happened to mention that he had heard that *Fretilin* had compiled a list of Europeans whose heads they intended to cut off,[64] a statement that *União Democrática Timorense* supporters eagerly seized upon and embellished with an announcement that *Fretilin* was about to stage a coup. And so it was that, on the morning of August 11, just as José Ramos-Horta was about to drive to Darwin airport for his return flight to Baucau, and he heard news of an insurrection on the radio, his first thought was that it was his own party that had staged it.[65]

Notes

1 Hamish McDonald (1981: 200) suggests that one reason for the "propaganda offensive" might have been the start of village elections on February 26, which continued until July, and whose few eventually published results, he remarks, showed little party polarization. However this may be, they demonstrated that the integration option had not caught on with the general population.
2 McDonald (1981: 200) believes this was most likely to have been an Indonesian colonel by the name of Alex Dinuth.
3 Jolliffe (1978: 117); Thomaz (1977: 68). However, President Suharto, had not yet committed Indonesia to a forced annexation of East Timor.
4 Nicol (1978: 85).
5 Nicol (1978: 85).
6 Ramos-Horta (1996: 51).
7 Carrascalão (2006: 52–63). He provides the details of the text of the accord the two parties reached.
8 Ramos-Horta (1996: 51). Whatever that might have been!
9 Ramos-Horta (1996: 51–52).
10 Ramos-Horta (1996: 52). Ramos-Horta states that the two Timorese "were the targets of outright bribes," though he offers no evidence to support his claim.
11 Ramos-Horta (1996: 52).
12 Transcribed in Jolliffe (1978: 339–340). As with the party manifestos, it is unclear in what language it was written (probably Portuguese). Nor is the translator or translators identified.
13 Ramos-Horta (1996: 36).
14 Ramos-Horta (1996: 36).
15 CAVR (2006 Part 3: 34).
16 CAVR (2006 Part 3: 34).
17 Ramos-Horta's (1996: 69–71) is the principal source here.
18 Ramos-Horta (1996: 69–70).
19 An observation I am grateful to one reviewer for pointing out.
20 Such as happened in Uato Carabau and Uato Lari (see pages 176–187).
21 Gari-Wai *suku* was a case in point (see page 176).
22 Thomaz (1977: 69).
23 Thomaz (1977: 69–70).
24 Biddlecombe (Interview 2005).
25 Biddlecombe (Interview 2005).
26 Ramos-Horta (1996: 66).
27 Ramos-Horta (1996: 65).
28 Ramos-Horta (1996: 66).
29 Ramos-Horta (1996: 66–67).

30 Jolliffe (1978: 113).

31 Ramos-Horta (1996: 52).

32 See Lopes da Cruz (1999: 68) for his account of the break-up (*bubar*) of the coalition.

33 Ramos-Horta (1996: 52).

34 Ramos-Horta (1996: 52–53).

35 Ramos-Horta (1996: 52–53).

36 Ramos-Horta (1996: 53–54) characterizes this failure as a tactical political error for which he never found "an intelligent explanation," and contends that it fueled the anti-*Fretilin* propaganda machine, which was given further justification for describing *Fretilin* as a group of communist radicals. In 2005, when I questioned his absence at Macau and remaining there for a month to celebrate that country's independence, Amaral told me, a trifle defensively, or so it appeared, that he had been advised by a leading Mozambique politician to keep a low profile. He added that on his return journey he cut short his visit to Australia because he had heard rumors of an impending attack by the *União Democrática Timorense* (Amaral Interview 2005).

37 Ramos-Horta (1996: 54).

38 Dunn (1996: 80).

39 Conboy (1983: 208).

40 There appears to be little solid information about where these elections were held or what the results were. Conboy (1983: 208) does mention that 55 percent of the voters voted for *Fretilin* with the *União Democrática Timorense* coming in second and *Apodeti* winning just one seat. But no source for these results is given. In the event, very few elections appeared to have been held, though one, at least, was held in Lospalos.

41 Quoted in Conboy (1983: 208).

42 Thomaz (1977: 22).

43 Thomaz (1977: 72).

44 Cf. the twice-washed away bridge over the River Laklo. The Timorese penchant for the bizarre continued after independence. On January 4, 2004, in the wake of the tsunami that devastated Aceh, Thailand, Sri Lanka, and other coastal areas of South and Southeast Asia on December 26, 2004, the rumor spread that Dili was about to experience a tsunami of its own. The capital was seized by a panic that was followed by chaos. A sizeable proportion of the population fled to the hills south of the town, filling the streets with people struggling to reach higher ground. Twenty persons were believed killed in the mad scramble on the jammed roads, a few cars crashed into each other, and several pregnant women were said to have given birth on the way. Miles to the south, the men of Aileu or Maubisse (it is unclear which it was or indeed, whether both sub-districts were involved) attired themselves in traditional warrior garb, and armed with machetes readied themselves to confront "the Tsunami," which they had mischaracterized as a new group of militias that had re-emerged after five years under a new name. According to information I received from one photojournalist who covered the scene, she was told the tsunami was making its landfall at Tasi Tolu, a beach situated at the western environs of Dili. Upon finding no evidence of its presence, she was next informed the landfall was not there but at Arreia Branca, a beach at the eastern end of the capital. There, too, she found nothing. The owner of a local bar was on his boat fishing offshore at the time and affirmed that a wave of unusually large dimensions did indeed move across the bay, but with experience of the Dili tides to call upon, characterized it as nothing remotely phenomenal. Upon returning to their homes some of the refugees discovered they had been burgled, a misfortune that retrospectively gave birth to a second rumor. This alleged that the first rumor had been invented and disseminated by the burglars to get people to quit their homes! (The foregoing account is based on information given me on January 24 and 25, and February 1 and 5, 2005, by Geoffrey Etches, Gil Fawset, Rosaley Forganes, and Kym Miller).

45 Thomaz (1977: 72–73).
46 They may have feared they would be physically assaulted.
47 Nicol (1978: 63).
48 Nicol (1978: 64–65).
49 Nicol (1978: 66).
50 Nicol (1978: 67).
51 Nicol (1978: 65–66).
52 Ramos-Horta (1996: 65).
53 Nicol (1978: 66–67).
54 Nicol (1978: 67).
55 The party was protected by the *Forças Armadas Portuguêses em Timor* garrison.
56 One later consequence of this disjunction was that in some sub-districts, the aftermath of Carrascalão's would-be coup witnessed intimidations, assaults, and killings on a bloodier scale than previously. The violence, as we shall see, culminated in the atrocities in the sub-districts of Maubisse and Same.
57 Nicol (1978: 301).
58 Dunn (2003: 140).
59 CAVR (2005, Part 3: 158). Testimony of João Carrascalão.
60 Dunn (2003: 140–141).
61 Dunn (2003: 141).
62 Thomaz (1977: 78–79).
63 Thomaz (1977: 79–80).
64 Pires (1991: 191).
65 Ramos-Horta (1996: 54).

References

Conboy, Ken. 2003. *Kopassus Inside Indonesia's Special Forces*. Jakarta & Singapore: Equinox Publishing (Asia) Pte. Ltd.

Cruz, Francisco Xavier Lopes da. 1999. *Kesaksian: Aku Dan Timur Timur*. Jakarta, Indonesia: Yayasan Tunas Harapan Timor Lorosae.

Dunn, James. 1996. Timor: *A People Betrayed*. 2nd edition. Sydney, Australia: ABC Books for the Australian Broadcasting Corporation.

Jolliffe, Jill. 1978. *East Timor: Nationalism and Colonialism*. Brisbane: University of Queensland Press.

Favaro, Frank. 2003. Interview in Clive Schollay, *East Timor Reconciliation: Scenes from Timor, September 1975* [video].

Feijó, Rui Graça. 2009. "Elections and Social Dimensions of Democracy, Lessons from Timor-Leste," in Christine Cabasset and Frederic Durand (eds.). *East Timor: How to Build a New Nation in Southeast Asia in the 21st Century?* pp. 123–138. Research Institute on Contemporary Southeast Asia (IRASEC & CASE): Bangkok, Thailand.

McDonald, Hamish. 1981. *Suharto's Indonesia*. Blackburn, Victoria, Australia: The Dominion Press and Fontana/Collins.

Nicol, Bill. 1978. *Timor: The Stillborn Nation*. Melbourne: Widescope International Publishers Pty Ltd.

Pires, Mário Lemos. 1991. *Descolonização de Timor: Missão Impossível?* 3rd edition. Lisbon: Publicações Dom Quixote, Lda.

Ramos-Horta, José. 1996. *Funu – The Unfinished Saga of East Timor*. Lawrenceville, N.J.: The Red Sea Press, Inc.

Thomaz, Luís Filipe F.R. 1977. *Timor: Autopsia de Uma Tragedia*. Lisbon, Portugal: Author, distributed by Dig/livro.

Interviews

Amaral, Francisco Xavier do. Interview 2005.
Biddlecombe, Maria Rosa. Interview 2005; Interview 2007.
Etches, Geoffrey. Interview 2005.
Fawset, Gil. Interview 2005.
Forganes, Roseley. Interview 2005.
Miller, Kym. Interview 2005.

7 Words and deeds: Dili, August–December 1975

1974–1975

In the mountains the Central Committee of FRETILIN proclaimed a state of "general armed insurrection against the traitors of the homeland and for the genuine liberation of the Maubere people." The text read:
"Considering that:

1   *There is a necessity to impede the advance of the reactionary forces, which with the system of terror are prolonging the system of domination and exploitation of the Maubere people;*
2   *The local Government, which the mounting arrests, is in the position of having looked on at the pillaging, assassinations, rape of women, etc. ... and is responsible for the arming (supply of arms, training of forces) of the UDT and permitting also, the reaction and terror which spreads to all corners of our country of East Timor...*

The Central Committee ... proclaims ... at ... 15 hours and 45 minutes on 15 August 1975 a general armed insurrection against all traitors and enemies of the people..."

(Translation of the "Text of the Proclamation of General Armed Insurrection Against the Traitors of the Homeland and for the Genuine Liberation of the Maubere People" *Timor Leste* (extra) December 4, 1975, quoted in Jolliffe [1978: 124.])

2008

At the time of writing in April 2008 many details remain sketchy of the death of Alfredo Reinado and the attempted assassination of President Ramos-Horta the February before. The train of events that led to Reinado's death can be traced back to early 2006 when tensions within the East Timorese armed forces resulted in nearly 600 soldiers – around one-third of the military – abandoning their barracks over accusations of discrimination. They claimed that the military was dominated by the lorosa'e, *a term describing those from the three eastern-most districts of Timor-Leste, who were said to be discriminating against* loromonu, *namely those from the ten western districts...*

(Grenfell 2008: 91)

João Carrascalão's assault on the Dili army garrison was, in part, the result of his frustration at the success *Fretilin*'s leaders and youthful followers had had in dominating the campaign. Also, anger at the heated verbiage directed at them; and fear that if his party did not "clean up" its own "backyard" of communist elements, that Indonesia would invade. Carrascalão also suspected *Fretilin*'s language portended violence against his party and bore in mind what the generals had said about the impending August 15 coup. Substantiation seemed to come in yet another rumor, one about a hitlist. The story was that when Francisco Xavier do Amaral arrived at the Dili airport upon returning from celebrating Mozambique's independence, he was so overwhelmed by the welcome his enthusiastic supporters demonstrated that he left his briefcase unattended on a seat when he left the plane. It so happened that the aircrew was *União Democrática Timorense*, and upon catching sight of the document case, one of them decided to riffle though its contents. He discovered what he later described as plans for a *coup d'état* and a list of *Fretilin* members who would be given positions in a *Fretilin* government. Tucked in among the documents he spied a list of the ~~names of those~~ *União Democrática Timorense* ~~leaders~~ *Fretilin* ~~had marked down for assassination.~~[1] Xavier do Amaral denied the allegation in our interview, dismissing it as a Mário Carrascalão fabrication and observed that during the CAVR inquiry when he had challenged Carrascalão to prove the list's existence, the latter was unable to do so. If a *Fretilin* coup had been planned, Xavier do Amaral said, *he* had never heard of it.[2]

An insurrection was being planned, however, ~~as João Carrascalão and Domingos do Oliveira were creating a new political entity which they called the "Anti-Communist Movement"~~ (*Movimento Anti-Comunista* or *MAC*), later renamed the "Anti-Communist Movement of August Eleventh" (*Movimento Anti-Comunista de Onze de Agosto*), the "UDT Movement" (*Movimento da UDT*). Its commander (*comandante*) was Carrascalão himself. The movement was launched it on Saturday, August 9, as the *União Democrática Timorense* staged rowdy demonstrations on the streets of Dili. These continued the following day, and were a prelude to what was to happen later that night. In his all-too-brief account of that memorable day, Lopes da Cruz[3] draws attention to the absence of Pires (in Lospalos), Jonátas (in Ermera), and Xavier do Amaral (in Aileu) shortly before the attack, and suggests that their absence facilitated it.

According to Mário Pires, August 10 started out like any other day.[4]

> The situation in Dili [...] was apparently that of a normal Sunday, although some rumors about an action by the *União Democrática Timorense* had begun to circulate. Deep down no one really believed the UDT would carry out an act of violence.[5]

Accordingly, he saw no reason why he should not continue with his official visit to Lospalos that he had planned weeks before in connection with the *Comissão Administrativa Regional de Lautem*. When his plane landed at Dili airport, on his return later that same afternoon, however, Pires was met by a group of agitated men that included the *Chefe de Estado-Major*, the *Chefe de Gabinete*, and Police Commandant Gouveia, who told him he must take the rumors seriously. He told Pires that, in his opinion, the *União Democrática Timorense* was going to strike that night, and that the police headquarters (*Comando da Polícia*) was targeted. Gouveia added, however, that, although it was a bit late in the game, if the governor acted fast enough, their plan might yet be thwarted. Governor Pires, though, contented himself with instructing Gouveia to ensure that the *Comando da Polícia* was prepared for any eventuality and that Gouveia was to liaise with the *Quartel-General* and his office. The governor was inclined to dismiss the rumors, but prudence dictated he issue an alert to reinforce the military garrison in Taibesse and he informed Gouveia that he wanted continual updating. This was just as well, because, in a foretaste of the violence to come, at around ten o'clock, a pair of armed *União Democrática Timorense* men tried to seize the garrison. This was to be the first assault of the night, and only a quick reaction by one of the guards who had been alerted to the threat, repelled them. At 11.30, the telephone connection linking the governor's residence to the rest of Dili was severed. A second attack came 30 minutes later. This time it was on the *Comando da Polícia*, and the attackers occuped the building and grabbed whatever weapons they found stacked inside.[6] Some of the assault troops marched to the governor's palace, which they surrounded, and others occupied key strategic points in the capital, the port, airport, official radio station, central telephone office, Marconi telecommunications post, reservoir, and electricity station. Whether by inclination or prudence, most of the officials the rebels confronted opted to join them, and they surrendered to them whatever weapons were on hand. Some did refuse to join, though, and they managed to escape before heading over to Pires' house to tell him what had happened. Police Commandant Gouveia was not so fortunate. He and a few other loyalists in the *Comando da Polícia* were taken prisoner by the rebels.[7] By now, blood had already been shed. In the raid on the airport, one *União Democrática Timorense* attacker had been injured and a man who had defended the *Comando da Polícia* had been killed.

The two ringleaders hoped that the majority of *Fretilin*'s *comité central* would join them in eliminating its "communist elements," but the leadership remained united and instead demanded that the governor suppress the uprising,[8] even as the *União Democrática Timorense* began to detain hundreds of *Fretilin* members, including some its leaders, at its headquarters in Palapaço, where acts of cruelty became commonplace and where some of the captives died in circumstances that have still to be determined.[9]

Mário Pires has given a summary of what he takes to have been the *União Democrática Timorense's*[10] plan of operations.[11] The conspirators, he writes, had scribbled the scheme's details over a dozen pages, and these pages had been discovered after the rebellion by the *Forças Armadas Portuguêses em Timor*. The document they amount to itemizes the rebels' selected targets and specifies their final objective.[12] The latter was "To totally eradicate Communism"; bring about national liberty for all Timorese in unity; and "total independence." Under the title "Note for the Day"[13] was listed the following:[14]

> We are in control and totally dominate the situation.
> We have eliminated the Fretilin Marxists from the political scene of Timor.
> We are imposing upon the Portuguese government the following:
>
> • Immediate transmission of power.
> • Withdrawal of all Portuguese communists in Timor.

Pires relates how he was eventually able to glean a clearer notion of what was going on from the *Chefe do Estado-Maior* and from the "guiding force"[15] of the "*Movimento da UDT*," João Carrascalão, "the person in charge of the party's external relations," as Pires puts it. When the rebel arrived at his house, the governor's greeted him with the words, "You have destroyed your independence hypothesis [option]."[16] He reports that Carrascalão was not "firm"[17] as to the movement's intentions, but said that the objectives of the rebellion[18] were to eliminate the *Fretilin* leaders and to expel the communists from the administration.[19] The movement did not demand that other administrative officers leave the country, however, and Carrascalão said that he wished the Portuguese to continue governing. As to the Timorese Army, the movement demanded only that it would not intervene. Pires believed what Carrascalão said about the *União Democrática Timorense* not wanting to overthrow his administration. Indeed, "It appeared that UDT wanted to be joined with the government in accomplishing its objectives of destroying Fretilin and the "communists" or, at least, that it would permit them – the UDT – to do it."[20] The governor refused to go along with Carrascalão's proposals, nevertheless, and demanded that Maggiolo Gouveia be freed immediately, and that the rebel force be disbanded. Only then would he permit Carrascalão to make a presentation of his organization's demands – and it must be a formal one.[21] Declining these conditions, Carrascalão left, whereupon Governor Pires assembled members of the *Comissão de Descolonização de Timor* to assess the situation. Although the commission had carefully considered its limited range of options, the governor declared himself determined to prevent, at all costs, the shedding of blood. He also insisted on guaranteeing the security of the Europeans in the colony, an objective that, as he pointed out, might result in all European families having to be evacuated. In the morning, he sent a message to President Costa Gomes summarizing what he knew of the situation facing him, and informing him that, to avoid bloodshed, he was talking to João Carrascalão and the other insurgents.

Later on Monday morning, Pires reiterated his decision not to resort to violence to quell the rebellion and restore what authority remained to him. His decision was consistent with a strategy the government had decided upon earlier. This went by the term "*apartidarismo*," by which was meant that the Timorese Army would not take political sides in the campaign.[22] Yet although the weapons taken from the *Comando da Polícia* gave the *União Democrática Timorense* temporary control of Dili, and even though the Timorese Army had been drastically downscaled, Governor Pires's position was not hopeless. The Baucau military units, like those in Dili, appeared loyal, and, despite the rebels' claim they did not control the territory. The *União Democrática Timorense* is unlikely to have had much more than 100 armed men in the capital, whereas Pires could summon what remained of the *Forças Armadas Portuguêses em Timor*, the parachutists, and the *Companhia de Polícia Militar*. Had Pires requested assistance, he might have found recruits among the 200 Portuguese civilians residing in the capital who could have offered auxiliary assistance, and even this task force might have been augmented by the 500 or 600 Timorese civilians in Dili loyal to the Portuguese. But the governor stuck to his guns, so to speak. Reflecting later upon his decision, Pires listed what he understood to be his options, or "hypotheses," as he preferred to call them, on the morning of August 11. One option was to accede to Carrascalão's demands. The second option was to confront the *União Democrática Timorense* with what men he could muster up and try to fight them into submission. The third option was to try to negotiate with both parties in hopes of bringing about peace through a political solution. Governor Pires, as he said when Carrascalão visited him, would not accept the first option and he fretted that the second option might result in Timorese fighting Timorese or Timorese fighting Europeans. Even the nightmarish prospect of Europeans fighting Europeans passed through his mind.

Added to these worries might have been a sense of insecurity. While he might have more men at his disposal than Carrascalão, when push came to shove, might Timorese men prove to be more loyal to the *União Democrática Timorense* than to his administration? President Suharto, too, had to figure into the governor's calculations. Would Suharto think the administration was fighting against the *União Democrática Timorense* and on behalf of what they called the "communist" *Fretilin*? If so, intervention by Indonesia was not inconceivable. So Pires settled on his third option. To some extent, one might sympathize with the governor. President Gomes, after all, was offering no advice or assistance. Since those euphoric days of the Carnation Revolution now receding ever more distantly into history, communication between the mother country and the colony had been sporadic. Now it had, for all intents and purposes lapsed almost totally. Between August and September Pires transmitted over 20 dispatches to Lisbon, 17 sent after he had abandoned Dili for Ataúro, and only one graced by a reply. Pires claimed that before August 11 he had "incessantly" requested military reinforcements, but to no avail.[23] The secretary of *Fretilin* might have sympathized; after the insurrection he dispatched over 400 telegrams to the Portuguese Government, and had not received so much as a single acknowledgement.[24] President Gomes and the Portuguese Foreign Ministry were too distracted by Portugal's own increasing political instability. While the

Portuguese Government did nothing, President Suharto and Prime Minister Whitlam reacted immediately. A pair of Indonesian warships and three Australian vedettes had been dispatched to the region; and it was rumored that the Indonesian Army was marshaling its troops along the border.

That the uprising was not intended as an anti-administrative coup or call for independence is shown by the rebels' continuing to fly the Portuguese flag. It served as symbolic affirmation of the iconic reverence in which this *lulik* artifact was enshrouded and a convenient index of their loyalty. In a message sent to Darwin on August 13, Francisco Lopes da Cruz, for the moment at one with his *União Democrática Timorense* colleagues, announced over the radio that he had proposed that the communist-leaning members of the cabinet be ousted, the more extreme *Fretilin* leaders held in check, and a "government of transition" take charge. The latter he envisaged as comprising the *União Democrática Timorense* and *Fretilin* moderates under the presidency of Governor Pires, in whom Lopes da Cruz declared his party continued to have confidence. To one demand the governor did accede. Francisco Mota and Silvério Jónatas left for Lisbon six days after the revolt.

In his account of the mission his government had entrusted him with, Mário Pires allocated the greatest share of blame for the rebellion on the Indonesian "hawks," who had acted, with "calculated coldness" to instigate the rebellion. As he saw it, their goal was to drag East Timor into chaos and deliver the *União Democrática Timorense* into its hands.[25] However, if the attack had not surprised the "hawks," the same could not be said for Mário Carrascalão. As Pires correctly remarked, João's brother was as surprised by the storming of the garrison as most other Timorese (including many *União Democrática Timorense*), a conclusion Mário subsequently affirmed in his political biography. In that book, Carrascalão speculates that had he been in Dili he could probably have prevented the revolt, but as it happened, he was in Natarbora, on the south coast, at the time.[26] At 6pm on August 12 Carrascalão, his wife, Milena, and their two children, Pedro and Sónia, heard the voice of Lopes da Cruz on the *Emissora da Rádio Difusão de Dili* announce (mendaciously) that the "*Movimento Anti-Comunista de Onze de Agosto*" was in control of the entire territory, and Carrascalão immediately set out for capital undertaking an arduous journey that lasted for several days, and achieved nothing.

In the aftermath of the rebellion there were doubts expressed about who masterminded the insurrection. Pires' account, however, leaves no doubt that its author was João Carrascalão. And Major António Barrento, an army officer who had talked with Carrascalão when the latter had returned from Jakarta on August 6, confirmed this. In an interview with Jill Jolliffe in Darwin in January 1976 he stated:[27]

> deeply influenced by what he had been told in Indonesia.... He they [UDT] were convinced there would be no independence for East Timor under FRE-TILIN and they were doubtful there would be independence even under UDT.

Perhaps this was important for the action they took. They were very conscious of ... the need not to offend Indonesia. Carrascalão was also convinced that a Communist-influenced East Timor could not survive next to Indonesia.

More evidence comes from Ramos-Horta. Carrascalão and Domingos de Oliveira, he maintained, had been duped by the Indonesian Government: "...[they] took a [*sic*] simplistic line that Indonesia would not invade East Timor if the threat of "communist" influence on the island were [*sic*] eliminated. They failed to understand that the Indonesian military were [*sic*] determined to incorporate the territory regardless."[28] The rebellion was Carrascalão's brainchild, he told me in our interview, and, "João Carrascalão has much blood on his hands."[29] Duped or not, by the time Carrascalão and Domingos de Oliveira had returned from Jakarta "the idea of the seizure of control of the main administrative centers was already well-formed in their minds."[30] Another man I interviewed, Jerry Desousa also identified João Carrascalão as the leader of the revolt, and attributed Carrascalão's rash action to his ego, aided by a "push" from friends, a combination that surmounted his common sense and made him oblivious of, or ignore, the support most non-commissioned soldiers in the *Forças Armadas Portuguêses em Timor*, by that time, were giving to *Fretilin*.[31] Ramos-Horta was of the opinion that Carrascalão and Domingos de Oliveira had counted on a popular uprising against *Fretilin*, and they hoped that the moderates in *Fretilin* would split off from the militants and open negotiations. Perhaps it was to show his willingness to reach some accommodation with the moderates that João Carrascalão placed Lopes da Cruz under house arrest for the first few days following the rebellion. Other remarks tells more about what was going on in Carrascalão's mind:[32]

> We want to be independent but only when we can see that we can support ourselves. We definitely want linkage with Portugal because we need their help, technically and financially plus the fact that the Portuguese language is spoken throughout the island.

He added:

> I decided to organize this movement who's [spirit] is unity, independence, and non Communists [*sic*] for Timor ... we had no arms and so decided to dominate the police by using strategy: we knew that all the police follow completely their comandante [Maggiolo Gouveia] and we invite [*sic*] him to our H.Q. and we put him in prison there. Then we went to the police and told them that their comandante was in prison and if they didn't surrender we will kill [him].... Then the police handed over all of their guns and ... 10% of them join [*sic*] our cause. After this we went to the Army H.Q. and we asked for the Second in Command of the Military for the Army not to interfere in our problem because all we want was to oblige [*sic*] Fretilin leaders to have talks with us without violence.

Dunn agrees with Pires, noting that,

> This coup leader [Carrascalão] later insisted to me that his and de Oliveira's aim was just that; to force Fretilin into talks, to expel the more radical elements of that party from East Timor and to then set up an anti-communist coalition that would head off Indonesian moves to intervene. His attitude to, and treatment of, Lopes da Cruz, [i.e., not taking the latter into his confidence when he was planning the revolt and then detaining him] support this contention.[33]

Why did the *Movimento Anti-Comunista de Onze de Agosto* assault fail? Part of the explanation is that, unknown to Carrascalão and Domingos de Oliveira, *Fretilin comité central* leaders had got wind of the plan, and, while some remained in the capital, others had left for the mountainous ramparts of the interior before the assault came. There they established themselves in the town of Aileu, which became their headquarters, and from which they planned a reprisal and, as noted earlier, issued a call for peace talks. When he heard of this stipulation João Carrascalão dismissed it.

Another contributor to the failure of the armed movement was a shortage of weapons. The rebels had some, but by failing to capture the Dili garrison and stealing the weapons stashed away in its armory they not only handicapped their operation, they left the weapons available to their opponents. Then, again, the *ema foho* did not get behind them, as perhaps a more astute leadership might have anticipated given the apolitical attitudes of the rural population. The escape of the *Fretilin* leaders into the hills around Dili and up through the "liberated zone" to Aileu town without meeting any opposition, demonstrated that. They had scattered pockets of sympathizers, but these were too uncoordinated to be assembled into a fighting force at short notice and with no leaders to organize them. Nor had Carrascalão and Domingos de Oliveira ever taken the trouble to woo villagers, or inform potential leaders in the sub-districts of their scheme; and after the rebellion, poor communications prevented João Carrascalão from keeping in contact with supporters the party had. The only support was in Lospalos, where *Capitão* Vasco Lino da Silva, of the *Exército Português*, Carrascalão's brother-in-law, was able to assemble some men for a march upon Dili. At first, his makeshift army started out imposingly enough, all the more so after Baucau men added to it as they made their way to Dili. But from that district onwards, as the contingent marched along the north coast, men kept drifting away with the result that by the time the band arrived in the capital it was down to about one-third of its original size. Then, once in Dili, instead of confronting the enemy immediately, the men contented themselves with parading around the streets in a show of "strength" that only served to fuel antagonisms.[34] Freed from custody by this time, Maggiolo Gouveia used his remaining influence to support the rebels; but elsewhere European officers and sergeants gave up their weapons and left their men free to team up with whichever army they wished. Most threw their lot in with *Fretilin*'s, which gave its army the weapons the *União Democrática Timorense* had neglected to expropriate.[35]

The seven days that followed were anxious ones for Europeans and ordinary Timorese residents alike, as an expectant Dili remained becalmed, but alert. The majority of Portuguese who had remained working in administration had, by August 18, found sanctuary in the *bairro* of Faro, where many of their homes were located, and this location, near the wharf and guarded by the paratroopers, formed the core of a zone that had been declared neutral.[36] Nothing constructive came from either the governor or the two political parties even as sporadic fighting began breaking out in the *foho* between men who, genuinely or not, claimed to be fighting on behalf of one party or other. Some were true loyalists; others simply disguising their craving to satisfy old grievances or improve upon new ones, as opportunity arose. As Rogério Lobato himself later said about the factors that helped bring about the violence:[37]

> Sometimes this wasn't because they had a problem with them about this [political] situation, but from an old problem. I know that sometimes it was because someone had taken someone else's girlfriend and so now he used it as a chance to beat him. I know this. People took advantage of this war to beat others and to take justice into their own hands. But some did beat others because they were angry at them due to the war ... I want to say that in this process of war so many died.... It is true that Fretilin killed many UDT prisoners ... UDT also killed Fretilin prisoners.

From its base *Fretilin*'s *comité central* issued a list of 13 conditions before its members would participate in negotiations with the governor. One was the disarming of the *União Democrática Timorense* and another was entrusting security, not to the police, but to "patriotic" Timorese soldiers, whose leader, of course, was Rogério Lobato. The list was signed by Nicolau Lobato.[38] The governor's reaction was to send Rogério Lobato as his emissary to *Fretilin*'s *comité central* up in the highlands. When he got there, however, Lobato used his prestige to convince most of the garrison to throw in their lot with *Fretilin*, and, on the night of August 18, he returned from the Aileu garrison and headed towards the capital with a company of soldiers from the *Forças Armadas Portuguêses em Timor*,[39] entered Dili and headed straight for the Taibesse *quartel geral*. Upon his arrival, Lobato set about persuading the *Fretilin* sergeants, who had been confined to their quarters by their officers, to join his band.[40] He succeeded in his persuasions, and, on August 20, at 1am, Lobato, in command of what had just become transformed into *Fretilin*'s army, *Falintil*, led its attack on the *União Democrática Timorense*.[41]

Rogério Lobato proved his military instructors' judgment right about his leadership potential. Under his command, the *Fretilin* army was soon mounting rigorous attacks upon whatever enemy clusters they could find. Over the course of the next two days – when the *Fretilin comité central* returned from Aileu to Dili – Dili saw some deadly street engagements as each army carved out positions in various areas in the town and strove to consolidate them into strongholds. The *União Democrática Timorense's* stronghold was near the airport, in the western part of Dili; *Fretilin*'s was in the town's eastern quarters. The front line between the combatants was at first in Colmera *bairro*, but during the two weeks the fighting lasted it spread throughout the capital.[42] Although the time had passed for Governor Pires to serve as a credible mediator, a courageous one did emerge, *Dom* José Joaquim Ribeiro, Bishop of Dili. Gaining the trust of the leaders of both sides, he succeeded in establishing a neutral zone between the western and eastern enemy sections. This was the wharf, outside the perimeter of which people were now being wounded or killed on a daily basis. There were many unnecessary deaths and injuries, mainly because the regular military troops each side possessed had been supplemented by hundreds of young men more accustomed to machetes than firearms. Some were ignorant of the mechanics of firing, and occasionally wounded their companions or even shot themselves. Killing, though, was what they wanted to do, and observers have described how the young men slaughtered without giving any thought to the needless destruction they were wreaking. Revenge killings occurred daily and houses were torched. The carnage continued for a further eight days, until Lobato's troops dislodged the *União Democrática Timorense* army from its position and drove it into the hills and out of Dili. One former member of the *União Democrática Timorense* contingent provided me with a grim account of their retreat.[43] He described how, in a rearguard action, as they were forced into the hills behind Dili, he and his comrades fired fusillade after fusillade at hordes of young, bare-chested men and bare-breasted women who stormed towards their guns in suicidal waves.[44]

Two victims' testimonies at the CAVR's hearings give some idea of the whimsical character of the misery innocent people experienced in the capital and, a short while later, in the *foho*. The first, that given by Florentino de Jesus Martins, a *Fretilin* man, describes how he was captured by the *União Democrática Timorense* on August 11 in Dili.[45] Nine days later, after *Fretilin* had won control over Dili, he and his fellow prisoners were transported to Ermera, where he witnessed *União Democrática Timorense* troops executing more than 75 persons. When *Fretilin* troops took the town on September 5 they retaliated by executing *União Democrática Timorense* supporters.

On August 10, António Amado J.R. Guterres left Laklo, in Manatuto district, with the intention of studying in Dili, where he stayed with relatives in the *bairro* of Balide.[46] The day following his arrival, while he was smoking a cigarette in front of the neighborhood market, a car-full of shouting men passed by. They gestured to him, as though they were *Fretilin*. Guterres responded as a *Fretilin* man would have done, but he quickly learned he had been tricked. The *União Democrática Timorense* driver halted the car and he was shoved inside and taken to Palapasu *bairro* where he was incarcerated. Next day he was released, but five days later, his former captors came for him and took him back so he could receive a *União Democrática Timorense* identity card. On August 19, he heard gunfire in Taibesse and when the shooting spread closer he left Palapaço *bairro*. Nine days later he was caught and taken back to Bidau where he came to learn about the death of a man called Augusto Metan, who was shot by

Fretilin in front of the primary school in that *bairro*. On September 20, he returned to Laklo, where the East Timor's future president, Alexandre (Xanana) Gusmão, served as the local *Fretilin* commander. Since he had now become identified as a *União Democrática Timorense* man, he secluded himself in the house of a man called Vitor da Costa Oliveira that night, but three *Fretilin*, armed with a G3 firearm and two Mausers, found him. They battered him unconscious. Four days later, *Fretilin* interrogators questioned him about the rebellion, but when he told them he knew nothing, they allowed him to go.

The *comité central* of neither party could keep abreast of what was going on in the sub-districts,[47] and had conditions permitted them to do so, they probably would have contained the wanton violence that took place to some degree. But, on the other hand, atrocities alleged to have been committed against their people did not incline leaders to turn the other cheek either. José Xanana Gusmão, who only joined *Fretilin* after August 11, declared as much:[48]

> Political parties had no energy to contain the violence ... political party leaders were happy when they heard reports from the ground that they had beaten up people ... when they heard of a political party in one place, they sent their people ... and they would fight when they got there ...

Fretilin's ace in the confrontation between the two parties was *Falintil*, whose troops were energized by calls upon all "patriots of the Army" to crush the *União Democrática Timorense* "reactionaries," who were now, by this time, reduced to clutching at diplomatic, as well as rhetorical, straws. Carrascalão, Mousinho, Domingos de Oliveira, and Lopes da Cruz, hastily dispatched requests to a number of countries to intervene, condemning the "left-wing officers" of the garrison for putting weapons into *Fretilin* hands and claiming the *União Democrática Timorense* still owned territory they had quite obviously ceded. More forebodingly, the Indonesian Government took the opportunity to intervene as broker by disingenuously urging the Portuguese Government to resume its responsibilities. But Lisbon made no attempt to regain control over its colony, and continued to ignore Pires' cables. For his part, besides sending these messages, the governor continued to play a passive role. Now, President Gomes realized East Timor's growing crisis gave President Suharto a pretext for intervention, and he offered to mediate personally between the two parties, but nothing that changed the situation came of his initiative.

Continuing with his policy of non-interference, yet hoping some party might yet seize the initiative and open negotiations, Governor Pires did, at least, make one serious attempt to broker a deal. He sent an emissary to Aileu in one of the Alouette helicopters with proposals from the *União Democrática Timorense*. *Fretilin* leaders rejected them, and detained the helicopter and its pilot.

If Pires could not muster the resolve to take an active role in the challenges facing the residents of the capital, the same could not be said for two foreign skippers who came to play a sterling role in the history of the evacuation.[49] Captain Fred Dagger commanded the *MacDili*, a small merchant freighter that on August 11 happened to be berthed in Dili Harbor on its way to Darwin. When European families, Chinese families, and tourists requested a passage to Darwin, he obliged, but there were no Timorese aboard when, next day, the *MacDili* weighed anchor and sailed on what was to be the first of its two rescue missions. Captain Dagger brought his ship back to pick up more refugees by August 20, and this time shared the harbor with a 9,000 ton Norwegian freighter, the *Lloyd Bakke*, which was embarking Timorese that afternoon. Boarding for the latter continued until the early hours of the following morning, and, carrying 1,115 refugees, mainly Timorese women and children, but with some Portuguese and Chinese. Among them was a young man called Jerry Desousa.

We get some idea of the chaotic conditions the insurrection caused by an account given me by this man whose origins lay in the countryside.[50] As it did almost every other resident of Dili, the raid on the *Comando da Polícia* took Jerry Desousa, supervisor of the Port Authorities on Dili's wharf, chief officer responsible for the town's water supply, and custodian of its electricity plant, by surprise. The evening of August 10 had seen him at a party and sleeping the night in Taibesse *bairro*, with the intention of going to the wharf in the morning and switching off the lights he had kept on overnight. He awoke to the sound of gunfire and was advised by his housemates to stay where he was. Desousa did not listen to them, and went out into the streets on his way to work. Before he had gone far, another person told him he might get shot, but he was now in Kuluhun *bairro*, and was determined to show up for work. For the next hour or so, he cautiously threaded his way westwards, through a labyrinth of narrow streets until he reached the wharf. Entering its gates, he crossed the open ground that formed a compound in front of the generator building, and went inside and switched off the lights. Desousa's original thought was that he had discovered a hideaway where he could take refuge for a few days to avoid any stray bullets that might be flying about, but on August 19, Rogério Lobato's soldiers attacked the airport and the area around the wharf, two key *União Democrática Timorense* strongholds. The desultory skirmishing had evolved into a full-scale war, and when he heard on the radio that *Dom* Ribeiro had brokered a deal between *Fretilin* and the *União Democrática Timorense*, he decided his smartest course of action was to take advantage of the provision that the wharf would be treated as neutral territory, and so he decided to remain sequestered there until it was safe to go out. Events, however, brought about another change in his plans. Jerry Desousa was about to transform his personal hideaway into a place of refuge for dozens of victims of the fighting and stage a massive, one-man rescue operation that would attract international attention.[51]

As a politically disengaged, yet discerning man-of-affairs whom fate had embroiled in the violence of those days, Desousa's views about the politics of the time are well worth registering. Although not foreseeing Carrascalão's revolt, about four days after it had taken place he was quite sure it would be met by a *Fretilin* counter-attack, and sensed that the *Forças Armadas Portuguêses em Timor*, predominately Timorese by this time, of course, would throw its weight behind *Fretilin*, bringing about a shift in the balance of military power that would prove decisive. He was not in the least surprised, therefore, that within a few days the *Fretilin* army had moved out from their base in Taibesse and advanced on the neutral area around the wharf, adjacent to where the *União Democrática Timorense* troops had been holding out. Most, though not all, of these troops abandoned the area and retreated westwards to the adjoining *bairro*s of Palapasu and Mandarin, "running away," as Desousa put it, because they "were overwhelmed." Notwithstanding the neutrality deal, the wharf had become one of *Fretilin*'s satellite bases, although the continuing presence of some *União Democrática Timorense* nearby meant that a certain amount of sporadic shooting went on.

Since the rebellion, Desousa's boss, Lieutenant Daniel Soto Braga, whose office was at the wharf, had not come to work, and Desousa was anxious about his safety. So, two days before Lobato's counter-attack, on August 17, before the serious fighting began, he set out to learn what had happened to the man who had given him his start in colonial service. Requisitioning a government car that he found at the Port Authority, he left his sanctuary and cautiously made his way eastwards to his boss' home, which was in a building today known as the Boca Doce, an area swarming with *Fretilin* supporters. Before the rebellion, *Fretilin* people who knew Jerry Desousa understood that he was non-political, but they looked upon him as a "sympathizer," he told me. When he was accosted on the streets during that first expedition, he was able to greet them as "comrades" and ingratiate himself, and upon arriving outside Braga's house, where some *Fretilin* youth challenged him, he convinced them of his loyalty to the party, so much so that they permitted him to knock on the front door. A series of bangs elicited no response, so Desousa kicked in the door, called out for Braga, and received a tentative, plaintive, "Is that you, Jerry?" by way of response. Desousa ordered him to remain silent, and noticed that in his bedroom Braga had several suitcases packed for a rapid departure. He picked up one in each hand and started out of the house, but had hardly crossed its threshold before one of the *Fretilin* lads asked, "Comrade what are you doing?" Desousa told him, "Look, I'm taking my boss' things to the Port. He's gone, now. I've got to send it after him. He's gone. His wife has gone. They have all gone. They all ran away, so I ... I've to go..." "Oh!" said a couple of the soldiers in unison, "Oh! You don't have to send...." Thinking fast, Desousa interrupted them. He explained that Braga had given him some money to send on the cases and that he was obligated by his sense of honor to keep his word. He told them that as soon as he had finished loading the cases into the vehicle they could go into the house and take everything they fancied. This response satisfied them, and they were content to remain outside until he had finished. When he had placed all the suitcases in the car, Desousa returned for a final entry into the house. He enveloped Braga in some bedding, and, under the noses of the gang waiting outside, carried him to the car, and concealed him on the back seat under more layers of cloth. He then invited the young men to enter the house, and as they did, he started the car and drove Braga to the wharf.

Desousa now faced a new problem. His tenure had depleted the wharf's supply of food, so he got in the car and drove to a Chinese shop where he "commandeered a number of boxes" containing cans of sausages, sardines, and other edibles. While he was at it, he also helped himself to some cases of wine and cartons of beer.

A few hours later, some Portuguese soldiers from the garrison, looking "scared" (he said) because of the violence, summoned the courage to defy the *Fretilin* soldiers outside and pushed their way into the wharf, a show of force, Desousa said, that later led to their claim that they had "liberated" the wharf. Once installed in the buildings around the compound they began helping themselves to Desousa's provisions.

After several days, Braga grew anxious about his colleagues. He reminded Desousa that he had been befriended by other Portuguese officials as well as by himself, especially a man called Reis. Braga asked Desousa what he was going to do about *his* plight for, as a European, he was a standing target for every anti-colonial gunman in town. In response, Desousa sallied forth. Fortunately, he had only to run the gauntlet of *Fretilin*, by now, since the handful of *União Democrática Timorense* who had remained near the wharf were intent on keeping a low profile and almost everywhere else *Fretilin* had a solid purchase on the capital. Arriving at Reis' house, near the Chinese cemetery, in Taibesse, Desousa found that "it was all surrounded by the people [*Fretilin* troops who had come with Lobato] from Aileu, Maubisse." He had the impression they had never held guns in their lives, "so you know it was very dangerous.... They might not want to shoot you, but [out of sheer ineptitude] they might!" He went up to Reis' door and kicked it in, as he had Braga's, and found himself eyeball to eyeball with his patron's eldest son. Unlike his father, who had not taken sides, the son and his siblings were *Fretilin* supporters, not that this sympathy did him any good, however. "The problem was that they were white and the people that were surrounding them were the people [from the *foho*] that didn't know them. And being a *malai* could put you very much at risk ... you being a white person you could be at risk." Desousa pointed out that the "mentality of *Fretilin*" – the "doctrine" – was that the Europeans had been exploiting the Timorese for 500 years. He turned around, went up to one of the gang whom he took to be the commander of the "fighters," as Desousa called them, and put a few coins in his hand. "Go buy some bananas," he told him. When the men were safely removed from the scene, Desousa went into the house. "[I] loaded up Mr. Reis, his son, and then I put the old ladies and the daughters on the top of them and I took them to the wharf." His reason for piling the females on top of the two men was that *Fretilin* (and the few *União Democrática Timorense* soldiers outside the wharf, for that matter) had adopted a policy of preventing "able-bodied men" from attempting to get on the ships and leave East Timor. Inside the gates of the wharf, Desousa conducted the frightened people to Braga who was "so happy" at seeing Reis and his family safe, he gave Desousa a massive hug.

The next excursion came soon after he had rescued Reis. Desousa recalled another European benefactor, Jack DeFilippi, chief of the X-ray Department at the hospital. DeFilippi had looked after him during the time he had a broken leg, and his house was located across the road from a leading Dili landmark, the Hotel

Resende. Although DeFilippi's two brothers and sister were sympathetic to the *União Democrática Timorense* cause, his wife and children were *Fretilin*, but as Reis' family had discovered, this did them no good. Desousa reached DeFilippi's house easily enough, but when he told DeFilippi he was going to take him and his family to the wharf, DeFilippi refused to go without his siblings who lived further to the south, in Lahane *bairro*. Desousa promised to do his best to rescue them, and his word was enough to convince DeFilippi to come with him to the wharf. At the wharf, Desousa was about to head out in search of the siblings, when a disturbing thought shadowed his mind. Were his constant "comings and goings," as he put it, getting "too dicey," perhaps? If so, was there any precaution he could adopt that might deflect any suspicions his excursions might arouse? As he was thinking what he could do, his gaze alighted on the flag of Portugal raised on the flagpole standing on the wharf. The red in its combination of colors, gave him an inspiration. Desousa ran the flag down, spread it upon the ground, and began slicing out strips from the red parts. While he was engrossed in this task, a major from the paratroopers, who had joined the Portuguese soldiers in the wharf a few days before, approached him. He saw what Desousa was doing, and ordered, "Don't do that! That's my flag; you're pulling it into pieces." Desousa replied that there were Timorese men, women, and children dying out in the streets as they were speaking, and that the integrity of "his" flag was nothing compared to human lives. The major backed off, but asked Desousa to give him the *quinas* in the design.[52] Desousa told him he was welcome to everything except for the red strips he was cutting out. After he had finished, Desousa went into the wharf's storeroom, grabbed a couple of white bed sheets, and sewed the red strips into the form of a cross. He now had a pair of crude International Red Cross flags at his disposal. He walked over to his car, tied one "flag" across its hood and the other he attached to its trunk. Then he was off to retrieve DeFilippi's kin. As it turned out, his instinct to buy insurance had come none too soon. As he approached the DeFilippi residence some *Fretilin* gunmen blocked the road when they spied him coming and he stopped his car. Had his rescue attempts come to an end, he wondered? Apparently not, it seemed. When the men realized what the flag signified they told him he could continue on his way. But the display of rifles and machetes unnerved Desousa, and he called out, "Comrades, get into the car, right now! Everyone! Let's go to Taibesse [where, of course, the *Fretilin* armory was located] and get some guns!"[53] Eager to acquire more weapons, they accepted Desousa's invitation. Half dozen piled into the car while the remainder (there were too many for everyone to ride inside) either threw themselves across the roof or hung onto to the doors as Desousa took off. When they reached Taibesse, full of eager anticipation, the soldiers jumped down from the car and formed a line to go into the armory. Desousa made sure he kept in the rearguard, and because the opportunity to get the weapons preoccupied them they failed to see him slip back inside the car. He revved it up, shouting back at his erstwhile soldiers-in-arms as he accelerated away that he was off "to get more comrades." These "comrades" he duly picked up in DeFilippi's house and took them to the wharf.

Rescues of this kind continued for another four days or so, until at last, at one of the checkpoints Desousa was accustomed to slipping through without much fuss, a guard told him he had "woken up" to Desousa's "antics." The *Fretilin* man did not "mince words." In no uncertain terms, he warned Desousa not to "push his luck." The next time he was stopped, the guard would "put him to rest." Desousa surmised that the commander's suspicions might have been aroused by observers reporting an unexpectedly large number of men behind the walls of the wharf compound. But, whatever the reason, Desousa obviously had to come up with an alternative ploy, and at this point Rogério Lobato's name slipped into his mind. He wrote what purported to be an official authorization permitting him to continue his rescue operations, and although he had never seen Lobato's signature, signed it in the commander's name, hoping that whoever challenged him at the roadblocks had not have seen it either. The authorization read: "*I hereby declare that Comrade Jerry Desousa is allowed to circulate in Dili.*" At each checkpoint, when he heard the words, "Comrade, you are not allowed to circulate anymore!" Desousa would produce the fake authorization, thrust it in the face of his interrogator, and say it came straight "from the head-quarters of the counter-revolutionary counter-*coup d'état.*" The fraudulent piece of paper proved to be his passport through every checkpoint, with guards waving him through without further ado ("Oh! Oh! Oh! Oh! Please, please, go!"). Eventually, having "finished" off the Taibesse area, Desousa moved into a locale where the *União Democrática Timorense* was still fighting, and where bullets had to be dodged. A close friend had asked him to bring his mother from a cluster of buildings the United Nations was later to convert into the future *Obrigado Barracks*, where she lay in hiding.[54] This site lay just west of the Vila Verde *bairro*, and his was the only car on the streets. Desousa rescued the woman, but his luck almost ran out when, as they were speeding back to the wharf a bullet fired by a *União Democrática Timorense* sniper only just missed him. For another four or five days and nights, Desousa continued to transport Europeans and Timorese, sustaining his strength between excursions with biscuits and sardines taken from the Chinese shops, as the number of refugees at the wharf gradually mounted. To alleviate the risk of any stray bullets hitting them while they were in the wharf, Desousa used a forklift that he discovered in the wharf's storeroom to pile up crates that he placed at judicious points around the buildings housing his guests. As early as August 14, or thereabouts, Dili's electricity supply had failed but, although the town was deprived of electricity, there was electricity in the wharf whenever Desousa decided to turn it on, and even the paratroopers acknowledged his authority over it.[55] He was the wharf's "master of light."

The wharf's neutrality prevented the two armies from bothering the refugees, but because the agreement did not permit younger men to seek refuge or to leave on either of the two ships, Desousa took care not to allow them to join his party – save for exceptions he granted friends. Nevertheless, he was growing concerned about the increasing number of younger men who had independently managed to make their way onto the wharf, and was apprehensive that, with the

Lloyd Bakke soon beginning to take on aboard authorized refugees, the *Fretilin* troops just outside might take it into their heads to ignore the neutrality agreement, enter the wharf, and carry out a thorough search of its premises. To avoid this occurring, he took the pre-emptive step of inviting the respective commanders of both armies to supervise the refugees as they embarked on the barges that took them to the freighter. They could also, he told them, remove any unauthorized person from the compound, and *Fretilin* inspectors came into the wharf and started doing exactly that, with considerable enthusiasm.[56] Soon however, Desousa realized he had created a problem for himself. He had planned to escape on a barge and board the *Lloyd Bakke*, but the inspectors had now taken it into their heads to scrutinize every person, one by one, that sought to get onto the gangway. After some thought he hit upon a scheme that, with luck, he believed, might just work. But it meant that a "master of light" had to turn into a "master of darkness."

Desousa's preliminary gambit was to assume the mantle of a *Fretilin* patron gifted with a sense of unbounded generosity. He ransacked every shop he could to provision the troops with all the food they might wish, and encouraged them to make free with bottles of Portuguese brandy and cases of expensive "Dutch Three Horse" beer to which he found they were particularly partial. In no time at all, the troops came to regard him as a generous fellow, and his ability to find alcohol in limitless amounts showed him he was a man who knew how to get things done. Like the paratroopers before them, the *Fretilin* militia came to regard Desousa as something of an unofficial leader, even to the extent of addressing him as "chief!" Thus, by the afternoon of August 25, when the first refugees were clambering into the *Lloyd Bakke*, Desousa had become a most trusted ally of the *Fretilin* inspectors, regarded by all with collegial respect. Disillusionment was not long in coming.

Desousa was concerned about his chances of slipping through under the eyes of the inspectors, but since he realized a successful outcome would be dependent upon quick wits, a silver tongue (qualities he possessed in abundance) and control over the generator (which he also had) he was confident he could make his scheme work. Throughout the evening of departure, the line of refugees piling into the barges continued, and when darkness fell, Desousa switched on the all-revealing lights. Then, just after midnight passed, the last barge arrived at the wharf-side. During the previous 12 hours, as the barges were filling up, Desousa had been more lavish than ever with his gifts of alcohol, so by the time the last batch of refugees arrived at the gangway, the inspectors were seriously the worse for wear. Desousa's moment had arrived, and he was not a man to let an opportunity slip away. He authoritatively shouldered his way through the refugees, walked with a commanding assurance he did not feel to the inspectors guarding the head of the gangway. He told them he had detected a malfunction aboard the barge that might require his assistance. "Bloody hell! I think they want me in the boat! There is something that is not going very well." The commandant told him he had better see what the matter was. None of the troops could go. They were needed to keep watch for the unauthorized. "Well. That's what *I* worry about," retorted Desousa. The chief inspector told his colleagues Desousa had to go over to the barge to fix a problem. They didn't want to spend all night and the next day on watch, did they? They just wanted to "have a drink and stop all this nonsense." So Desousa walked over to the small room that housed the generator and turned off the tap that supplied fuel to the filter, leaving just enough to last a few more minutes. Picking up a pair of pliers and a screwdriver, Desousa returned to where the inspectors were standing at the entrance to the gangway. Promising the repair would take no more than 20 minutes or so, he nonchalantly strolled past them and onto the gangway. One of them grunted, "Yeah. Yeah. You don't have to fix [the barge] very properly. Just make it move." "Okay! No problem!" As quickly as he dared, Desousa made his way across and stepped into the barge. As soon as he did so, he ordered the skipper, "Start this thing up." The man hesitated and Desousa shouted, "Start!" whereupon the small craft began to inch its way slowly through the water and merge into the blackness of night. Only when its speed kept increasing did the drunken inspectors realized their "chief" was not about to return, but before they could decide how to stop him, the wharf plunged into darkness. The fuel in the generator had run out. The men scrambled about searching for illumination of some kind, and Desousa was amazed to hear them actually calling for him to put things "right!" A few more minutes and the barge was maneuvering itself against the side of the *Lloyd Bakke*, and Desousa was scrambling over the rail. The reception that greeted his arrival on board was hardly one that befitted a hero. As his feet met the deck, and he lurched into the crowd of women and children jammed along the passageway, one among them, a woman he knew to have *União Democrática Timorense* sympathies, identified him as a *Fretilin* supporter, and demanded that he return to the wharf. Desousa told her she should go back herself. What help had *she* given her fellow refugees? He had done something for people. All she had done was run away. The woman turned away from him, but their heated exchange had warned him that he was not yet out of the woods and that his situation remained precarious. Circumspect as ever, he decided not to take any chances. He needed to hide until the *Lloyd Bakke* was on the high seas and too far out for the captain to turn around. A hideaway had to be found where no *Fretilin* search party might discover him if the ship's departure was delayed. And quickly, since the *Fretilin* guards, intoxicated and certainly angry, might even now be on their way. Included among the ship's cargo were bulldozers and a fork-loader, and it was the fork-loader Desousa settled upon as his place of refuge. He slid under its bulk, intending to position himself between the engine at the back and the business end at the front; but it was dark on deck, and hardly any light illuminated the fork-loader, and as he was groping his way towards it, his hands felt a warm body. "Bloody hell!" he thought, "What's this?" It turned out to be yet another of his many Portuguese friends, a man called Pereira, who had been employed as a mechanic in veterinarian services. After a hushed exchange of reintroductions, explanations, and mutual congratulations Pereira extended himself across the top of the engine starter while Desousa settled down uncomfortably under the fork. Desousa's emotional ordeal was still not over, though, because the ship's engines had not yet started up, and every moment the pair feared that the inspectors would show up and haul them back. Tense and apprehensive, they stuck it out hour after hour, until, seven hours after Desousa had embarked their ears heard the glorious sound that their by-now shredded nerves had convinced them they were never going to hear. The engines, deep in the bowels of the ship, revving up and the anchor being weighed. They were safe. They were on their way to Darwin. "What a relief!" Jerry Desousa told me.[57]

Now that his mental anguish had abated, so he began to feel hungry. As the ship began plowing its way eastwards through the waters of the Wetar Strait and along the northern coast of Timor, he left his hideaway to search for something to eat. He knew that none of the refugees had been able to find food, but he was determined to try his luck and, with characteristic initiative, located the ship's kitchen. He stepped inside, and there found a Chinese cook preparing meals for the crew. Desousa attracted the man's attention by calling out "Hallo! Hallo! Hallo! *Hallo!*" Busily at work, the cook turned around for an instant, only to summarily wave him away. Desousa rubbed his hand over his stomach, affected a pained grimace, and pointed to a loaf of bread on a table. He kept miming until the cook gave it to him. After he had wolfed down the bread, he realized he was thirsty, but, uncertain about trusting the ship's water, his eyes lighted upon a two-liter bottle of milk in the kitchen. Once more, the cook gestured Desousa to depart, but he again persisted with mimicry until the cook, wanting to be rid of the nuisance, poured out two-thirds of the bottle into a jug, gave him the rest of the bottle, and pushed Desousa (who was repeating "Thank you! Thank you") out of the door, with the words, "Go! Go! Go!" As he was being propelled towards the deck, the thought occurred to him that he might have landed himself with another problem. When the other refugees saw his prize they were definitely going to demand a share! As it chanced, just the other side of the door was a foyer, which afforded sufficient privacy for Desousa to drink as much milk and gorge as much bread as he could. When he emerged on deck and his fellow passengers swarmed around, Desousa was glad-handed with his trophies. Before hunger and thirst returned, the *Lloyd Bakke* had docked in Darwin later that same day.

The end of a European colony: exiled in Ataúro

However spectacular Jerry Desousa's departure from Portuguese Timor, from the perspective of the colony's history, the most momentous departure was that of Governor Mário Lemos Pires, who had come to the conclusion that prudence necessitated that he and his administrative team leave the main island.[58] By August 26, with *Fretilin* in control of Dili, and such key towns as Same and Turiscai, and still receiving no advice from Gomes, Pires decided to seek sanctuary on Ataúro. The obliging Captain Dagger, who had brought his vessel back to Dili from Darwin, added his name to the burgeoning passenger list.[59] At 3:30 a.m. on August 27, the *MacDili* weighed anchor in the harbor for the second time, but on this occasion towing a military barge, the *Loes*, with the last governor of Portuguese Timor aboard. Accompanying Pires were a few administrative officers and the remnants of the European *Forças Armadas Portuguêses em Timor*. After dropping off the barge on Ataúro, and in the wake of the *Lloyd Bakke*, the *MacDili* headed eastwards, rounded the eastern part of the island, and crossed the Timor Sea to Darwin. The following day, Governor Pires received a belated response from Lisbon in the shape of a delegation, led by Almeida Santos, chief spokesmen for the government, with Brigadier Oliveira Rodrigûes, Major Faria Ravara, and Dr. Melo Gouveia, the Portuguese Consul in Sydney.[60] They accomplished nothing and soon departed for Lisbon. By this time there was not much they could do.

A small number of officials remained closeted in the Dili garrison, but with Pires' departure they and the sub-district administrators and European chiefs of post were at liberty to leave Timor. By whatever means they could. One was the administrator of Cova Lima, António Oliveira.[61] At the time of the rebellion Administrator Oliveira had been in Dili, but instead of joining the fugitives in the barge, decided to travel independently for Kupang. So, too, did the remaining Europeans, except for those whom the *Fretilin* army detained. Of the Portuguese community in East Timor, only one member opted to remain with the Timorese: Bishop, *Dom* José Joaquim Ribeiro.

After its troops had been driven out of Dili and into the hills, the fighting continued to go badly for the *União Democrática Timorense*, and its leaders decided to make a break for the frontier and seek sanctuary in Indonesian Timor. They headed west along the northern road towards Batugadé, a town about half a mile inside the frontier, and, after managing to fight their way through a wedge of *Fretilin* troops separating them from another battalion of *União Democrática Timorense* troops following the southern route, via Suai, to the border, they were able to cross.[62]

On the same day the governor left for Ataúro, a third ship was spied cutting through the waters of the Wetar Strait and into Dili harbor. This visitor was much less welcome than the other two, however. It was an Indonesian warship, *Monginsidi*, which landed solders to repatriate the staff from the Indonesian Consulate: a foretaste of what was to come.

Notes

1 Thomaz (1977:79). Dr. Werner Kraus (personal communication 1989) pointed out to me that the "hitlist" is a common motif in Indonesian political folklore, and he was dubious about its authenticity in this instance.
2 Xavier do Amaral (Interview 2005).
3 Cruz (1999: 69).
4 The following account of what happened that night is based upon Pires (1991: 192–199).
5 Pires (1991: 192):

> *A situação en Dili [...] foi a de um aparente domingo normal, tendo mesmo militares e civis frequentado a praia como habitualmente, ainda que alguns rumores sobre uma acção da UDT tivessem começado a circular. No fundo, ninguém acreditava muito numa iniciativa violenta por parte da UDT.*

6 See Cruz (1999:69). Considering the prominent part Lopes da Cruz played in the political events leading up to, during, and after the coup, it is surprising that in his *Kesaksian Aku dan Timor Timur*, he merely summarizes what, in his opinion, was going on rather than provide a more substantial "testimony."

7 He did not remain a prisoner for long. On August 14, Gouveia publicly announced his resignation from his official position as police chief and his decision to join the *Movimento Anti-Comunista* (Pires 1991: 214–218), decisions Pires attributes to Gouveia's mental instability, which had been indicated by his behavior days before the insurrection.

8 CAVR (2006 Part 3: 41).

9 CAVR (2006 Part 3: 41).

10 Strictly speaking, the *União Democrática Timorense* was, by this time, incorporated into the *Movimento Anti-Comunista*, with João Carrascalão as its *Comandante Operacional do Movimento Anti-Comunista*; but it has become accepted practice for writers to designate the combined grouping by the name of the dominant party, and I shall tend to follow the convention here, the context making it clear whether reference is being made to the "former" *União Democrática Timorense* or to the *Movimento Anti-Comunista*.

11 Pires (1991: 193–194).

12 *"Objectivo Final."*

13 *"Nota do Dia."*

14 *"Consequimos controlar e dominar totalment a situação.*
Eliminámos a marxista Fretilin da cena politica de Timor.
Impomos ao Governo português o sequinte:

• *Transmissão imediate de poderes;*
• *Retirada imediata de todos os comunistas portugueses em Timor."*

15 *"principal dirigente."*

16 *"Vocês acabam de destruir a vossa hipótese de independência."*

17 *"firme."*

18 *"golpe."*

19 See Cruz (1999: 70) for his reasons for supporting the coup.

20 *"Parecia que a UDT vinha procurar junto do Governo que este realizasse os seus objectivos de destruir a Fretilin e os "comunistas" ou, no mínimo, que lhe permitisse, a ela, UDT, que o fizesse."*

21 Pires (1991: 195).

22 Generally speaking this policy was respected by officers and men, but there were individuals who did take sides.

23 Pires (1991: 197).

24 Ramos-Horta (1996: 58).

25 Pires (1991: 196).

26 Carrascalão (2006: 82).

27 Jolliffe (1978: 117–118).

28 Ramos-Horta (1996: 54, 56).

29 Ramos-Horta (Interview 2005).

30 Dunn (2003: 142).

31 Sousa (Interview 2005).

32 Dunn (2003: 143).

33 Dunn (2003: 143).

34 Texeira (Interview 2005).

35 Thomaz (1977: 85).

36 CAVR (2006 Part 3: 42).

37 CAVR (2006 Part 3: 43).

38 The complete transcript is to be found in Pires (1991: 205).

39 Hill (2010: 142).

40 The support of both garrisons resulted from the persuasive tongues of Nicolau Lobato, Alarico Fernandes, and Mari Alkatiri, who had solicited them three or four months earlier (Fernandes 1975).

41 CAVR (2006 Part 3: 42). This defection of the Timorese Army garrison in Dili to *Fretilin* signaled the establishment of *Falintil*, whose official founding has been celebrated ever since as August 20. The name is an acronym for *Forças Armadas da Libertação Nacional de Timor-Leste* or the "Armed Forces for the National Liberation of East Timor." By the time the Indonesian army invaded East Timor *Falintil* numbered around 20,000 soldiers, of whom 2,500 were regular troops, 7,000 were men who had had trained under the Portuguese, and another 10,000 were soldiers had attended brief military instruction courses (Timor Archives).

42 CAVR (2006 Part 3: 42).

43 Assis (Interview 2007).

44 Mr. Assis added the surmise that the young people might have been excited into their self-destructive advance by dosing on drugs supplied them by the Chinese who, he suggested, had in 1975 promised support to *Fretilin* (Assis Interview: 2007). This association between China and *Fretilin* was the subject of propaganda on the part of their rivals and seemed to have been fueled by Bishop of Dili, José Joaquim Ribeiro.

45 CAVR (2005: 18–19).

46 CAVR (2005: 24–25).

47 Ramos-Horta (Interview 2005).

48 CAVR (2004: 14).

49 Cf. Jolliffe (1978: 122–123, 139–140).

50 Desousa (2005 Interview). This account is based on two interviews Mr. Desousa granted me in 2005 in Dili. The first, an informal one, was at the Acait Restaurant on January 12. The second interview, which was taped, was held on August 16, 18, or 19 in his office in Taibesse. Both interviews were conducted in English.

51 *Fretilin*'s and *União Democrática Timorense's* agreement that the wharf would be neutral territory, excluded from the combatant zone, made it a natural congregation point for women, children, and elderly men who wished to take advantage of the unexpected docking of the ship *Lloyd Bakke* as a way of escaping Timor.

52 The five blue and white shields in the Portuguese flag that represent the five Moorish kings defeated by the first king of Portugal, *Dom* Afonso Henriques, at the Battle of Ourique.

53 Probably from the *Fretilin* headquarters, the former army camp.

54 After the United Nations had established itself in East Timor.

55 In a lead article published in a Darwin newspaper on August 28, 1975, describing his exploits, the writer actually identified him as an "electrician" so closely had he become associated with the generator (White 1975).

56 It is unclear what happened to the young men Desousa had befriended. Presumably, like the European colonial officers, they enjoyed the protection of the paratroopers and other European soldiers in the former Timorese Army.

57 Happily though he recollected that night, in his interview he could not refrain from reiterating his contempt for the Portuguese soldiers and paratroopers, the self-declared "protectors" of the fleeing governor. A thousand or so "heroes," he sarcastically remarked, who had deployed their guns well enough to force their way through the *Fretilin* inspectors, but who had done nothing to assist any refugees.

58 Pires (1991: 253).

59 Hill (2002: 143).

60 Pires (1991: 271). A first-hand account of the circumstances of the governor's arrival on the island and his departure is given in Pires (1991: 267–347).

61 Oliveira (2005).

62 Assis (Interview 2007).

References

Carrascalão, Mário Viegas. 2006. *"Timor: Antes Do Futuro."* Dili, Timor-Leste: Livaria Mau Huran.

CAVR. 2005. *Timor-Leste Massacres: Audiência Pública Nacional*, 19–21 Novembro 2003, 2005 Comissão de Acolhimento, *Verdade e Reconciliação de Timor-Leste (CAVR)*.

Cruz, Francisco Xavier Lopes da. 1999. *Kesaksian: Aku Dan Timur Timur*. Jakarta, Indonesia: Yayasan Tunas Harapan Timor Lorosae.

Dunn, James. 2003. *East Timor: A Rough Passage to Independence*. New South Wales, Australia: Longueville Books.

Fernandes, Alarico. 2003. Interview in Clive Schollay. *East Timor Reconciliation: Scenes from Timor, September 1975* [video].

Grenfell, Damian. 2008. "Governance, Violence and Crises in Timor-Leste: Estadu Seidauk Mai," in David Mearns (Steven Farram, assistant editor). *Democratic Governance in Timor-Leste: Reconciling the Local and the National*. pp. 85–97. Darwin, Australia: Charles Darwin University Press.

Hill, Helen. 2002. *Stirrings of Nationalism in East Timor: Fretilin 1974–78, The Origins, Ideologies and Strategies of a Nationalist Movement*. Kuala Lumpur and Díli. Contemporary Otford, Otford Press, Ortford (Sydney).

Jolliffe, Jill. 1978. *East Timor: Nationalism and Colonialism*. Brisbane: University of Queensland Press.

Kraus, Werner. 1989. Personal Communication.

Pires, Mário Lemos. 1991. *Descolonização de Timor: Missão Impossível?* 3rd. Edition. Lisbon: Publicações Dom Quixote, Lda.

Ramos-Horta, José. 1996. *Funu – The Unfinished Saga of East Timor*. Lawrenceville, N.J.: The Red Sea Press, Inc.

Thomaz, Luís Filipe F.R. 1973. *O Problema Politico De Timor*. Braga: Editora Pax. Rua do Souto.

Timor Archives. Available at: http://timorarchives.wordpress.com/2012/08/21/falintil-archival-record. Accessed February 13, 2014.

Interviews

Amaral, Francisco Xavier do. Interview 2005.

Assis, Rudy de. Interview 2007.

Desousa, Jerry. Interview 2005.

Oliveira, Fernanda. Interview 2005.

Ramos-Horta, José. Interview 2005.

Souza, Domingos de. Interview 2005.

Texeira, José. Interview 2005.

White, Ken. 1975 (Thursday, August 28). "Jerimias de Souza – HERO!" *The Northern Territory News*, Vol. 24, No. 141: 1. Darwin, Northern Territories, Australia.

8   Words and deeds: the *foho*

1974–1975

> *The strange thing is that, without in most cases any socio-economic, ethnic, or religious motives that might explain why a social unit supported one rather than another party, all East Timor was politicized–and fanatically so. Without ideological preparation or historical traditions to discuss programs or confront possible solutions, the parties involved themselves in a shameless washing of dirty linen, in body to body personal attacks, in a genuine civil war of words. It would not be just to blame the parties exclusively for what happened; the greater part of the blame must be laid on the policies that were followed.*
>
> (Thomaz 1977: 63–64; translation supplied)

2006–2007

> *The violence that consumed East Timor between April 2006 to December 2007, in what is often referred to as "the Crisis", opened multiple fracture lines in East Timorese society, pitting neighbor against neighbor, friend against friend and family against family. The repercussions for the international aid community were equally salutary. In the space of two months, from April to May 2006, East Timor's reputation had traversed the full spectrum between U.N. success story to failed state.*
>
> (Scambary 2011: 59)

Idées reçues to the contrary, killings were not the norm in the majority of sub-districts, a surprising fact, perhaps, considering the fighting between *Fretilin* and the *União Democrática Timorense* is typically characterized – incorrectly – as a "civil war." We are unlikely ever to know with any exactitude how many people lost their lives, but more deaths occurred in the hinterland than in the capital,[1] and relatively few occurred in the eastern districts and Oe-Cussi. The violence was most extreme in Liquiça, Ermera, Ainaro, Manufahi, and Manatuto, "where tensions based on long-standing clan feuds and personal grudges, intensified by more recent militant party ideological divisions, exploded into violence."[2] Some of the most anguished fighting was in Maubisse sub-district, where hundreds of men, women, and children were reportedly slain.[3] CAVR recorded the testimonies of many Timorese on the impact the conflict had on their lives:

> The brutality of East Timorese people against each other in this brief conflict has left deep wounds in East Timorese society which continue to be felt to this day. UDT members were responsible for the killing of Fretilin prisoners in a number of places in August, as it became clear that Fretilin forces were gaining control. 348 killings during the period of the internal conflict were reported to the Commission through its statement-taking process. Based on its research, the accounts given to it by contemporary accounts such as the ICRC who were based in Timor-Leste the Commission estimates that the [*sic*] between 1,500 and 3,000 were killed during the internal armed conflict.... The Commission's data indicate that the majority of the killings were perpetrated by Fretilin, though mass killings were also committed by members of the UDT.... On 28 August, as Fretilin forces neared the UDT stronghold of Ermera, 20 people whom UDT had taken prisoner after the armed movement were killed.[4]

The corridor formed by the north-south road that links Same town with Dili includes the small towns of Ainaro, Aileu, and Maubisse, and a few other places that had witnessed several brutal confrontations before August 11, but generally speaking, noisy demonstrations, verbal threats, minor physical intimidations, and brief skirmishes, were customary. Even these tended to be fairly subdued, and many sub-districts stayed comparatively tranquil. Mário Pires recorded of his visit to Lospalos the day before the revolt that the sub-district was very quiet. He writes that he carried out his task of formally empowering the *Comissão Administrativa Regional de Lautem* in the presence of representatives of the three political parties, and describes how they cooperated in a sentimental display of fraternity. "This act, at which were present delegates of the three parties, ended in an emotional day of fraternization, in striking contrast with the atmosphere in Dili."[5] There, all was anything but "peace and light," as the governor found out.

Fretilin retaliates

In the days immediately following the rebellion, even as *Fretilin* supporters fled Dili for Aileu, they had some grounds for optimism. Although the town and the sub-district in which it was situated were regarded as a *União Democrática Timorense* stronghold it housed the largest *Forças Armadas Portuguêses em Timor* garrison outside of the capital, and most sergeants seemed inclined to support the *União Democrática Timorense*, the soldiers[6] were not as committed to the party as were their sergeants, and even the latter had recently displayed signs of volatility in their political loyalty. And whatever the inclination of the sergeants might be, the men would follow their lead. After their strenuous three-day trek from Dili uphill to Aileu, the band of *Fretilin* supporters and non-political refugees arrived at the town and immediately the sergeants were urged to support their cause. The sergeants resisted their pleas until August 17, when news reached the garrison that *União Democrática Timorense* troops had assaulted *Fretilin* soldiers in Dili. At once the sergeants switched allegiances and, predictably, the soldiers joined them. They jailed their European officers and Timorese sergeants and solders who refused to join *Fretilin*, using the excuse that they had to protect local villagers from *União Democrática Timorense* supporters who, so they alleged, had been killing villagers.[7] They then shored up the town's defenses. In a video made by Clive Scollay, an Australian filmmaker, which depicts the progress of the war in August–September 1975 and includes interviews with such figures as José Ramos-Horta and Alarico Fernandes, the latter contrasts the restrained behavior of *Fretilin* troops with what he claims to have been the murderous actions of the *União Democrática Timorense*. He asserts that the latter slaughtered people wholesale and burned down houses, whereas with *Fretilin* troops "no house was burned," and certainly, in the scenes shown, buildings do appear undamaged. "Nothing at all happened here," i.e., no retaliatory massacres, he adds. With Aileu secured so rapidly and easily, the following day the soldiers of *Fretilin* were emboldened to attack Maubisse, to the south. Like Aileu had been – and Ermera continued to be – Maubisse was a *União Democrática Timorense* town.[8] *Fretilin* soldiers, some using bows and arrows or throwing stones, quickly took Maubisse, without, the *Fretilin* spokesman emphasized, torching any houses; but they put those *União Democrática Timorense* supporters they could catch in the local jail. Maggiolo Gouveia, who was captured by *Fretilin* men on September 20, later joined the prisoners. In the Scollay video, Ramos-Horta, with the victorious *Fretilin* forces in Maubisse, points to a crèche in the town, remarking, with evident satisfaction, that *Fretilin* created it to accommodate the hundreds of children allegedly made orphans by the *União Democrática Timorense* troops.

By August 30 *Falintil* controlled most of the colony, but the fighting was still going on, and Almeida Santos, now back in East Timor, asked Ramos-Horta, who had returned from Australia during the second week of August, if he would undertake the job of "sounding out" his colleagues' attitudes to peace negotiations with the *Movimento Anti-Comunista*. Again, nothing came from these overtures.

Now, on a roll, the *Fretilin* Army attacked Liquiça, on September 7, and Baucau the following day. Liquiça fell on the September 11, followed quickly by Baucau. The *Movimento Anti-Comunista* troops made a few desultory stands and rearguard forays during their retreat along the northern road to Batugadé – at Maubara, at Atabae, and at Balibo – but the oncoming *Fretilin* tide overwhelmed them. On September 24, at the tiny border town, their force, badly depleted and their morale in the doldrums, the largest remaining contingent of the *Movimento Anti-Comunista* Army made its last stand. In the group were Mário Carrascalão, Domingos de Oliveira, Captain Lino, the *liurai* of Maubara, Gaspar Nunes, about 900 soldiers, and 28 prisoners (23 Portuguese from the Bobonaro garrison and five *Fretilin* men). Included also were a handful of *Apodeti, Klibur Oan*

Timur Asuwa'in, and *Partido Trabalhista* men, who had joined them in Batu-gadé. This group of fugitives provided President Suharto's justification for claiming to President Ford and Secretary of State Kissinger that the tattered contingent represented the entire Timorese people and thus had the authority to speak on their behalf. The multi-party group was in pretty bad shape now, and the *Fretilin* troops had no trouble in giving it one last thrust over the border. The survivors struggled on until they reached the nearest town, Atapupu, and sanctuary while 200 of their companions opted to remain in East Timor and surrender to *Fretilin.* With the removal of their rivals' last remaining toe-hold in the country, Francisco Xavier do Amaral's party was now in charge of East Timor. For the time being.

One curious aspect of the fighting was that the political parties allied with one another in all possible combinations, as Mário Carrascalão testified at the National Public Hearing on The Internal Political Conflict:[9]

> We saw a different approach there [in the districts].... In Atsabe we saw Fretilin together with UDT against Apodeti. Apodeti in Same was different, it was with UDT against Fretilin. In Dili it was Fretilin and Apodeti against UDT.

A *Fretilin* government

Once the *Movimento Anti-Comunista* contingent had crossed the border into Indonesian Timor and was effectively in Indonesian custody, *Fretilin* wasted little time consolidating its hold on the capital and the hinterland, and, with Mário Pires' on Ataúro, *Fretilin* had little choice but to assume the responsibility of administering the country. The process of decolonization was reaching its final stages. Dili was quiet, and Francisco Xavier do Amaral, Nicolau Lobato, Alarico Fernandes, and the rest of the *Fretilin* leadership set about the difficult task of trying to impose order on the country. With elan and lightening promotions, they began by allocating offices.[10] Ramos-Horta's later characterization of *Fretilin*'s brief administration as having functioned "reasonably well" is, if anything, insufficiently appreciative, for although the party's campaign had been marred by impetuous language, and its younger devotees had behaved irresponsibly, in their new capacity as leaders of a country, *Fretilin* politicians rose to the occasion. They displayed a political maturity absent from their campaign. East Timor faced formidable problems that even today have not been solved, yet the young men of *Fretilin* succeeded in restoring a limited degree of political stability. However, in saying that the "people" were motivated to work hard and volunteer their labor because of "the euphoria of the victory and the prospect of a free and independent East Timor within a short period of time," Ramos-Horta[11] went too far. The apolitical "people" were not the *Fretilin comité central* and farmers had had their lives thrown into too much turmoil for them to feel elated because one of the political parties had managed to defeat its rivals. The unsettled conditions of August and September had prevented households from preparing their gardens for the next seasons' crop, a failure that would later cost lives.[12] Rather than enthusiastically working towards creating a nation-state, ordinary folk desired nothing more than the restoration of peace and being left alone, though in some subdistricts this did not happen. In Viqueque, to take one sub-district as an example, *Fretilin*'s victory encouraged its local supporters to wreak vengeance, albeit not of a particularly violent nature, on neighbors against whom they held grievances that had nothing to do with the struggle between the parties. In his account of what occurred in Viqueque town during those days, Domingos de Sousa, a member of a *liurai* family, recounts being confronted by a *Fretilin* cadre, guarding him while he was a captive, who gloated that he was getting even with all who were of *liurai* rank, because of an incident that had transpired years before in Dili.[13] It seems the cadre had begged some food from Sousa when the latter was having a meal in a restaurant, and Sousa had curtly sent him on his way.

We have already seen how the parties took revenge against those whom they captured, but after its won power, *Fretilin* did a fairly reasonable job of complying with the Geneva Conventions, and the de facto government granted unencumbered access to prisons and anywhere else the agents of the International Committee of the Red Cross (*Internationale Comité de la Rouge-Croix* [*ICRC*]), requested to visit after they arrived in Timor. Given his penchant for public relations and facility with the English language, the man for this kind of job was Ramos-Horta, who became official *Fretilin* spokesman for the press.[14] Its findings were, on the whole, favorable to *Fretilin*, but some prisoners, nevertheless, did receive abusive treatment, and one of them, Jaime Mousinho, a worker in the customs, alleged that he and more than 30 other men, Europeans and *mestiços* alike, had been confined in a small room, given no food, and beaten. Later, after the tensions of battle had diminished somewhat, *Fretilin* guards adhered to International Red Cross protocols more scrupulously. With the exception of Maggiolo Gouveia, who had been a prisoner since the first few days of the fighting and was a man *Fretilin* had not forgiven for having been a key player for the *Movimento Anti-Comunista*, *Fretilin* freed its Portuguese captives. The ever-present threat of the *Angkatan Bersenjata Republik Indonesia*, however, meant the *Apodeti* leaders, still incarcerated in the old World War II Japanese garrison in Dili, remained imprisoned, and they were still there when the Indonesian military arrived in Dili and freed them.

Although *Fretilin* leaders in the capital had declared a policy of not inflicting revenge upon their enemies, the same could not be said of some local leaders, who often handled their captives callously, sometimes because they bore them personal grudges, as in the "payback" incident at Viqueque. Typically, the victims were put on show trials or, pending a public trial, detained in prison. In some instances, they were beaten. There were few murders, though, perhaps because of the occasional intercession of Bishop Ribeiro, whose decision not to flee with the other Europeans had conferred upon him prestige no other European enjoyed.[15]

Nowhere did the rural population attempt to impede *Fretilin*'s assumption of power, nor did farmers resist its administration. Despite there still being *União Democrática Timorense* supporters in the land, Australian relief workers, who visited numerous sub-districts in October, reported, without any exception, no evidence of hostility towards the new government. Jill Jolliffe found that its leaders were warmly and spontaneously welcomed by crowds of Timorese,[16] a response Bill Nicol accounts for in terms of a reversal in policy by the two parties.[17] The *União Democrática Timorense*'s initial strength, he speculates, came because it had advocated retaining colonial ties, but by staging the rebellion the party had severed those ties, whereas, regardless of *Fretilin*'s earlier agenda, as a government, it had continued to accept Portugal's legal jurisdiction, so it could be argued that it was *Fretilin* that was now the party fighting for Portugal's authority to govern the country. Accordingly, *Fretilin* was "able to gain the support of many tribal [*sic*] chiefs who had at first opposed it. Added to the impact of *Fretilin*'s propaganda and earlier campaign methods, the support of these chiefs provided the key to the party's victory." Nicol adds the caveat that *Fretilin*'s victory "did not end the animosity between tribes [*sic*] and the threat of war at village level persisted."[18]

Therefore, even as *Fretilin* leaders looked upon their party as the only legitimate representative of the people, they continued to urge President Gomes and Governor Lemos to reassume their administration of the country, and a transitional period of three years was what they had in mind. Ramos-Horta kept regularly in touch with Pires, Almeida Santos, and the negotiators on Ataúro before he left for Darwin, where he worked out of an office in a hotel.[19] To these officials and to the "aloof" Portuguese ambassador in Canberra, Ramos-Horta "always stressed" *Fretilin*'s willingness to resolve the conflict through negotiation. Following Ramos-Horta's arrival in Dili during the second week of September, *Fretilin*'s *comité central* had issued a number of *communiqués* that consistently supported the calling of *any* (Ramos-Horta's own emphasis) peace conference.[20] One, written on September 16 by Ramos-Horta, had summarized *Fretilin*'s position, and been unanimously endorsed by the *comité central*:

1. The affairs of East Timor must be decided by the Timorese people within the national territory, without external pressures. *Fretilin* recognizes Portugal's sovereignty over East Timor and seeks talks with the Portuguese government's representatives on September 30, 1975, in Baucau.
2. The *comité central* of *Fretilin* would welcome a joint conference with representatives from Portugal, Australia and Indonesia, and the leaders of East Timor in order ... to promote friendship and cooperation amongst the people of the region.

To demonstrate *Fretilin*'s good will towards the mother country, the *comité central*[21] unconditionally handed over to the International Committee of the Red Cross several of those Portuguese officers and men *Fretilin* had taken prisoners when the garrison rebelled. Ramos-Horta believed that talks between *Fretilin* and the Portuguese, and perhaps even with the *Movimento Anti-Comunista*, were essential if East Timor were to be viable as an independent state because they would provide a legal foundation for what was certain to be a protracted process towards the completion of the decolonization. Although the Portuguese kept stalling – "always asking for postponements" – the main stumbling block, was the refusal of the *Movimento Anti-Comunista*, now to all intents and purposes at the beck and call of the Indonesian Government, to discuss terms anywhere but in Bali, where they would have been closely monitored by the Indonesian Government. Dili, Indonesia would not accept; and Ramos-Horta's suggestion of Darwin was also rejected. In the capital, Ramos-Horta had contacted several *Movimento Anti-Comunista* leaders captured by *Fretilin*, César Augusto Mousinho, among them, urging them to disavow their colleague's pro-Indonesian stance and thereby help the negotiations move forward. The prisoners responded in a *communiqué* asserting that only they, and not those who had crossed the border and collaborated with the Indonesians, represented the *União Democrática Timorense's* authentic platform. For his part, President Gomes chose to ignore *Fretilin*, and his refusal to negotiate played directly into President Suharto's hands. It prompted Governor Pires to fly to Lisbon on September 23[22] to talk personally with government officials in a ten-day sojourn that bore no fruit. "I returned frustrated and empty handed to Ataúro." For Portugal's president domestic problems were more compelling than the problems of remote East Timor.

This indifference was consistent with Lisbon's demonstrated attitude to the colony. As remarked earlier, the Portuguese Government knew that Indonesian agents were engaged in subversive activities in the colony, yet did nothing to stop them, and in June 1974, when the United Nations dispatched its Special Committee on Decolonization to Lisbon, Spínola had not invited any Timorese leader to meet with them. Nor did Portuguese ambassadors in Canberra or Jakarta display interest and now the "creeping administrative paralysis" in Lisbon prevented President Gomes from taking an active role in events even had he wished.[23] It was only with the first intimation of political stability in Portugal, when General António dos Santos Ramalho Eanes became the first freely elected President of Portugal, that some serious response to the plight of the Timorese people might have been forthcoming from Lisbon.[24] But that happened on July 14 of the following year, by which time East Timor had already been incorporated into Indonesia.

Despite receiving no response from Lisbon, the de facto Timorese Administration demonstrated, like the *Movimento Anti-Comunista* before it, formal deference to Portuguese symbols of authority, particularly the flag, which continued to fly over the government's palace in acknowledgement of Portugal's *de jure* sovereignty. The governor's official Mercedes was not driven, banks remained closed, and a "strict respect" for protocols applied to the Indonesian and Taiwanese consulates.[25]

Although domestic troubles in Lisbon distracted President Gomes from dealing with *Fretilin* or Mário Pires, they did not prevent him from opening negotiations with the Indonesian Government. In the first two days of November, his representative, Foreign Minister Major Ernesto Melo Antunes met with Adam Malik in Rome. This conference was a meeting to which some of the *Movimento Anti-Comunista* fugitives, who had very quickly become disenchanted with their Indonesian host, like Mário Carrascalão, hoped they would be invited. But they were not; and neither was *Fretilin*.[26] The Indonesian Government refused to permit their participation, and the Portuguese did not demur.[27] However, both governments wanted *Apodeti*. Gomes' view was that Indonesia was the agency most relevant to resolving the crisis; its government he regarded as "a *more* principal [*sic*] party than the East Timorese themselves!"[28] The excuse the two governments offered was that they needed to quell the violence and complete the process of decolonization in an orderly manner, even though the violence had already ended. East Timor had a stable administration that was working, even if it was a de facto one, and it would appear, to all intents and purposes, that the country had already been decolonized. The term "armed strife" was included as part of the propaganda the two governments issued in their joint *communiqué* after the meeting, but this "strife" resulted from the *Angkatan Bersenjata Republik Indonesia's* covert military operations. The *Memorando de Roma* that emerged from the meetings bore the signatures of Antunes and Malik, and its terms made clear that *Fretilin* would not – nor never would – be permitted the opportunity to argue its case for independence in an international forum.[29] Then, as in President Suharto's December meeting with President Ford and Secretary of State Henry Kissinger, the Indonesian Government's position was that the *União Democrática Timorense, Apodeti, Oan Klibur Asuwa'in*, and the *Trabalhista* represented the majority of the Timorese people. Therefore, its leaders were "fully entitled" to form a provisional government which would be endowed with the necessary authority to request integration. The president claimed they had already formally done so, and that this request Indonesia was thereby authorized to accomplish militarily.

On November 11, a second glimmer of hope for *Fretilin* and the *Movimento Anti-Comunista* dissidents came with a political bombshell from Canberra. Prime Minister Gough Whitlam's Labor Government had been ousted, and a caretaker government installed under Malcolm Fraser, with a general election set for December 13. The transference of power did not, as it turned out, change the political landscape. Prime Minister Fraser continued to toe the Jakarta line as tenaciously as had his predecessor. *Fretilin* stood alone.

Recolonization

President Suharto took his time before committing himself to an invasion of Portuguese Timor. As early as the second week in August during successive meetings of the Cabinet on August 15 and 18, Maraden Panggabean, Benny Murdani, and Surono Reksodiredjo had forcefully urge their president to intervene militarily, though in a limited way, and occupy Dili. Yoga Sugama and Adam Malik had seconded their arguments.[30] The plan was to use a single battalion, around

500 men, and after the occupation the Portuguese would be invited to resume their responsibility as the decolonization authority. Ali Murtopo, though, favored the more subtle strategy of his *Operasi Komodo*, and Suharto stayed his hand and refused to take decisive action. Hamish McDonald suggests that he was aware that Indonesia needed to retain the confidence of the western countries and was undoubtedly mindful of the warnings he had received from Whitlam about "a hostile public reaction" among his countrymen. The latter, however, also sent the Indonesian President a private message to the effect that nothing he had said earlier to Suharto should be understood as a veto on whatever actions Suharto might take "in the changed circumstances."[31] Suharto also realized that, however much Lisbon might wish to rid itself of the colony, the Portuguese Government could not turn a blind eye to what it would see as an affront to its authority. There was also another factor at work in the president's decision not to seize Dili. His preferred strategy was to win, not by personally defeating his opponents, but trust that events would play into his hands. In the present crisis, Suharto's natural disposition harmonized with that of an adviser, Lieutenant General Sujono Humardani, who argued that the colony was certain to fall into Indonesia's hands eventually.[32]

By November Indonesia was now able to direct its propaganda and diplomacy on a single political party, and denounced the *Fretilin* Government ever more stridently as it continued to castigate the party as an irresponsible collection of socialists-cum-communists. Complementing Indonesia's denunciations, and beginning in September the *Angkatan Bersenjata Republik Indonesia* carried out a series of armed incursions into East Timor.[33] At first, these were sporadic; but by the following month increased in number and intensity and resulted in the capture of several towns, with *Fretilin* resisting tenaciously. At the same time, Indonesian authorities repeatedly denied their troops were involved.[34] They claimed that the fighting inside the border resulted from Timorese partisans attempting to repel *Fretilin* incursions into Indonesian Timor. On October 15 *Angkatan Bersenjata Republik Indonesia* battalions from the 2nd Infantry Brigade attacked Balibo, an attack in which five foreign journalists were killed, and on October 16 Balibo and Maliana were captured, forcing *Fretilin* to shift its front line to Bobonaro and Atabae. Unlike the attack on Atsabe, the attack on Balibo included few partisans. Other Kopassandhra-led forces attacked during October, but were pushed back. The incapacity of the *Kopassandra* troops to retain land they had seized was clearly evident, and the onset of the wet season aided *Falintil*, which put up stern resistance for a while. There was a lull in the fighting until November 20 when, for the first time, Indonesian naval and air support was brought in to help, with Atabae as the target.[35] The small town fell on November 28.

The United States Central Intelligence Agency had been monitoring events in Timor for months, so the White House was current with what was going on. On September 10, the agency announced that "serious fighting between the factions [*sic*] [had] evidently ended," adding that "Meanwhile, the leftists [i.e., FRETI-LIN] have publicly abandoned their demand for immediate independence and are calling for a gradual decolonization program similar to the one announced by Portugal in June." A CIA report eight days later announced that,

> Indonesia continues to follow a two-track approach toward the Timor problem. Publicly, Jakarta denies any intention of unilateral intervention and calls on Lisbon to move faster in arranging talks between the Timorese parties. Privately, Jakarta has stepped up covert military operations inside Timor, including use of Indonesian special units...

A September 26 CIA briefing disclosed that: (a) *Fretilin* seemed to possess the capacity to repel the Indonesian army's attacks; (b) *União Democrática Timorense* personnel, fighting alongside the soldiers of *Angkatan Bersenjata Republik Indonesia*, were unable – left to their own resources – to retain the positions captured once the *Angkatan Bersenjata Republik Indonesia* withdrew from the sites in East Timor it had captured; and (c) Malaysia had provided arms for the Indonesian troops.[36] The reports stated that "Indonesian special forces have taken casualties in recent fighting in Portuguese Timor [and that] [s]ome Indonesian soldiers have been captured." They added that *Fretilin*'s "efforts to stir up an international outcry by publicizing Jakarta's involvement have evoked little response." The reference to the *Angkatan Bersenjata Republik Indonesia* prisoners most likely identified the 30 or so Indonesian commandos *Fretilin* captured near Bobonaro in mid-September. These included a corporal who was taken to Dili and exhibited for the benefit of the foreign press. *Fretilin* advised the International Red Cross of its willingness to surrender the prisoner for repatriation, but Jakarta refused to admit his existence, since to have acknowledged this would have implicated Indonesia in the attacks. Ramos-Horta has recorded that, as early as October, in an attempt to publicize Indonesia's involvement in the fighting, he cabled newspaper offices around the world, issuing them a carte blanche invitation to visit Timor. He even included *Antara*, which refused on the grounds that its correspondent was on "another assignment."

Aside from minor border violations, the *Angkatan Bersenjata Republik Indonesia* did not make sustained assaults on East Timor until after the *Movimento Anti-Comunista* troops had crossed the border, a development that that gave the Indonesian Army the political cover it required for initiating serious incursions. It did so through *Operasi Flamboyan*, which was a combined operation between 300 Indonesian commandos (*Sandi Yudha*) and members of the *Anti-Comunista Movimento*. It began on October 5 and ended with the invasion itself on December 7. The brainchild of Benny Murdani, it entailed covert, border crossings into East Timor by deploying Indonesian troops under the pretext they were assisting the "partisans" of the four political parties. Thus, whereas Ali Murtopo's *Operasi Komodo* was a strategic intelligence operation, that of Benny Murdani's was a tactical combat intelligence operation preparatory to a direct military invasion. Colonel Dading Kalbuadi, an old colleague of Murdani's, was asked by the latter to start the operation.[37] Indonesia claimed, as the pretext for the participation of its troops, that the *Angkatan Bersenjata Republik Indonesia* was merely assisting the legitimate leaders of East Timor "regain" control of the country. Its commandos were allegedly present solely in the capacity of advisers (*"voluntáros"*) to the Timorese partisans (*"os partisans"*) – "partisans" who included the likes of Tomás Gonçalves (*Apodeti*), João da Silva Tavares (*União Democrática Timorense*), Francisco Lopes da Cruz (*União Democrática Timorense*), and Guilherme Maria Gonçalves (*Apodeti*), all of whom had given "unconditional and subservient" support to the Indonesian military.[38] The Indonesian-Timorese force attacked Batugadé on October 6, supported by a tank which kept firing from the west at the town. The *Fretilin* army offered little resistance, and its troops retreated to Balibo, allowing the invaders to enter Batugadé the next day without loss of life.[39] The town immediately became a training base for the joint army while an Indonesian warship stood off the coast unloading tanks, vehicles, and other military equipment for deployment against Balibo and Maliana, and later, the more distant Atabae town. A few days after taking Batugadé, the invasion army removed João Carrascalão from his position as *Comandante Operacional do Movimento Anti-Comunista* and transferred their Timorese captives into a new fighting unit called the *"Pasukan Sukarelawan"* ("Voluntary Force") under the command of Colonel Dading Kalbuadi. The force included *Angkatan Bersenjata Republik Indonesia* soldiers disguised as civilian "volunteers," with Tomás Gonçalves as commander of the Timorese contingent, which had previously included João Carrascalão and Lino da Silva. In the meantime, to pump up a sense of impending catastrophe, the *Antara* made sure its Indonesian and foreign readers heard Jakarta's version – and only Jakarta's version – of what was happening in East Timor. It portrayed a country racked by looting, arson, assaults, and murder; disasters brought about by Timorese fighting one another.

Nine days after it took Batugadé, the hybrid force began its assault on Maliana and Balibo. This time, however, the 40 troops that comprised *Fretilin*'s army put up sterner resistance, and only after the two armies had exchanged ground several times for more than a week did the two towns eventually succumb.[40] The attack on Balibo differed from that on Batugadé, however, in that it had fateful international consequences that continue to the present day. As the 300 troops under Field Commander, Colonel Dading Kalbuahi, with Major Yunus Yosfiah as the leader of the actual assault, entered the town on October 16, Indonesian soldiers executed five journalists based in Australia, Greg Shackleton, Tony Stewart, Malcom Rennie, Brian Peters, and Gary Cunningham. Major Yosfiah, who according to Mário Carrascalão had disguised himself in civilian clothing and assumed the *nom de guerre* of "Andreas," seems to have been the individual responsible for sanctioning the slaughter, and, although they were on hand, it appears Tomás Gonçalves and João da Silva Tavares did nothing to prevent it.[41] Far from it. Mário Carrascalão reports that,

> Later, in Kupang, in the Hotel Flobamor, João da Silva Tavares showed me a wrist watch that he said belonged to one of these journalists and which he would keep as a souvenir of his participation in the "elimination of these enemies."[42]

The *Angkatan Bersenjata Republik Indonesia* continued to advance towards the capital. The third assault, under bombardments from the warship in the first week of November, was on Atabae, whose defenders held their ground until November 26. On this occasion, the Indonesian Government did not bother attributing the attack to the Timorese partisans, and it was this lack of pretense that convinced Francisco Xavier do Amaral and Nicolau Lobato that a full and overt invasion was imminent. Only President Gerald Ford and Henry Kissinger, stood in the way, and, faced by the threat of impending invasion, *Fretilin* leaders made one final attempt to internationalize their predicament in hopes that, by securing some manner of international recognition they might yet deter Suharto. Two days after Atabae fell the *Fretilin* Government declared independence; and on November 28, the first Democratic Republic of East Timor came into being.

Operasi Seroja

Indonesia's generals had drawn up their plans for invading East Timor months before the declaration of independence. It was to be a three-pronged attack along the north coast: one prong would be a land assault, moving east from Mota'in, a small community in Indonesian Timor, near Atambua; another would consist of a para-commando drop on Dili; the third was to be an attack on Baucau. The operation was given the code name *Seroja*.[43] President Suharto might have refused to give the go-ahead at that time; but now, with the declaration of independence, the die was cast: "Although Suharto had been delaying approval for *Seroja* since August, procrastination was no longer an option."[44]

International response failed to justify the hopes of the *Fretilin* Government, for only Mozambique and China recognized the new state. The declaration, however, did produce an immediate reaction from the Indonesian Government. The following day Louis Taolin and Colonel Sugiyanto (the go-between between the Indonesian Government and the *Movimento Anti-Comunista*) forced Guilherme Gonçalves (*Apodeti*), Lopes da Cruz (*União Democrática Timorense*), António Santos (*Trabalhista*), João Tavares (*União Democrática Timorense*), and José Martins (*Klibur Oan Timur Asuwa'in*) to endorse the "integration declaration," that is to say, the "Balibo Declaration."[45] This was formally executed at that town and dated November 30, 1975, but was actually issued at Batugadé on the same day.[46] The document proclaimed East Timor's integration into the Republic of Indonesia, a proclamation Indonesian rhetoric wasted no time using as its justification for the planned invasion.[47] The momentum was now unstoppable. A few days later, Adam Malik made a brief visit to Atambua and told representatives of the four parties that his country was going to "use full force," adding that "The solution to the East Timor problem is now the front line of battle."[48]

President Suharto knew Portugal's continued instability and lack of troops made military intervention by Lisbon unlikely. He understood, too, that Australia's government had always concurred with his views, and that even though these would now result in a full-bodied invasion, Canberra would not throw a wrench into his plans. As for the United Nations, since the world body had declined to intervene in any meaningful way so far, it was unlikely to challenge what he was about to do.[49] There remained only one more ally to persuade.

Briefed up to the minute by the CIA, Gerald Ford and Henry Kissinger realized exactly where Suharto was coming from when they conferred with him on December 6, in Jakarta. The two allies found several international concerns to reach agreement on, among them Vietnam (Saigon had fallen several months before), Thailand, Malaysia, and the general political situation in Southeast Asia. Thus, by the time the question of East Timor came up, all three were consulting the same map. As the epigraph that heads the Introduction to this book suggests, the United States Government gave its *imprimatur* for a full and overt military action by the Republic of Indonesia, so that, emboldened by the American "go ahead," Suharto needed to expend no more time on argument.[50] Smoke and mirrors was done with, and the *Angkatan Bersenjata Republik Indonesia* could now just get on with its job.

With Air Force One just having cleared Indonesian airspace, the long anticipated, but no less dreaded, onslaught on Dili began. The invasion was under the overall command of Major General Benny Murdani, though it appears the officer in charge of the actual operation was Major General Suweno, Commander (*Panglima*) of *Kowilhan II* (the Indonesian armed forces' "Regional Defence Command, Number 2"). Ten thousand troops from *Kopassandha* ("Special Forces Command"), *Kopasgat* (*Komando Pasukan Gerak Tjepat* (the "Rapid Action Forces"), *Korps Marinir* (the "Marines"), and battalions from the *Siliwangi* (West Java) and *Brawijaya* (East Java) divisions participated.[51] On December 7 at around 1:30 a.m. a marine reconnaissance team landed on the beach slightly west of the capital to lay markers along the shore preparatory to an amphibious assault at dawn.[52] However, anticipating an attack, the de facto government suddenly extinguished all the town lights before the force could leave. Meanwhile, 16 Indonesian warships remained over the horizon, requesting permission to start shelling Dili. This was duly granted, by Major General Suweno, and, at 2 a.m. the ships began bombarding *Fretilin* positions east and west of the town, where *Angkatan Bersenjata Republik Indonesia* intelligence had determined artillery batteries were located.[53] Meanwhile, nine C-130 transports of the Indonesian air force were fast approaching from the west, and when they arrived near Dili they banked clockwise, to come in from over the hills to the east and make a westward run down the center of the town. The plan was that, after having dropped the soldiers, they would then fly on to Kupang where they would take on other *Kostrad* paratroopers for a second drop. At 5:30 a.m. the first para-commanders began exiting the leading Hercules. Since the sun was only starting to come up and the town had no lights, they dropped towards a town shrouded in complete blackness. Troops from the other transports followed, as flashes of gunshots from the ground told the troops that *Falintil* had begun its defense. With the softening up completed, just before dawn *Kopassandha* paratroopers dropped along the waterfront area of the capital.

President Suharto's conviction that the Portuguese Government would not intervene proved well founded. But in a defiant charade of vestigial colonial authority, a pair of Portuguese corvettes (the *João Roby* and the *Afonso Cerquiera*) remained at anchor off Ataúro, and from its beaches the European troops watched the fires raging all over Dili until night fell. Next day, the two vessels weighed anchor and carried the Europeans to Darwin, leaving behind a platoon of Timorese soldiers to the mercy of the invaders.[54] In just over 20 months, the people of East Timor had seen two administrations come to an end. One was a long-standing colonial hegemony; the other, a short-lived indigenous government. A third administration was on its way; and it was to bring with it the recolonization of East Timor.

The districts

Luís Thomaz's observation that "We must not forget that rivalries between families, *suku* and kingdoms were not less than four centuries old, and that the barbarity of ancient times was much less dead than slumbering,"[55] is correct. It is perhaps surprising, therefore, that after the rebellion, bloodshed in the sub-districts was not more widespread. Indeed, most were free of wholesale slaughter. Dili had witnessed the first serious killings, and, while reverberations of one sort or another were experienced in virtually all sub-districts, outside the capital most deaths, as we have seen, took place in the Same-Aileu-Maubisse-Dili zone and along the northern road down which the *União Democrática Timorense* army fled. Sporadic skirmishes, rather than slaughter, were what the majority of sub-districts east of Dili and in Oe-Cussi experienced, and, as ever, webs of kinship and marriage averted or ameliorated bloodshed on many an occasion. In Viqueque, *Fretilin* and *União Democrática Timorense* supporters agreed to avoid violence, and the pact was only broken after *Fretilin* troops from Dili entered the town. None of the ten *liurai* in the local sub-district was of *Fretilin*, and all were imprisoned in a makeshift jail in Olobai, a hamlet on the outskirts of the town; but the conditions of their confinement were not unduly harsh. As the aforementioned Domingos de Sousa, one of the prisoners, noted, although some cases of minor abuse occurred, there was no serious physical violence and differences in political ideology never became an issue.[56] On the contrary, local *Fretilin* leaders feared their superiors in Dili would order them to convey their prisoners to the capital, where they might have to share the same fate as that inflicted on *União Democrática Timorense* supporters in Aileu and Maubisse. Other sub-districts, too, showed how far local political reactions could differ from those in Dili.[57]

Party loyalties in these sub-districts could be ambiguous, and although the political geography was "never ... clear-cut,"[58] as I indicated earlier, we can discern a rough pattern. Throughout most of the campaign, the *União Democrática Timorense* had significant support in the sub-districts of Maubara, Ainaro, Aileu, Laclubar, and Liquiça;[59] Same;[60] Lospalos; and Viqueque.[61] For *ema lisan* in Ainaro, the name of *Dom* Aleixo Corte Real helped the *União Democrática*

Timorense, as did the influence of the firmly committed pro-Portuguese *liurai* Gaspar Nunes in the Tokode-speaking sub-district of Maubara. Villagers residing in Laclubar sub-district, an Idate-speaking region, were subject to the influence of *Liurai* Moniz, as were e*ma foho* in certain *suku* in the Mambai-speaking sub-district of Maubisse, where some *liurai* remained loyal to the Portuguese and supported the *União Democrática Timorense*, even though their sons might be members of *Fretilin*.[62] Of the ten *suku* in Viqueque sub-district, nine followed their respective *liurai* in supporting the *União Democrática Timorense*, while one, *suku* Uma Kik, followed its *liurai*, Miguel Soares, an *Apodeti* man.[63] *Apodeti* strength, of course, was considerably more restricted, besides existing in Uma Kik, occurring only in Atsabe and Uato Lari. Surprisingly, considering its geographical placement in Indonesian Timor, Oe-Cussi gave *Apodeti* virtually no backing. The *União Democrática Timorense* found some support there, but that district was either *Fretilin*, or else showed no particular political preference.[64]

Moderation, of course, did not prevail in all sub-districts, and the poor communications between the capital and the *foho* did nothing to help party leaders keep their more violent supporters under control, a problem Ramos-Horta candidly admitted.[65] While crediting the *União Democrática Timorense* leaders, "by and large," with behaving with restraint during their occupation of Dili and humanely treating their several hundred *Fretilin* captives, he noted that self-control was not observed in all sub-districts, as the Same executions demonstrated.[66] Having said as much, though, he conceded that *Fretilin* had more "hotheads," including some "real opportunists," who used party credentials to fuel "personal vendettas among rival families and tribes [*sic*] who used the war to settle old accounts." Thus, when *Fretilin* turned the tables on the *União Democrática Timorense* and captured hundreds of its leaders, cadres, and supporters. "It was time for revenge," and even *União Democrática Timorense* supporters innocent of any killings were held to account for what had happened, and a man's capture might result in beatings and death. Some were outright massacres.

In his testimony to CAVR in November 2003, Alexandre da Costa Araújo, a *União Democrática Timorense* supporter described two incidents of multiple slaughters.[67] The first was an episode that took place at Aisirimou, in the district of Aileu. Araújo said that, when the rebellion happened, he was living in the nearby *suku* of Saboria, and had no idea what it was about. During the *Fretilin* reprisals he was caught by *Fretilin* troops in Aisirimou, and interrogated. He was confined with hundreds of other prisoners from various regions and was made to work in the communal gardens run by *Fretilin*. After a time, he was freed and permitted to live in his own house until, at 11 p.m. one night, a man knocked at his door and ordered Araújo to come with him. The man escorted him to where a truck containing prisoners was waiting, and, with Araújo watching, told his men to make the captives get out. When they had obeyed, he ordered them to form a line. They were given time to pray, and were then shot. All died instantly. One of the *Fretilin* troops told local villagers to bury the corpses. The second massacre Araújo described also occurred near his *suku*. One night, he said, its residents heard what turned out to be over 100 men being escorted from Aileu prison to a nearly site called Aisirimou-Manifunihun. It seemed to them that something dreadful was about to happen, so they followed along quietly. When the group reached their destination, the watchers caught sight of the captives from a distance. None of them could see exactly what was going on, but they heard shots and the sound of cries. The fusillade lasted about a quarter of an hour, and when the cries stopped, they returned to Saboria. It has never been determined precisely how many persons were killed, but estimates range from about 90 to around 160.

If the principals in the party echelons were distanced from the party's local leaders in the sub-districts, as much could be said about the local leaders' links with their party's ordinary, or nominal, supporters. Although individuals lent support to one or other party either by conviction or, like Jerry Desousa, for personal reasons, others – and, given the general population's conservatism, almost certainly a substantial majority – did so under pressure. In this respect, the *ema lisan's* instinct for survival-by-dissimulation, reinforced by the lessons taught them by 300 years of colonialism, served them well.[68] We see one example of this in the way they manipulated the party membership cards that each of the three main parties required people to produce on demand. When challenged by party inspectors checking party affiliation at roadblocks, they produced whichever card favored the moment. Illiterate persons used various mnemonic devices to aid them in distinguishing among the three cards. One device frequently resorted to by men wearing trousers took advantage of the garment's pockets. Challenged by *Fretilin* operatives, a man would pull out the card he had in his left pocket. He had heard that *Fretilin* was the party of the left. If the inspectors were *União Democrática Timorense*, then the man would withdraw the card he had in his right pocket. He had been told this was the party of the right. At an *Apodeti* roadblock, the card would come from his back pocket: "The shit's in the back pocket."[69]

Same sub-district

Of all the massacres that followed in the wake of the rebellion, none gained more notoriety than that inflicted by *União Democrática Timorense* diehards on eight *Fretilin* students of the *União Nacional de Estudantes Timorense*, who had taught in *Fretilin*'s literacy program. The murders took place in the sub-district of Same, on August 28, and were the killings to which Ramos-Horta referred.[70] Today, the remains of the victims lie buried in five graves a few meters from the Timor Sea in a cemetery dedicated to them at a site called We Dau Berek, to the south of Same town. Among the names poignantly inscribed on the only five crosses that were standing when I visited the site on February 27, 2007 were those of Domingo Ribeira (younger brother of Alkatiri's wife), Sabinos Pereira, Ponciano C. Ribeiro, a "Domingos," who lacked a surname on his cross, and a Lobato brother. The youngest was 16 years old.

In his testimony at the CAVR hearings, Ilídio Maria de Jesus, a *Fretilin* man, provided his own perspective, describing how, at the end of August, *União Democrática Timorense* troops, fleeing from *Fretilin* forces, took 11 *Fretilin* persons they had captured to Natarbora and Besusu, on the south coast.[71] The group included his father, José Maria; a man called Ponciano, who was the regional secretary of *Fretilin*; Sabino Soares Pereira, vice-secretary of the party; Bernardino Hornai, another vice-secretary; António Guterres, a sub-delegate; Domingos Lobato, president of the *União Nacional de Estudantes de Timor*; and Quiquito Kaduak, Francisco, Domingos Ribeiro, Alexandre da Costa, and Tonito Ribeiro. Tonito and Domingos Ribeiro, Ponciano's sons, were taken away by truck and executed near Meti-Oan Beach. He saw his father's corpse, sometime later, and the hands covered the man's intestines that oozed out of the bullet holes in his stomach. One of Domingos Ribeiro's hands had been sliced off.

Atsabe sub-district

Atsabe was a sub-district whose *liurai* constantly changed their political loyalties, sometimes supporting the colonial administration, and, at other times, opposing it. In World War II, the Gonçalves family began by lending support to the Japanese, but as soon as the invaders looked like they might lose, the family switched to the Portuguese cause. When Guilherme Gonçalves helped found a pro-Indonesian party it was therefore no surprise, though, as remarked in Chapter Three, that not all the residents of Atsabe followed their *liurai's* choice.[72]

Gari-Wai *suku*

Gari-Wai, a *suku* on the border between the two sub-districts of Baucau and Venilale, in Baucau district, included a community called Mau-Kali, the inhabitants of which had, for several years, held grievances against their neighbors and for years had been contriving an excuse to secede from the *suku*. When, therefore, the population of Gari-Wai decided to support the *União Democrática Timorense*, the residents of Mau-Kali took advantage of the political cover afforded by party allegiances to throw in their lot with *Fretilin*. This defining statement of alienation provoked some Gari-Wai residents to trespass upon Mau-Kai land, smash pots, and inflict other nuisance damage. They shed no blood; but they had made their point.[73]

Uato Lari sub-district and Uato Carabau sub-district

The present account has called attention to the sub-districts of Uato Lari and Uato Carabau in the context of their histories of 1959 on several occasions. As Francisco Xavier do Amaral had found inspiration from the curious episode of that year, and Abílio Araújo chose to consider the event something of a "landmark" in the growth of political opposition to Portuguese colonialism,[74] so did *Apodeti* leaders find ammunition for rhetorical broadsides, including a resort to hagiography, in the person of one António da Costa Soares.[75] Given the wide-spread lack of support for *Apodeti* throughout the colony, one can argue that, *pace* Xavier do Amaral and Araújo, the so-called "uprising" was of relatively greater significance for *Apodeti* than for *Fretilin*.[76]

In no sub-district did ideological orientation mask local grudges more than in these two adjoining sub-districts. Party affiliation cloaked long-held antagonisms between clans, lineages, families, and individuals; and the roots of some were deeply entrenched in the bloody soils of the Japanese occupation, and kept on the boil by more contemporary grievances, for which 1959 served as a trope to further incitement.[77] As Janet Gunter remarks, "the events of 1974–1975 effectively aligned the rebellion of 1959 with the pro-Indonesian clans of eastern Timor."[78] As the Portuguese flag had served as a tangible metaphor for the *União Democrática Timorense* in the first year of the campaign, so did the year 1959 assume intangible iconic status in the verbal imagery of *Fretilin* and *Apodeti*, as *liurai*, among others, manipulated it to serve their respective interests locally.[79] There is no consensus among those who have written of the affair about the details of what occurred, nor their relative significance, but what we do know suggests that what happened hardly merited the epithet "uprising."[80]

On March 2, 1959, 14 members of an Indonesian secessionist movement called *Piagam Perdjuangan Permesta*, the "Charter of the Common Struggle," allegedly in fear of retaliation by the Indonesian Government, fled from Kupang and crossed over the border into Oe-Cussi where they requested political asylum from the colonial authorities.[81] Asylum was duly granted, and the administration allowed the men to make their way to Dili. Although it has never been determined whether the Indonesian consul encouraged whatever anti-colonial subterfuge they may have been scheming, it was common knowledge that, after leaving the capital, they began a campaign of intrigue that involved contacting whatever anti-colonial elements they could unearth among the Timorese. The administration got wind of what was going on, and the police commander in Dili arrested several of them. Five days later, on June 6, in Viqueque town, the administrator, Artur Ramos, tried to detain a suspect implicated in the network the Indonesian refugees had established, a man called António da Costa Soares, but he eluded capture, and escaped to Uato Lari. There, he linked up with some of the Indonesian refugees and certain disaffected Timorese whose possible goal was to embarrass the colonial government in that sub-district and in its neighbor, Uato Carabau. Cutting telephone lines, they isolated the two sub-districts, sowing seeds for a wild succession of violent acts in which houses were set on fire and the Portuguese flag was dragged down from its post. Ossu, Viqueque town, and Uato Lari were also targeted, and the general mayhem caused Governor Filipe José Freire Temudo Barata to dispatch *Segunda Linha* troops billeted in Lospalos sub-district to Viqueque district. Thus reinforced, the administration restored its authority and order returned, though at the cost of several hundred lives. In the aftermath, 58 of the local rebels were exiled to Angola, Mozambique, and Lisbon,[82] but most were eventually permitted to return home, and, 15 years later, some of these became *Apodeti*'s strongest supporters.[83]

On the surface, the uprising would have seemed ideological, but ideology was shaped by the politics of competition for land between Makassai and Naueti families, and in 1974–1975 *Apodeti* and *Fretilin* partisans in the two sub-districts did not let the history of this competition go to waste. They encouraged Naueti families to see in *Apodeti* a vehicle providing them with a more principled justification for their enmities than festering grudges about resources, and disaffected Naueti channeled their hostility towards Makassai families they thought had taken advantage of their exile in 1959 to usurp their land and otherwise benefit at their expense from their enforced absence. Memories of that year made Makassai families disinclined to throw themselves behind the pro-Portuguese *União Democrática Timorense* party, and so those wishing to align themselves with some party opted for *Fretilin*. Nevertheless, as Janet Gunter suggests, it would be too simplistic to view the hostilities entirely through the lens of ethnicity. She correctly regards "the struggle over resources," by which she means buffaloes and rice in Uato Lari sub-district, as the prime cause of hostility,[84] an assessment that correctly highlights the social geography of ill-will, in which Naueti families residing in the lowlands arrayed themselves against Makassai families residing in the mountains. Inflecting the social complexity was the variation in the wider political geography of the two sub-districts. On the whole, Uato Carabau sub-district may have tended towards *Apodeti*, whereas Uato Lari generally inclined to *Fretilin*.[85,86]

Modifying Janet Gunter's analysis somewhat, a prominent member of a *liurai* family in Viqueque town, Luís Gonzaga Soares, stressed the influence of ethnicity and politics.[87] In his interview, he described the relationship between the two ethnolinguistic groups in Manichean-like terms, and, by way of emphasizing this characterization, pointed to what had occurred after *Fretilin* had run the *União Democrática Timorense* out of East Timor. *Fretilin* rewarded the Makassai of Uato Lari and Uato Carabau by giving them land that belonged to Naueti families, as well as jobs. No retaliatory murders, however, were reported. With the advent of the Indonesian Army, *Apodeti* came into its own, and the Naueti were privileged. When the *Angkatan Bersenjata Republik Indonesia* left East Timor in 1999, the Makassai regained their political advantages, and their properties were restored. This dialectical conundrum has yet to be resolved within the legal system.

Viqueque sub-district

After the new protocols of "decolonization" went into effect in the *suku* of Viqueque sub-district in 1975, local elections were held to "democratize" the system. Every one of the "traditional" incumbents was returned to power, nine of them, of course, *União Democrática Timorense* members. The exception, *liurai* Miguel Soares, supported *Apodeti* because of affinal bonds; his daughter, Mariazinha, having married *Apodeti*'s *secretário geral*, José Fernando Soares.[88]

Once news of the revolt in Dili reached Viqueque, the administrator, Alfredo Lemos Pinto, wasted no time heading for the capital, leaving his duties to be assumed by his *secretário do posto*, Anacleto, a Timorese,[89] his rapid exit said to have been prompted by his having no resources to prevent any fighting that he suspected might break out between local *União Democrática Timorense* and *Fretilin*. Pockets of *Fretilin* supporters, sufficiently numerous to have caused real trouble, were present; but by late August, even *União Democrática Timorense* villagers had come round to the view that independence (*ukun rasik-an*) should be their preferred goal, a rethinking that brought the two parties into closer alignment than had been the case in Dili during the coalition. When I interviewed Viqueque town residents in 2005, they were proud of the irenic atmosphere that had obtained between the parties in their sub-district 30 years previously, and contrasted it with the poisonous hostility that dominated in Dili, Aileu, and Maubisse. There was some violence, however, and even a few deaths, but reliable statistics are lacking, and estimates of how many people lost their lives vary. One interlocutor mentioned a single killing, of a man in Barique, a *suku* in Lacluta sub-district;[90] another told me there had been "a lot."[91] Unsurprisingly, given the political landscape of Viqueque, all attributed the death, or deaths, to *Fretilin*, and, while persons with different party loyalties generally left each other alone, a careless word could lead to a brawl.

When *Fretilin* troops from the capital arrived soon after August 11, and their commanders arrested all the *liurai*, the general comity in the town appreciably declined. Families having connections with the *União Democrática Timorense* or otherwise wary of *Fretilin* intentions, prudently decided to hide in the forests outside the town, and only during the third week of December, when the *Angkatan Bersenjata Republik Indonesia* battalion entered town, did they return.[92] The newcomers appointed an Ossu native, Jaime Carvalho, as acting administrator of the Viqueque district, chosen because he was of *Apodeti* and had been with the *Movimento Anti-Comunista* when it fled crossed the border.

Whereas the response of the upperclass Domingos de Sousa, when he knew the *União Democrática Timorense* had lost the war, was one of resignation, the reaction of another Viqueque man, an *ema foho* villager, José Pereira, when *he* was overtaken by events, was anything but passive. In his quick-witted response to the rebellion and its aftermath, Pereira demonstrated the purposeful initiative we saw in Jerry Desousa. I first came to know him in December 1966, when he was a *suku* lad of 14 years old who lacked any influential connections, and with a limited elementary education appeared to have no opportunity for social advancement.[93] With the rebellion his chance came, and 39 years later he described how he had taken advantage of it and had used the event to transform his life, opening doors to opportunities he had never imagined possible for a boy born to a *foho* family.

Social elevation and economic advancement were far from his mind, however, when the shooting began that August morning: his thoughts were on "survival."[94] Conscripted into the *Forças Armadas Portuguêses em Timor* two years earlier, Pereira had carried out his military training in Aileu before being posted to Dili at a time when the army could still be counted on as being loyal to the *União Democrática Timorense*. He chose, therefore, to identify himself as

União Democrática Timorense. On the morning of the rebellion, Pereira was with his fellow soldiers in Dili, and, since he had a nose for danger, decided to head for Viqueque on the fastest vehicle he could find. Finding a military truck, he rounded up a few like-minded soldiers, and told his commanding officer he needed to protect them; "protection" for Pereira meant escorting the men to Viqueque town where his family resided. When the little group arrived, they were brought to a halt by three *Fretilin* soldiers who had noticed Pereira was not attired in the fatigues *Fretilin* militia customarily wore. They questioned him, and, suspicious about his alleged *Fretilin* bona fides, decided to detain him in the former Administrator Pinto's house under armed guard, together with a man called Anacleto and one other suspect. Pereira, though, is a plausible character, and he convinced his captors he was truly *Fretilin.* Won over, they inducted him into the local contingent of the *Segunda Linha* and made him responsible for guarding the town's telecommunications centre at the airport on the edge of the town. José Pereira continued playing the part of a committed member of *Fretilin* until the news reached Viqueque that the *Angkatan Bersenjata Republik Indonesia* was only 60 kilometers away in Baucau and approaching fast. Since prospects looked grim for any *Fretilin* supporter, Pereira abandoned the town for the adjacent village of Mamulak, where he closeted himself in his family's hamlet of Baria Laran.[95] Apprehensive his former comrades would find him if he stayed in his parental house, he decided to camp out at night in a succession of local gardens. His betrayal had infuriated his former comrades so much that they were determined to spare no pains finding him, and relentlessly searched the gardens for what they described as "this dangerous man."[96] For greater safety, Pereira decided to head northwards into the ragged fastness of the Mundo Perdido Mountain, with his parents. There, they remained until word reached them that the first Indonesian troops had entered Viqueque town and that they numbered among them colleagues he had known in the Timorese Army. He made up his mind to go back to the town. Arriving there, he recognized a group of his old army mates from the Dili garrison, and hailed them. They told him they had been among the *Movimento Anti-Comunista* troops who had fled over the border after *Fretilin* had taken Batugadé, but were now with the *Angkatan Bersenjata Republik Indonesia.* Pereira reciprocated with a suitably tailored account of his own adventures, and so impressed them that in no time at all they welcomed him into their company. Before long, the newcomers discovered that their prodigal brother-in-arms had greater fluency in *Bahasa Indonesia* than they, and that they now had a trustworthy interpreter who could help them deal with the Indonesian commandant, who had not been impressed by their command of his national tongue. They took Pereira to the officer and introduced him as one of their own. Pereira's personality and ability to speak Indonesian caused the commandant to bring the young man to the attention of his fellow officers, and they came to like Pereira so much they invited him to join the Indonesian Army. Not possessing "the heart of a military man," he declined; but when they asked him if he would like to become an agricultural officer for Viqueque district he did say "yes." Pereira knew nothing about agronomy, but that did not matter: the officers were willing to sponsor his training in agrarian science in Java. So off to Java he went. When he completed his course of studies, Pereira returned to East Timor to spend the duration of the Indonesian occupation working in various jobs, and when the United Nations Transitional Administration in East Timor (UNTAET) assumed responsibility for running the country in 1999 the organization found a ready use for his knowledge of languages and common sense. By 2009, Pereira was working for the *Deutsche Gesellschaft für Technische Zusammenarbeit (GTZ)* an NGO[97] for which he became a well-established employee, possessed of ample wealth and respected by all as a man of substance. Having earlier married into to the da Costa Soares family, the most prestigious *liurai* family in Viqueque, José Pereira had emerged as a man of distinction.

Oe-Cussi district

There was little violence in Oe-Cussi, possibly because of its remoteness from the other districts. A minor, international, incident did occur during the first few days of August 1975, which Mário Pires describes as being caused by the Indonesian Army's firing off guns along the border in a possible attempt at intimidating local farmers, but peace was restored in a cordial exchange of letters between the two respective governors.[98] In any case, the confrontation was not between Timorese; and Oe-Cussi remained undisturbed by the battle of words for the entire 20 months. Even the Indonesian invasion scarcely ruffled the tranquility of a district that, given its location, one might have supposed would have been dominated by *Apodeti*. But then, it might have been that the Indonesian Government regarded its geographical propinquity to the Republic sufficient to make that party's presence unnecessary.

Notes

1 CAVR (2006 Part 3: 42).
2 CAVR (2006: 42). Testimony of Francisco Xavier do Amaral.
3 Nicol (1978: 303).
4 CAVR (2006 Part 3: 43).
5 "*Este acto, a que estiveram presentes delegados, dos três partidos terminou em emotiva jornada de confraternizção, em contrast flagrante com o ambiente de Díli…*" Pires (1991: 192).
6 Alaríco Fernandes later described these men as the "real fighters" (Schollay 2003).
7 The administrator of Ainaro district, reputedly a *União Democrática Timorense* man, was utterly ineffectual, according to the report of a Portuguese prisoner interviewed in the Schollay video. When *Fretilin* took Ainaro, the administrator was on his way to Dili after having received a telephone call from a source well connected with *União Democrática Timorense* advising him to go to Dili "very quickly." He set out for the capital and in Maubisse talked with the captain of the battalion stationed there. He then returned to the local guesthouse (*pousada*), where his party (which included the interviewee) was staying and announced that they were remaining in Maubisse. After the news of the attack on the garrison came through, the group sought protection from the captain, but was refused on the grounds that were he to accept them then he would

have to accept the Chinese who lived in the town. When *Fretilin* took over Maubisse he was interrogated by the secretary-general of *Fretilin*, who informed him that while he had nothing personally against him, because his interrogator had seen his mother in Dili with a friend who was in the *União Democrática Timorense*, the secretary-general would have to have him committed to the officers' mess, which served as Maubisse's makeshift prison.

8 Madeira (Interview 2009).

9 CAVR (2006 Part 3: 42).

10 Whoever reads the *Timor-Leste*, a publication published by *Fretilin* during this period, contends Thomaz (1977: 86), cannot fail to detect a certain sense of juvenile adventure about the zestful activities of the *Fretilin* leaders. And why not? Their quick triumph over their rivals had conferred upon them a sense of well-deserved brio.

11 Ramos-Horta (1996: 55).

12 Cf. Hicks (2004: 49).

13 Sousa (2003).

14 "We did not restrict foreigners in East Timor" (Ramos-Horta 1996: 55).

15 As it turned out, from this time on, the Church, which in all its hundreds of years' of proselytizing had never succeeded in converting the large numbers of Timorese pagans it aimed for, began its spectacular emergence as the first pan-East Timorese institution the country had ever known, its clergy and nuns sustaining the *ema foho* with moral, emotional, and educational support throughout the Indonesian occupation.

16 Jolliffe (1978: 161).

17 Nicol (1978: 304–305).

18 Nicol (1978: 304–305). This statement contradicts the claim Suharto made to Ford and Kissinger that "The local kings are ... on our side."

19 Ramos-Horta (1996: 58–59).

20 Ramos-Horta (1996: 58).

21 Acting, Ramos-Horta says, upon his personal recommendation.

22 Pires (1991: 296, 300).

23 Willenson and Acoca (1975: 45). Though he might, at least, have replied to some of the cables coming from Governor Pires and, later, from the *Fretilin* de facto administration.

24 He served two terms in office. The first was from 1976 to 1981, and the second was from 1981 to 1986.

25 Ramos-Horta (1996: 59).

26 Carrascalão (2006: 118).

27 As he had all along, Suharto was strongly opposed to including the United Nations in any discussions about East Timor.

28 Ramos-Horta (1996: 60).

29 It included a statement that the Indonesian Government "reiterates" its position that recognizes Portugal as the only authority in Portuguese Timor until "the moment" that the people of Portuguese Timor exercise their "legal rights of self-determination" (*Relatório do Governo de Timor* 1981: 307). The memorandum is reproduced in *Integrasi* (1976: 319).

30 McDonald (1981: 207–208).

31 McDonald (1981: 207).

32 McDonald (1981: 208).

33 CAVR (2006 Part 3, pages 46, 48).

34 The following account relies on CAVR (2006 Part 3, pages 51–52).

35 Atabae is considerably nearer the north coast of Timor than Atsabe.

36 The source for these extracts is Ramos-Horta (1996: 72).

37 CAVR (2006 Part 3: 33).

38 Carrascalão (2006: 116).

39 Even before *Fretilin* occupied Batugadé in mid-September, the *Movimento Anti-Comunista* forces stationed in Balibó had already abandoned Balibó whose residents, including Chinese merchants, had already crossed into Atambua (Carrascalão 2006: 112).

40 Dunn (2003: 199–201).

41 Carrascalão (2006: 116).

42 "*Mas tarde, em Kupang, no Hotel Florbamor*, João da Silva Tavares *mostrou-me um relógio de pulso que, disse, ser pertença de um desse jornalistas e que o iria guarder como uma recordação da sua participação na 'eliminação desses inimigos'*" (Carrascalão 2006: 116).

43 Conboy (2003: 239). *Seroja* is the Indonesian word for "lotus."

44 Conboy (2003: 240).

45 The document bears the signatures of Guilherme Maria Gonçalves who signed on behalf of *Apodeti*; Francisco X. Lopes da Cruz and Oliveira who signed on behalf of the *União Democrática Timorense*; José Martins who signed on behalf of *Klibur Oan Timur Asuwa'in*; and Domingos C. Pereira who signed on behalf of the *Partido Trabalhista* (Noor 1977: 22–24).

46 Enclosure of the Annex to Letter dated December 4, 1975 from the permanent representative to Indonesia addressed to the secretary-general, A/C. 4/808 (Krieger, ed., 1997: 40).

47 Prior to the Balibo Declaration there were three other documents declaring or requesting integration with Indonesia: the Suai Declaration, the Bobonaro Declaration, and the Batugade Petition. Indonesian agents were involved in drafting at least the first two and put pressure on some of those Timorese to sign (CAVR 2006 Part 3: 57).

48 Dunn (1996: 277).

49 Only after the invasion was a fait accompli did the Security Council bestir itself. But by then, all the world organization could do was to denounce the Indonesian invasion and for the next 24 years continue to insist – futilely – that Portugal was the legitimate agency representing East Timor.

50 The two American leaders, it will be recalled, had reservations about the Indonesian army using weapons supplied by the United States.

51 Dunn (2003: 243–244).

52 Conboy (2003: 245).

53 Conboy (2003: 245).

54 Thomaz (1977: 94).

55 "*Não esqueçamos, porém, que as rivalidades entre famílias, sucos e reinos não eram menores que há quatro séculos, e que a barbárie dos antigos tempos estava muito menos morta do que adormcida…*" (Thomaz 1977: 25).

56 Sousa (2003).

57 The prisons in Dili and Aileu witnessed some ugly scenes, according to Ramos-Horta (Interview 2005).

58 Ramos-Horta (Interview 2005).

59 Ramos-Horta (Interview 2005).

60 Texeira (Interview 2005).

61 Soares (Interview 2005).

62 Ramos-Horta (Interview 2005).

63 Soares (Interview 2005).

64 Ramos-Horta (Interview 2005).

65 Ramos-Horta (Interview 2005).

66 See below.

67 CAVR (2005: 22–23).

68 As it would, again, under the Indonesian occupation.

69 Ramos-Horta (Interview 2005). As one reviewer has pointed out, Timorese did not know the Western political spectrum of "left" and "right," so the story may be apocryphal.

70 By which time, the *União Democrática Timorense* was already a spent force.
71 CAVR (2005: 16–17).
72 Soares, Fernando (Interview 2005); Ramos-Horta (Interview 2005); Texeira (Interview 2005).
73 Ramos-Horta (2005 Interview).
74 Hill (2002: 51).
75 See page 190.
76 Sousa (Interview 2005) suggested that most villages in the sub-districts were *Fretilin*.
77 Gunter (2007: 33).
78 Gunter (2007: 36–37).
79 Sousa (Interview 2005).
80 Among the most useful sources on this event are Chamberlain (2009), Gunn (2014), Gunter (2007), Hill (2002: 49–51), and Jolliffe (1978: 48–49).
81 Gunter (2007: 27). Her "Communal Conflict in Viqueque and the 'Charged' History of '59" contain an abundance of valuable information on the events of that year.
82 Hill (2002: 50).
83 For an Indonesian slant on the so-called "uprising" see Tomodok (1994: 61).
84 Gunter (2007: 36).
85 Mário Carrascalão expressed this opposition in absolute terms (CAVR 2004: 19).
86 But see Nicol (1978: 290).
87 Soares (Interview 2007).
88 Soares (Interview 2005).
89 An alternative source cites a member of the *liurai* family of the da Costa Soares – Luís Gonzaga Soares – as having stepped into the breach (Sousa Interview 2005).
90 Sousa (Interview 2005).
91 Soares [Simões] (Interview 2005). Included among the victims was a maid who had been in Luís Gonzaga Soares' family for a long time and who, when Soares was in the Olobai prison, took him food.
92 See the history of José Pereira below.
93 Our friendship is discussed in the first edition of *Tetum Ghosts and Kin* (Hicks 1976).
94 Pereira (Interview 2005).
95 Cf. Hicks (2004: 20).
96 In one of his interviews with me he remarked that a friend of his had told him that it is "the brave people who are killed" – redundant advice, I suspect.
97 Non-government Organization.
98 Pires (1991: 187–188).

References

Carrascalão, Mário Viegas. 2006. *"Timor: Antes Do Futuro."* Dili, Timor-Leste: Livaria Mau Huran.
Chamberlain, Ernest. 2009. *Rebellion, Defeat and Exile: The 1959 Uprising in East Timor*. Revised 2nd edition. Point Lonsdale, Australia: Ernest Chamberlain.
Conboy, Ken. 2003. *Kopassus Inside Indonesia's Special Forces*. Jakarta & Singapore: Equinox Publishing (Asia) Pte. Ltd.
Gunn, Geoffrey C. nd. "Revisiting the Viqueque Rebellion of 1959." Available at: http://geoffreycgunn.com/material/draft_viquequerebellion.pdf. Accessed May 17, 2014.
Gunter, Janet. 2007. "Communal Conflict in Viqueque and the 'Charged' History of '59." *The Asia Pacific Journal of Anthropology* 8, no. 1: 27–41.
Hicks, David. 1976. *Tetum Ghosts and Kin: Fieldwork in an Indonesian Community*. Palo Alto: Mayfield Publishing Company.
Hicks, David 2004. *Tetum Ghosts and Kin: Fertility and Gender in East Timor*. Waveland Press, Inc.: Prospect Heights, Illinois. 2nd edition. 2004.

Hill, Helen. 2002. *Stirrings of Nationalism in East Timor: Fretilin 1974–78, The Origins, Ideologies and Strategies of a Nationalist Movement*. Kuala Lumpur and Díli. Contemporary Otford, Otford Press, Ortford (Sydney).

Jolliffe, Jill. 1978. *East Timor: Nationalism and Colonialism*. Brisbane: University of Queensland Press.

Integrasi: Kebulatan Tekad Rakyat Timor Timur. 1976. Jakarta, Indonesia: Yayasan Parikesit.

Krieger, Heike (ed.). 1997. *East Timor and the International Community: Basic Documents*. Cambridge: Cambridge University Press.

McDonald, Hamish. 1981. *Suharto's Indonesia*. Blackburn, Victoria, Australia: The Dominion Press and Fontana/Collins.

Nicol, Bill. 1978. *Timor: The Stillborn Nation*. Melbourne: Widescope International Publishers Pty Ltd.

Noor, Machmuddin, Slamet Moeljono, and Sujamto and H. Soemarno (eds.). 1977. *Lahirnya Propinsi Timor Timur: Dokumentasi Tentang Proses Dekolonisasi Timor Timur Dan Pembentukan Propinsi Daerah Tingkat I Timor Timur*. Jakarta: Badan Penerbit Almanak Republik Indonesia/BP Alda Jalan Tambak 12A.

Pires, Mário Lemos. 1991. *Descolonização de Timor: Missão Impossível?* 3rd edition. Lisbon: Publicações Dom Quixote, Lda.

Ramos-Horta, José. 1996. *Funu – The Unfinished Saga of East Timor*. Lawrenceville, N.J.: The Red Sea Press, Inc.

Relatório do Governo de Timor. 1981. Presidência do Conselho de Ministros: Lisbon, Portugal.

Scambary, James. 2011. *"Anatomy of a Conflict: The 2006–7 Communal Violence in East Timor,"* in Vandra Harris and Andrew Goldsmith (eds.). *Security, Development and Nation-Building in Timor-Leste: A Cross-sectoral Assessment*. pp. 59–79. London and New York: Routledge.

Schollay, Clive. 2003 (24 October). *East Timor Reconciliation: Scenes from Timor, September 1975* [Video]. Screen Sound Australia Video, National Screen and Sound Archive, VHS C10131, I.D. 50112–01–5 Reels, 153 minutes 30 seconds.

Sousa, Domingos de. 2003. *Olobai 75. Baucau, East Timor: Gráfica Diocesana Baucau.*

Thomaz, Luís Filipe F.R. 1977. *Timor: Autopsia de Uma Tragedia*. Lisbon, Portugal: Author, distributed by Dig/livro.

Tomodok, E.M. 1994. *Hari-Hari Akhir Timor Portugis*. Jakarta: Pustaka Jaya.

Interviews

Madeira, Maria. Interview 2009.
Pereira, José Henriques. Interview 2005.
Ramos-Horta, José. Interview 2005.
Soares, Luís Francisco de Gonzaga. Interview 2005.
Soares, Luís Francisco de Gonzaga. Interview 2007.
Soares, Tereza da Luz Simões. Interview 2005.
Sousa, Domingos de. Interview 2005.
Texeira, José. Interview 2005.

9   Rhetoric

1974–1975

*What really divided these two centrist parties [UDT and Fretilin], however,
were the militant ideologues on their extremes who accused each other, and
by extension, each other's parties of being "fascist' or "communist."*

(CAVR 2006 Part 3: 24)

2012

Press release

FM [Fundasaun Mahein] Calls for an End to Inflammatory Rhetoric

*In late February of this year, Fundasaun Mahein (FM) condemned PNTL
General Commander, Longuinhos Monteiro's order to his officers to shoot
on sight anyone trying to derail the general elections following the actions
of unknown persons who threw Molotov Cocktail bombs at the offices of the
Secretariat For Technical Electoral Support (STAE). We argued that this
was another demonstration that the PNTL was not a 'community-oriented'
police force and that the PNTL had once again proven to be a typical reactionary force, always reacting with excessive force after a crime has been
committed. (PNTL commander accentuates the rise of violence, 23rd of
February: www.fundasaunmahein.org/2012/02/23/komandu-pntl-haforsa-
numeru-violensia/). Last week, local media (DN Independente 04rd of
March quoted the Timorese Defense Force (F-FDTL) Commander, Major
General Lere Anan Timur giving out a similar statement, threatening to
shoot dead anyone who will commit acts of violence during the general
election period. Once again FM laments the very violent tone of this
comment, which serves only to accentuate tensions and increase trauma and
fear among the general population. This also serves as a barrier to ordinary
citizens to actively participate in the democratic process of choosing our
country's next head of state. FM would like to remind the commanders of
both security forces of the rights of citizens as enshrined in the relevant laws
and Constitution of the RDTL. The role of the F-FDTL & PNTL is to protect*

and serve the community and to uphold the rule of law. We have a system of justice and our security forces cannot take the law into their own hands by applying the system of shoot first, ask later. FM calls on both security forces to actively engage with communities instead of using such violent rhetoric. The traditional Timorese form of dialogue Nahe biti Boot could be used as a model for both the F-FDTL & PNTL when engaging with the community. Their role is to maintain order and security while upholding the rule of law and FM once again calls for greater integration of both force's operations and activities during this election period. FM also recommends that commanders of both the police and army instead make statements that are problem solving oriented. They could use their positions of influence to call attention to politicians to steer away their militants from confrontation so as to create a peaceful democratic process. Timor-Leste is a small nation but nonetheless well known internationally and FM hopes our country can set an example to other post-conflict countries.

(Fundasaun Mahein March 9, 2012)

Politicians of all the parties struggled to convince people of the superior merits of their different platforms, and understood that myths, clichés, catchwords, and sound-bites that make up the stuff of international political rhetoric could also serve as their own tools of persuasion. Accordingly, they sold their platforms using whatever verbal imagery seemed appropriate to their audiences in the capital and in the *foho*.

Narratives

Susan Rodgers has described how oral narratives facilitate political rhetoric in non-literate societies; Robert Paine has shown the authority of language in instigating political action;[1] and Murray Jacob Edelman has argued that what may be called political "events" are often no more than fabrications made by the language used to "describe" them for constituencies not directly observing them. He reminds us that what may be experienced as a disorderly multitude of impressions requires to be ordered if meaning is to be discerned in them: "Language performs a crucial function by creating shared meanings, perceptions, and reassurances among mass publics."[2] Combined with these suggestions of Rodgers and Paine, Edelman helps us understand rather more clearly how politicians use language to create illusions – "smoke and mirrors" – as they persuade others to support their agendas. In East Timor, the capital politicians' fabrication of "instant" myths to authenticate their respective visions of the future is once such instance, and I shall return to this matter later in the present chapter.[3] *Fretilin* and *Apodeti* narratives took advantage of both the Aristotelian political and forensic modes of rhetoric in their anticipating an imagined "mythological future," while, at the same time, retrospectively glancing back to an invented past that had never existed, but which, they contended, sanctioned their visions of the future. The *Klibur Oan Timur Asua'in's* own version of this Janus model envisioned a future that revivified its leaders' imagined recollections of a past that was as different from its rivals as it was as illusory. Not to be outdone, the *União Democrática Timorense* employed forensic rhetoric to represent the past-as-the-present. On the other hand, and in contrast with the language emanating from Dili, the verbal arts by which the *foho* convinced its denizens of the merits of their *lisan* required no newly-minted narratives. The "words of the ancestors," issuing forth from the primordial past, sufficed for their understanding of the meaning of their existences, or so they believed. Whether in the guise of Malinowskian "charter myths" or as Hobsbawmian "invented traditions," the language of the ancestors was, for them, the source of all knowledge that was authentic. In *lisan* the present, the future, and the past blended into a single time-less vision refracted through the prism of myth as well as that of narratives of more recent vintage, many of which bespoke of *suku* rivalries and personal grievances.

Years earlier and thousands of miles away, rhetoric employed by the Viet Minh had secured the support of the peasants of the Vietnam hinterland because the nationalistic aspirations of the party had already seeped into their local traditions.[4] In the Portuguese Timor of 1974 this had not occurred. Instead, the colony found itself somewhat in the condition of the Dutch East Indies at the beginning of the nineteen century, where "...there was no ground on which a national spirit could take roots, no strong links, even including the common enemy of the Dutch, to enable people to conceive of themselves as a nation."[5] The Timorese, likewise, had not had enough time to bridge the gap between the values of the capital and the institutions of the *foho*, and although claims of kinship and affinal alliance might have served as conduits between the two poles, disparities between the two were too extreme. So, even as they were in vogue among the political class in Dili, narratives possessed of a "national" or, more plausibly, a quasi-national slant, attracted less support within the narrow circum-scriptions of *suku* life. Party leaders domiciled in Dili, and the Indonesian opera-tives working out of Kupang, accordingly, had no alternative but to tap sympathetic *suku* for local leaders (some from *liurai* families; others of non-*liurai* descent) who might be willing to serve as brokers in recruiting villagers, *Liurai* Gonçalves being a case in point. By evoking collective memories of a period in Timor's past when his family's prestige was at its apogee in Atsabe sub-district,[6] the *liurai* was able to convince some of his several *suku* to join him in buying into the future *Fretilin* visualized.[7] But for all that, of course, some vil-lagers declined to follow him into that vision. We have also seen how the Uato Lari incident of 1959 was mined by both *Apodeti* and *Fretilin* for imagery that might persuade, even as the *União Democrática Timorense's* close ties with the colonial administration prevented that party from exploiting *that* particular narrative.[8]

Peel's suggestion that "fashioning a future social order entails a constant revaluation of the past"[9] finds exemplification in the language in which both *Fretilin* and *Apodeti* wove their own meanings into the past. By reinterpreting the past to suit its goal of a future independent state that would be grounded in socialistic principles,[10] ~~*Fretilin* sought to persuade, not only *suku* chiefs, but~~ ~~other locally ambitious men to subvert the status quo in those *suku* that~~ ~~remained loyal to the Portuguese.~~ Where village constituencies permitted, these chiefs and ambitious men willingly allowed their *suku* to be seduced by the *Fretilin* vision in anticipation of future political preferment in an independent nation. They hoped for huge improvements in education and agricultural practices, land reform, and jobs substantial enough to reward the efforts they were expending on their party when it became the government. ~~Central to~~ ~~*Fretilin*'s persuasive strategy was a forensic narrative "proving" that *Fretilin*~~ ~~was merely restoring to eastern Timor a unity, a nationalistic inclusiveness,~~ ~~which the Portuguese had vitiated, even though the myth was at odds with~~ ~~eyewitnesses' reports of inter-kingdom fighting from the time the first missionary, Friar António Taveira, began his pastoral work in Lifão in the middle~~ ~~of the sixteenth century.~~[11] Although kingdoms had been knitted together by kinship, affinity, and political alliances before the advent of the Europeans, *Fretilin*'s narrative of a unified polity covering all of East Timor was refuted by history.[12] "Fiction acting as history" also forestalled a myth contrived by *Apodeti* that told of the entire island of Timor (east no less than west) being encompassed by a greater Indonesian state, the celebrated Majapahit of the thirteenth and fourteenth centuries, a claim that found useful material for embellishing the events of 1959.[13] A brochure entitled *O célebre massacre de Uato-Lari e Uato-Carabau Verificado No Ano de 1959*, written by Loyola Jordão de Araújo,[14] and published in Jakarta, casts the events of March to June of that year in such a way as to define the incident as the founding moment, even the founding "movement," for the integration of Portuguese Timor into Indonesia.[15]

Just as the two anti-Portuguese parties fabricated pseudo-histories to suit the demands of their respective platforms, so did the *Klibur Oan Timur Asuwa'in* use events endowed with more historical credibility to make the past serve the interests of the present. On January 26, 1975, its leaders ostentatiously proclaimed their platform at the party's inauguration in a ritual dramatizing their "Message ... for the Portuguese People:"

> In the Oath celebrated between the *régulo* (rajas) [i.e., *liurai*] and the Portuguese of the bygone era, figured a compromise of honour undertaken to carry out [*sic*] by both parts equally. From the Timorean [*sic*] part, there was a performance of compromise as sealed up by the Timorean régulos of yore with the first Portuguese callers who set their feet on this land. The Oath was accomplished with blood-letting of both Timorean régulos and the Portuguese elements present, mixed with wine, and such mixed wine was shared and drunk by all jurors, thus sealing the Pact of Eternal Alliance amongst the peoples who made contact and got known. In compliance of their compromise, Timorean [*sic*] people have show their almost religious and undying love and consecration to the Flag of Portugal, including sacrifices in holocaust on the altar of the Portuguese Fatherland, throughout the

history of colonisation ... Timor is a unique case in the history of peoples – it is a unique fact that testifies the presence of Portugal in this place.

(Nicol 1978: 53)

Rather more attuned with ethnographic reality than the narratives of the other two parties it may have been, but the ritual it dramatized had nevertheless been consigned to folk memory for centuries, in a somewhat similar fashion to the Angkola Batak, of northern Sumatra, who also used political language to evoke the past. Their "old ... chiefdoms and village alliances [had] largely ceased to exist as temporal, political realities," writes Susan Rodgers, "but ... continued to exist in the [speech-making sessions] as essentially kingdoms of words."[16]

Eva-Lotta Hedman and John Sidel have pointed out that false reconfigurations of the past (sometimes invented by the colonialists themselves) are common features of rhetoric in post-colonial Southeast Asia.[17] On Java, the Dutch encouraged the local aristocracy to elaborate their presumed "Javanese" court culture "in accordance with Dutch Javanologists' advice and authority." In the Federated Malay States, the British "inspired" local sultans to codify and regulate Islamic law and *adat*; and French authorities, bewitched by Angkor's beautiful monuments, went so far as to chide the "Khmers" for not living up to "their" glorious heritage. There were, naturally, exceptions to such evocations of the past. Like East Timor at the time of the Carnation Revolution, "a deafening silence reigned" across the Philippines.

In harnessing the past to serve their platforms of the present, the parties found stellar names to suit the purposes of hagiography. *Dom* Aleixo Corte Real, acclaimed by the Portuguese as a great patriot, was the *União Democrática Timorense's* luminary, and *Fretilin's* national hero was the anti-Portugal *liurai*, Dom Boaventura. Not to be outdone, sifting through the murky detritus 1959, *Apodeti* unearthed the name of António da Costa Soares and transformed an otherwise insignificant "Timorese political actor" into a figure of heroic stature:[18] "The party attempted to present itself as a product of the first legitimate Timorese political actors, pre-dating the 'new' parties established in 1974 [...] language [that] helped provide the justification for the annexation of Timor" (Gunter 2007: 35–36). Costa Soares, however, was not some remote figure culled from a distant past, but a flesh and blood contemporary hero whose apotheosis came in August 1975 when *Fretilin* men executed him in Aileu during the war, thus giving *Apodeti* a martyr to match those of its two rivals. Transcending past, present, and future, "His death 'martyred' him for his support for Indonesia. From then on, his famed role in the 1959 rebellion became retrospectively associated with his pro-Indonesian stance of 1975."[19]

Like the language of the capital, that of *lisan* also contained tropes of violence. Bloody kingdom and *suku* feuds nourished many an *ema foho* narrative, and some of the stories I collected in Viqueque were of this genre. Villagers recalled, with relish, the days when their ancestors followed the king of Viqueque into battle against the queen of neighboring Luka kingdom,[20] or challenged another neighbor, Queen Hare-Manek of Bibiluto, whose kingdom had allied itself with those of Luka, Lacluta, and Ossu.[21] Although such stories did not incite violence at the time of the campaign, in the adjacent Ossu sub-district, as the administrative authority was fast disintegrating, these legendary rivalries were reflected in hotly charged verbal assaults between adherents of the three political parties. There, as in several other sub-districts, J. Stephen Hoadley's prediction, made before any intimation of war, that "Another fear expressed by the Indonesians is that rural strife will break out ... between ethnic groups..." proved prescient, though the author laid too much stress on the notion of "ethnic group."[22] Even between the Naueti and Makassai ethnolinguistic groups in Uato Lari and Uato Carabau or the Kemak and Bunaq further west, the violence resulted mainly from disputes about property rather than Dili politics, as men who had been exiled to Angola for their participation in the revolt tried to wrest back their expropriated rice fields and livestock when they came home.[23] "What had begun as basically a local domestic issue had become a clash between two political parties, with some violence resulting. It was the same elsewhere."[24]

Catchwords and slogans

Mauberism

Experimenting to find the most effective verbal formula to win over the *ema foho*, *Fretilin* hit upon what proved to be the most flamboyant verbal inspiration of the campaign. Although its influence has been overrated, the slogan, "*Mauberism*," emerged as its prime verbal shibboleth. The word itself was a masculine personal name used by the Mambai, but residents of the capital, borrowing it, converted the word into something of a derogatory antonomasia for all those who lived in hinterland. The circumstance under which it was adopted and adapted for propaganda purposes is disputed. Jorge Duarte bestows the honors for the invention upon Abílio de Araújo, but Ramos-Horta, as we have seen, claims paternity, having, so he says, glimpsed its persuasive possibilities for convincing *ema foho* to look upon themselves as *the* "*maubere*," downtrodden members of an "oppressed" class, "exploited" men and women who had suffered under the colonial yoke. But whoever was the inventor, the catchword offered a snappy complement to Abílio de Araújo's prolix pronouncements:[25]

> *Maubere* is a personal name such as 'John' or 'Mary' and is very common in East Timor. Relatively speaking there were in Timor more individuals with the name *Maubere* than 'John' or 'Mary' in Portugal. Because of this the colonialists used the name *Maubere* for any non-literate individual, a semantic expansion. In the last years of Portuguese domination, the man of the interior, one who resisted the cultural domination of colonialism, came to be called indiscriminately *Maubere*. Because *Maubere* is, in short, the Timorese man who resisted colonial acculturation, one who was the true bearer of popular culture and because of this suffered in his 'meat and bones' the worst effects of colonization.

The acerbity of Araújo's language joined with the compelling force of his convictions, to impress fellow *Fretilin* leaders and their student cadres; but his refashioned history fails the test of any close scrutiny. Unless he is referring to the incident in Uato Lari, where, incidentally, the word "*maubere*" seems not to have been used, it is difficult to know what Araújo means when he describes the Timorese as having resisted colonial acculturation. This factual shortcoming may partly help to explain why the word *mauberism* never really caught on among the *ema lisan*. The insularity of rural society meant that village people were to take much longer than the campaign lasted to even begin identifying themselves with *Fretilin*'s collective entity, "*the Maubere*." In 1974–1975 they may have seen through the catchword and recognized it for the misleading political rhetoric it was.

The conviction some writers about the period have that the word "*maubere*" referred to the *ema foho*, results in part from the assumption that the term was widely used throughout the country.[26] Jill Jolliffe,[27] for example, who numbers among its gloss the referents "poor" and "ignorant," appears to have relied upon Araújo's charge that the Europeans customarily used the term to deprecate Timorese dwelling in the hinterland. For my part, I can affirm that I have never once heard the term used in a derogatory sense by either a European or a Timorese.[28] Nor have heard it uttered by a *mestiço* or non-*mestiço*. In its official documents, the bureaucracy typically classified the *ema foho* as either "*não-civilizados*" ("non-civilized") or *atrasados* ("backward" or "undeveloped"). Paradoxically, had the term *maubere* circulated as a verbal derogation before 1974–1975, the people finding employment for it would most likely have been the *Fretilin* leaders themselves, since, unlike the *União Democrática Timorense*, some of them had little time for *lisan*. Except when they had no choice but to conform to its protocols, as with the matter of party leadership and relative age. Furthermore, by their own admission, they attempted to change *lisan* by imparting to it notions from the *malai* world. In the self-image they cultivated, the Dili elite portrayed themselves as too enlightened for *lisan* to have claims on them: *lisan* was for the illiterates in the *suku*. But they saw "*mauberism*" as a handy verbal weapon by which to excite anti-colonial sentiment in the promotion of nationalism. Jorge Duarte, himself a Mambai, queried *Fretilin*'s arrogation of the word, which in his view not only corrupted his mother tongue, but debased the dignity of the Timorese:

> If I may comment very summarily on the pretensions of *Fretilin* in presenting to national and international public opinion the people of East Timor as "*Povo Maubere*." This code word disfigures and even debases with impunity the identity of this people in view of the fact that "*Maubere*" is not an ethnonym. It is a personal name, not a generalization, only adopted in some regions of the country and used in the Portuguese of Timor [i.e., Tetum Praça] as a term of deprecation. To designate, therefore, the Timorese people as "*Povo Maubere*" is the equivalent of identifying the Portuguese people as "*Povo Zé ninguém*" ["Joe nobody"] or "*Povo Zé*" ["the Joes"].[29]

Significantly, the self-acknowledged author of the catchword is himself not all that far removed from endorsing Duarte's implied accusation of semantic speciousness. "Though vaguely defined without any serious theoretical basis," Ramos-Horta tells us, *Maubere* and *Mauberism* proved to be the single most successful political symbol of our campaign."[30] Contradicting Jorge Duarte, Ramos-Horta continued to assert ownership 30 years after its genesis, elaborating upon its history in the following words:

> I wrote an article in a journal in Timor [*Seara*], not in 1975 or in 1974, but in 1973.... When we began ASDT, in a meeting of ASDT/Fretilin, I explained that all political parties needed an image. That if we wanted to convince the electorate we could not do this with complicated philosophy.... So I said it would be good if we could identity Fretilin with Maubere like a slogan, a symbol of Fretilin's identity. It is clear that 90% of Timorese are barefoot, no papers, but they all called themselves Maubere.... It is important [to understand] there was no other philosophy to this term, it was a party identity.[31]

Ramos-Horta's claim finds a skeptical audience in Bill Nicol, who, while willing enough to embrace Ramos-Horta's authorship, nonetheless surmises that the evolution of the term *maubere* into *mauberism* had a precursor in former Indonesian President Sukarno's *marhaenism*. "Sukarno's [philosophy] was known as *marhaenism*. Ramos-Horta's was *mauberism*."[32] Ramos-Horta, for his part, though, denies even knowing of the word, *marhaenism*. Still, regardless of origins and semantics, *Fretilin* leaders saw in the suffix a useful plus for their campaign.

Fretilin's claim to represent "*the maubere*" went so far as to confer upon its members *maubere* status; an arrogation writers and Timorese alike have all-too readily accepted.[33] Jolliffe, for one, describes one supporter of the *Klibur Oan Timorense Asuwa'in* party as being only "superficially inaccurate" when he said that many *liurai Fretilin* leaders were really *maubere*.[34] He was, Jolliffe contends, merely giving vent to a "fundamental truism." In other words, although *Fretilin* leaders were decidedly *not* "*maubere*" in any sociological sense, they were entitled to self-identity (for political advantage) as *maubere* on the grounds that they *claimed* to empathize with those of lower social status. *Fretilin* tried to exploit this identity in order to justify its claim to represent the *ema lisan* and speak on their behalf. Like his fellow elite, José Ramos-Horta saw nothing inconsistent in his asserting that he and his colleagues "spoke the language of the people," and claiming his colleagues' right to speak on their behalf.[35] Araújo and Xavier do Amaral supported these claims in evocative language: "Are we human beings or a sack of potatoes to be sold away to another country?"; "Do you ask a slave if he wants to be free?"; "Should we crawl after the *malae*?"; "Aren't we men enough to govern ourselves?"; "Why should we remain as horses, first of the Portuguese and tomorrow of the Indonesians?"[36] In their determination to lead the *maubere*, *Fretilin* leaders revealed their own intellectual certitude, an attitude villagers would have caught and been sensitive to when they heard speeches by *Fretilin* leaders, like Francisco Xavier do Amaral, or their student followers. The peasants were only too cognizant of the enormous sociocultural gulf separating these Dili people from themselves.

Elizabeth Traube gives an instructive *aperçu* into Mambai attitudes to *Fretilin* at the time she left Timor at the end of 1974:[37]

> In Mambai ritual centres, people rallied around a traditional, back-looking ideology of domination, in defence of the hierarchical values and political arrangements that colonial practice had cumulatively eroded.... Among the demands most vociferously, not to say petulantly, articulated was that Mambai ritual leaders be consulted to legitimize any new claimants to power. In this respect, many people nurtured a sense of grievance against Fretilin for what they perceived as the party's disregard for traditional authorities.

Sensing that a catchphrase might add some punch to their own campaign, the *União Democrática Timorense* leaders made an attempt to invent some phrase of their own to rival *Fretilin*'s, but, lacking a champion word-spinner endowed with the talents of Ramos-Horta, the best they could come up with was the bland *maun-alin*. Although "elder brother-younger brother" denoted a fundamental kinship relationship, it was too commonplace to attract attention, and as a genuine term defined by an institutional referent it lacked pungency.[38]

Political novelty, of course, did not play well in the *foho*, where the insularity of the population encouraged a parochialism that proved a major hindrance to *Fretilin*'s goal of uniting hundreds of variegated local communities into a nation-state.[39] Slogans and catchwords that aspired to advance the cause of nationalism were not as effective in the *suku* as in the capital. Even the myth of the imagined Belu confederation of the sixteenth century could not induce *suku* folk to transcend the compulsive claims of their various *lisan* and begin to envision themselves as citizens of a nation-state. In October 1975, António Carvarino had urged Timorese to overcome traditional local prejudices and think in more inclusive terms. Like his kindred spirit, Abílio de Araújo, Carvarino identified "divisionism" as the Timorese people's recurrent impediment to national unity; segmentation he believed had brought about their ancestors' subjugation to the Europeans. Jill Jolliffe elaborates upon this thesis: "much *Fretilin* work [was] devoted to combating 'divisionism,' 'tribalism and regionalism'..."[40] Yet Timor's history shows that although inter-*suku* antagonisms did play some part in the colonial conquest, these were not "tribal" wars, since Timor does not have what anthropologists conventionally mean by "tribes."[41] Carvarino also applied the notion of "divisionism" to the alleged political opposition between "westerners" and "easterners." "One of the variations of tribalism," he says,

> is the division of the population into 'Loro Mono' and 'Loro Sae,' into 'Kaladis' and 'Firakus' ["westerners" and "easterners" respectively], and the

belief that some groups are superior than [*sic*] the others. Still, today, in spite of a year of clarification, we frequently hear our friends saying that 'the Firakus are better than the Kaladis' or that 'the Loro Mono are not good, the Loro Sae are the ones that are good.'[42] These ideas … in no ways help our struggle … *Fretilin* wants the unity of the people and this is only possible by eradicating the false ideas [*sic*] which come from a colonial and traditional [*sic*] society.[43]

As with Araújo, one can only wonder why Carvarino is so emphatic about a putative opposition that never became a campaign issue, and only emerged as a relevant "talking point" in January 2006 when soldiers from the western districts complained to President José Ramos-Horta that their colleagues from the eastern districts of the country received preferential treatment from the government. More recently, this issue has attracted attention from foreign scholars and Timorese intellectuals, and one conclusion reached was that this alleged "duality" was exaggerated, with insufficient ethnographic data to give it convincing sociological substance.[44] This is not to say that people did not resort to pejoratives in speaking about other ethnolinguistic groups. In the languages of their respective neighbors, the Fataluku were called "Dagadá"; the Makassai, "Firaku"; the Galoli, "Gari"; and the Mambai, "Kaladi." But such tags did not necessarily translate into political antagonisms and were less commonly resorted to than identification by place of birth or place of residence.[45] In the Tetum language, for example, an individual was identified as "*ema*+[locality]," so that a person born in Viqueque would be called *ema Wekeke*; someone living in Maubisse, *ema Maubisse*; and a man or woman from Baucau, *ema Baucau*.

Nevertheless, unnecessarily careless with the ethnography of Timorese ethnicity, language, and history, *Fretilin* leaders kept admonishing the uneducated for continuing to follow their *lisan*, which, in addition to being divisive, they regarded as outdated. At the same time, they appeared unaware that their rhetoric, in addition to reinforcing such divisions as might have existed, actually helped open up new rifts. *Fretilin* also contradicted itself. The party denounced the Portuguese for depriving the Timorese of their *lisan* while, simultaneously criticizing them for not having developed the country, a process which would have inevitably undermined *lisan*.[46] *Fretilin*'s most consequential verbal image was its adoption of the designation "*frente*" ("front"), a term resounding with possibilities, and – to more conservative ears – ominous ones. Bolstering their argument that a national consciousness actually existed, and that *Fretilin* was its political incarnation, once its leaders had changed their party's name from the *Associação Social Democratic Timorense* to *Fretilin*, in September 1974, they insisted that they alone possessed the authentic legitimacy to represent the people of Timor, a presumption that found ready verbal expression in this word.[47] *Fretilin* was no mere party. It was a *movement* representing *all* Timorese.

Invective

That the tone that marked campaign language exceeded the bounds of reasonable political discourse had already been anticipated in Abílio de Araújo's, *Timorese*

Elites. Not content with criticizing what he identified as the elite social groups in Timor, and emphasizing their negative influence on its history, Araújo misrepresented the facts of history. Araújo also dismissed those of his fellow students who preferred to continue with their studies in Portugal rather than return to East Timor and engage in political activism. They were "unfortunates" and "traitors." And, in promoting his central thesis, he did not attempt to persuade his readers by coordinating his propositions into a coherent argument. Instead, the verbal strategy he adopted was to evoke an assortment of clichéd tropes such as "colonial yoke," "exploited and oppressed people," "neo-colonialist elements," "oppressed majority," "wars of liberation," and "colonialism through its faithful lackeys and servants." These "lackeys and servants" were the *ema foho* who, he contends, were really nationalists under the skin, yearning – had they but known it – to be set free from their shackles. They had been unable to see themselves as exploited because, he implies, their devotion to *lisan* rendered them passive. Now, although it was obvious that some of the educated were dissatisfied with their lot under the Portuguese – Araújo, for one – and that others were driven by an ambition to run their country, the same could not be so unequivocally asserted for the so-called "oppressed." Most Timorese wanted nothing more than to live their lives as they had always done, working in their gardens and fields, negotiating marriage alliances, performing collective rituals, exchanging the latest *suku* gossip, and carrying out the other activities that made up the daily round of life in the *foho.* As the popular reception that greeted Dr. António de Almeida Santos, when he deplaned in Dili after his flight from Lisbon, demonstrated,[48] and as Elizabeth Traube has noted,[49] the *ema foho* wanted their "younger brothers," the Portuguese, to remain in Timor. Indeed, since various Lusitanian institutions had been integrated into "traditional" Timorese institutions to the extent that people considered them "traditional," it might be argued that the *ema foho* considered the radical culture of *Fretilin* to be more alien than Portuguese culture.

In the later stages of the campaign, of course, the language to which the *União Democrática Timorense* resorted assumed a tone as uncompromisingly divisive as that of *Fretilin*, and the "facts" it adduced as specious, as those of its rival. But if the party was unsuccessful in coming up with an effective catchword, it did succeed in smearing *Fretilin* with a label that in the long run proved decisive. A goal of *União Democrática Timorense* intention was to cast *Fretilin* as a party of communists and left-wing extremists, and a vehicle for this accusation was a polemical, anonymous, leaflet that appeared in Dili in mid-May 1975. Demanding that *Fretilin* expel four members it regarded as communist, the *União Democrática Timorense's* missive ran: "[Jorge Tomás] Carapinha, Roque [Rodrigûes], [António] Carvarino and Vicente Reis are Communist-Maoist extremists ... Mauberism is synonymous with Maoism!"[50] They were billed as "lackeys, ignorant defenders of the MRPP[51] in Timor.... The people demand the immediate expulsion of these real malefactors, because they are also traitors ... OUT WITH THE TRAITORS! He who hesitates doubts the Maubere people."[52] The leaflet was signed *"Das Armas"* ("From those who are armed"). Aimed at persuading people outside the *União Democrática Timorense*, these defamations also came to exert persuasive force on the thinking of the *União Democrática Timorense* party leaders themselves, especially on João Carrascalão and Domingos de Oliveira, who, two months later, expanded the *União Democrática Timorense* into the *Movimento Anti-Comunista de Onze de Agosto*.

While the principal executives of central *Fretilin*'s policy, Francisco Xavier do Amaral, José Ramos-Horta, and Alarico Fernandes, were not reticent about asserting their convictions as social democrats or socialists, it was the uncompromising language of António Carvarino, Roque Rodrigûes, Vicente dos Reis, Mari Alkatiri, and, Abílio de Araújo, that came to define the party's public image. Their extravagant onslaught on their rivals opened the way for President Suharto – intent auditor of every piece of provocative statement that vented forth from Dili – to successfully brand the new *Fretilin* Government as "communist" when it came into power, and proved a stigma the new government never succeeded in shaking off. *Fretilin*'s self-identification as a "front," and the hirsute appearance and military fatigues sported by most of the leaders, further consolidated its image as a party of irresponsible, dangerous, young men.[53] That this impression was false counted little at a time communists had united the two Vietnams and the specter of Chinese expanding influence in Southeast Asia caused disquiet in Washington and Jakarta. President Suharto did not encounter any difficulty turning the *Fretilin* radicals' words against the party, and characterize it as a threat to the region's stability, a threat Gerald Ford and Henry Kissinger willingly accepted. Portuguese conservative scholars also joined these world leaders in denouncing the party as communist. Luís Thomaz, for one, argues that by mid-1975 *Fretilin*'s "language" and modus operandi revealed it to be a "real" communist movement ("*um verdadeiro movimento comunista*"),[54] although Araújo has denied this label. In a newspaper interview he gave 30 years later, he stated, "The political program of *Fretilin* which I completed in its entirety, in Aileu, with my wife, Dr. Guilhermina Araújo, and was later unanimously approved by the *Comité Central da Fretilin*, is not and cannot be confused with a Marxist political program."[55]

President Suharto's denunciation of *Fretilin* climaxed a campaign of distorted propagnda that had been steadily intensifying after September 1974 in response to the first students' arrival in Dili from Portugal and started attracting notoriety in Jakarta; and anti-*Fretilin* propaganda assumed an ever-increasing stridently with the passing of the months. By January, *Operasi Komodo* was sending menacing transmissions from the Kupang radio station into the colony, misrepresenting *Fretilin* as communist and accusing the Portuguese Administration of victimizing what was characterized as the pro-Indonesian majority. By late February, as noted in Chapter Six, the Indonesian Government's press agency, *Antara*'s propaganda had reached a heightened pitch. Still, the impact this propaganda had on the Timorese was probably slight since the broadcasts were in Tetum and Portuguese, which the majority of the population did not readily understand.[56] The Australian media, meanwhile, quoted Canberra intelligence sources that suggested Jakarta might be preparing to invade.

Indonesia's narrative concerning the entire island of Timor being part of the mythical Majapahit Empire – one shared with *Apodeti* – was complemented by metaphors of kinship that included a trope reminiscent of the Mambai metaphor of elder brother/younger brother. This cast the Indonesians and the Timorese as "brothers," who "had once belonged together but had been separated by the European colonizers."[57] Another trope likened the Timorese to "lost children returning to their family" (i.e., the Indonesians). Another invited the Timorese to "return to the lap of Mother Earth," i.e., the mythological united Majapahit. On the other hand, the arguments intended for consumption by heads of government and the international press were couched in milder tones of diplomacy. It was this style of speech that reaped the greatest rewards, since it convinced Prime Minister Gough Whitlam to discount the authenticity of the Timorese politicians and persuaded João Carrascalão to attempt his foolhardy attack on the police headquarters, an action that proved the most consequential act in the whole campaign.[58] Nor was this all. For, notwithstanding *Fretilin*'s clamorous advocacy of an imaginary national movement and its self-styled championing of *the maubere*, it was the nationalistic rhetoric of Suharto, president of a genuine and well-entrenched nation-state, quietly and discreetly fed into the confiding ears of the two most powerful politicians in the world, that ultimately triumphed. The momentous meeting between Ford, Kissinger, and Suharto that day in Jakarta, December 6, 1975, brought the war of words to an end, and prepared the stage for a war of deeds that was about to commence.

Notes

1 Paine (1981).
2 Edelman (1981: 65).
3 See also Chapter 4.
4 Keyes (1977: 9).
5 Vickers (2005: 73).
6 Cf. Atkinson (1984).
7 Peel (1984: 128–129).
8 Cf. Atkinson (1984) for a very different rhetorical style of persuasion employed by an ethnic group in the Indonesian archipelago to those displayed during the Timorese campaign.
9 Peel (1984: 129).
10 Cf. Peel (1984: 128).
11 Jolliffe (1978: 134), picking up on the nationalist theme, asserts that "tribal conflict" constantly blighted "Timorese *hopes* [my italics] of national unity since Portuguese occupation."
12 Boxer (1960: 352).
13 Jolliffe (1978: 134).
14 Araújo (1974).
15 Gunter (2007: 35; see also Hill 2002: 50).

16 Rodgers (1983: 23).

17 Hedman and Sidel (2000: 142–143).

18 Gunter (2007: 32). He was also known as António Metan ("Black" António). In Viqueque town, during my first spell of fieldwork, he was described as a "bad" man. Hence his sobriquet.

19 Gunter (2007: 36).

20 Hicks (1984: 7–8).

21 Hicks (1984: 8).

22 Hoadley (1975: 25).

23 There is some evidence that ethnicity did play a role in local skirmishes at one time in West Timor, though, as H.G. Schulte Nordholt (1971: 328) notes, "During the brief political vacuum after the Japanese defeat and before the return of the Colonial Government, the Belunese [i.e., the western Tetum] perpetrated scores of cattle raids," on their neighbors, violence that prefigured the anarchy that would erupt when Portuguese control was later withdrawn in the east. Schulte Nordholt added that "The deeper cause [of warfare] was … a historically grown hostility which was likely to spark off a war at the slightest provocation."

24 Nicol (1978: 290).

25 Quoted in Duarte (1988a: 18):

> *"Maubere é um nome próprio como João ou Maria, muito comum em Timor-Leste. Relativamente havia mais individuos com o nome de Maubere em Timor que João ou Maria em Portugal. Por isso os colonialistas chamavam Maubere a qualquer nativo iletrado, uma evolução semântica. Nos últimos anos da dominação colonial portuguesa, o homen do interior, aquele que resistiu a dominacão cultural do colonialism passou a ser chamado indiscriminadamente por maubere. Pois maubere é, em resumo, o homen timor que resistiu culturalmente ão colonialism, aquele que era o verdadeiro portador da cultura popular e, por isso mesmo, sofreu na carne e ossos os piores efeitos da colonização."*

26 Cf. Jolliffe (1978: 105); Nicol (1978: 134–137, 147, 152–153); Ramos-Horta (1996: 37n). Examples of common names for a man in Viqueque sub-district are "Funo," "Lequi," "Kai," "Loi," and "Naha."

27 Jolliffe (1978: 105).

28 But see Traube (2007: 9).

29

> *Seja-me consentido apostilar, muito sumariamente, a pretensão da Fretilin em apresentar á opinião pública nacional e internacional o povo de Timor-Leste como "Povo Maubere." Esta designacão-código desfigura e até avilta impunemane a identidade desse povo. Porquanto "Maubere" não é um etnónimo. É sim, um antropónoimo, não generalizadao, mas apenas adoptado nalgumas zonas daquele território, e usado, em português de Timor, como term depreciativo. Designar, portanto, o povo Timorense de "Povo Maubere" equivale a identificar o povo Português como "Povo Zé ninguem," ou "povo Zé"*

(Duarte 1988a: 18)

30 Ramos-Horta (1996: 37n).

31 Ramos-Horta (CAVR 2006: 27). Ramos-Horta claims he invented the term *maubere* in 1973, which, of course, would have predated the formation of the parties by many months.

32 Nicol (1973: 134–137).

33 Later on, of course, the term *mauberism* would win considerably wider acceptance among a significant part of the population as a genuine term connoting Timorese solidarity.

34 Jolliffe (1978: 105).

35 Ramos-Horta (1996: 38).
36 A reference to *kuda reino*, a derogatory Luso-Tetum term by which members of the *ema reino* rank were called. *Kuda* or "horse"; the metaphor conveys the image of commoners acting as beasts of burden for the *dato* and *liurai* ranks.
37 Traube (1995: 53).
38 Nicol (1978: 152–153).
39 For an arresting example of how local antagonisms could merge with wider political loyalties, the reader may recall the incident, described in Chapter Five, of the house of the Portuguese loyalist, António Verdial, being destroyed by *Fretilin* marauders from Same.
40 Jolliffe (1978: 185, 313).
41 Cf. "Tribalism [sic] in East Timor was a contentious question in the period of the *União Democrática Timorense* coup, with some commentators denying its existence and others treating it as an explanation of political events" (Jolliffe 1978: 313).
42 One may remark that he fails to suggest what the connection between this dualism and colonialism might be.
43 Quoted in Jolliffe (1978: 313–314).
44 Hicks (2009).
45 Sá (1961: xxvi).
46 See Traube above.
47 As Mário Carrascalão remarked (CAVR 2004).
48 See Chapter 5.
49 Traube (1986: 52).
50 Jolliffe (1978: 115).
51 The Revolutionary Movement of the Portuguese Proletariat, a Maoist party in Portugal.
52 Note how the term "*maubere*" has been appropriated!
53 As José Pereira belatedly discovered, military fatigues were de rigueur if you were a *Fretilin* leader.
54 Thomaz (1977: 40).
55 Araújo (2005:7). "*O programa Político da FRETILIN que acabei por redigir na integra, em Alieu, com a minha mulher Dra. Guilhermina Araújo e foi posteriormente aprovado por unanimidade pelo Comité Central da FRETILIN, não é nem pode ser confundido com un Programa Politico marxista.*"
56 See Cabral (2000: 70).
57 The following material is from van Klinken (2001: *passim*).
58 "Most consequential" because it brought about the violent conflict between *Fretilin* and the *União Democrática Timorense* and initiated the chain of events that culminated in the Indonesian invasion.

References

Araújo, A. Loyola Jordão de. 1974. *O Célebre Massacré de Uato-Lari e Uato Carabau Verificado No Ano de 1959*. Jakarta: A. Loyola Jordão de Araújo.

Araújo, Abilio de. 1975. *Timorese Elites*. J.M. Alberto (translator). Jill Jolliffe and Bob Reece (eds.). Canberra: Jill Jolliffe and Bob Reece.

Araújo, Abilio de. 2005. "É um imperativo rever a nossa Constituição." *Jornal Nacional Semanário*. 28 May. pp. 1, 6–7. Dili, Timor-Leste.

Atkinson, J.M. 1984. "Wrapped Words," in Donald Lawrence Brenneis and Fred R. Myers (eds.). *Dangerous Words: Language and Politics in the Pacific*. pp. 33–68. New York: New York University.

Boxer, Charles. 1960. "Portuguese Timor: A Rough Island History." *History* 10: 349–355.

Burke, Kenneth. 1950. *A Rhetoric of Motives*. New York: George Braziller, Inc.

CAVR (Commision for Reception, Truth and Reconciliation). *c.*2006. Chega! *Final Report of the Commission for Reception, Truth and Reconciliation in Timor-Leste (CAVR)*. Available at: www.etan.org/news/2006/cavr.htm. Accessed February 8, 2014.

Edelman, Murray Jacob. 1971. *Politics as Symbolic Action: Mass Arousal and Quiescence*. Institute for Research on Poverty Monograph Series. Chicago: Markham Publishing Company.

Duarte, Jorge Barros. 1988a. Timor: *Um Grito*. Odivelas, Portugal: Pentaedro Publicidade e Artes Gráficas, Lda. e Jorge Barros Duarte.

Fundasaun Mahein. March 9, 2012. Available at: www.fundasaunmahein.org/2012/04/09/fm-calls-for-an-end-to-inflammatory-rhetoric/. Accessed: May 17, 2014.

Gunter, Janet. 2007. "Communal Conflict in Viqueque and the 'Charged' History of '59." *The Asia Pacific Journal of Anthropology* 8, no. 1: 27–41.

Hedman, Eva-Lotta E. and John T. Sidel. 2000. *Philippine Politics and Society in the Twentieth Century*. Politics in Asia Series. London and New York: Routledge.

Hicks, David. 1984. *A Maternal Religion: The Role of Women in Tetum Myth and Ritual*. DeKalb: Northern Illinois University Center for Southeast Asian Studies.

Hicks, David. 2009. "'*Ema Lorosa'e*', '*Ema Loromonu*': identity and politics in Timor-Leste," in Christine Cabasset and Frederic Durand (eds.). *East Timor: How to Build a New Nation in Southeast Asia in the 21st Century?*" pp. 81–94. Research Institute on Contemporary Southeast Asia (IRASEC & CASE): Bangkok, Thailand.

Hill, Helen. 2002. *Stirrings of Nationalism in East Timor: Fretilin 1974–78, The Origins, Ideologies and Strategies of a Nationalist Movement*. Kuala Lumpur and Díli. Contemporary Otford, Otford Press, Ortford (Sydney).

Hoadley, J. Stephen. 1975 (March). *The Future of Portuguese Timor. Occasional Paper, No. 27*. Singapore: Institute of Southeast Asian Studies.

Jolliffe, Jill. 1978. *East Timor: Nationalism and Colonialism*. Brisbane: University of Queensland Press.

Keyes, Charles F. 1977. *The Golden Peninsular Culture and Adaptation in Mainland Southeast Asia*. New York: Macmillan Publishing Co. Inc.; London: Collier Macmillan Publishers.

Paine, Robert (ed.). 1981. *Politically Speaking: Cross-Cultural Studies of Rhetoric*. Philadelphia: Institute for the Study of Human Issues.

Peel, J.D.Y. 1984. "Making History: The Past in the Ijesha Present." *Man (n.s.)* 19: 111–132.

Rodgers, Susan. 1983. "Political Oratory in a Modernizing Southern Batak Homeland," in Rita Kipp Smith and D. Richard Kipp (eds.). *Beyond Samosir: Recent Studies of the Batak Peoples of Sumatra. Ohio University Papers in International Studies 62*. pp. 21–52. Athens, Ohio: Ohio University Press.

Sá, Artur Basílio de. 1961. *Textos em Teto Literatura Oral Timorense*, Vol. 1. Lisbon: Junta de Investigações do Ultramar.

Schulte Nordholt, H.G. 1971. *The Political System of the Atoni of Timor*. Translated by M.J.L. van Yperen. Verhandelingen Van Het Koninklijk Instituut Voor Taal-, Land- en Volkenkunde 60. The Hague: Martinus Nijhoff.

Thomaz, Luís Filipe F.R. 1977. *Timor: Autopsia de Uma Tragedia*. Lisbon, Portugal: Author, distributed by Dig/livro.

Traube, Elizabeth G. 198.6 *Cosmology and Social Life: ritual exchange among the Mambai of East Timor*. Chicago: University of Chicago Press.

Traube, Elizabeth G. 1995. "Mambai Perspectives on Colonialism and Decolonization," in Peter Carey and G. Carter Bentley (eds.). *East Timor at the Crossroads: The Forging of a Nation.* pp. 42–55. Honolulu, Hawai'i: University of Hawai'i Press.

Traube, Elizabeth G. 2007. "Unpaid Wages: Local Narratives and the Imagination of the Nation." *The Asia Pacific Journal of Anthropology* 8: 1, 9–25.

Van Klinken, Helene. 2012. "The New Order in East Timor," in *Making Them Indonesians: Child Transfers out of East Timor.* Melbourne: Monash University Publishing. pp. 1–19. Available at: http://books.publishing.monash.edu/apps/bookworm/view/Making+Them+Indonesians%3A+Child+Transfers+out+of+East+Timor/169/mti11001-a.html. Accessed February 16, 2014.

10 The legacy of 1974–1975

1974

In August [1974], UDT and ASDT supporters organised a series of meetings to form a coalition, but again failed to agree on a common platform.... The two parties quickly descended into public verbal attacks on each other and aggressive rhetoric which was socially divisive and helped prepare the ground for the violence that followed...

(CAVR 2006 Part 3: 25)

2012

TMR and Bishop Nascimento Call On Political Parties To Avoid Provocative Words

President of the Republic Taur Matan Ruak (TMR) and Bishop for Baucau Diocese, Monsignor Basilio do Nascimento have called on the political parties not to provoke each other. President TMR and Bishop Nascimento made the call regarding the political parties' political campaigns which would be begun today (5/6). Bishop Nascimento said it was important for all the political parties to focus and convey their planned programs during their political campaigns and should not insult and provoke other parties. "Tomorrow ... the electoral campaigns by the political parties for the legislative election will be started. Therefore all the political parties should be aware of themselves to respect their rivals and do things that include in their concepts, programs and their thoughts and this is important," Monsignor Nascimento said. Meanwhile President of the Republic Taur Matan Ruak recently has called on the young Timorese and all the political parties not to use provocative words which would appear undesirable thing in the country.

(Timor Newsline: News for Change, June 5, 2012) (www.timornewslineida. com/government/160-tmr-and-bishop-nascimento-call-on-political-parties-to-avoid-provocative-words)

Parliamentary Election Test For Political Parties' Responsibility

MP Teresa Maria de Carvalho from Democratic Party (PD) said the parliamentary election which would be conducted on the upcoming July 7

should be peaceful and be successful. Ms. Carvalho called on all the polit-
ical parties not to provoke one another as this was a good manner to avoid
acts of violence during the campaigning. "We should not provoke other
people as the communities are scared and are traumatic with the political
crisis in 2006," MP Carvalho said. She said the community of [Uato Lari
Sub-District] [sic]urged for[sic] the Timorese National Police (PNTL) to
set up security posts in the area before [the] parliamentary election due to
[sic] they felt scared because a numbers of violence [sic] had happened
there.

(*Suara Timor Lorosae*, June 5, 2012
(http://twitter.com/CJITL/statuses/209911612595908608))

Independence has reshaped East Timor in ways undreamed of by the politicians of the capital and the ordinary residents of the *foho* in the mid-1970s.
The introduction of democracy, the adoption of a new currency, adjustments
in gender attitudes, and numerous other novelties have secured for the nation-
state a place in the family of nations. One indication of changing social attitudes may be glimpsed in the system of social hierarchy. We have seen how
party rhetoric used hagiography to identify cultural heroes whose personalities
embodied their respective ideologies and whose bold actions served as models
for the new leaders' own campaigns. Significantly, these heroes of the past
came from *liurai* stock. However, the mid-1970s produced cultural heroes
from the *ema foho*, men like Jerry Desousa and José Pereira, who not only
stamped their personalities onto the period, but continue doing so to this day.[1]
This is hardly surprising, for in contemporary East Timor the present shadows
the past. Politics is very personal, the language of politics inclines to be undisciplined, and when verbal persuasions fail, the threat of violence lurks in the
background. The period's most striking resonance from those earlier days,
however, lies in its leadership. Despite internecine war, foreign invasion,
occupation, exile, the involvement of the United Nations, the introduction of
democracy, and independence, many of the same cast of characters continues
in the public eye. José Ramos-Horta, Mari Alkatiri, Roque Rodrigûes, Abílio
de Araújo,[2] Rogério Lobato, and Mário Carrascalão are no longer Young
Turks, and they display rather more *gravitas*. Yet their bellicosity has mel-
lowed little, and when they have the chance they still harangue each other,
employing whatever words seem most apt in the context of the time. As in
earlier times also, their less mature young followers are on hand to transform
words of inducement into more physical forms of persuasion, a potential threat
that now and then casts a shadow upon Timor-Leste's future.

The most disturbing resonance from those years, though – "disturbing"
because it challenges the conventional model of a nation-state – is the disjunction that continues between the capital and *foho*.[3] Attempts have been made, and
continue to be made, to reconcile the two polarities, and since independence,
decrees, mandates, and laws have been promulgated aplenty by the government:
and, hand-in-hand with the United Nations and international agencies,

government leaders work to achieve *Fretilin*'s goal of transforming peasants into citizens. But *ema foho* remain almost as resistant to the contemporary purveyors of the latest injunctions as they did before, and, like its predecessor, today's government underestimates the persuasive force *lisan* exerts. For those bound by its precepts, the words of Luís Thomaz are as apt today as when he penned them four decades ago: "[I]t is well known that in Timor, for the majority of persons, the most appreciated liberty is the power of not doing anything."[4]

Current debates about the nature of the relationship between citizenship and the nation-state typically include reassessing how realistically applicable to post-colonial polities are such notions as "civil society" and "citizen" and the processes by which peasants become converted into citizens. One implication of this rethinking is that, as Max Weber's "legal authority" and "traditional authority" models[5] were later modified from the "pure" categories of polity typology he initially envisaged to more sophisticated modes, so has the notion of "civil society," a child of early modern European political thought, also been subject to revision. Thus, while scholars like Gary Wilder,[6] continue to advocate for its value, others, remarking how disparate are the ways in which the term is used, join Kumar[7] in concluding that the term has little use as an analytical tool, and Adam Seligman[8] has gone so far as to dismiss the term as "a [mere] slogan,"[9] a skepticism also embracing the concept of "citizen" itself, but a position one might regard as excessively negative. However the concept is defined, though, if they are to have pragmatic value, the terms "citizenship" and "citizen" need to include the notion of the individual recognizing a responsibility to some abstract entity of a higher order than the mere physical space occupied by his or her local community. Looking at the way *ema lisan* perceive themselves today, we see that, while there might be something of a trend towards accepting this new classification, the ordinary Timorese's notion of "citizenship" probably accords more with Rousseau's notion of a citizen than Wilder's,[10] which grants to the individual the right to participate in government, at the same time as it acknowledges the individual's right to remain untouched by the authority of the state.

In this context, one might wonder whether "a global order in which nation-statehood is mandatory"[11] is a realistic possibility at all for all post-colonial nation-states, and consider how the case of Timor-Leste might be relevant for arguments that question the universality of this model. More especially is this a concern since the United Nations once pronounced Timor-Leste to be a "poster boy" for its mandate to "nation-build." Eric Hobsbawm[12] and Ernest Gellner,[13] after all, have argued that the concept of a nation-state, deriving, as it does, from Western experience, may be unsuited to the political diversities of Third World post-colonial countries, while Basil Davidson[14] pushes this proposition further with regard to Africa, arguing that the nation-state paradigm has proved unfeasible on that continent. When they carved out their colonies, the Europeans ignored ethnic divisions; and when they left, their places at the top of the political system were filled by a small number of elite from advantaged ethnic groups whose legitimacy was questioned by those less privileged. In East Timor, ancestral authority, reinforced by difficult communications and illiteracy provided the principal banes to the evolution of a national consciousness and the development of something akin to a Ben Anderson "imagined community." Today, while the two latter influences are more attenuated than in the 1970s – there are television sets, phones, and a better infrastructure, and the majority of Timorese are literate – the ancestors still remain an obstacle to a more cohesive national integration.[15] This is certainly not to underrate the feelings of national awareness that distinguishes the Timor-Leste of today from the East Timor of 1975. The Indonesian occupation succeeded in making Timorese, in the hinterland as well as in the capital, aware that there was something that united them – the brutal impositions of "The Indonesian Other," and a growing sense of national consciousness facilitated by the Catholic Church. The Timor-Leste of today more closely resembles a nation in Kingsbury's sense than at any time in history. But, for all that, its future as an integrated nation-state, faces difficulties, some of which José Ramos-Horta forthrightly discussed in his article, "East Timor is Not a Failed State."[16]

Although, as Hans Antlöf[17] has depicted in the case of Java, the lack of cohesion between what Edward Shils[18] has distinguished as "the centre" and "the periphery"[19] is not inevitable in post-colonial nation-states, it is a concern for some governments, and should be for the government of Timor-Leste.[20] In Burma, as was noted, certain peripheral areas, like that controlled by the Kachin, have become so alienated from the capital as to have become practically faux-states in their own right,[21] and in eastern Indonesia, Patricia Spyer, in discussing the role of modernization in Aru, has detected certain tensions not unlike those described in the present study.[22] As yet, the Democratic Republic of Timor-Leste has nothing approaching the degree of alienation of Burma's, nor can it be characterized as another Southeast Asian "Zomia,"[23] but for Timor-Leste to evolve into a more effectively integrated nation-state its leaders will need to demonstrate a firmer commitment to bringing about reconciliation between the country's capital and its interior hinterland. They and the United Nations and other international agencies, should allow themselves to be guided by more realistic approaches to *lisan*, which would mean investing less trust in the classic "top-down" model of development, and giving more weight to a "grassroots" alternative. As one agency report, more perceptive than most of its ilk, states, "The governments' [*sic*] failure to conduct public 'consultations' in the process of drafting new laws also contributes to the lack of local ownership and understanding on how the law can provide justice to the people."[24] In turning to the grassroots paradigm, government and agencies should seek advice from, among others, the *liurai* rather than depend on some "representative" pool of informants selected by the bureaucratic mindset. This is not to say that *liurai* are popular in all *suku* or necessarily influential everywhere; but they do know their people, their *lisan*, and their needs. They are placed in a position to know what ordinary people want. Nevertheless, with or without input from the *liurai*, a necessary part of a grassroots' initiative would be consulting *ema foho* to learn what exactly they wish for their futures. The government might then be able to tap into the local dynamism now expended on such *lisan* activities as the rebuilding of *uma lulik*, an enterprise the U.S. Ambassador Hans Klemm apparently admired so much, and diverting it into channels more relevant for the needs of an emerging nation-state. Doing so would demonstrate that the leaders of today's Timor-Leste have learned something from the mistakes made by their *Fretilin* and *União Democrática Timorense* predecessors.

But the legacy of the "past-in-the-present" makes this easier said than done. Several years ago, my wife and I were driving from Dili to the urban center of one of the districts on the south coast. Along the way we were obliged to negotiate several deep potholes, a circumstance that delayed our arrival in the town. Later, when I explained our tardiness to our hostess, she pointed out that the district *had* received funds from the capital to maintain the roads, but that the administrator was not disposed to allocate them. He, a resident in the *foho*, was *Fretilin*; Prime Minister Gusmão, in Dili, was of a rival political party. Why let him take the credit? As Bu Wilson put it, in the epigraph that heads the Introduction, "1974 is still alive."

Notes

1 See Chapter 8.
2 In an interview he gave to the Dili newspaper, the *Jornal de Semanário*, in 2005, Araújo attributes the course of action espoused by *Fretilin* leaders to the radically-charged atmosphere of the 1970s (Araújo).
3 Hicks (2007).
4 "...*é bem sabido que em Timor, para a major parte das pesssoas, a liberdade mais apreciada ainda é a de poder não fazer nada...*" (Thomaz 1977: 25).
5 Weber (1978: 12–13).
6 Wilder (1999: 66–67). He would include in the definition of the term "civil, political, and social rights ... liberal rights and civic obligations; legal protection and political participation ... territory or genealogy; and ... a juridico-political status that may be ascribed at birth, legally petitioned for, and secured through struggle."
7 Kumar (1993: 392).
8 Seligman (1992: 201–206).
9 Cohen and Arato (1991), on the other hand, are willing to take the concept of "civil society" seriously enough to elaborate its meaning by including within its definitional framework what they call "spheres," such as the family and voluntary associations.
10 Wilder (1999: 51).
11 Karlström (1999); Mann (1993).
12 Hobsbawm (1990).
13 Gellner (2008).
14 Davidson (1992).
15 See Leach, Michael, James Scambary, Matthew Clarke, Simon Feeny and Heather Wallace (2013) for a recent and exceptionally revealing survey of tertiary students' attitudes to nationalism and nation-building.
16 Ramos-Horta (2006).
17 Antlöf (1995).
18 Shils (1975).
19 Shils' well-known model of center/periphery has received considerable attention. The contrast is also hinted at in Comaroff and Comaroff's (2007) aforementioned discussion of the attempts by nation-states to convert "people" into "citizens" and the increasing "juridicalization" trend they detect in contemporary assertions of nation-state authority. Given the distinction between the capital and *foho* this model might seem applicable to East Timor. However, Dili (Shils' would-be "center") is not

208   *The legacy of 1974–1975*

regarded by those residing in the *foho* ("periphery") as an exemplary model deserving emulation. Quite the opposite.
20 A similar dynamic between local ideologies and national ideologies, is discernible in today's Latin America, where it exercises a significant influence on the ongoing process of nation-building (Radcliffe and Westwood 2005).
21 Smith (2006: 20).
22 Spyer (2000).
23 Scott (2009).
24 Asia Foundation (2004 [ca.]: 12).

References

Antlöf, Hans. 1995. *Exemplary centre, administrative periphery: Rural Leadership and the New Order in Java.* Nordic Institute of Asian Studies Monograph Series, No. 68. Richmond, Surrey: Curzon Press.

Araújo, Abilio de. Araújo. 2005. "É um imperativo rever a nossa Constituição." *Jornal Nacional Semanário.* May 28. pp. 1, 6–7. Dili, Timor-Leste.

Asia Foundation. 2004 (ca.). *Law and justice in East Timor: a survey of citizen awareness and attitudes regarding law and justice in East Timor.* San Francisco: The Asia Foundation.

Bompadre, Viviana Andrea. 2003. *Sources and Processes of Cultural Innovation: A Comparison Between Center and Border Communities in the Making of Mercosur.* Ph.D. Diss. Chicago.

CAVR (Commision for Reception, Truth and Reconciliation). *c.*2006. Chega! *Final Report of the Commission for Reception, Truth and Reconciliation in Timor-Leste (CAVR).* Available at: www.etan.org/news/2006/cavr.htm. Accessed February 8, 2014.

Cohen, Jean L. and Andrew Arato. 1992. *Civil Society and Political Theory.* Cambridge: The MIT Press.

Davidson, Basil. 1992. *The Black man's Burden: Africa and the Curse of the Nation-State.* New York: Times Books, Random House.

Gellner, Ernest. 2008. *Nations and Nationalism.* 2nd edition. Ithaca, N.Y.: Cornell University Press.

Hobsbawm, E.J. 1990. *Nations and Nationalism Since 1780: Programme, Myth, Reality.* Cambridge: The Press Syndicate of the University of Cambridge.

Hicks, David. 2007b. "Community and Nation-State in East Timor: A View from the Periphery." *Anthropology Today* 23, no. 1, 13–16.

Karlström, Mikael. 1999. "Civil Society and its Presuppositions: Lessons from Uganda," in Jean Comaroff and John Comaroff (eds.). *Civil Society and the Political Imagination in Africa: critical perspectives.* pp. 104–123. Chicago: University of Chicago Press.

Kumar, K. 1993. "Civil Society: an enquiry into the usefulness of an historical term." *British Journal of Sociology* 44 (3): 375–395.

Larsen, M.T. 1979. *The Tradition of Empire in Mesopotamia, in Power and Propaganda: A Symposium on Ancient Empires,* Vol. 7 of Mesopotamia: Copenhagen Studies in Assyriology. pp. 75–103. Copenhagen: Akademisk Forlag.

Leach, Michael, James Scambary, Matthew Clarke, Simon Feeny, and Heather Wallace. 2013. "National identity in fragile states: insights from tertiary students in Melanesia and Timor-Leste" *Commonwealth & Comparative Politics,* 51: 4, 447–478, DOI: 10.1080/14662043.2013.841004. Available at: http://dx.doi.org/10.1080/14662043.2013.841004. Accessed February 16, 2014.

Mann, Michael. 1993. "Nation-States in Europe and Other Continents: Diversifying, Developing, Not Dying." *Daedalus* 122 (2): 115–140.

Queer Space: Centers and Peripheries Conference. 2006. Available at: www.dab.uts.edu.au/conferences/queer_space/. Accessed May 17, 2014.

Radcliffe, Sarah, and Sallie Westwood. 2006 (1996). *Remaking the Nation: place, identity and politics in Latin America.* Taylor and Francis e-Library, Routledge: London and New York.

Ramos-Horta, José. 2006. "East Timor is Not a Failed State." *The Wall Street Journal,* June 9, p. A14. New York.

Scott, C. James. 2009. *The Art of Not Being Governed: an anarchist history of Upland Southeast Asia.* New Haven: Yale University Press.

Seligman, Adam B. 1992. *The Idea of Civil Society.* New York: The Free Press.

Smith, M. 2006. "The Paradox of Burma: conflict and illegality as a way of life." *International Institute for Asian Studies (IIAS) Newsletter* 42: 20–21.

Spyer, Patricia. 2000. *Memory of Trade: modernity's entanglements on an eastern Indonesian Island.* Durham, NC: Duke University Press.

Thomaz, Luís Filipe F.R. 1977. *Timor: Autopsia de Uma Tragedia.* Lisbon, Portugal: Author, distributed by Dig/livro.

Timor Newsline: News for Change. "TMR and Bishop Nascimento Call On Political Parties To Avoid Provocative Words." June 5, 2012. Available at: www.timornewslineida.com/government/160-tmr-and-bishop-nascimento-call-on-political-parties-to-avoid-provocative-words. Accessed May 17, 2014.

Weber, Max. 1978. *Economy and Society.* Guenther Roth and Claus Wittich (eds.). Berkeley: University of California Press. Vol. One.

Wilder, Gary. 1999. "Practicing Citizenship in Imperial Paris," in Jean Comaroff and John Comaroff (eds.). *Civil Society and the Political Imagination in Africa: critical perspectives.* pp. 44–71. Chicago: University of Chicago Press.

A note on sources

This monograph is based upon three sources: interviews conducted in East Timor itself and in Portugal; other primary sources (published and unpublished), and secondary sources. The following includes a selected compilation of some of the most important primary and secondary sources I have used.

1 Interviews

Amaral, Francisco Xavier do. Interview 2005.
Assis, Rudy de. Interview 2007.
Biddlecombe, Maria Rosa. Interview 2005.
Biddlecombe, Maria Rosa. Interview 2007.
Desousa, Jerry. Interview 2005.
Etches, Geoffrey. Interview 2005.
Fawset, Gil. Interview 2005.
Forganes, Rosaley. Interview 2005.
Freitas, Sidónio. Interview 2005.
Kammen, Douglas. Interview 2005.
Madeira, Maria. Interview 2009.
Miller, Kym. Interview 2005.
Oliveira, Fernanda. Interview 2005.
Pereira, José Henriques. Interview 2005.
Pereira, José Henriques. Interview 2007.
Ramos-Horta, José. Interview 2005.
Soares, Fernando da Costa. Interview 2005.
Soares, Luís Francisco de Gonzaga. Interview 2005.
Soares, Luís Francisco de Gonzaga. Interview 2007.
Soares, Tereza da Luz Simões. Interview 2005.
Soares, Rosa Maria da Costa. Interview 2005.
Soares, Rosa Maria da Costa. Interview 2007.
Soares, Teresa da Luz Simões. Interview 2005.
Soares, Teresa da Luz Simões. Interview 2007.
Sousa, Domingos de. Interview 2005.
Texeira, José. Interview 2005.

2 Primary published/unpublished sources

Three first-hand accounts by foreign journalists provide copious information regarding the events and personalities of the period. Jill Jolliffe's excellent account, *East Timor: nationalism and colonialism*,[1] was the first book about the period to be published, an eyewitness portrait based on her three months' stay, from September to December 1975. During this period Jolliffe traveled extensively and witnessed events of importance and interviewed some of the more prominent history-makers as well as others involved in lesser capacities. Her second book, *Timor: terra sangrenta* (1989), amplifies her earlier study with biographies of six Timorese. In contrast with Jolliffe, whose sympathies favor *Fretilin*, Bill Nicol writes his *Timor: The Stillborn Nation* (1978), more in sympathy with one of the minor parties, *Klibur Oan Timur Asuwa'in*, and is rather less anti-*União Democrática Timorense*. Imparting an idiosyncratic flavor to the events and personalities involved, including José Ramos-Horta, he and his interviews provide an important eyewitness record that complements that of Jolliffe. One of my own interviewees, the *União Democrática Timorense* supporter, Mrs. Rosa Maria Biddlecombe, considered that Nichol's book gave the most accurate account of any she had read. He seems to have arrived in Timor in January 1975. The third book, *Timor Leste: O Dossier Secreto 1973–1975*, tells us what was going on before the two journalists arrived on the scene, giving an almost month-by-month account of the period from September 1973 to April 1975, by the editor of the Dili newspaper, *Voz de Timor*, J. Chrys Chrystello. Supplementing this printed journalism is the film made by Clive Scollay, which I was able to see in the archives of CAVR. It depicts the progress of the war in August-September 1975 and includes interviews with such figures as José Ramos-Horta and Alarico Fernandes.

Seven personal accounts have been published by the political elite or individuals who played one role or other in the events of the time. The most informative is that of José Ramos-Horta, who knew everyone of note and was ubiquitously involved in several critical events, including participating in the birth of the *União Democrática Timorense* and *Fretilin*. His book *Funu: the unfinished saga of East Timor*, which originally appeared in 1987 and reprinted in 1996, is a personal account of his maneuvers, and provides intimate insights into what his colleagues and rivals were up to. While allowing due weight for his own political and personal bias, I consider his account especially enlightening, for besides enabling us to share in the events as they were going on and the activities its author took upon himself to engage in, it gives us a wider perspective on the campaigning than most other sources. Mário Viegas Carrascalão's *Timor: antes do futuro* (2006) describes what occurred from the viewpoint of the most astute of the *União Democrática Timorense* leaders. For obvious reasons, Mário Lemos Pires' *Descolonização de Timor: Missão Impossível?* (1994), the Portuguese governor for most of the period discussed here, merits the closest of scrutiny. The author makes use of three earlier accounts he submitted as official reports: *Relatório do Governo de Timor*, 1981; *Relatório da*

CAEPDT (*Comissão de Análise e Esclarecimento do Processo of Descoloniza-ção de Timor*), 1981; and an unnamed and otherwise unspecified document. Francisco Lopes da Cruz's *Kesaksian: aka dan Timor Timur* (1999) describes what occurred from the perspective of a man who was both a *União Democrática Timorense* leader and Indonesian operative. *Olobai 75* by Domingos de Sousa (ca. 2003) discusses the aftermath of August 11 in one particular sub-district, Viqueque, from the perspective of an ordinary *União Democrática Timorense* supporter; and an Indonesian perspective comes from Elias M. Tomodok, Indonesian consul in Dili, who in his *Hari-Hari Akhir Timor Portugis* (1994) gives us some idea of the official thinking of his government. Finally, the *Autobiografia de Abílio de Araújo* provides, among many other things, an insid-er's view of the lives of the students in the *Casa de Timores*, by the most pub-lished intellectual in *Fretilin*.

Compiled after the Indonesian Government left East Timor, the various reports of *The Commission for Reception, Truth and Reconciliation in Timor-Leste* provide a source of substantial data, based, as they are on testimonies from over 7,000 eyewitnesses, including political leaders, ordinary party members, and innocents accidently ensnared in the troubles. The commission is more com-monly referred to by its Portuguese acronym of CAVR (*Comissão por Alcolhi-mento, Verdade, e Reconciliação de Timor-Leste*), an independent, statutory authority whose brief was to investigate the nature of the conflict in 1974–1975, uncover the truth regarding the violence the Republic of Indonesia visited upon East Timor, and help reconcile Timorese with one another. On October 31, 2005 CAVR presented its final report to the president of Timor-Leste, Alexandre "Xanana" Gusmão, who on November 28, 2005, as stipulated by Timorese legis-lation, submitted it to the parliament and cabinet of Timor-Leste and subse-quently, on January, 20, 2006, to the secretary-general of the United Nations, Kofi Annan. The report was made public on January 30, 2006. Complementing its massive data set is the most reliable chronological and analytical summary yet published of the period under discussion. CAVR had previously produced an update on its activities, "CAVR Update/Dec 2003–January 2004" (including Appendix 2: Report on Hearing on Internal Political Conflict, December 15–18, 2003. 2004.) They include testimonies by João Carrascalão, Mário Carrascalão, José Ramos-Horta, Mari Alkatiri, and Mário Lemos Pires. In addition, in 2005 CAVR published a slimmer compendium of testimonies bearing the title, *Timor-Leste Massacres: Audiência Pública Nacional, 19–21 Novembro 200. Comissão de Acolhimento, Verdade e Reconciliação de Timor-Leste* (CAVR). They include further narratives recounting the experience of five men from the coun-tryside – three Fretilin supporters, Ilídio Maria de Jesus, Mateus Soares, and Florentino de Jesus Martins; a *União Democrática Timorense* follower, Alexan-dre da Costa Araújo; and one unfortunate trapped between both of these parties, António Amado J.R. Guterres, each of whom found himself caught up in waves of violence not of their doing following the failure of the coup. Reading their testimonies and comparing them with those given by the men who aspired to lead East Timor into the future as a nation-state gives us a salutary lesson in the extent to which ordinary persons in the hinterland paid for the ambitions of the privileged in the capital. In 2005 a third report entitled *Timor-Leste Massacres: Audiência Pública Nacional*, November 19–21, 2003 was published as a booklet. The material in all three reports is of exceptional value.

Also previously inaccessible has been the resources of the United States National Intelligence, and published in the *National Intelligence Bulletin*. The Freedom of Information Act (FOIA) has made available documents of the period from the Central Intelligence Agency that were previously secret. Among the documents is a copy of the telegram reporting the secret negotiations between President Gerald Ford, Secretary of State Henry Kissinger, and President Suharto in Jakarta, on December 6, 1975, regarding the invasion of East Timor, relevant parts of which appear as an epigraph to the Introduction.

3 Secondary sources

The writings of Portuguese scholars have been almost entirely ignored by English-speaking authors, yet two scholars, Luís Thomaz and the late Father Jorge Barros Duarte, offer insights into the history of the times that are all the more authoritative for being grounded in an intensive, first-hand, experience of the country and its inhabitants acquired as the result of years of residence in Portuguese Timor before the April revolution. Both are political conservatives, and so their regard for the *União Democrática Timorense* is higher than for *Fretilin*. Four months before August 11, Thomaz had published *O Problema Político de Timor* (1975), a small book in which he speculated about the future of East Timor, and two years later followed up with *Timor: autópsia de uma tragédia*, a collection of articles he had contributed to the Portuguese journal *O Dia* between December 1975 and September 1976. Jorge Barros Duarte was born in 1912 in the town of Same, where he spent 33 years as a Catholic missionary. His mother was Timorese and his father a European. Among the Timorese languages he spoke were Tetum, Mambai, and Galoli, and he may be credited with the most authoritative knowledge of the Timorese. For this reason, his observations on their institutions carry singular weight, and certain of these appear in his *Timor: um grito* (1988).

Like Portuguese sources, those emanating from Indonesian sources, such as the aforementioned Elias M. Tomodok's, have not been used by previous writers, except for Sue Rabbitt Roff, whose *Timor's Anschluss: Indonesian and Australian Policy in East Timor 1974–1976*, published in 1992, gives information regarding Indonesian attitudes, including that of the press. The Indonesian Government published a wealth of detailed material intended to justify the case for intervention and this provides an alternative slant. *Integrasi*[2] is a massive compilation of documents and photographs, and is usefully supplemented by *Lahirnya Propinsi Timor Timur*.[3] Also from Indonesia, but in English, is *The Question of Portuguese Timor*, which appeared in November 1975 just before the invasion, and summarizes the situation as seen from Jakarta at the time.[4]

Of the secondary sources in English, the book that includes the most general account of the period is *Timor: a people betrayed*, by James Dunn, which originally appeared in 1983 and was followed two further editions in 1986 (reprinted in 1996) and 2003, under a new title: *East Timor: a rough passage to independence*, as the author expanded his account to take in the later years of the Indonesian occupation and the eventual emergence of East Timor as an independent nation-state. Dunn served as Australian consul stationed in Dili from January 1962 to 1964, returning in 1974 as a member of a fact-finding mission sent by the Australian Government. He again went back in October and November of the following year as the leader of the Australian Council for Overseas Aid (ACFOA) which performed relief work following the civil war, and attempted to assess what the longer-term aid requirements of the Timorese might be. His book describes the political life of the capital and his portrait of Portuguese colonial life furnishes us with an authentic portrait of the political elite. Dunn makes no bones about ascribing much of the culpability for what occurred to the governments of Indonesia and Australia, as well as providing an unmatched analysis of the diplomatic maneuvers of the two successive Australian administrations. Another excellent general account that takes the reader beyond the time of the invasion is John Taylor's *Indonesia's Forgotten War: the hidden history of East Timor* (1991), which includes a comprehensive chronology. Helen M. Hill's *Stirrings of Nationalism in East Timor: Fretilin 1974–78: the origins, ideologies and strategies of a nationalist movement* is the published version of her Master of Arts dissertation[5] which was based on her three-month spell in East Timor between January and March 1975. With its exclusive depiction of the history of one of the contending parties, her monograph is the most focused of all the books published on this period, and is an essential mine of information on *Fretilin*, providing a shrewd scrutiny of its leaders. Although restricted in its scope, it remains the only scholarly monograph on the history of East Timor from 1974 to 1975.

Notes

1 Jolliffe (1978).
2 Yayasan Parikesit (1976).
3 Noor *et al.* (1977).
4 Department of Foreign Affairs, Jakarta (1975).
5 Hill (1978).

References

Anderson, Benedict R.O'G. 1972. *Java in a Time of Revolution: occupation and resistence, 1944–1946*. Ithaca and London: Cornell University Press.
Anderson, Benedict R.O'G. 1991. *Imagined Communities: reflections on the origin and spread of nationalism*. Revised and extended edition. London: Verso.
Antlöf, Hans. 1995. *Exemplary centre, administrative periphery: Rural Leadership and the New Order in Java*. Nordic Institute of Asian Studies Monograph Series, No. 68. Richmond, Surrey: Curzon Press.

Appadurai, Arjun. 1981. "The Past as Scarce Resource." *Man (n.s.)* 16, no. 2: 201–219.

Araújo, A. Loyola Jordão de. 1974. *O Célebre Massacré de Uato-Lari e Uato Carabau Verificado No Ano de 1959.* Jakarta: A. Loyola Jordão de Araújo.

Araújo, Abilio de. 1975. *Timorese Elites.* J.M. Alberto (translator). Jill Jolliffe and Bob Reece (eds.). Canberra: Jill Jolliffe and Bob Reece.

Araújo, Abilio de. 1977. *Timor Leste: os loricos voltaram a cantar* 1977. Publisher: author.

Araújo, Abilio de. 2005. "É um imperativo rever a nossa Constituição." *Jornal Nacional Semanário.* May 28. pp. 1, 6–7. Dili, Timor-Leste.

Araújo, Abilio [sic]. 2012. *Autobiografia de Abílio Araújo: Dato Siri Loe II.* With José de Assunção Gonçalves. Lisbon: Alétheia Editores.

Aristotle. 1924. *Rhetorica.* W. Rhys (editor and translator). Translated into English under the editorship of W.D. Ross Robert. *The Works of Aristotle, vol. 112.* Oxford: Clarendon Press.

Asia Foundation. 2004 (ca.). *Law and justice in East Timor: a survey of citizen awareness and attitudes regarding law and justice in East Timor.* San Francisco: The Asia Foundation.

Atkinson, J.M. 1984. "Wrapped Words," in Donald Lawrence Brenneis and Fred R. Myers (eds.). *Dangerous Words: Language and Politics in the Pacific.* pp. 36–68. New York: New York University.

Australian Government Department of Foreign Affairs and Trade. n.d. *Historical Documents Volume 23: Australia and the Indonesian Incorporation of Portuguese Timor, 1974–1976.* Available at: www.dfat.gov.au/publications/historical/volume-23/. Accessed February 14, 2014.

BBC. 1974. "On this Day April 25, 1974." Available at: http://news.bbc.co.uk/onthisday/hi/dates/stories/april/25/newsid_4754000/4754581.stm. Accessed May 17, 2014.

Bertrand, Jacques. 2004. *Nationalism and Ethnic Conflict in Indonesia.* Cambridge: Cambridge University Press.

Bompadre, Viviana Andrea. 2003. *Sources and Processes of Cultural Innovation: A Comparison Between Center and Border Communities in the Making of Mercosur.* Ph.D. Diss. Chicago.

Boxer, Charles. 1960. "Portuguese Timor: A Rough Island History." *History* 10: 349–55.

Burke, Kenneth. 1950. *A Rhetoric of Motives.* New York: George Braziller, Inc.

Burr, William and Michael L. Evans (eds.). 2001 (December 6). "East Timor Revisited: Ford, Kissinger and Indonesian Invasion, 1975–76," in *National Security Archive Electronic Briefing Book No. 62.* Available at: www.Gwu.Edu/~Nsarchiv/NSAEBB/NSAEBB62/. Accessed May 17, 2014.

Cabral, Estêvão. 2000. "The Indonesian Propaganda War against East Timor," in Paul Hainsworth and Stephen McCloskey (eds.). *The East Timor Question The Struggle for Independence from Indonesia.* pp. 69–84. London and New York: I.B. Tauris Publishers.

Carrascalão, Mário Viegas. 2006. *Timor: Antes Do Futuro.* Dili, Timor-Leste: Livaria Mau Huran.

Carrithers, Michael. 2005a. "Why Anthropologists Should Study Rhetoric." *The Journal of the Royal Anthropological Institute (N.S.)* 11, no. 2: 577–583.

Carrithers, Michael. 2005b. "Anthropology as a Moral Science of Possibilities." *Current Anthropology* 46: 433–446.

Cascais, António M. Cravo. 1977. *Timor: Quem é o Culpado?* Portugal: Braga Editora, LDA.

Catholic Institute for International Relations. 1995. *International Law and the Questions of East Timor.* Nottingham, UK: Russell Press.

216   *A note on sources*

CAVR (Commision for Reception, Truth and Reconciliation). 2004. "CAVR Update/Dec 2003-January 2004" (including Appendix 2: Report on Hearing on Internal Political Conflict) December 15–18, 2003. Available at: www.cavr-timorleste.org/updateFiles/english/cavrUpdate-Dec03Jan04-en.pdf. Accessed February 7, 2014.

CAVR (Commision for Reception, Truth and Reconciliation). 2005. *Timor-Leste Massacres: Audiência Pública Nacional.* November 19–21, 2003. Timor-Leste: CAVR.

CAVR (Commision for Reception, Truth and Reconciliation). ca. 2006. Chega! *Final Report of the Commission for Reception, Truth and Reconciliation in Timor-Leste (CAVR).* Available at: www.etan.org/news/2006/cavr.htm. Accessed February 8, 2014.

Central Intelligence Agency Reports. Available at: www.foia.cia.gov/. Accessed May 17, 2014.

Chamberlain, Ernest. 2009. *Rebellion, Defeat and Exile: The 1959 Uprising in East Timor.* Revised second edition. Point Lonsdale, Australia: Ernest Chamberlain.

Chrystello, J. Chrys. 1999. *Timor Leste: 1973–1975, O Dossier Secreto.* Matosinhos, Portugal: Contemporânea Editora.

Coèdes, Georges. 1968. *The Indianized States of Southeast Asia,* 3rd edition. Honolulu: East-West Center.

Cohen, Jean L. and Andrew Arato. 1992. *Civil Society and Political Theory.* Cambridge: The MIT Press.

Cohen, Jean L. and Andrew Arato. 1999. *Civil Society and the Political Imagination in Africa: critical perspectives.* Chicago: University of Chicago Press.

Cohen, Jean L. and Andrew Arato. 2007. "Law and Disorder in the Postcolony." *Social Anthropology,* 15 (2): 133–152.

Comaroff, Jean and John Comaroff. 2007. Law and Disorder in the Postcolony. *Social Anthropology,* 15 (2): 133–152.

Conboy, Ken. 2003. *Kopassus Inside Indonesia's Special Forces.* Jakarta & Singapore: Equinox Publishing (Asia) Pte. Ltd.

Cortesão, A. (ed.). 1944. *The Suma Oriental of Tomé Pires.* London: Hakluyt Society, Series 2: 89.

Costa, Francisco Borja da. 1976. *Revolutionary Poems in the Struggle Against Colonialism.* Translated by Jill Jolliffe (editor) and James J. Fox. Sydney: Wild and Woolley.

Costa, Luís. [Synopsis of a Paper]. 1992. In António (ed.). *East Timor: Land of Hope Second Symposium on Timor Oporto University (28 April–1 May 1990).* pp. 146–147. Barbedo de Magalhães. Oporto, Portugal: President's Office, Oporto University.

Cruz, Francisco Xavier Lopes da. 1999. *Kesaksian: Aku Dan Timur Timur.* Jakarta, Indonesia: Yayasan Tunas Harapan Timor Lorosae.

Cunningham, Clark. 1972. "Atoni," in Frank M. LeBar (ed.). *Ethnic Groups of Insular Southeast Asia, Volume I: Indonesia, Andaman Islands, and Madagascar.* pp. 103–105. New Haven: Human Relations Area Files Press.

Cunningham, Clark. 1967. "Soba: An Atoni Village of West Timor," in Koentjaraningrat (ed.). *Villages in Indonesia.* pp. 63–89. Itahaca: Cornell University Press.

Davidson, Basil. 1992. *The Black man's Burden: Africa and the Curse of the Nation-State.* New York: Times Books, Random House.

Defert, Gabriel. 1992. *Timor-Est: Le Génocide Oublié; Droit d'un Peuple et Raisons d'États.* Paris: Éditions L'Harmattan.

Delegação de Timor do Instituto Nacional de Estatística. 1973. Instituto Nacional de Estatístic: Lisbon.

Decolonization in East Timor. 1977. Department of Foreign Affairs. Jakarta.

Department of Foreign Affairs. 1975. *The Question of Portuguese Timor, September.* Jakarta: The Department of Foreign Affairs, Republic of Indonesia.

Department of State, U.S. 1975. Department of State Telegram, dated December 1975 and Issuing from Jakarta, Indonesia.

Duarte, Jorge Barros. 1988a. Timor: *Um Grito.* Odivelas, Portugal: Pentaedro Publicidade e Artes Gráficas, Lda. e Jorge Barros Duarte.

Duarte, Jorge Barros. 1988b. *Timor Jeremiada.* Lisbon: Pentaedro Publicidade e Artes Gráficas, Lda. e Jorge Barros Duarte.

Dunn, James. 2003. *East Timor: A Rough Passage to Independence.* New South Wales, Australia: Longueville Books.

Dunn, James. 1996. *Timor: A People Betrayed.* 2nd edition. Sydney, Australia: ABC Books for the Australian Broadcasting Corporation.

Durand, Frédéric. 2002. *Timor Lorosa'e Pays Au Carrefour de l'Asie et Du Pacifique Un Atlas Géo-Historique.* Marne la Vallée Cedex 2; Bangkok, Thailand: Press Universitaires de Marne-la-Vallée; IRASEC [Institut de Recherche sur l'Asia du Sud-Est Contemporaine], Bangkok, Thailand.

Durand, Frédéric. 2006. *Timor: 1250 750 ans de cartographie et de voyages.* Editions Arkuiris, Espace, Asie, Toulouse, France; IRASEC [Institut de Recherche sur l'Asia du Sud-Est Contemporaine], Bangkok, Thailand.

Durkheim, Émile. 1960. *Les structures élémentaires de la vie religieuse; le système totémique en Australie.* Paris: Bibliothèque de Philosophie Contemporaine Fondée par Felix Alcan, Press Universitaires de France. 4th edition.

Edelman, Murray Jacob. 1971. *Politics as Symbolic Action: Mass Arousal and Quiescence.* Institute for Research on Poverty Monograph Series. Chicago: Markham Publishing Company.

Evans, Grant. 1975. "Eastern (Portuguese) Timor: Independence or Oppression?" Australian Union of Students, Melbourne.

Favaro, Frank. 2003. Interview in Clive Schollay, *East Timor Reconciliation: Scenes from Timor, September 1975* [video].

Feijó, Rui Graça. 2009. "Elections and Social Dimensions of Democracy, Lessons from Timor-Leste," in Christine Cabasset and Frederic Durand (eds.). *East Timor: How to Build a New Nation in Southeast Asia in the 21st Century?* pp. 123–138. Research Institute on Contemporary Southeast Asia (IRASEC & CASE): Bangkok, Thailand.

Felgas, Helio A. Esteves. 1956. *Timor Português.* Lisbon: Agencie Geral do Ultramar.

Fernandes, Alarico. 2003. Interview in Clive Schollay, *East Timor Reconciliation: Scenes from Timor, September 1975* [video].

Figueiredo, Fernando Augusto de. 2011. *Timor A Presença Portuguesa (1769–1945).* Lisbon: Centro de Estudos Históricos Universidade Nova de Lisboa.

Fundasaun Mahein. (March 9, 2012). Available at: www.fundasaunmahein.org/2012/04/09/fm-calls-for-an-end-to-inflammatory-rhetoric/. Accessed May 17, 2014.

Gellner, Ernest. 2008. *Nations and Nationalism.* 2nd. Ithaca, N.Y.: Cornell University Press.

Gominho, Adriano de Almeida. 2006. *Timor Parais odo Oriente (Memórias de um malaio – estranho).* Ebook by author.

Grenfell, Damian. 2008. "Governance, Violence and Crises in Timor-Leste: Estadu Seidauk Mai," in David Mearns (Steven Farram, assistant editor). *Democratic Governance in Timor-Leste: Reconciling the Local and the National.* pp. 85–97. Darwin, Australia: Charles Darwin University Press.

Gunn, Geoffrey C. nd. "Revisiting the Viqueque Rebellion of 1959." Available at: http://geoffreycgunn.com/material/draft_viquequerebellion.pdf. Accessed May 17, 2014.

Gunter, Janet. 2007. "Communal Conflict in Viqueque and the 'Charged' History of '59." *The Asia Pacific Journal of Anthropology* 8, no. 1: 27–41.

Guterres, Apolinário, and João dos Santos. 1992 [Synopsis of a Paper]. In António Barbedo de Magalhães (ed.). *East Timor: Land of Hope Second Symposium on Timor Oporto University (28 April–1 May 1990)* p. 145. Oporto, Portugal: President's Office, Oporto University.

Greenfield, Liah and Martin Michel (eds.). 1988. *Center: Ideas and Institutions.* Chicago and London: The University of Chicago Press.

Hastings, Peter. 1975 (April). "The Timor Problem." *Australian Outlook.* 29 (1): 18–33.

Hedman, Eva-Lotta E. and John T. Sidel. 2000. *Philippine Politics and Society in the Twentieth Century.* Politics in Asia Series. London and New York: Routledge.

Hicks, David. 1976. *Tetum Ghosts and Kin: Fieldwork in an Indonesian Community.* Palo Alto: Mayfield Publishing Company.

Hicks, David. 1978. *Structural Analysis in Anthropology: Case Studies from Indonesia and Brazil.* Studia Instituti Anthropos, vol. 30. St. Augustin bei Bonn, Germany: Anthropos-Instituts.

Hicks, David. 1983. "Unachieved Syncretism: The Local-Level Political System in Portuguese Timor (1966–1967)." *Anthropos* 78: 17–40.

Hicks, David. 1984. *A Maternal Religion: The Role of Women in Tetum Myth and Ritual.* DeKalb: Northern Illinois University Center for Southeast Asian Studies.

Hicks, David. 1988. "Literary Masks and Metaphysical Truths." *American Anthropologist* 90: 807–17.

Hicks, David. 1990. *Kinship and Religion in Eastern Indonesia.* Gothenburg Studies in Social Anthropology 12. Gothenburg: Acta Universitatis Gothoburgensis.

Hicks, David. 2004. *Tetum Ghosts and Kin: Fertility and Gender in East Timor.* Waveland Press, Inc.: Prospect Heights, Illinois. 2nd edition.

Hicks, David. 2007a. "The Naueti Relationship Terminology: A New Instance of Asymmetric Prescription from East Timor." *Bijdragen tot de Taal-,Land- en Volkenkunde* 163 (2/3): 239–262.

Hicks, David. 2007b. "Community and Nation-State in East Timor: A View from the Periphery." *Anthropology Today* 23, no. 1, 13–16.

Hicks, David. 2008. "Afterword: Glimpses of Alternatives: The *Uma Lulik* of East Timor," in Simon Coleman and Galina Lindquist (eds.). "Against Belief?" *Social Analysis* 52 (1): 166–180. Special Issue. London.

Hicks, David. 2009. "'*Ema Lorosa'e*', '*Ema Loromonu*': identity and politics in Timor-Leste," in Christine Cabasset and Frederic Durand (eds.). *East Timor: How to Build a New Nation in Southeast Asia in the 21st Century?* pp. 81–94. Research Institute on Contemporary Southeast Asia (IRASEC & CASE): Bangkok, Thailand.

Hicks, David. 2013. "Adat and the Nation-State in Timor-Leste: Opposition and Synthesis in Two Political Cultures," in Michael Leach and Damien Kingsbury (eds.). *The Politics of Timor-Leste.* pp. 25–43. Ithaca, N.Y.: Cornell Southeast Asia Program.

Hill, Helen. 2002. *Stirrings of Nationalism in East Timor: Fretilin 1974–78, The Origins, Ideologies and Strategies of a Nationalist Movement.* Kuala Lumpur and Díli. Contemporary Otford, Otford Press, Ortford (Sydney).

Hobsbawm, Eric and R. Terence (eds.). 1983 *The Invention of Tradition* (Cambridge and New York, Cambridge University Press).

Hobsbawm, E.J. 1990. *Nations and Nationalism Since 1780: Programme, Myth, Reality.* Cambridge: The Press Syndicate of the University of Cambridge.

Hull, Geoffrey. 1998. "Basic Lexical Affinities of Timor's Austronesian Languages." *Studies in Languages and Cultures of East Timor* 1: 97–202.

Hull, Geoffrey. 2000. "Historical Phonology of Tetum." *Studies in Languages and Cultures of East Timor* 3: 158–212.

Hull, Geoffrey. 2004. "The Papuan Languages of Timor." *Studies in Languages and Cultures of East Timor* 6: 23–99.

Hoadley, J. Stephen. 1975 (March). *The Future of Portuguese Timor. Occasional Paper, No. 27.* Singapore: Institute of Southeast Asian Studies.

Integrasi: Kebulatan Tekad Rakyat Timor Timur. 1976. Jakarta, Indonesia: Yayasan Parikesit.

Jenkins, David. 1984. *Suharto and His Generals: Indonesian Military Politics 1975–1983.* Monograph Series (Publication no. 64) Cornell Modern Indonesian Project. Southeast Asia Program, Cornell University, Ithaca, New York.

Jolliffe, Jill. 1976. "Introduction," in Francisco Borja da Costa. *Revolutionary Poems in the Struggle Against Colonialism.* pp. 7–18.

Jolliffe, Jill. 1978. *East Timor: Nationalism and Colonialism.* Brisbane: University of Queensland Press.

Jolliffe, Jill. 1989. *Timor, Terra Sangrenta.* Colecção Memória Memórias. Lisbon, Portugal: O Jornal.

Jornal Nacional Semanário. 2005 (May 28). "Dr. Abilio Araújo: É Um Imperativo Rever a Nossa Constituição." *Jornal Nacional Semanário* 1, No. 70: 1, 6–7.

Kahin, George McTurnan. 1966 (1952). *Nationalism and Revolution in Indonesia.* Ithaca, New York: Cornell University Press.

Karlström, Mikael. 1999. "Civil Society and its Presuppositions: Lessons from Uganda," in Jean Comaroff and John Comaroff (eds.). *Civil Society and the Political Imagination in Africa: critical perspectives.* pp. 104–123.

Keyes, Charles F. 1977. *The Golden Peninsular Culture and Adaptation in Mainland Southeast Asia.* New York: Macmillan Publishing Co. Inc.; London: Collier Macmillan Publishers.

Kimura, Tomohiko. 2012. *Australian Foreign Policymaking Towards the East Timor Question From April 1974 to January 1978: a re-examination.* Unpublished Doctor of Philosophy thesis. Canberra: University of New South Wales.

King, Margaret. 1963. *Eden to Paradise.* London: Hodder & Stoughton.

King, Victor T. 1985. *The Maloh of West Kalimantan.* Verhandelingen van het Koninklijk Institut voor Taal-, Land-en Volkenkunde 108. Dordrecht-Holland/Cinnaminson--U.S.A.: Floris Publications.

Kingsbury, Damien. 1998. *The Politics of Indonesia.* 1st edition. South Melbourne, Australia: Oxford University Press.

Kingsbury, Damien. 2005. *The Politics of Indonesia.* 3rd edition. Oxford: Oxford University Press.

Kraus, Werner. 1989. Personal Communication.

Krieger, Heike (ed.). 1997. *East Timor and the International Community: Basic Documents.* Cambridge: Cambridge University Press.

Kumar, K. 1993. "Civil Society: an enquiry into the usefulness of an historical term." *British Journal of Sociology* 44 (3): 375–395.

Larsen, M.T. 1979. *The Tradition of Empire in Mesopotamia, in Power and Propaganda: A Symposium on Ancient Empires*, Vol. 7 of Mesopotamia: Copenhagen Studies in Assyriology, pp. 75–103. Copenhagen: Akademisk Forlag.

Lazarowitz, Toby Fred. 1980. *The Makassai: complementary dualism in Timor.* Unpublished Ph.D. dissertation, State University of New York at Stony Brook.

Leach, Michael, James Scambary, Matthew Clarke, Simon Feeny, and Heather Wallace. 2013. "National identity in fragile states: insights from tertiary students in Melanesia and Timor-Leste" *Commonwealth & Comparative Politics*, 51: 4, 447–478, DOI: 10.1080/14662043.2013.841004. Available at: http://dx.doi.org/10.1080/14662043.201 3.841004. Accessed February 16, 2014.

Loch, Alexander. 2009. "Nation Building at the Village Level: First the House, then the Church and finally a modern state," in Christine Cabasset and Frederic Durand (eds.). *East Timor: How to Build a New Nation in Southeast Asia in the 21st Century?* pp. 95–104. Research Institute on Contemporary Southeast Asia (IRASEC & CASE): Bangkok, Thailand.

Mann, Michael. 1993. "Nation-States in Europe and Other Continents: Diversifying, Developing, Not Dying." *Daedalus* 122 (2): 115–140.

Martinho, José Simões. 1947. *Vida e morte do régulo timorense D. Alexio*. Lisbon.

Matos, Artur Teodoro de. 1974. *Timor Português 1515–1769: Contribuçâo Para a Sua História*. Lisbon: Faculdade de Letras da Universidade de Lisboa Instituto Histórico Infante Dom Henrique.

Mauss, Marcel. 1968. *Oeuvres: 1. les fonctions sociales du sacré*. V. Karady (ed.). Paris: Les éditions de Minuit.

Maxwell, Kenneth. 1975 (April 17). "The Hidden Revolution in Portugal." pp. 29–35. *New York Review of Books*. New York.

McDonald, Hamish. 1981. *Suharto's Indonesia*. Blackburn, Victoria, Australia: The Dominion Press and Fontana/Collins.

Metzner, Joachim. 1977. *Man and Environment in Eastern Timor*. Development Studies Centre, Monograph 8. Canberra: The Australian National University.

Molnar, Andrea. 2009. *Timor Leste: Politics, History, and Culture*. London and New York: Routledge.

Moreira, Adriano. 1956. "The 'Elites' of the 'Tribal' Provinces." *UNESCO International Social Science Bulletin* 8, no. 3: 458–81.

Nicol, Bill. 1978. *Timor: The Stillborn Nation*. Melbourne: Widescope International Publishers Pty Ltd.

Nixon, Rod. 2012. *Justice and Governance in East Timor: indigenous approaches and the "new subsistence state"*. Abingdon and New York: Routledge Contemporary Southeast Asia Series.

Noor, Machmuddin, Slamet Moeljono, and Sujamto and H. Soemarno (eds.). 1977. *Lahirnya Propinsi Timor Timur: Dokumentasi Tentang Proses Dekolonisasi Timor Timur Dan Pembentukan Propinsi Daerah Tingkat I Timor Timur*. Jakarta: Badan Penerbit Almanak Republik Indonesia/BP Alda Jalan Tambak 12A.

Ormeling, F.J. 1956. *The Timor Problem: A Geographical Interpretation of an Undeveloped Island*. Groningen and Jakarta: T.B. Wolters, 1956.

Paine, Robert (ed.). 1981. *Politically Speaking: Cross-Cultural Studies of Rhetoric*. Philadelphia: Institute for the Study of Human Issues.

Passes, Alan. 2004. "The Place of Politics: Powerful Speech and Women Speakers in Everyday Pa'ikwené (Palikur) Life." *The Journal of the Royal Anthropological Society (N.S.)* 10, no. 1: 1–18.

Peel, J.D.Y. 1984. "Making History: The Past in the Ijesha Present." *Man (n.s.)* 19: 111–132.

Pélissier, René. 1996. *Timor en guerre. Le crocodile and les Portugais (1847–1913)*. Orgeval: Pélissier.

Pires, Mário Lemos. 1991. *Descolonização de Timor: Missão Impossível?* 3rd edition. Lisbon: Publicações Dom Quixote, Lda.

Pires, Paulo. 2013. *Timor: Labirinto da Descolonização*. Lisbon: Edições Colibri.

Queer Space: Centers and Peripheries Conference. 2006. Available at: www.dab.uts.edu. au/conferences/queer_space/. Accessed May 17, 2014.

Radcliffe, Sarah, and Sallie Westwood. 2006 (1996). *Remaking the Nation: place, identity and politics in Latin. America*. Taylor and Francis e-Library, Routledge: London and New York.

Ramos-Horta, José. 1996. *Funu – The Unfinished Saga of East Timor*. Lawrenceville, N.J.: The Red Sea Press, Inc.

Ramos-Horta, José. 2006. "East Timor is Not a Failed State." *The Wall Street Journal*, 9 June, p. A14. New York, New York.

Ramos-Horta, José. 1994. *Timor Leste: Amanhã Em Dili*. Lisbon, Portugal: Publicações Dom Quixote, Lda., Portugal.

Relatório do Governo de Timor. 1981. Presidência do Conselho de Ministros, Lisbon, Portugal.

Relatório da CAEPDT (Comissão de Análise e Esclarecimento do Processo of Descolonização de Timor). 1981. Presidência do Conselho de Ministros, Lisbon, Portugal.

Rodgers, Susan. 1983. "Political Oratory in a Modernizing Southern Batak Homeland," in Rita Kipp Smith and D. Richard Kipp (eds.). *Beyond Samosir: Recent Studies of the Batak Peoples of Sumatra*. pp. 21–52. *Ohio University Papers in International Studies* 62. Athens, Ohio: Ohio University Press.

Roff, Sue Rabbitt. 1992. *Timor's Anschluss: Indonesian and Australian Policy in East Timor 1974–1976*. Lewiston, New York; Queenton, Ontario; Lampeter, Wales: The Edwin Mellen Press Ltd., Lampeter, Wales, UK.

Rousseau, Jerome. 1990. *Central Borneo: Ethnic Identity and Social Life in a Stratified Society*. Oxford: Clarendon Press.

Sá, Artur Basílio de. 1961. *Textos em Teto Literatura Oral Timorense*, Vol. 1. Lisbon: Junta de Investigações do Ultramar.

Sahlins, Marshall. 1981. *Historical Metaphors and Mythical Realities: The Early History of the Sandwich Islands Kingdom*. Ann Arbor: The University of Michigan Press.

Schulte Nordholt, H.G. 1971. *The Political System of the Atoni of Timor*. Translated by M.J.L. van Yperen. Verhandelingen Van Het Koninklijk Instituut Voor Taal-, Land- en Volkenkunde 60. The Hague: Martinus Nijhoff.

Schollay, Clive. 2003 (24 October). *East Timor Reconciliation: Scenes from Timor, September 1975* [video]. Screen Sound Australia Video, National Screen and Sound Archive, VHS C10131, I.D. 50112–01–5 Reels, 153 minutes 30 seconds.

Scott, C. James. 2009. *The Art of Not Being Governed: an anarchist history of Upland Southeast Asia*. New Haven: Yale University Press.

Scambary, James. 2011. *"Anatomy of a Conflict: The 2006–7 Communal Violence in East Timor,"* in Vandra Harris and Andrew Goldsmith (eds.). *Security, Development and Nation-Building in Timor-Leste: A Cross-sectoral Assessment*. pp. 59–79. London and New York: Routledge.

Seligman, Adam B.B. 1992. *The Idea of Civil Society*. New York: The Free Press.

Shea, Michael. 1989. *Influence*. London: Sphere Books Ltd.

Shils, Edward. 1975. *Center and Periphery: Essays in Macrosociology*. Chicago and London: University of Chicago Press.

Silva, Kelly Cristiane da. 2010. "Processes of Regionalisation in East Timor Social Conflicts," in Paulo Castro Seixas (ed.). *Transition, Society and Politics in Timor-Leste*. pp. 123–136. Porto: Universidade Fernando Pessoa.

Spínola, António de. 1974. *Portugal e o Futuro. Análise da conjuntura nacional*. Lisbon: Arcadia.

Spyer, Patricia. 2000. *Memory of Trade: modernity's entanglements on an eastern Indonesian Island*. Durham, NC.: Duke University Press.

Sousa, Domingos de. 2003. *Olobai 75. Baucau, East Timor: Gráfica Diocesana Baucau.*

Smith, M. 2006. "The Paradox of Burma: conflict and illegality as a way of life." *International Institute for Asian Studies (IIAS) Newsletter* 42: 20–21.

Strecker, Ivo. 2005 (August-October). "On Anthropology as a Moral Science of Possibilities." *Cultural Anthropology* 46, no. 4: 650.

Suara Timor Lorosae. 2012. "Parliamentary Election Test For Political Parties." *Responsibility.* June 5, 2012. Available at: http://twitter.com/CJITL/statuses/209911612595908608. Accessed May 17, 2014.

Suttles, G.D. 1976. "Urban Ethnography: Situational and Normative Accounts." *Annual Review of Sociology* 2 (August): 1–18.

Tanter, Richard. 2001. "East Timor and the Crisis of the Indonesian Intelligence State," in Richard Tanter, Mark Selden, and Stephen R. Shalom (eds.). *Bitter Flowers, Sweet Flowers: East Timor, Indonesia, and the World Community.* pp. 189–207. New York: Rowman & Littlefield Publishers, Inc.

Tarczynski, Stephen de. 2009. Australia: Complicit in East Timor – Records. January 27. Available at: www.globalissues.org/news/2009/01/27/448. Accessed February 15, 2014.

Taylor, John G. 1991. *Indonesia's Forgotten War: The Hidden History of East Timor.* London and New Jersey: Zed Books Ltd./Pluto Press Australia.

Taylor, John G. 1995. "The Emergence of a Nationalist Movement in East Timor," in R.H. Barnes, Andrew Gray, and Benedict Kingsbury (eds.). *Indigenous Peoples of Asia.* pp. 323–343; 436–438. Ann Arbor: The Association for Asian Studies. Monograph and Occasional Paper, Number 48.

Thomaz, Luís Filipe F.R. 1973. *O Problema Politico De Timor.* Braga: Editora Pax. Rua do Souto.

Thomaz, Luís Filipe F.R. 1977. *Timor: Autopsia de Uma Tragedia.* Lisbon, Portugal: Author, distributed by Dig/livro.

Timor Archives. 2012. Available at: http://timorarchives.wordpress.com/2012/08/21/falintil-archival-record. Accessed February 13, 2014.

Timor Newsline: News for Change. 2012. "TMR and Bishop Nascimento Call On Political Parties To Avoid Provocative Words." June 5, 2012. Available at: www.timornewsline-ida.com/government/160-tmr-and-bishop-nascimento-call-on-political-parties-to-avoid-provocative-words. Accessed May 17, 2014.

Tomodok, E.M. 1994. *Hari-Hari Akhir Timor Portugis.* Jakarta: Pustaka Jaya.

Traube, Elizabeth G. 1986. *Cosmology and Social Life: ritual exchange among the Mambai of East Timor.* Chicago; University of Chicago Press.

Traube, Elizabeth G. 1995. "Mambai Perspectives on Colonialism and Decolonization," in Peter Carey and G. Carter Bentley (eds.). *East Timor at the Crossroads: The Forging of a Nation.* pp. 42–55. Honolulu, Hawai'i: University of Hawai'i Press.

Traube, Elizabeth G. 2007. "Unpaid Wages: Local Narratives and the Imagination of the Nation." *The Asia Pacific Journal of Anthropology* 8: 1, 9–25.

United Nations. 1976 (August). *Decolonization.* A publication of the United Nations Department of Political Affairs, Trusteeship and Decolonization. No. 7.

United States Embassy Jakarta Telegram 1579 to Secretary State. December 6, 1975. [Text of Gerald Ford-Henry Kissinger-Suharto Meeting], Secret/Nodis (24). Gerald R. Ford Library, Kissinger-Scowcroft Temporary Parallel File Box A3, Country File, Far East-Indonesia, State Department Telegrams 4/1/75–9/22/76. See William Burr and Michael L. Evans. 2001. "East Timor Revisited Ford, Kissinger and the Indonesian Invasion," 1975–1976. December 6. www.gwu.edu/~nsarchiv/NSAEBB/NSAEBB62/. Accessed April 28, 2014.

United States Embassy. 2010 (April 23). Press Release: Sacred House Inaugurated in Hatobuilico, Embassy News. Available at: http://timor-leste.usembassy.gov/ (U.S. Embassy, Dili, Timor-Leste). Accessed February 17, 2014.

Van Klinken, Helene. 2012. "The New Order in East Timor," in *Making Them Indonesians: Child Transfers out of East Timor.* Melbourne: Monash University Publishing. pp. 1–19. Available at: http://books.publishing.monash.edu/apps/bookworm/view/Making+Them+Indonesians%3A+Child+Transfers+out+of+East+Timor/169/mti11001-a.html. Accessed February 16, 2014.

Wallace, Alfred Russel. 1883. *The Malay Archipelago: The Land of the Orang-Utan and the Bird of Paradise, a Narrative of Travel, with Studies of Man and Nature.* London: Macmillan and Co.

Wallace, Anthony F.C. 1956. "Revitalization Movements." *American Anthropologist* 58, no. 2: 264–281.

Way, Wendy (ed.). (Damien Browne & Vivianne Johnson, assistant editors.). 2002. *Australia and the Indonesian Incorporation of Portuguese Timor, 1974–1976.* Documents on Australian Foreign Policy. Department of Foreign Affairs and Trade. Melbourne: Melbourne University Press.

Weber, Max. 1971. "Class, Status, and Party," in K. Thompson and J. Tunstall (eds.). *Sociological Perspectives.* pp. 250–264. Harmondsworth: Penguin Books.

Weber, Max. 1978. *Economy and Society.* Guenther Roth and Claus Wittich (eds.). Berkeley: University of California Press. Vol. One.

Weissleder, Wolfgang. 1979. "The Promotion of Suzerainty Between Sedentary and Nomadic Populations in Eastern Ethiopia," in S. Lee Seaton and Henri J.M. Claessen (eds.). *Political Anthropology: The State of the Art.* pp. 157–171. The Hague, Paris, New York: Mouton Publishers.

White, Ken. 1975 (Thursday, August 28). "Jerimias de Souza – HERO!" *The Northern Territory News,* Vol. 24, No. 141: 1. Darwin, Northern Territories, Australia.

Whitlam, E.G. 1975. Unpublished Letter dated April 22, 1975 to Senator Arthur Gietzelt quoted in Dunn (2003: 129).

Whitlam, E.G. 1980. "Indonesia and Australia: Political Aspects," in Ross Garnaut, James J. Fox, Peter McCawley (eds.). *Indonesia: Australian Perspectives.* Canberra: Research School of Pacific Studies, The Australian National University.

Wilder, Gary. 1999. "Practicing Citizenship in Imperial Paris," in Jean Comaroff and John Comaroff (eds.). *Civil Society and the Political Imagination in Africa: critical perspectives.* pp. 44–71. Chicago: University of Chicago Press.

Wikipedia. Available at: http://en.wikipedia.org/wiki/Falintil. Accessed November 30, 2013.

Willenson, Kim (with Miguel Acoca). 1975 (September 15). "Portugal's Turning Point." *Newsweek,* p. 45.

Wilson, Bu. 2009. Personal Communication.

Appendix A

Glossary

ABRI	*Angatan Bersenjata Republic Indonesia* (Indonesian Armed Forces).
ANP	*Acção Nacional Popular* (government-backed political party during the Salazar regime).
ACFOA	Australian Council for Overseas Aid.
Aditla	*Associação Democrática Integração Timor-Leste-Australia* (Democratic Association for Integration of East Timor with Australia).
Aiti	*Associação Para a Integração de Timor na Indonesia* (Association for the Integration of Timor into Indonesia); renamed *Apodeti.*
Antara	the official Indonesian Government news agency.
Apodeti	*Associação Popular Democrática Timorense* (Timorese Popular Democratic Association).
ASDT	*Associação Social-Democrática Timorense* (Timorese Association of Social Democrats); renamed *Fretilin.*
ASEAN	Association of South East Asian Nations.
ASIAT	Australian Society for Inter-Country Aid (Timor).
APMT	*Associação Popular Monarquia* (Popular Monarchic Association of Timor); renamed *Klibur Oan Timur Asuain*, or *Kota.*
BAKIN	*Badan Koordinasi Intelijen Negara* (Indonesian State Intelligence Coordinating Agency).
Concelho	a district; the largest administrative unit into which Timor was divided.
Ema	people; also an alternative name for the Kemak people.
Ema foho	people who inhabit the interior of the country; see *ema lisan.*
Ema lisan	people who follow customary "traditions," see *ema foho.*
Falintil	*Forças Armadas de Libertação Nacional de Timor-Leste* (Armed Forces for the National Liberation of Timor-Leste).
Foho	mountain, hill, uplands, interior of East Timor.

Frelimo	*Frente de Libertação de Moçambique* (Mozambique Liberation Front).
Fretilin	*Frente Revolutionária de Timor-Leste Independente* (Revolutionary Front for an Independent East Timor).
Fulin	*Frente Unida para a Libertação e Independência Nacional* (Front for National Liberation and Independence).
ICRC	*Internationale Comité de la Rouge-Croix* (International Committee of the Red Cross).
Kopassandha	*Komando Pasukan Sandi Yudha* (Special Warfare Force Command); before February 17, 1971 known as *RPKAD*; after 1985 known as *Kopassus;* an army para-commando unit.
Kopassus	*Komando Pasu Pasukan Khusus* (Special Forces Command); before 1985 known as *Kopassandha*.
Kopkamtib	(*Komando Operasi Pemulihan Keamanan dan Ketertiban*, the Operational Command for the Restoration of Security and Order).
Kostrad	*Komando Cadangan Strategis Angkatan Darat* (Army Strategic Reserve Command).
Kota	*Klibur Oan Timur Asuain*, glossed by some commentators as the "Sons of the Mountain Warriors"; Jorge Duarte provides the gloss, "Association [or Congregation] of the heroic sons of Timor."
Lesvalt	League of Students for the Appreciation of Timor.
Liurai	A local king or chief of a *suku*.
MAC	*Movimento Anti-Communista* (Anti-Communist Movement).
MFA	*Movimento das Forças Armadas* (Armed Forces Movement).
MPLA	*Movimento Popular de Libertação de Angola* (Popular Movement for the Liberation of Angola).
NGO	Non-government Organisation.
Operasi Komodo	A clandestine campaign, created in October by General Ali Murtopo to undermine the stability of Portuguese Timor.
Operasi Flamboyan	A campaign, created by Benny Murdani, to covertly cross the border into Portuguese Timor by deploying Indonesian troops under the pretext they were assisting the partisans of the four political parties to regain their rightful authority in Portuguese Timor.
Operasi Seroja	Indonesia's generals' plans for a full-scale invasion of Portuguese Timor drawn up around November 1975.
Opsus	*Operasi Khusus* (Special Operations); an independent intelligence unit headed by Ali Murtopo with responsibilities for covert operations.
OPMT	*Organização Popular da Mulher Timor* (Popular Organization of Timorese Women).
PAIGC	*Partido Africano da Independência da Guine e Cabo Verde* (African Party for the Independence of Guinea and Cape Verde).

PPP	*Partai Persatuan Pembangunan*, the Development Unity Party, an amalgamated Muslim party.
Partido Trabalhista	Workers' Party.
PIDE	*Polícia Internacional e de Defendo Estado* (International and State Defence Police), the political police force during the Salazar regime.
Posto	a sub-district under the directed of a *chefe do posto* (chief of the post).
Rai	a "traditional" kingdom; also known as *reino*.
Reino	a "traditional" kingdom; also known as *rai*.
Rádio Dili	Housed in Dili, this radio station broadcast the propaganda of the three main East Timorese parties, and then, after the installation of the *Fretilin* Government that of *Radio Kupang Fretilin*.
Radio Kupang	Housed in a building situated on high ground above Kupang, this radio station broadcast pro-Indonesian propaganda. It came later to be known also as *Radio Kupang* and *Radio Kupang*.
RPKAD	*Resimen Para Komando Angkatan Darat* (Army Commando Paratroop Regiment) of the Republic of Indonesia.
SAPT	*Sociedade Agricola Patria e Trabalho* (a business enterprise half-owned by the Portuguese Government in which coffee was a dominant commodity).
Sandi Yudha	an Indonesian special warfare military unit within *Kopassandha*.
SOTA	*Sociedade Orientale do Transportes e Armazens* (a government-sponsored wholesale and retail business enterprise).
Suku	a sub-division of a *posto*; in past times a sub-division of a *reino* and glossed as "princedom."
UDT	*Unão Democrática Timorense*.
UNETIM	*União Nacional de Estudantes de Timor* (National Union of Timorese Students).

Appendix B

Some principal personalities

Supporters of the four main political parties

União Democrática Timorense

Francisco Xavier Lopes da Cruz, (editor of *A Voz de Timor*), President, customs officer former representative of the ANP
César Augusto da Costa Mousinho, Vice-President, Mayor of Dili, senior officer in the administration
Domingos de Oliveira, Secretary-General
Mário Viegas Carrascalão
João Manuel Viegas Carrascalão, leader of the rebellion of August 11
Gaspar Nunes, *Liurai* in Maubara
Rui Alberto Maggiolo Gouveia, a lieutenant-colonel in the Timorese Army and Police Commandant in Dili
Vasco de Lino, leader of the task force that advanced on Dili in August 1975
João da Silva Tavares, a partisan operative

Associação Social-Democrática Timorense/Fretilin

Francisco Xavier do Amaral, President
Nicolau dos Reis Lobato, Vice-President
Alariço Jorge Fernandes, Secretary-General
Mari Alkatiri
Rogério dos Reis Lobato
José Manuel Ramos-Horta
Abílio de Araújo
Guilhermina dos Santos Araújo
Francisco Borja da Costa
Mau Lear (António Duarte Carvarino)
Vicente Sahe (Vicente dos Reis)
Roque Rodrigûes
Justino Mota

Hermeneguildo Alves
Rosa Muki Bonaparte, secretary of the *Organização Popular da Mulher Timor*
Maria do Céu Pereira
Isobel dos Reis Lobato, wife of Nicolau Lobato
Fernando Carmo

Apodeti

Arnaldo dos Reis Araújo, President and first governor of East Timor under the Indonesian Administration
José Hermenegildo Martins, Vice-President
Casimiro dos Reis Araújo
José Fernandes Osório Soares
Guilherme Maria Gonçalves, *Liurai Dom* of Atsabe, and second governor of East Timor under the Indonesian Administration
Lucio Gonçalves, son of Guilherme Gonçalves
Tomás Gonçalves, son of Guilherme Gonçalves

Kota

José Martins, President
Francisco Ximenes, Vice-President
Tomás Ximenes

Other leading participants

Portugal

Marcelo Caetano, Prime Minister
Francisco da Costa Gomes, Prime Minister
António de Spínola, Prime Minister
Vasço dos Gonçalves, Prime Minister
António dos Santos Ramalho Eanes, President
Mário Soares, Foreign Minister
Vitor Alves, Minister without portfolio
António Carlos Arnão Metelo, *Estado-Maior do Comando Militar de Timor* ("Chief of Staff") and *Chefe do Estado Maior das Forças Armadas* ("Chief of the General Staff of Armed Forces"; said to be "*Apodeti*'s father"
Níveo Herdade, de facto Governor of Portuguese Timor
Alves Aldeia, Governor of Portuguese Timor (1971–1972)
Mário Lemos Pires, last Governor of Portuguese Timor
Adelino Coelho, *chefe de cabinete* in Dili
Capitão António Ramos, Information Officer in Dili *cabinete*
Francisco Mota, Chief of the Cabinet for Political Affairs and a leading member of the Decolonization Commission

Silvério de Costa Jonátas, Chief of the Social Communications Bureau and a leading member of the Decolonization Commission
António de Almeida Santos, Minister for Interterritorial Coordination
António Soares, head of a negotiating team sent to Dili in August 1975 to help restore peace
Melo Antunes, Foreign Minister (1974; 1975)
Dom José Joaquim Ribeiro, Bishop of Dili

Indonesia

Suharto, President of Indonesia
El Tari, Governor of Nusa Tenggara Timor
Louis Taolin, son of the *raja* of Insana, in West Timor, and a local agent of *Bakin*
Elias M. Tomodok, Indonesian consul in Dili
Adam Malik, Indonesian Minister for Foreign Affairs
Ali Murtopo, Lieutenant General; Deputy head of *Bakin*
Benny Murdani, Lieutenant General, assistant for intelligence to the minister of defense; long time advocate for the use of military force in Portuguese Timor and inspiring force in *Operasi Komodo*
Aloysius Sugiyanto, a colleague of Murtopo's and an officer in *Kopassus*; co-framer with Louis Taolin of the "Integration Declaration" at Atambua
Maraden Panggabean, General, Minister of Defence; commander-in-chief of *ABRI*
Surono Reksodiredjo, Deputy Commander in Chief of *ABRI*
Yoga Sugama, head of *Bakin*
Aloysius Sugianto, a colonel in *Kopassus*; negotiated with *União Democrática Timorense* and *Apodeti comité central* members
Dading Kalbuadi, Colonel, field commander of October 1975 assault on Maliana and Balibo
Yunus Yosfiah, Major, an officer in the Strategic Reserve Command who led the assault on Balibo

Australia

Gough Whitlam, Prime Minister
Malcolm Fraser, Prime Minister
Andrew Peacock, Foreign Affairs Minister in the caretaker Liberal Government
Richard Woolcott, Australian Ambassador to Indonesia

United States

Gerald Ford, President
Henry Kissinger, Secretary of State

Index

*Page numbers in **bold** denote figures*

232   *Index*

with João Carrascalão 140; political attitudes 75, 107, 108; undertakings 42, 43, 104–6, 107, 108, 109, 116, 117, 122, 125, 127, 131, 133, 161, 181; visit to Lisbon 166

Polícia Internacional e de Defendo Estado (PIDE)

political center 6, 7, 83, 206, 207n19

political elites xii, 6, 7, 8, 10, 12n29, 26, 31, 35, 42, 45, 54, 68, 72, 73, 83, 84n10, 97, 105, 127, 129, 192, 195–6, 205, 211, 214

political periphery xii, 6, 7, 8, 10, 11n19, 15, 25, 27, 31, 36, 38, 39, 46, 67, 69, 81, 82, 83, 99, 109, 118, 119, 121, 131, 160, 163, 188, 191, 192, 200, 206, 207n19, 208n19, 213

population statistics 40, 59n3

Portugal: flag of 7, 14, 27, 66, 72, 79, 83, 102, 111n61, 142, 151, 158n52, 166, 177, 189

Rádio Dili 76, 80, 92, 99, 100, 103, 104, 105, 111n49, 119, 129, 139, 142, 148, 227

Radio Kupang 76, 116, 125, 129, 197, 227

rai see reino 19, 20, 22, 183n55, 200n36, 227

Ramelau 16, 69

Ramos-Horta, José Manuel: and Adam Malik 1, 46, 91–2; career summary 50–2; and founding of *Fretilin* 72–4; and founding of the *União Democrática Timorense* 70–1; meeting with Whitlam 94; meetings with Tomodok 89; visit to Australia 94; visit to Jakarta 91–2, 132

Reception, Reconciliation and Truth Commission *see* CAVR

Reis, Vicente dos 4, 12n29, 24, 46, 47, 53, 54, 61, 68, 74, 91, 100, 125, 130, 196

Reksodiredjo, Surono 123, 167, 230

resemblances between Portuguese Timor in 1974–1975 and Timor-Leste today

Resimen Para Komando Angkatan Darat (RPKAD) 110n12, 227

Revolução dos Cravos see Carnation Revolution

rhetoric i, vi, xii, 5, 7–8, 15, 26, 64, 71, 78, 84n13, 88, 109, 194, 205, 119, 191–6, 195; *see also* forensic rhetoric 6–7, 15, 187, 188, 189; hagiography 7, 177, 190, 204; political rhetoric 7, 15, 26, 78, 84n13, 187, 188, 189

Ribeiro, Dom José Joaquim 50, 146, 148, 156, 158n44, 164, 230

ritual house *see uma lulik*

ritual speech *see* rhetoric

rituals 14, 15, 18, 19, 23, 26, 27, 28, 31n1, 79, 121, 189, 190, 194, 196

Rodgers, Susan xiii, 187, 190, 199n16

Rodrigûes, Roque 4, 9, 12n29, 46, 54, 68, 74, 91, 96, 97, 100, 103, 104, 111n39, 125, 130, 156, 196, 197, 204, 228

Roff, Sue Rabbitt 110n24, 213

Rome talks 1, 167

Rousseau, Jean Jacques 205

Sá, Artur Basílio de 200n45

Sahe, Vicente *see* Vicente dos Reis

Sandi Yuha 96, 169, 226

Santos, António de Almeida 94, 101, 111, 120, 126, 156, 162, 165, 196, 230

Scambary, James 160, 207

Schollay, Clive 181n6, 181n7

Schulte Nordholt, H.G. 23, 32n26, 199n23

Scott, C. James 208n23

Seara 48, 49, 60n55, 193

Segunda Linha 20, 21, 42, 131, 177, 180

Seligman, Adam B. 205, 207n8

Sentenca Arbitral 16

Shils, Edward 206, 207n18, 207n19

Silva, Celestino da 38

Silva, Kelly Cristiane da 64, 88

Smith, M. 11n17, 208n21

Soares, António 177, 190

Soares, José Fernandes Osório 23, 57, 58, 71, 77, 128, 129, 229

Soares, Mário 102, 120, 229

social hierarchy 19, 20, 25, 48, 204

social status 19, 55, 56

Sociedade Agricola Patria e Trabalho (SAPT) 40, 41, 96, 227

Sociedade Orientale do Transportes e Armazens (SOTA) 40, 227

Soibada 27, 47, 48, 49, 50, 52, 54

Sousa, Domingos de xiii, 24, 164, 173, 179, 182n13, 183n56, 184n76, 184n79, 184n89, 184n90, 212

Spínola, António de 2, 3, 43–5, 71, 75, 83, 93, 103, 104, 105, 112n81, 166, 229

Spyer, Patricia 206, 208n22

Strecker, Ivo 11n23

students 10, 49, 52, 53, 54, 55, 59n3, 61n74, 85n31, 97, 98, 99, 111n56, 122, 127, 131, 175, 176, 192, 194, 196, 197, 207n15, 212, 226, 227

Sugama, Yoga 90, 167, 230

Sugiyanto, Aloysius 77, 92, 123, 127, 131, 132, 171, 230